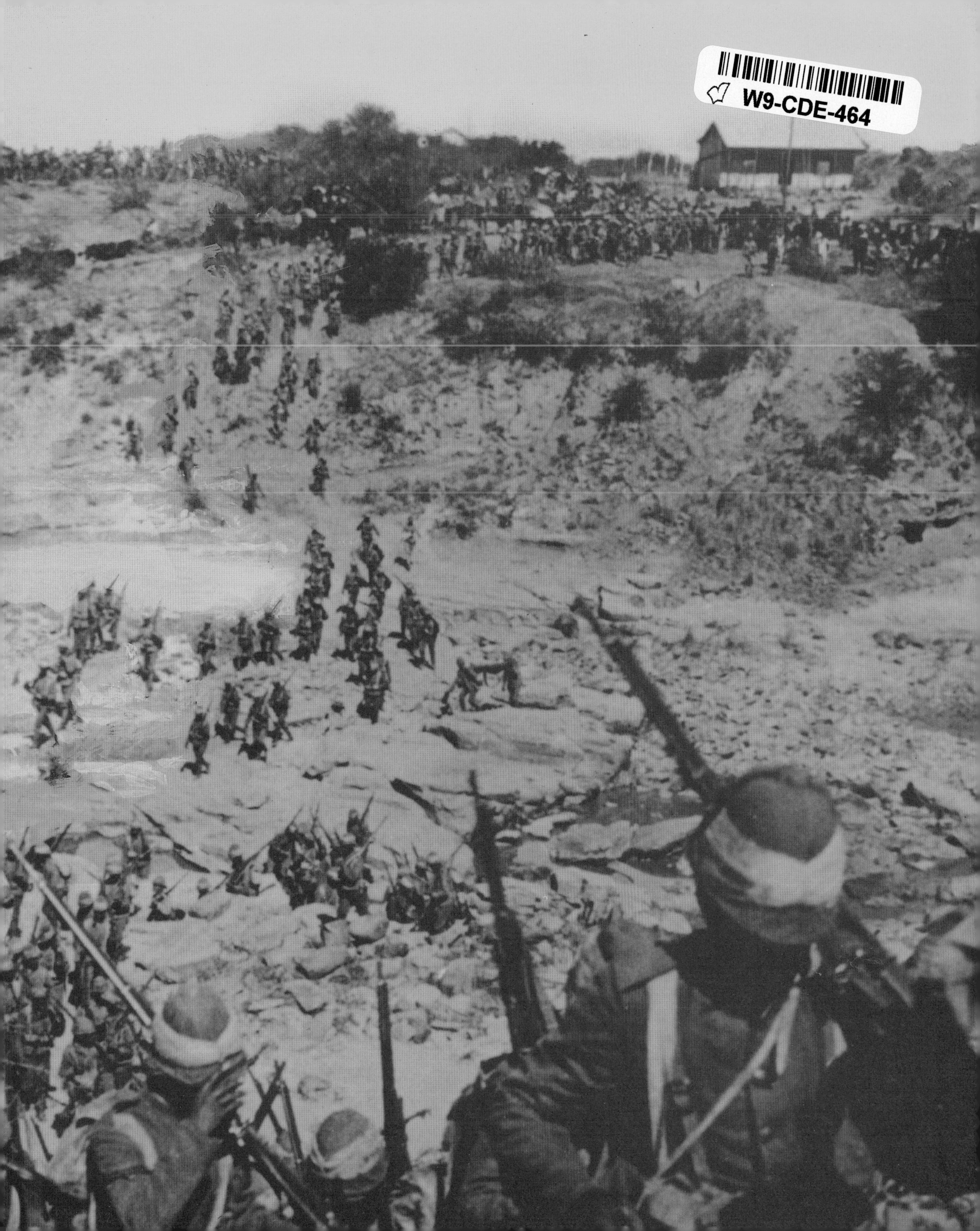

The Boer War

'Look back over the pages of history;
consider the feelings with which we now regard
wars that our forefathers in their time
supported . . . see how powerful and deadly are
the fascinations of passion and of pride.'

W. E. Gladstone, 26 November 1879,
condemning the first annexation of the Transvaal

The Boer War

Illustrated Edition

THOMAS PAKENHAM

'Won't be happy till he gets it.'

RANDOM HOUSE
NEW YORK

For Val, in gratitude once again.

*And to the memory of the war veterans who told me
what it was like to be there.*

❖

All rights reserved under International and
Pan-American copyright conventions. Published
in the United States by Random House, Inc.,
New York.

This work was originally published in different
form in 1979 by George Weidenfeld & Nicolson Ltd.,
London in Great Britain, and Random House, Inc.,
New York, in the United States.

This illustrated edition is published in Great Britain
by George Weidenfeld & Nicolson Limited, a division
of The Orion Publishing Group, London.

Library of Congress Cataloging-in-Publication Data
Pekenham, Thomas, 1933–
    The Boer War/Thomas Pakenham.—Illustrated ed.
        p.   cm.
    Includes bibliographical references and index.
    ISBN 679-43047-4
    1. South African War, 1899–1902.   I. Title.
DT1996.P35   1994
968.04′8—dc20   93-26234

Printed in Great Britain
98765432
First Illustrated US Edition

Front endpaper The Guards Brigade
splashing across the Zand River on 10 May
1900.

Back endpaper 'The Camp for
Undesirables.' One of the British
concentration camps in which some 20,000
Boers and 12,000 Africans died of epidemics
caused by neglect.

Frontispiece Europe stands aloof from the
struggle while the Boer bull (President
Kruger) tosses the effete British lion.

CONTENTS

Introduction   9

Historical Note   11

Prologue: Rhodes's 'Big Idea':   13
    Pitsani Camp (Bechuanaland border), Mafeking (Cape Colony
    border) and Transvaal, 29 December 1895–2 January 1896

PART I – MILNER'S WAR   19

  1 Out of the Abyss: 20
     SS *Scot* and South Africa, 18 November 1898 and before;
     London, 22 November–December 1898

  2 Champagne for the Volk: 29
     Pretoria, 23–29 December 1898;
     Johannesburg, 23 December 1898–28 March 1899

  3 'Working up Steam':   35
     Cape Town, 31 March–9 May 1899;
     The Orange Free State, 30 May–6 June 1899

  4 Milner's Three Questions: 40
     Pall Mall, London, 8 June–19 July 1899

  5 Preparing for a Small War: 45
     Cape Town, London and Natal, 20 July–7 October 1899

  6 The Ultimatum: 52
     Pretoria and the Transvaal, 1–12 October 1899;
     Cape Town and Ladysmith, 14–20 October 1899

PART II – BULLER'S REVERSE   67

  7 White Flag, *Arme Blanche*:   68
     Dundee, North Natal, 20 October 1899;
     Elandslaagte, near Ladysmith, Natal, 21 October 1899

  8 The Whale and the Fish: 86
     SS *Dunottar Castle* and the Cape, 14 October–26 November 1899

  9 Botha's Raid: 93
     South Natal, 9–30 November 1899

10 The Lights of Kimberley: 99
The Western Frontier, Cape Colony, 20–28 November 1899

11 Breakfast at the Island: 107
Modder and Riet Rivers, Cape Colony, 28 November–
10 December 1899

12 Marching up in Column: 115
Magersfontein, 9–12 December 1899

13 'Where are the Boers?':   118
Tugela River, near Ladysmith, 11–15 December 1899

14 'A Devil of a Mess':   123
Colenso, Natal, 15 December 1899;
British Isles, 16 December 1899–1 February 1900

15 'Are We Rotters or Heroes?':   139
Pretoria, 12 December 1899–1 January 1900;
Ladysmith, 2 November 1899–6 January 1900

16 An Acre of Massacre: 146
Natal, 6–24 January 1900;
Spion Kop, Natal, 24–25 January 1900

PART III – ROBERTS'S ADVANCE   161

17 The Steam-Roller: 162
The Western Front, 11–15 February 1900

18 The Siege within the Siege: 166
Kimberley, 9–17 February 1900;
Paardeberg, 17–27 February 1900

19 The Key Turns: 180
The Tugela Line and Ladysmith, 12–28 February 1900

20 The Handshake: 185
Across the Tugela, 27 February–15 March 1900

21 The Plague of Bloemfontein: 192
The Orange Free State, 13–28 March 1900;
Northern and Eastern Free State, 17 March–April 1900

22 'The White Man's War':   205
Mafeking (Cape Colony border), 30 April–May 1900

23 Across the Vaal: 216
The Orange River Colony and the
Transvaal, 31 May–June 1900

24 'Practically Over':   226
The Ex-Republics, 8 July–September 1900

PART IV – KITCHENER'S PEACE   237

25 The Worm Turns: 238
    South Africa, 30 October–16 December 1900

26 Disregarding the Screamers: 244
    Cape Town and Beyond, 17 December 1900–28 May 1901;
    London and South Africa, 1901

27 Raiding the Colonies: 256
    Cape Colony and Natal, 3 September–December 1901

28 Blockhouse or Blockhead?:   263
    The New Colonies, November 1901–March 1902

29 Peace 'Betrayed':   273
    Pretoria, 11 April–June 1902

Epilogue: 'Winners and Losers'   287

Important Dates Before and During the Boer War   291

Acknowledgements   295

Picture Sources   295

Index   297

LIST OF MAPS

South Africa, 1899   14
Boer invasion of Natal, 11 October–23 November 1899   70
Kimberley under siege, 1899–1900   103
Battles of Modder River, 28 November 1899,
and Magersfontein, 11 December 1899   110
Battle of Colenso, 15 December 1899   123
Ladysmith under siege, 1899–1900   138
Battle of Spion Kop, 24 January 1900   147
Battle of Paardeberg, 18 February 1900   174
The Breakthrough, 14–27 February 1900   182
Mafeking under siege, 1899–1900   206
Blockhouse system, 1902   267

INTRODUCTION

THE WAR DECLARED BY THE BOERS on 11 October 1899 gave the British, in Kipling's famous phrase, 'no end of a lesson'. The British public expected it to be over by Christmas. It proved to be the longest (two and three-quarter years), the costliest (over £200 million), the bloodiest (at least twenty-two thousand British, twenty-five thousand Boer and twelve thousand African lives) and the most humiliating war for Britain between 1815 and 1914.

I decided to try to tell the story of this last great (or infamous) imperial war, taking as my raw material the first-hand, and largely unpublished, accounts provided by contemporaries.

It was an ambitious idea, to base the book largely on manuscript (and oral) sources. No one had made the attempt for seventy years. In the decade after 1902, the public suffered a barrage of Boer War books. This culminated in a bombardment from the Long Toms, as it were: the seven-volume *Times History of the War in South Africa* (1900–1909), edited by Leo Amery, and the eight-volume (Official) *History of the War in South Africa* (1906–1910), edited by General Maurice and others. (In spelling South African place-names I have used the contemporary forms adopted by the *Official History*, not the modern Afrikaans forms.) These two massive works have dominated Boer War studies, and remain indispensable to the historian. They incorporate, often anonymously, a vast mass of original material. Understandably, as they were completed seventy years ago, both have their limitations.

In due course I began to read the confidential War Office files – those that survived a bizarre decision to 'weed' them in the 1950s – the files on which much of Amery's and Maurice's work had been based. I was fortunate enough to be able to dig up, often in odd places, the private papers of most of the generals and politicians on the British side. So there was no shortage of new raw material. I stumbled on the lost archives of Sir Redvers Buller, the British Commander-in-Chief in 1899 – battle letters of Buller's which had remained hidden under the billiard table at Downes, his house in Devon, and in Lord Lansdowne's muniment room at Bowood; I sifted through the trunk-loads of Lord Roberts's papers rescued by the National Army Museum from the care of one of his most recent biographers, David James (who claims to have burnt every scrap of paper Lord Roberts ever wrote to his wife); I discovered a *Secret Journal* of the war, written by the War Office Intelligence Department, running to nearly a million words; I saw the private papers of the War Minister, Lord Lansdowne, and other members of Lord Salisbury's Cabinet. And I traced over a hundred unseen sets of letters and diaries, written by British officers and men who served in the war; these were generously lent to me by their descendants. I was also privileged to capture on my tape-recorder the memories of fifty-two men who had actually fought in the war, the youngest of whom was eighty-six when I tracked him down.

Young urban Boers pose with flowers in their buttonholes.

9

I have been extremely fortunate in the help I have received from modern South African historians. I owe a great debt to Godfrey Le May's incisive study *British Supremacy in South Africa, 1899–1907*. I have also borrowed freely from the work in Afrikaans of the Transvaal State Archivist, Dr J. H. Breytenbach, who has already completed four volumes of his monumental history of the war, based on the state archives, *Die Geskiedenis van die Tweede Vryheidsoorlog*. I have plundered many other works in Afrikaans, especially Dr J. A. Mouton's study of Joubert, and Professor Johann Barnard's seminal work on Botha, *Botha op die Natalse Front, 1899–1900*.

Among the themes in this story I should like to emphasize four in particular.

First, there is a thin, golden thread running through the narrative, a thread woven by the 'gold-bugs': the Rand millionaires who controlled the richest gold mines in the world. Their secret support, I believe, gave Milner the strength to precipitate the war.

Second, there is a broader strand in the story involving Sir Redvers Buller, who has passed into folklore as the symbol of all that was most fatuous in the late-Victorian British army. I have tried to place Buller in context, and to show that this judgement is largely unjust.

A third strand to the story involves the invisible majority of South Africans: the blacks. Their part – and there may have been as many as a hundred thousand of them serving both sides – has been all but forgotten. Yet in general it was the Africans who had to pay the heaviest price in the war and its aftermath.

A fourth strand involves the plight of the Boer civilians, women and children caught up in the guerrilla war, and especially those removed to the 'concentration camps'. The conscience of Britain was stirred by the holocaust in the camps, and if the guerrillas in South Africa lost the war, they won the peace.

Thomas Pakenham   1979

To make possible this illustrated edition, two thirds of the original text had to be cut. Toby Buchan has wielded the scalpel. I should like to thank him for making the surgery almost painless.

I should also like to thank Kevin MacDonnell and Ryno Greenwall, who provided me with many of the best illustrations in this book from their own collections.

Other acknowledgements will be found at the back.

I have not included a new bibliography or new notes on sources. These are best consulted in the original edition.

1993

HISTORICAL NOTE

THE CRISIS IN THE TRANSVAAL at the end of the nineteenth century was the culmination of two and a half centuries of Afrikaner expansion and conflict with Africans and British.

In 1652 the Dutch East India Company founded a shipping station at the Cape of Good Hope. The settlers, who from the first were outnumbered by their coloured servants, were mainly Dutch Calvinists, and brought to Africa a tradition of dissent and a legacy of resentment against Europe. They called themselves 'Afrikaners' or 'Afrikanders', and spoke a variant of Dutch that came to be called 'Afrikaans'. The poorest and most independent of them were the *trekboers* (alias Boers), wandering farmers whose search for new grazing lands took them progressively deeper into African territory.

In 1806, during the Napoleonic Wars, Britain took permanent possession of the colony. The aim was strategic, for the Cape was a naval base on the sea route to India and the East. But the colony was too arid to tempt many British immigrants. The Afrikaners remained the majority – of the whites. Most of them were prepared to submit to British Crown rule, but a republican-minded minority resented imperial interference, especially over their ill-treatment of the Africans. In 1834 Britain abolished slavery throughout the Empire. This precipitated the Great Trek: the exodus in 1835–7 of about 5,000 Boers (with about 5,000 Coloured servants) across the Orange and Vaal rivers beyond the colony's frontiers. The *voortrekkers* (pioneers) shared one article of faith: to deny political rights to Africans and Coloured people of mixed race.

For years the British government blew hot and cold in its dealings with the Boers. In 1843 Britain created a secondary colony by annexing Natal, one of the voortrekker areas; in 1852 and 1854 she recognized the independence of the two new Boer republics, the Transvaal and the Orange Free State; then in 1877 she annexed the Transvaal, the first step in an attempt to federate South Africa. In 1880 the Boers under Paul Kruger rose in revolt against their new government, and within a few weeks inflicted three small but shattering reverses on the British army, culminating in the Battle of Majuba in British territory, just inside the borders of Natal.

By this time, Gladstone had returned as Prime Minister for the third time. He was quick to seize on a compromise. His Liberal government agreed to withdraw the large British force (led by the then Sir Frederick Roberts) hurrying to the rescue, and also restored complete internal self-government to the Boers, thus reversing the annexation. Although Britain still claimed her status as paramount power in South Africa, and reserved to herself ultimate control over the Transvaal's foreign affairs, she did not now claim the republic as a colony, or even as a member of her Empire.

Kruger, under pressure, consented to this arrangement, which was formalized as an international treaty by the Convention of Pretoria, 1881, and the Convention of London, 1884. But Kruger, elected President of the restored republic, made no secret that he signed under pressure, and would do everything to remove the shadow of British paramountcy from the Transvaal's independence. On their part, many British soldiers felt deeply humiliated by the settlement. In Britain, it served to quicken the rising spirit of jingoism – not least because Majuba had gone unavenged.

In 1895 two multi-millionaires, Cecil Rhodes and Alfred Beit, conspired to take over the Transvaal for themselves and the Empire. The outcome of their conspiracy provides the Prologue of this book. By now two great mineral discoveries had turned the political map upside down. In 1870 began the diamond rush to Kimberley, on the borders of Cape Colony, which smoothed the colony's path to successful self-government within the Empire. Diamonds also made Rhodes's and Beit's fortunes. Rhodes became Prime Minister at the Cape, and with Beit founded a new British colony, in African territory to the north of the Transvaal, re-named Rhodesia. In 1886 began the gold-rush to the Witwatersrand in the Transvaal. But this did not smooth the Transvaal's path. Gold made it the richest and militarily the most powerful nation in southern Africa. But gold also made, for the second time, the fortunes of Rhodes and Beit – especially Beit. And it precipitated a collision between the Boers and Uitlanders: the new immigrants, mainly British, swept along in the gold-rush. The situation of the Uitlanders was unique. They were believed to outnumber the Boers, yet by means of a new and restrictive franchise law, the Boers kept them starved of political rights. In 1895 it was the political hunger of the Uitlanders – backed by Rhodes's and Beit's millions – that seemed to offer the British a chance of taking the Transvaal back.

PROLOGUE

Rhodes's 'Big Idea'

Pitsani Camp (Bechuanaland border),
Mafeking (Cape Colony border) and Transvaal,
29 December 1895–2 January 1896

'Johannesburg is ready ... [this is] the big idea which makes England
dominant in Africa, in fact gives England the African continent.'

Secret letter from Cecil Rhodes to Alfred Beit in August 1895,
when they hatched the plot to create a revolution at
Johannesburg supported by a raid from Pitsani and
Mafeking led by Dr Jameson

JOHANNESBURG WAS NOT READY. That was the message of the last six code telegrams to Dr Jameson at Pitsani, his camp in Bechuanaland. They confirmed his fears, as did a special messenger sent by the Johannesburg 'Reform Committee', the leaders of Rhodes's and Beit's revolutionary movement in the Transvaal. The rising, in which they proposed to seize Johannesburg, was going to be a flop. For twenty minutes on that hot Sunday afternoon, 29 December 1895, Jameson paced up and down. Then he decided. He was going in, despite everything; he'd 'lick the burghers all round the Transvaal'. If the fellows at Johannesburg wouldn't start the rising as agreed, their hands would have to be forced. It was a chance of a lifetime.

Jameson had nearly four hundred Rhodesian mounted police at Pitsani, belonging to the Chartered Company. (It was this company, created by Cecil Rhodes and Alfred Beit, that administered the new British colony of Rhodesia under Crown Charter.) He had another one hundred and twenty volunteers twenty-five miles away at Mafeking – just within the borders of Cape Colony. That brought the total of the Chartered Company force up to about six hundred if one counted the Cape Coloured 'boys' who led the spare horses. He had originally planned to invade the Transvaal with fifteen hundred. After six months' work, he had scraped together six Maxim machine-guns, two 7-pounder mountain guns and a $12\frac{1}{2}$-pounder field-piece. Otherwise, apart from a few comforts, they had cut the baggage train to the bone. The plan was to make a three-day dash for Johannesburg, before the Boer commandos could mobilize. Unfortunately, 'blabbing' about the rising had already reached the local papers. It was now or never.

The troopers saw Dr Jameson step into the sunlight, the great Dr Jim,

13

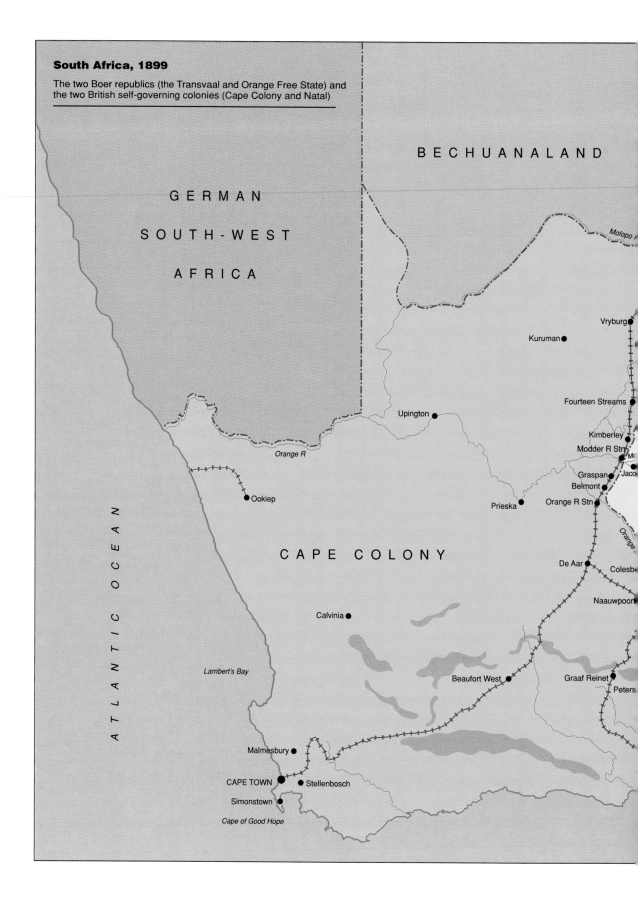

South Africa, 1899

The two Boer republics (the Transvaal and Orange Free State) and
the two British self-governing colonies (Cape Colony and Natal)

BECHUANALAND

GERMAN

SOUTH-WEST

AFRICA

Molopo

Vryburg

Kuruman

Fourteen Streams

Upington

Kimberley

Modder R Stn

Orange R

Mo

Graspan   Jaco

Belmont

Ookiep

Prieska   Orange R Stn

Orange

ATLANTIC OCEAN

CAPE COLONY

De Aar   Colesb

Naauwpoor

Calvinia

Lambert's Bay

Beaufort West   Graaf Reinet

Peters

Malmesbury

CAPE TOWN   ● Stellenbosch

Simonstown

Cape of Good Hope

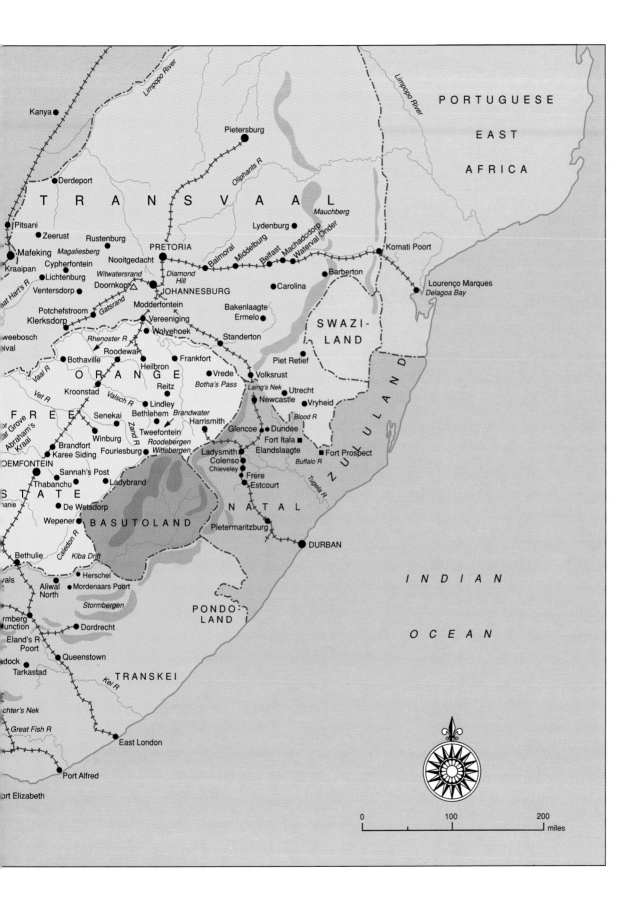

pioneer Administrator of the Chartered Company in Rhodesia, Rhodes's right-hand man. He took a crumpled paper out of his pocket and began to read aloud in his nervous voice. It was a letter of invitation from the committee of Uitlanders in Johannesburg organized by Rhodes and Beit – the mine-executives, miners and others who comprised the British and foreign business community of the Transvaal. 'All the elements necessary for armed conflict. . . . The one desire of the people here is for fair play. . . . Thousands of unarmed men, women and children of our race will be at the mercy of well-armed Boers. . . .' This was stirring stuff about the women and children, but not the precise truth. The letter, written a month before and left undated, was supposed to be kept until *after* the Johannesburg rising had begun. It would cover them with both the Chartered Company and the imperial government if there were awkward questions. Without it, they might have looked like pirates. As it was, the three senior officers – Colonels Johnny Willoughby, Raleigh Grey and Bobby White – were worried about the risk of losing their dormant commissions in the British army. Jameson had reassured them; they took it that Joseph Chamberlain (the Colonial Secretary) and the British government must be in the know.

One last precaution: they must cut off communications with the Cape. Working for Rhodes in these last years in Rhodesia had taught Jameson when to turn a blind eye to instructions; provided that they were not signed by Rhodes. Each stage of the collapse of the movement in Johannesburg had been reported to him by way of Rhodes's office, but not one telegram was signed 'Rhodes'. He had left the final decision to Jameson. Well, there would be no more orders to anyone at Pitsani for some time. Troopers smashed down the telegraph poles and cut the cable. Jameson's other contingent were doing the same near Mafeking.

Of course it was a wild gamble, but then so was much of the work of Rhodes's company. If Jameson gambled and won – if they could rush Johannesburg into a rising and take over the Transvaal – they would be forgiven the illegality. If they lost – well, the usual penalty was death. Death, but not necessarily defeat. It was one of the lessons of history that it needed a disaster to make the British interested in their Empire: they seemed to prefer dead generals to living, and avenged them by completing their work. Already that was happening in the Transvaal – ever since the Battle of Majuba, where General Colley and four hundred men had been cut up by the Boers fourteen years before. Jameson knew that his staff officers, all from decent regiments, took the shame of Majuba personally, especially the shame of those who had raised the white flag. Majuba was 'unfinished business' for the British army.

There could be no going back now. Jameson, mounted on a black stallion, took off his hat, and there were three ringing cheers for the Queen. Then they trotted out of Pitsani, followed by the African servants and the mule-carts. Soon the column was engulfed in dust.

The morning of 2 January 1896 found Jameson's column halted close to a small whitewashed farm south of a kopje called Doornkop, in the brown, grassy hills of the Rand. They had ridden 170 miles into the Transvaal, with hardly a halt for sleep. Ahead was their goal, Johannesburg, only a couple of hours' ride. As dawn broke, they could see the lunar mining landscape of the Golden City.

Betrayal was the only word for it. Johannesburg had not risen. Their friends had made their peace with President Kruger and his Boers. Not one armed volunteer had ridden out to join the column. Now Jameson's path was barred by a relentless and invisible enemy.

For two days they had carried on a running fight against the commandos. The Boers had got wind of them from the first. Jameson's men had cut the telegraph wire at Malmani, but too late. At first the Boers had hung on their tail, picking off stragglers. Jameson's men had fought back, but the only dead were British. How could they fight mere puffs of smoke? That last night they had huddled together in a rough square formed by the wagons and horses, firing into the darkness across their saddles. At dawn Jameson sent a final laconic message to the men in Johannesburg: they would like a little help.

If help didn't come, he and his officers well knew what England expected of them. This was the moment they had been trained for ever since boyhood. The Last Stand. The Colonel grasps his sword; the little band sings 'God Save the Queen'; and, one by one, they fall.

By eight o'clock the little band had suffered sixty-five killed and wounded. Then reality at last broke in to Jameson's world of make-believe. Someone lifted a white flag. The firing ceased. From all around them, Boers rose up out of the ground 'like ants'. They disarmed the British, assisted the wounded and seized the baggage. In White's black tin box were found the code telegrams from Rhodes in the Cape and from the other plotters in Johannesburg. There was a spare copy of the 'women-and-children' letter, and, among the empty champagne bottles, the code book to go with the code telegrams.

The humiliation was complete when the dead were counted before burial. The British had lost sixteen, the Boers one man – one less than they had lost at Majuba. Weeping, Jameson was led away to the gaol at Pretoria.

'The Jameson Raid was the real declaration of war in the Great Anglo-Boer conflict. . . . And that is so in spite of the four years truce that followed . . . [the] aggressors consolidated their alliance . . . the defenders on the other hand silently and grimly prepared for the inevitable.'

Jan Smuts, 1906

PART I
Milner's War

CHAPTER ONE

Out of the Abyss

SS *Scot* and South Africa,
18 November 1898 and before;
London, 22 November–December 1898

'As he spoke his eyelids seemed to tremble and to fall a little over his keen
grey eyes. In a flash the phrase of Scudder's came back to me, when he
had described the man he most dreaded in the world. He had said that he
"could hood his eyes like a hawk". Then I saw that I had walked straight
into the enemy's headquarters.'

John Buchan (Sir Alfred Milner's Private Secretary in
South Africa, 1901–3), *The Thirty-Nine Steps*

IN THE SMALL HOURS, Sir Alfred Milner, High Commissioner for South
Africa and Lieutenant-Governor of Cape Colony, was woken by a bright
light in his eyes. That must be the Ushant lighthouse, the first land they had
sighted since Madeira. If the 7,000-ton *Scot* kept this up, he would be in time
to see Chamberlain at the Colonial Office on the 22nd.

After eighteen gruelling months at the Cape, Milner felt he had earned a
holiday in England, even if it was to be a working holiday. He had been sent
out in 1897 to pick up the pieces after that most extraordinary business, the
Jameson Raid. The 'Higher Powers' (as he donnishly put it) seemed to have
achieved a miracle for the Afrikaners twice; first at Majuba, then at
Doornkop. How to avoid their winning a third time? He had increasingly
strong views about that, although these had to remain, for the time being, his
own private heresy.

People generally thought Milner shy, austere, melancholy. With his long,
thin face and downcast eyes, he looked older than his forty-four years, and
sadder than a brilliantly successful diplomatist should be. Was this really the
man chosen by Joe Chamberlain to cut President Kruger down to size? To the
few friends who knew him intimately he showed a side of his nature that was
both ardent and affectionate. His parentage was unusual. He was the son of a
feckless half-German medical student and an English gentlewoman who had
come to Germany in straitened circumstances. His upbringing was divided
between Germany and England (he retained a faint trace of a German
accent), and his heart was still to some extent divided between the two. His
English mother was the driving force behind his life, though she died when he
was fifteen. At eighteen he won a senior scholarship to Oxford, an unheard-

Previous page Boer commando, against a background of mine chimneys at the Rand, leaving for the front in September 1899.

Below left Joseph Chamberlain, Colonial Secretary in Salisbury's Government. The Jameson Raid had nearly ended his political career. Now he had decided to play safe with a 'no-war' policy.

Below right Sir Alfred Milner, British High Commissioner for South Africa and Governor of Cape Colony, sketched at his desk in Cape Town by Mortimer Menpes. He was determined to 'burst the mould' in South Africa.

of feat for a boy from a London day school. He carried off a whole litany of prizes, becoming the most brilliant son of Balliol, where Dr Jowett held court among a golden generation of undergraduates.

Against his feckless father he was in complete reaction, it seemed, though not at all disloyal or unfilial. That relentless capacity for work, that single-minded devotion to a cause – it was almost as though young Alfred was doing penance for the sins of his father. Yet behind this paragon of English Victorian virtues, people occasionally detected something different. There was a frighteningly strained air to his self-control, as though most of his life was lived against the grain of his nature. He had strange, keen grey-brown eyes which he could hood like a hawk's. Inside Milner, concealed from all but his closest friends, was something of the spirit of his father – romantic, Bohemian, restless, perhaps even reckless.

Milner's rise to fame could, as he reckoned himself, be attributed to one thing above all: he was absolutely sound and reliable. This was why he had proved so useful to the leading men in both political parties: as private secretary to Goschen, the Conservative Chancellor of the Exchequer; next, as financial secretary to Sir Evelyn Baring (later Lord Cromer), the British ruler of Egypt; then, as Chairman of the Inland Revenue, right-hand man to Sir William Harcourt, the Liberal Chancellor.

In due course, he was promoted High Commissioner by Chamberlain, the man responsible for British colonies in South Africa. Britain had had enough of schoolboy heroes and bungling empire-builders like Jameson and Rhodes. Milner had a solid reputation in imperial questions. And he possessed both strength of character and patience. It was *im*patience that lay at the root of all Britain's mistakes in the past – from before Majuba to the Raid. Two years at

Cecil Rhodes and Alfred Beit, the two most powerful 'gold-bugs' in South Africa. Milner forged a secret alliance with Beit and his partner, Wernher, but not with Rhodes, who was too wayward to collaborate with the home government.

the Cape had taught Milner that his patience had a limit, however. The legacy of the past appalled him – not merely the Raid but the chain of mistakes that had preceded it. 'I hope South Africa is not going to be our one point of failure, but I feel very uneasy,' he wrote to Philip Gell, one of his closest friends, in April 1898. 'The more I know about it, the more profound is the abyss of our blunders in the past.'

Milner confessed that he could not see two sides to the imperial question. In his eyes the nineteenth century in South Africa was a century of struggle for supremacy between Britain and Boer – and of abysmal imperial blunders.

During most of the century British policy was weak and vacillating, like British imperial policy in general. On three occasions a positive attempt was made to solve the Boer question by adopting an active 'forward' (that is, expansionist) policy. On each occasion, and for various reasons, the policy ended in disaster. Yet the alternatives proved bigger blunders still: years of drift and compromise. All the time their Boer adversaries, expanding their strongholds in the interior, squeezing the natives into the poorest land, yet still leaving an Afrikaner (Afrikaans-speaking) majority at the Cape, grew richer and more numerous, more dangerous to Britain and her Empire.

To Milner, it was the whole annexation of the Transvaal, not just Majuba, that had been hopelessly bungled. And by settling for 'peace-under-defeat', Gladstone had taken another step in confirming the Transvaal as that dangerous anachronism, a quasi-independent nation in Africa. It was here that, for Milner, the 'great game' for South Africa emerged as part of the much greater struggle for world supremacy.

The phrases he used – 'imperial unity' and 'consolidating the Empire' – were conveniently vague. He flattered himself that he had no illusions about the true state of the British Empire. He was not misled by jingoisms. He was interested in power. Not merely for himself, but for England. This was the love of his life, pursued with a secret passion.

The years of drift and compromise in South Africa were, however, part of a general decline. Indeed, in the other settler colonies, for half a century there had not even been an *attempt* at a forward policy; *all* policy had been weak and negative. And gradually British power was eroded as, one by one, these colonies were granted self-government. As for the new black and brown colonies, no one could say whether they were to be a source of wealth or power. In Milner's eyes, and those of all the more sophisticated imperialists, Britain's main concern was not with the black Empire; it was with reasserting her power in the white Empire.

Milner believed that the answers would be found in South Africa, one way or another. He thought he knew the dangers. In his personal philosophy of aiming for the 'Big Things of life', big risks were unavoidable. Of one thing he was certain. The present backward policy of compromise offered no chance of restoring Britain's power. In 1886 gold had been discovered in the Transvaal hills called Witwatersrand – the Rand. It was gold that had lured Rhodes and Beit in 1895 to try to re-annex the Transvaal to the British Empire – a scheme in which Chamberlain and the imperial government claimed they had played no part. To the folly of Majuba had now been added the fiasco of the Raid.

Milner's own feelings towards the Raid and its political results were more complicated than towards the earlier blunders.

When the London Convention, by which Gladstone's government restored the Transvaal's independence, was signed in 1884, no one could have foreseen the discovery of the Rand two years later. The resulting explosion in the Transvaal's wealth had an explosive political result. Quite suddenly the Cape and Transvaal seemed to be exchanging roles, as political leadership of the sub-continent passed to the latter. There was a second anomaly: the Cape was a British colony, though the majority of the white inhabitants were Afrikaners; the Transvaal was still a Boer republic, though it appeared that the majority of its inhabitants were, by the mid-1890s, British.

When the Raid failed, Kruger was far too clever to take judicial revenge on the Raiders. He sent Jameson and the others to London, to be sentenced by a Crown court, to the great embarrassment of all concerned. Worse, Rhodes was proved to be the arch-plotter and arch-bungler of the whole affair by two official enquiries and two public trials, in London and South Africa. It could not be denied. Kruger had published to the world the code telegrams and other secret documents captured at Doornkop.

As the then Prime Minister at the Cape, as well as Chairman of the Chartered Company, Rhodes himself was forced to testify at the London enquiry – and a wretched figure he cut. It turned out that he and his multi-millionaire backer, Beit, had hopelessly overestimated the strength of

Boer commando, at the time of the Jameson Raid in January 1896, marching through Johannesburg to show the British would-be revolutionaries who was master.

Uitlander opposition to Kruger. A large minority were not British at all, but Cape Afrikaners, Germans, Frenchmen, even Americans. True, they had their grievances, including their lack of political rights. But they were earning good money in the goldmines, and were in no great hurry to overthrow the government. The same applied to many of the independent capitalists who had stakes in the Rand gold-fields. And even the Johannesburg 'Reformers' had not been able to agree on the crucial question: once they had toppled Kruger's republic of the Transvaal, what would they put in its place? An Uitlander republic? Or, as Rhodes and Beit had wanted, a British colony?

As for Rhodes, he was severely censured at both enquiries, and forced to resign as Chairman of the Chartered Company and as Cape Prime Minister.

Absurd as were the illusions of the conspirators in the Raid, the political consequences were real enough, as Milner knew to his cost: the imperial position in South Africa was disastrously weakened. In 1898 Kruger was re-elected President for a fourth term. He was now the hero not only of the Boers in the Transvaal, but of their fellow Afrikaners at the Cape. The bonds of a new kind of Cape colonial nationalism, which Rhodes had inspired, were now broken.

Milner had been sent to the Cape in 1897 with the task of restoring the world destroyed by the Raid. It was his job to be on good terms with all the pro-British party, especially the ex-German, naturalized British, millionaire 'gold-bugs' like Beit, though he privately thought that Rhodes's and Beit's plan for invading the Transvaal had been not only 'idiotic', but 'unscrupulous'. He did not now trust Rhodes (or his associates), and in any case would, he said (privately), 'rather it were Wernher, Beit and Transvaal things than . . . Rhodes and Rhodesian things.' It was for this – to concert a long-term strategy to deal with the Boers – that Milner had now come to see Chamberlain. He had no doubt of the lessons of the past. But the abject failure of the Raid and of the forward policy did not prove that intervention was the wrong policy. If Milner was to intervene, it must be on three conditions: that he had agreement of loyalists at the Cape, agreement with the Colonial Office at home, and the support of all shades of British public opinion.

He knew that the Colonial Office saw no need for a forward policy at all. Time was on their side, they claimed: only be patient and the Transvaal would fall into their lap. But time, Milner was sure, was *not* on their side: the Raid had strengthened Kruger's grip on his own people. Earlier that year (1898), Milner had written to London to ask for permission to 'work up to crisis', to force a show-down with Kruger. At the time Chamberlain, embarrassed by the enquiry into the Raid, had replied, politely but firmly, 'For the present at any rate our greatest interest in South Africa is peace . . . all our policy must be directed to this object.' But what was the policy now, in December?

Milner had a doubly delicate diplomatic mission during his working holiday in England. First, he must prove to Chamberlain and the Colonial Office that time was not on their side. Second, he must soften up the Press and politicians in general; he had no wish to end up sacrificed on the altar of public opinion. This in turn involved attendance at the dinner tables and house parties of the great political hostesses of the day.

That evening, 18 November, the train carrying Milner steamed into Vauxhall Station. He took a cab to his rooms at 47 Duke Street, where a stack of invitations awaited him. Everyone wanted to hear about South Africa.

Four days later, he arrived at the Colonial Office in Whitehall to see Chamberlain. He had every reason to feel depressed. He had just heard from friends in the CO: Chamberlain was sticking to the 'no-war policy'.

His own mind was made up. There were only two ways out of the abyss: either Kruger must make political reforms in his ramshackle republic or there must be a 'row'. To put it bluntly, the choice was between reform or war. And he believed 'war was more likely'.

Earlier that day, 22 November, the Colonial Secretary, Joseph Chamberlain, had briefed himself for Milner's visit.

If Queen Victoria was the symbol of the mother country, the Empire made flesh, her Colonial Secretary seemed to epitomize its other side, the dreadnought spirit. It was his strong hand that would pull the Empire together.

Such was the impression he conveyed – brilliantly. Yet, though less apparent, there was another Chamberlain: emotional, impulsive, moody, sometimes despondent. In 1895 he had been appointed Colonial Secretary by the Tory Prime Minister, Lord Salisbury. The frustrations of the last two and a half years at the CO had left their inner mark on him, as had the searing experience of the Raid, which he too had found an extraordinary business. Eighteen months afterwards, he would confess: 'The fact is that I can hardly say what I knew and what I did not.' Yet the evidence of his involvement *was* there, locked in his ministerial red boxes. Had it been published then, it would have destroyed him, and might well have changed the course of history.

Chamberlain's discomfiture certainly made him no more conciliatory to Kruger; he now had a personal score to settle with the old man. Nor had his sympathy for the Uitlanders increased with the Raid; and he regarded their leader, Rhodes, not only as a 'blunderer' who had alienated the Cape Afrikaners, but as a 'blackmailer' who had threatened to publish the missing telegrams if the Charter was revoked. Yet, since the Raid, these were Britain's only allies in South Africa.

One can well imagine Chamberlain's frustration. The Raid had made him keener than ever to cut the Transvaal down to size. By alienating the Cape Afrikaners, however, it had also deprived him of the means.

Chamberlain received Milner in his room at 2.30 p.m. on 22 November. The gap between them was as wide as ever.

Time was on the Boers' side, Milner claimed, as he put his case for 'working up to a crisis'. Kruger, re-elected President, was 'more autocratic and more reactionary than ever'. Now he was arming for the coming struggle with Britain. But either his government or the Uitlanders must rule in the Transvaal, and Milner saw no sign of Kruger's government removing itself.

To this, Chamberlain repeated his conviction that patience was now the *only* policy. First, because of the political effects of that 'accursed Raid'. It had placed the country in a 'false position'; the Afrikaners at the Cape had been alienated; he must wait until they resumed their confidence in him. Second, there were advantages in waiting. British influence was increasing all the time; internal opposition to Kruger must have time to develop.

Third and fourth, there were arguments against war. Chamberlain believed that military action would only arouse hatred and leave a legacy of bitterness, defeating their ultimate aim of a union in South Africa. If war had to come, Kruger must be the aggressor and the Cape Afrikaners – or at least a large part of them – on the side of the Empire. War would be 'extremely unpopular' in Britain, unless Kruger put himself blatantly in the wrong by committing a 'serious breach' of the London Convention .

Opposite The homely leader of the Transvaal, President Kruger, portrayed in London's *Vanity Fair*, summer 1899. The cartoonist noted the Good Book but gave him a rolled umbrella instead of a gun.

Above Cecil Rhodes, the ex-Colossus, sketched in Cape Town by Mortimer Menpes.

Give Kruger enough rope, Chamberlain seemed to be saying. To which Milner's reply was in effect that the old President had proved himself far too cunning to hang anyone, least of all himself.

If Milner's mission had resulted in anti-climax, he was not depressed. He had taken a hint from Joe that London's 'no-war policy' did not tie Cape Town's or Johannesburg's hands. To 'get things "forrarder" by my own actions,' was how he described his policy after the interview. It was in South Africa that a way of working up to the crisis must be found.

Meanwhile, he threw himself into the task of softening up public opinion at home, stamping 'on rose-coloured illusions about South Africa'. It was delicate work, for he had to catch up 'with *all* the leading politicians and pressmen – without seeming to run after them'.

Fortunately, Milner could rely on his vast network of influential friendships. At his first political house party that month, he bumped into Balfour, the Deputy Prime Minister, George Curzon (about to leave for India as Viceroy) and St John Brodrick, Under-Secretary at the Foreign Office. Curzon and Brodrick were Milner's own Balliol contemporaries; with Willie Selborne and Austen Chamberlain, they would soon come to dominate the Tory Party under Balfour.

The guests also included the Asquiths. Henry Asquith was now the leading Liberal after Sir Henry Campbell-Bannerman; it was essential, if Milner were to woo the Liberals, that he should keep in with him. And not only with Asquith and the Liberals. Milner's aim was to spread the word about South Africa as widely as possible, and if you wanted something shouted from the house-tops, you had only to tell it in strictest confidence to Asquith's wife, Margot, who was famous for her 'colossal indiscretions'.

That 'delightful' weekend set the pattern for the rest of Milner's trip. He saw George Buckle of *The Times*, and Spenser Wilkinson of the *Morning Post*. He was invited everywhere: by the Roseberys, the Rothschilds, not to mention the Queen, the Prime Minister, and the Prince of Wales.

Meanwhile, he was shaping his new political strategy. The 'no-war policy' did not tie his hands. Everything depended on the British subjects in the Transvaal. If they could be 'bucked up' and given competent leadership; if Wernher, Beit and the other 'gold-bugs' could be brought into line, too; if both their grievances could be presented to the British public in the correct light, in short, if the Uitlanders could be manoeuvred into the right, and the Boers into the wrong, they they could still 'screw Kruger'.

To arrange this himself he would have to wait till he reached the Cape. In the meantime he must pray that a premature crisis did not blow up in his absence.

CHAPTER TWO

Champagne for the Volk

Pretoria, 23–29 December 1898; Johannesburg, 23 December 1898–28 March 1899

> Geologist to Kruger in 1886: 'Mr President, the conglomerate gold-beds and enclosing sandstones and quartzites were sea-shore deposits formed during the subsidence of a coast line in . . .'
>
> Kruger to his wife: 'Mama, meet the gentleman who was there when God made the earth.'

WHILE MILNER might have been celebrating the quiet success of his efforts, a banquet was taking place in Pretoria in honour of the Transvaal Commander-in-Chief, Commandant-General Piet Joubert, and his commandos. They had returned safely after subduing, with the help of their Creusot artillery, a troublesome African chief.

It had been a triumphant evening for Joubert, the conquering hero, and 'Oom Paul' ('Uncle Paul') Kruger, the father of the republic. But the political realities were not so simple. Kruger was neither so unyielding nor so secure as he appeared. Joubert, the loyal general, opposed much of his policy. Behind Joubert there had gathered the 'Progressives', mustering about a third of the Raad (Volksraad, the Transvaal parliament), and determined to modernize the ramshackle republic before it was too late. Contrary to what Milner had told Chamberlain, change was in the air, radical change, supported (if reluctantly) by Kruger himself.

Chamberlain had called Kruger an 'ignorant, dirty, cunning' old man. Foreigners consistently underrated him. It is true that in some ways he appeared extremely crude. Yet those who knew him well knew also that his mind had its deep levels; that he was complex as well as crude.

By 1895 he seemed to be coming to the end of his tether. And then rescue came – from Dr Jameson.

The first great debt that Kruger owed Jameson was that the Raid united the volk behind the Transvaal government. The second was that it rallied the volk *outside* the Transvaal – especially in the Orange Free State, the sister republic, the first of the two voortrekker homelands. But the third debt,

Piet Joubert, Commander-in-Chief of the Transvaal army. Despite earlier bungling, the Boer army was fully armed with modern weapons by 1899.

Jameson's crowning achievement, was to teach Kruger how deplorable was the state of his own citizen army. The Raid brought to light a scandal. By law, every burgher had to provide himself with a rifle and ammunition. Of the 24,238 men liable to be commandeered, 9,996 were found to have no rifles; the rest had old or obsolescent weapons. There was only enough ammunition for a fortnight. The country, concluded Kruger, was 'practically defenceless'; 'the burghers had neglected their sacred duty to arm themselves'.

Kruger proceeded to re-equip the Transvaal army at a cost of over £1 million. Joubert had stupidly ordered some forty-odd thousand single-shot rifles, which had been superseded years before by new small-bore magazine rifles, the Lee-Metford in Britain and the Mauser in Germany. Kruger told him to buy a second rifle for each burgher, and made him import thirty-seven thousand Mausers.

Joubert was at least building up an excellent artillery corps. He was to order twenty-two of the most modern artillery pieces from Creusot in France, Krupps in Germany, and even Maxim-Nordenfeld in Britain. But the State Artillery Corps was still a midget by European standards. Joubert was told they needed another eight 75-mm Creusots. He delayed till it was too late.

Kruger had made some equally strange decisions. He commissioned four elephantine fortresses commanding Pretoria and the Rand, at vast cost. They offended the first principle of Boer tactics, mobility, and his object seems to have been political: to overawe the Uitlanders. But the fortresses had become the symbol of 'Krugerism', and the lesson the Uitlanders drew was the one he least wished them to: too weak to beat Kruger alone, they must summon the help of the imperial government.

Despite this blunder, and Joubert's bungling, Kruger had transformed the Transvaal's army since the Raid. The burghers could mobilize in a week: twenty-odd commandos armed with the most modern guns and rifles, an effective force of over twenty-five thousand fighting men – forty thousand including their allies from the Free State. The combined army was four times the size of the British garrisons in the two colonies, and the largest modern army in Africa.

Yet the future was still ominous. The basic dilemmas remained. Kruger must modernize the republic without alienating his deeply conservative burghers. He must make concessions to the Uitlanders without risking his country's independence. Above all, he needed a new convention with the British government in order to realize the dream of fully independent nationhood.

His first task was to try to sweep clean the Transvaal administration, which had long been both inefficient and corrupt. For this he relied on the young, brilliant, but totally inexperienced Jan Smuts. That year, 1898, he had boldly appointed him State Attorney. Just twenty-seven, Smuts had a reputation for academic brilliance combined with tact. But he would have to work fast if he was to pre-empt the Progressives, the Uitlanders and the imperial government. Kruger, like Chamberlain, believed that time favoured the British.

Jan Smuts, Kruger's 27-year-old State Attorney and right-hand man. He worked desperately to modernize the Transvaal before it was too late.

The trouble was that, at the root of most of the corruption and inefficiency, was the system of monopolies and concessions, in Kruger's eyes a 'cornerstone of his country's independence'. There was a purpose in allowing most of the huge profits of the dynamite monopoly to pass to German and French companies. By this means Kruger had built up one of the largest explosives factories in the world at Johannesburg, and he could also point to the useful political friends he had bought: German and French Uitlanders, foreign financiers and their governments. Kruger had in fact played off one set of Uitlanders, and one set of governments, against another. Smuts decided to try to settle the question of monopolies as part of a 'great deal' with the capitalists of the Rand.

In another field he *could* act swiftly: towards the regular Transvaal police. There had been several recent instances when the 'Zarps' (so called from 'Zuid Afrika Republik' on their shoulder flashes) had shot unarmed men – and not only 'Kaffirs' – when making arrests. The cause of Coloured people who were British subjects, and who had suffered at the hands of the Zarps, had been taken up by the acting British Agent in Pretoria, Edmund Fraser. He and Smuts accordingly met in Pretoria on 23 December 1898, the day of the great victory banquet. They discussed the Zarps and their treatment of Coloured British subjects amicably enough. Then Fraser suddenly launched into a bizarre outburst.

'Our own officials put us in a false position in the Raid,' he said; the time had come to take action. In handing back the Transvaal after Majuba, Gladstone had encouraged the idea 'of a great Afrikaner republic' throughout South Africa. Britain must now show who was boss; she was 'fed up' with the Boer 'maladministration', and especially ill-treatment of British subjects, and these were things (unlike abstractions such as suzerainty) the man in the street in Britain could understand. And, he added chillingly, Britain would 'go to war about things that everyone can understand'.

Smuts was left gasping. Was this the opening of a new and dangerous phase in the endless wrangle between the two governments? Were the British looking for a *casus belli*? If so, the ill-treatment of coloured British subjects would hardly wring the heart of everyone in England.

Smuts quickly learnt the meaning of the puzzle. Reports began to come in of a great protest meeting arranged to take place next day in Johannesburg. The British Uitlanders were in uproar. A young Englishman called Edgar had been shot by a trigger-happy Zarp. And the Uitlanders intended to petition the British government to intervene on their behalf.

It was little in itself, but it was the pebble that starts the avalanche.

People who came to Johannesburg saw one of the sights of Africa: a line of mine-wheels, mine-batteries and mine-chimneys spouting smoke and steam across thirty miles of the Rand. It was a geological phenomenon – too good to be true, it seemed at first. Other great gold-fields – the Klondyke, California, Australia – were notoriously fickle. The ore of the Rand conglomerate was not of a high grade, but its quality was uniquely uniform. And the sheer size

The greedy Boar (President Kruger) biting cruel Joe (Joseph Chamberlain, the British Colonial Secretary). From *The Political Struwwelpeter* by F. Carruthers Gould.

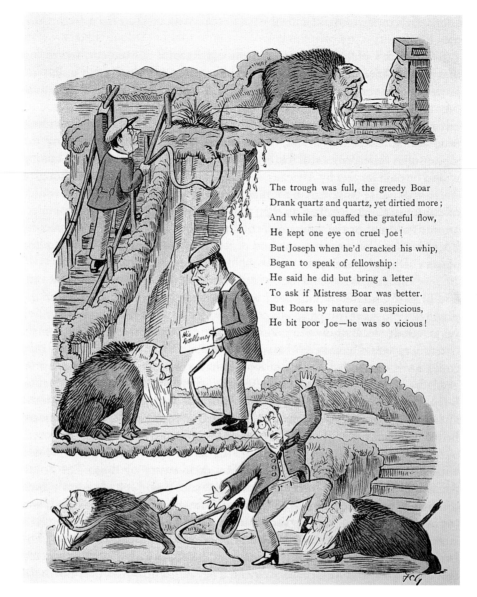

The trough was full, the greedy Boar
Drank quartz and quartz, yet dirtied more;
And while he quaffed the grateful flow,
He kept one eye on cruel Joe!
But Joseph when he'd cracked his whip,
Began to speak of fellowship:
He said he did but bring a letter
To ask if Mistress Boar was better.
But Boars by nature are suspicious,
He bit poor Joe—he was so vicious!

was a difficult stroke to counter. For three weeks Fitzpatrick played a double game, trying to get a deal for both the mining companies and the Uitlanders, and determined to fail. On 28 March he secretly caused the negotiations to collapse. Then he took to Cape Town the petition calling on the British government to intervene. Milner, now back in Cape Town, was being asked to forward it to London.

As the train crossed the bridge over the Orange River into British territory, Fitzpatrick crossed his Rubicon. The Raiders and Reformers had failed because they were divided and isolated. What Fitzpatrick could offer Milner was a powerful triple alliance: Britain, the mass of the Uitlanders, and Wernher-Beit, the giant of the Rand.

CHAPTER THREE

'Working up Steam'

Cape Town, 31 March–9 May 1899;
The Orange Free State, 30 May–6 June 1899

'If only the Uitlanders stand firm on the formula "no rest without
reform", we shall do the trick, my boy . . . And by the soul of St Jingo
they get a fair amount of bucking up from us all one way and another . . .'

Milner to his colleague, the Imperial Secretary
George Fiddes, 3 January 1899

MILNER HAD RETURNED from England in buoyant spirits. And he was
'*well pleased*', he told his friends, with the results of his trip.

That evening, 31 March, Fitzpatrick had arrived in Cape Town. The two
men talked far into the night, as Fitzpatrick poured out the story of the Great
Deal. First, Kruger was offering direct inducements to the mining houses,
concerned with preferential mining rights and lower mining taxes. Second – a
major concession – he was offering to restore the Uitlanders' right to vote
after five years' residence in the Transvaal. The Rand firms were required to
make some concessions in exchange: most important, the continuation of the
hated dynamite monopoly. Kruger also asked for pledges on a number of
political matters; including that they damp down the anti-Boer Press, and
repudiate the South African League.

It was an 'astonishing' offer, everyone agreed. But while Chamberlain
believed it to be genuine, Milner instinctively took the opposite view. Now it
turned out that Fitzpatrick had taken precisely the same line as Milner,
without any prompting from him.

The Great Deal, said Fitzpatrick, might be genuine as far as Boer civil
servants like Smuts were concerned. But Kruger himself had no intention of
giving a fair deal to the Uitlanders; besides, the Volksraad would never agree
to the concession. In thwarting it, Fitzpatrick had first obtained agreement
from his principals, Wernher and Beit, that Kruger's offer was a 'spoof'. He
had then set out to get the same agreement from the other great Rand firms,
especially Rhodes's Consolidated Goldfields, which was inclined to accept
the Great Deal. At the same time, Fitzpatrick broadened the base of his
campaign, seeking to unite the mass of ordinary Uitlanders behind the
capitalists.

That political support may have worked in his favour when he came to
deal with the Rand capitalists' representatives. At any rate, by 27 March they

President Steyn of the Orange Free State.
Until the last moment he believed war was
not inevitable.

had agreed to a joint resolution, of which the key demand was for the immediate and retrospective restoration of the original five-year franchise for those Uitlanders entitled to it. Despite opposition from Rhodes's local manager, this new 'Declaration of Rights' was handed to the Boer authorities, before Fitzpatrick had let the negotiations collapse.

Such was the inside story of the rise and fall of Kruger's Great Deal. In reply, Milner was equally frank. He explained that the next phase of their campaign would lie with the Press in Britain, before going on to discuss the possible replies of the imperial government. If the new petition was rejected, he would resign at once; fortunately, this possibility need not be considered. At the opposite extreme was the chance that Britain would send an ultimatum threatening war; but this would only be done if publication of the petition 'should so fire public opinion as to make it imperative'. Most likely was that Chamberlain would accept the petition, but postpone an ultimatum till Kruger had had more time to consider a climb-down.

As Milner had predicted, British public opinion did not lash itself into a frenzy over the Uitlanders. The Press took a broadly anti-Kruger line, but South African affairs did not long command the headlines. All he could do in the meantime was to keep the Uitlanders 'pegging away', and keep their cause well publicized. From mid-April, therefore, Fitzpatrick channelled the Uitlanders' grievances into mass meetings at mines all along the Rand, demanding restoration of the old five-year franchise.

Milner had also to work up the pressure on the British Cabinet to accept the Uitlanders' petition. His secret despatches to Chamberlain were masterly: no one could have guessed the intensity of his commitment to British intervention from these urbane and detached documents. By mid-April, however, as the British public continued to take no interest in *any* South African issue, his despatches became less urbane. Among other things, he warned Chamberlain that the Boers would yield to 'nothing less than the threat of war, perhaps not even to that'. By now, however, even Chamberlain had become disturbed by the lack of public interest in his South African policy. An urgent request was sent to Milner for a despatch for publication in Chamberlain's forthcoming Blue Book.

It was the chance Milner had been waiting for. A few days later he cabled back one of the most flamboyant despatches ever sent by a Viceroy, which came to be known as the 'Helot Despatch': 'The case for intervention is overwhelming. . . . The spectacle of thousands of British subjects kept permanently in the position of helots . . . calling vainly to Her Majesty's Government for redress . . .'

The British Cabinet was expected to decide for or against intervention on 9 May. It proved a difficult and anxious time for Milner.

Then, late on the 9th, the cypher cable from Chamberlain arrived: 'The despatch is approved. We have adopted your suggestion.' Milner had won, after all.

He was allowed no respite, however. A fortnight later he heard of another peaceful intervention: by Kruger's allies. William Schreiner and Jan Hofmeyr, leaders of the Cape Afrikaners, proposed that Milner meet Kruger and try to settle matters face to face; President Steyn offered Bloemfontein, the Free State capital, as the meeting-place. Milner regarded the conference as premature. But if he rejected Steyn's invitation, it would be 'too likely to lead to an outcry both here and in England that we *wanted war*'.

President Kruger had always been able to respond to a crisis. Now he scented battle. Although he had accepted Steyn's invitation to come to Bloemfontein for the conference, he was pessimistic about the outcome. Not that the truth about Milner was yet guessed by the Boers or other Afrikaners. The fiery 'Helot Despatch' was still unpublished. But Kruger was intensely suspicious of Chamberlain, and Milner was one of Chamberlain's men. Kruger now believed 'war is unavoidable or will soon become so . . . because the enemy is brazen enough not to wait for a cause'. Smuts, too, began to be haunted by doubts about Chamberlain's motives.

The special train from the Transvaal steamed into Bloemfontein on 30 May. Kruger shuffled out, and began his reply to the address of welcome. He would give 'everything, everything, everything' for peace, he said. But if 'they touch my independence, I shall resist'.

Chamberlain's *own* aims in the coming crisis preoccupied Milner and his Uitlander allies quite as much as Kruger and Smuts – and are puzzling even today. Milner knew the official (if private) answer. Since the crucial Cabinet meeting on 9 May, both Chamberlain and the government were committed to Milner's policy of imperial intervention on behalf of the Uitlanders.

But British demands – restoration of the five-year franchise, with a larger minority of seats in the Raad allocated to the Rand – would not give the British Uitlanders immediate collective supremacy. Would Chamberlain allow Milner to stiffen his demands? Not if Kruger conceded the five-year franchise, Milner believed. Chamberlain's aim – a limited settlement for the Uitlanders – was all British public opinion would accept.

Milner, however, had no intention of compromising with Kruger, and found Chamberlain's dependence on public opinion intensely frustrating. But a delicate plan, whose object had to be kept as secret from Chamberlain as from Kruger, was taking shape in his mind.

Chamberlain wanted a 'climb-down' by Kruger leading to a settlement; Milner, a war leading to annexation. These opposite strategies could be served by the same tactics. Chamberlain would agree to Milner turning the screw progressively tighter until Kruger climbed down. Milner would argue that to get a peaceful settlement they must first send out enough troops to frighten Kruger. Together the two screws – increased political demands and increased British garrisons – would precipitate war.

The Bloemfontein conference was, therefore, Milner's first step in 'screwing' Kruger. He would be 'studiously moderate', he had promised

Below President Kruger and his advisers in August 1899. It was his tragedy that he understood Chamberlain as little as Chamberlain understood him.

O!

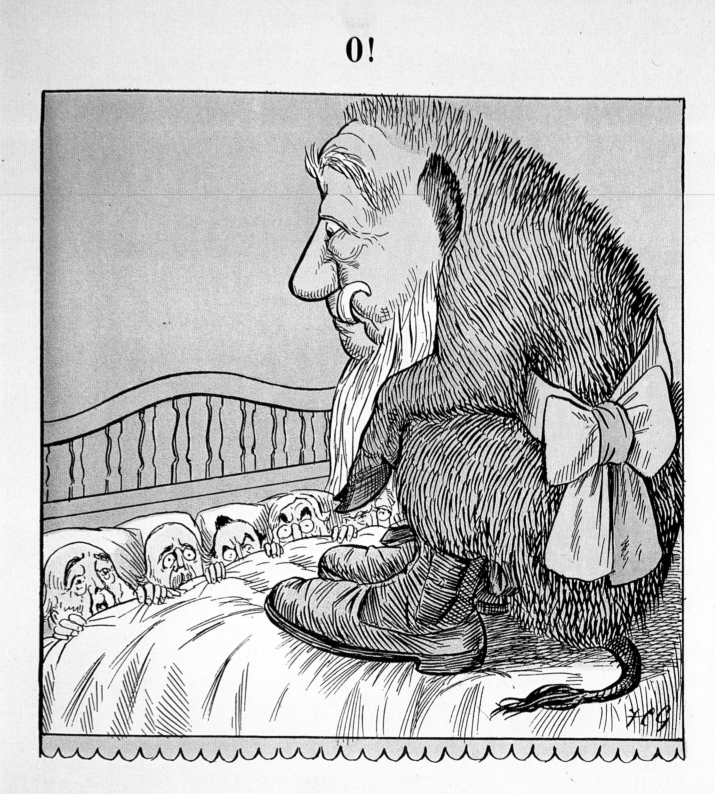

WHEN the children are in bed
O the Ogre shows his head,
Creeps along the rumpled sheet,
Tickling with his ghostly feet;
How can children take their rest
With an Ogre on their chest.

(15)

Kruger the Ogre terrifying the life out of the British Cabinet. Cartoon by F. Carruthers Gould.

Chamberlain. But once he had Kruger publicly seeking a settlement, the screw would tighten till it became unbearable. It was a trap out of which there was no escape, except a hopeless war – unless, horrible thought, Kruger agreed to the five-year franchise and accepted a settlement there and then.

He brushed aside Kruger's offered reforms with a counter-offer that could only infuriate the old man: some form of self-government for the Rand.

By Saturday 3 June, the stalemate remained unbroken. Milner produced his endless list of objections to Kruger's Reform Bill, and the conference adjourned till Monday. That afternoon he cabled to London: 'It seems that the conference will fail. . . . I have been studiously conciliatory. . . .'

Milner had failed to 'screw' Kruger, but he was not outmanoeuvred himself. He closed the proceedings with the chilling words: 'This conference is absolutely at an end, and there is no obligation on either side arising from it.'

In Milner's eyes, the moral of Bloemfontein was obvious. He had failed to frighten Kruger sufficiently. Now they must turn the 'war-screw'.

Specifically, Milner wanted the War Office to replace Lieutenant-General Sir William Butler as Commander-in-Chief in South Africa; he was thought to be 'pro-Boer', and was certainly anti-Uitlander. He also wanted competent officers sent out to organize the Cape border towns like Mafeking and Kimberley. And he wanted an *overwhelming* force pushed up into the dangerous northern triangle of Natal, where Colley had come to grief at Majuba, both to frustrate a Boer attack and to prove 'irresistible' as a political lever. These recommendations boiled down to detailed advice on three crucial military questions: how many troops to send out to guard the Cape and Natal; whom to appoint to organize and lead them; and how far forward to station them. If his advice was taken, he assured the Cabinet – disingenuously – there would be no war.

Kruger was, predictably, less reassured. His suspicions of Chamberlain were confirmed by Bloemfontein. Fortunately, his war preparations were nearly complete – apart from that important consignment of artillery which Joubert had failed to order in time. He knew he could have an overwhelming advantage if he chose to strike the first blow. However, the strategic key remained the Free State. Steyn had pressed Kruger to be generous to the Uitlanders, and Smuts, though swinging violently, after Bloemfontein, between his hopes for peace and his instinct for war, took a broadly similar line. Kruger did not doubt that, if war came, the Free State would fight shoulder to shoulder with the Transvaal. And he was more certain than ever that a collision with England was inevitable.

CHAPTER FOUR

Milner's Three Questions

Pall Mall, London, 8 June–19 July 1899

'It is perhaps not altogether remarkable under the circumstances described [the war inside the British War Office] that no plan of campaign ever existed for operations in South Africa.'

Report of the Royal Commission on the
South African War (1903)

THE BREAKDOWN at Bloemfontein had increased the risk of war. Not even Lord Lansdowne, the Secretary of State for War, could deny that. And for the first time he and his advisers at the War Office had to consider those three crucial military questions posed by Milner.

Milner's proposals were to send at once an '*overwhelming* force' – 'it may be perhaps 10,000 men'; to replace Butler with a British general politically and militarily capable of doing the job; to push most of the reinforcements forward into the frontierland of northern Natal. The Commander-in-Chief of the British army, Field-Marshal Lord Wolseley, took an even stronger line. On 8 June he proposed that they should mobilize the whole of General Sir Redvers Buller's 1st Army Corps and a cavalry division (about thirty-five thousand men in all) and make a 'demonstration' to overawe Kruger from Salisbury Plain.

In the growing South African crisis, the army needed a man of steel and fire at its head. 'Clan' Lansdowne – a former Viceroy of India, stylish, patrician, courteous – had neither, nor the faintest spark of imagination. The War Office was a laborious and antiquated department quite unfitted to controlling and directing Britain's new imperial army, and Lansdowne himself was utterly out of sympathy with Wolseley's soldiers around him. In the black months later that year, people were to blame Lansdowne, understandably, for the blunders of the War Office. And two other things, apart from his character, paralysed his war preparations.

First, his own Cabinet colleagues made their lack of confidence in the War Office abundantly clear. Lansdowne was kept on a tight rein financially, and the British army remained frail by international standards. Stretched by its commitments to garrisons all over the world and at home, the army had only

Below left The 5th Marquess of Lansdowne, British War Minister. The army needed at its head a man with fire and steel. Lansdowne had neither – nor a spark of imagination.

Below right Field-Marshal Lord Wolseley, British Commander-in-Chief and leader of the 'African Ring' in the British army. Lansdowne supported their rivals, the 'Indians'.

two corps and a cavalry division – about seventy thousand men – available for overseas 'demonstrations'. Moreover, it was seriously below strength, especially in artillery and cavalry, and short of essential supplies of every type, according to Wolseley.

The second reason for Lansdowne's inertia was his distaste for Wolseley and his supporters. The senior generals were split into two 'Rings' – Wolseley's 'Africans', and Field-Marshal Lord Roberts's 'Indians' – and the issue was still unresolved. The struggle left Lansdowne, who favoured Roberts and his 'Indians', alienated from Wolseley and most of the War Office. Diplomatic collaboration in India – Roberts as C-in-C, Lansdowne as Viceroy – had made the two men mutual admirers. Unfortunately for both, when Roberts returned to England after forty-one years' service in India, Lansdowne had failed to make him British C-in-C. The Cabinet had selected his rival, Wolseley. Roberts was fobbed off as C-in-C in Ireland – but he was still burning to snatch back the Horse Guards from the 'Africans'. Their second-in-command, and heir-apparent, Buller, blocked his way, however. So the 'Indians' waited their chance. The closer they drew to Lansdowne the worse for Wolseley, Buller and the efficiency of the army.

Lansdowne's reply to Wolseley's belligerent proposals was characteristically negative. He evaded Milner's three questions; it was too soon for 'open preparations for a row'. He turned down Wolseley's expensive proposal to

mobilize Buller's army corps. And he was unperturbed by the small number of British troops in South Africa, compared to the Boers' estimated forces. What was needed was to make sure the ten thousand men of the British garrison were in a 'thoroughly efficient state'.

In early July, Wolseley and his 'Africans' counter-attacked.

If Lansdowne found Wolseley rather trying, Wolseley regarded Lansdowne as more than a personal enemy. He seemed to epitomize the worst defects of the British military system, defects persisting despite the reforms Wolseley and his Ring had helped institute: reckless cost-cutting; pettifogging regulations and red tape; muddle and confusion in the War Office; above all, the encroachment of a civilian War Minister and his officials upon military matters.

Wolseley was not, of course, a mere theorist, but a famous fighting general. He had had an unbroken run of successes as a commander, and his name had become a by-word for military efficiency. But he was now sixty-six, and privately tormented by the idea that he ought to resign. At the same time he confessed to a hopeless longing to command an army in the field. But an expedition to South Africa would be led by his ex-protégé, Buller, six years his junior, and with a reputation for reform as brilliant as Wolseley's own. Wolseley was jealous; the magic had gone from the Ring.

His counter-attack on Lansdowne took the form of a salvo of minutes proposing a 'forward' policy. He repeated his earlier plan: mobilize Buller's 1st Army Corps; buy their transport for South Africa in case Kruger refused to be terrified. There was a second proposal: send out a first instalment of ten thousand men, as Milner had suggested. Lansdowne scoffed at this extravagant idea, and mustered other generals against Wolseley and Buller – especially one of the 'Indians'. In July, he had appointed Major-General Sir Penn Symons GOC in Natal, the more vulnerable of the two colonies. A more unsuitable choice would have been difficult to find; moreover Symons thought that a mere two thousand extra troops would make Natal safe.

In the absence of any support from Butler (who recommended *no* reinforcements *at all*) Wolseley turned to his old 'African' colleague, Major-General Sir John Ardagh, Director of Intelligence at the War Office. But Ardagh's forecasts were hesitant and conflicting, and Lansdowne easily brushed them aside.

The underlying strategic question was simple. On paper, the two republics outnumbered Britain's present garrison by five to one. Would they be powerful enough to drive deep into the two British colonies in strength? Or could they only adopt a raiding strategy, pushing a few thousand men beyond the border areas?

The Intelligence department's latest forecast was printed in a secret booklet, *Military Notes on the Dutch Republics* (largely unpublished even today), and predicted – correctly – that the Free State would throw in its lot with the Transvaal. Together, the two republics would have a potential invasion force of 34,000 men (including 4,000 Afrikaners from the colonies), leaving a balance of 20,000 to protect the homeland. They would be armed with the latest guns and rifles. There was a footnote about the possibility of a plan to attack Ladysmith, well inside Natal, from the Free State. But the general impression given in this and other Intelligence forecasts was that defending the colonies would be a question of checking 'raids' by up to three thousand Boers.

Military Notes gives the reason for this assessment, so astounding in the light of events: the Boers, were not regarded as a serious military adversary. The booklet concluded majestically: 'It appears certain that, after [one] serious defeat, they [the Boers] would be too deficient in discipline and organization to make any further real stand.'

The most important remaining member of Wolseley's Ring was Buller. Summoned by Lansdowne on 18 July, he proved to be even more alarmed than Wolseley about the defenceless state of both colonies. As the designated leader of the main expeditionary force, he might have to pay for those blunders with his own reputation – perhaps even with his life.

Then, suddenly and dramatically, the confused political situation seemed to clear. In mid-July Kruger made substantial political concessions, including a fully retrospective seven-year franchise. The crisis, according to *The Times*, was over.

Before Kruger's 'climb-down' was reported to the CO, Chamberlain had at last begun to see the real drift of Milner's policy (as had Smuts after Bloemfontein): to provoke a war and so annex the Transvaal. The gap between this policy and his own – to accept settlement on the franchise, if it was reasonable – had been widening since May. Chamberlain was displeased by the abrupt way Milner had broken off the talks at Bloemfontein; and still more displeased when he read Milner's immoderate despatches of May and June, which included the 'Helot Despatch'. The climax was reached when, to the CO's fury, Milner admitted that there *was* a case for war – it was the only way of getting annexation.

The danger of losing control of the situation alarmed Chamberlain. For, as a result of the activities of Milner and his capitalist allies (though Chamberlain cannot have known this), the tension had risen throughout South Africa. In the Transvaal, the Uitlanders stiffened their demands, and their new belligerence was echoed up and down British South Africa.

Then came the details of Kruger's offer of a retrospective seven-year franchise.

After the news of Kruger's 'climb-down', Chamberlain believed the crisis was over. But it was not in his nature to slacken his hold at the very moment he saw an adversary weakening. The diplomatic screw must be kept tight on Kruger until the settlement was finally arranged. And he insisted that a joint enquiry be held to establish whether the offer would give the Uitlanders 'immediate and substantial representation'.

It was a cool, rational way to end decades of wrangling between Britain

The 3rd Marquess of Salisbury, Prime Minister and Foreign Secretary. By September 1899 he realized he had been outmanoeuvred by Milner and his secret allies, the gold-bugs.

and the Transvaal. But Kruger did not trust Chamberlain, and claimed that an enquiry threatened his country's independence. As July passed into August, the air of uncertainty and deadlock drifted back.

Meanwhile, on 28 July, the House of Commons debated South Africa. Chamberlain had a delicate task. His speech must rouse his own imperialist supporters, of course, and continue to keep pressure on Kruger. Yet he must also reassure the centre Liberals, led by Campbell-Bannerman. In the event his speech was a triumph. He begged Parliament to support him and convince Kruger that he must yield before it was too late. Salisbury stood by Chamberlain, and Campbell-Bannerman made no attempt to deny the case for the Uitlanders, and was prepared to accept war as a means of achieving redress. The debate ended without a division, and the House broke up for its five-month holiday.

The Cabinet now reconsidered that tiresome business of military reinforcements for South Africa. Wolseley was still calling for ten thousand men, and Symons had raised his own estimate from two to five thousand. On 2 August Lansdowne conceded a token reinforcement: send a battalion (about a thousand men), add three batteries of artillery already under orders to go to Natal as reliefs, and shift five hundred men from the Cape – the total reinforcements would then be two thousand. Wolseley naturally protested that a relief was not a reinforcement, but the Cabinet took no notice. A few days later Lansdowne revealed that the War Office had at length worked out the contingency plan for putting the 1st Army Corps (the invasion force) on the Transvaal frontier. It would take four months, as matters stood – or three months, if a million pounds' worth of transport and equipment were ordered immediately.

This forecast of a four-month delay, during which they would be on the defensive, left the Cabinet aghast. How *could* Lansdowne have made such a hash of things? Salisbury, however, took the news more calmly. He had never doubted the 'futility' of the War Office. The question was: should they *now* spend the extra million in order to cut the delay? With splendid detachment, he replied that he thought it wiser not to incur any extra expenditure until war was certain; he considered the delay worthwhile if it concealed the 'scandal' of the state of Britain's military preparedness.

A few hours after Salisbury had made that decision, he received extraordinary news from Chamberlain. On 19 August, after further pleading from Afrikaner statesmen in the Cape, Kruger had made an offer that went, on the face of it, beyond the Bloemfontein minimum: a five-year franchise, with other complicated concessions thrown in.

In the light of Lansdowne's war preparations, this news was doubly welcome to the Cabinet. Salisbury congratulated Chamberlain, adding a sideways thrust at Milner, who was, predictably, trying to frustrate the new offer. Milner seemed to have been 'spoiling for the fight with some glee, and does not like putting his clothes on again'.

Peace flooded England, in that last golden summer of the century. While, in the South African winter, Milner saw hope at last – and the hope was war.

CHAPTER FIVE

Preparing for a Small War

Cape Town, London and Natal, 20 July–7 October 1899

'My own opinion is, as it has always been, that both Milner and the military authorities greatly exaggerate the risks of this campaign.'

Joseph Chamberlain, the Colonial Secretary, to Sir Michael Hicks Beach, the Chancellor of the Exchequer, 7 October 1899

THE 'CRISIS MAY BE REGARDED AS ENDED'. This time Kruger really did seem to have made his peace with Chamberlain. The appalling thought left Milner gasping. What could be more alarming than a settlement that he and every British South African were certain would prove to be a sham?

Chamberlain and the Cabinet had allowed the raging crisis to continue ever since Bloemfontein, and absolutely refused to adopt his next step: to turn the military screw and send out the troops. And while British ministers thus dragged their feet at home, the Cape ministers of the Crown appeared to have sided with the enemy.

For Milner, a long wrangle with Schreiner and the Cape Afrikaners had now reached an acutely painful stage. Schreiner's ministry was a child of the Raid: the result of Rhodes's downfall, and the polarization of Cape politics along the lines of the two communities, Afrikaner and British. Milner was trying to get Schreiner's support for the diplomatic campaign against Kruger – suitably negative support – to help prove that Kruger was irredeemable. But so far the Cape Afrikaners had been alarmingly successful in getting plausible-looking concessions from Kruger.

He also required positive military help from Schreiner. Instead, he had found his attempts to reinforce the frontier areas of the Cape actively obstructed by the Cape government. In early August Milner explained that Free State and Transvaal forces might be tempted to 'raid' Kimberley. Could Schreiner sanction reinforcements? Schreiner refused point-blank. Sending colonial (Cape government) troops would raise the political temperature and threaten the Transvaal negotiations then in progress, and their presence might unsettle the natives. In fact, Schreiner had correctly guessed one of Milner's motives: troops on the frontier *could* be used to invade the republics.

Matters then took a new twist with the revelation that the Free State was importing quantities of ammunition by way of Cape Colony, its chief trading partner. Milner was furious: his Afrikaner ministers left the colony defenceless, while giving every assistance to the enemy! To him the idea of the Cape's neutrality was preposterous, little short of a declaration of independence.

The row with Schreiner coincided with the announcement that, for the second time, the crisis was over. As well as the five-year franchise, Kruger was conceding ten seats (a quarter of the Raad) for the gold-fields: the same franchise as, and three more seats than, Milner himself had demanded at Bloemfontein. Milner had always recognized one fatal flaw in those terms: Kruger might actually accept them. The hope of annexing the Transvaal would die, for the Cabinet would never reject an unequivocal offer of a settlement.

All he could do was to use the same blocking tactics as he had used ever since Bloemfontein. He sent a snubbing cable to Conyngham Greene, the British Agent in Pretoria, who had personally negotiated the new offer with Smuts. He warned Chamberlain that the offer was, like its predecessors, full of traps and pitfalls. And, somehow, Greene's despatch to Chamberlain commending the offer arrived too late to influence him.

A week later Milner learnt Chamberlain's response. His warnings had been believed. At any rate, he had gained a respite. Now for a twist of the military screw, which he knew – despite what he told Chamberlain – would precipitate war. Furthermore, Milner had no intention of leaving the key to the success of his South African policy – political support at home – in the lap of the gods. He had many influential friends in Britain, among them senior politicians and powerful journalists and editors, who trusted him and supported him uncritically. In fact, their work at 'Headquarters' was beginning to take effect. The journalists, in particular, had taught British public opinion in the last few weeks of the dangers of delay, and of being fobbed off without a settlement on the franchise; indeed, *The Times* had taunted Chamberlain with weakness, as Milner could never have dared.

Still more active on Milner's behalf were his secret allies, the London 'gold-bugs' – especially the financiers of the largest of all the Rand mining houses, Wernher-Beit.

With the help of these new allies and old friends, Milner had been able to cultivate the ground at 'Headquarters', where he had 'sown the seed' himself earlier that year. Now a new, passionate friendship propelled him forward.

Among ten special service officers who had arrived in late July were Colonel Robert Baden-Powell and his second-in-command, Major Lord Edward Cecil, both destined to organize the force at Mafeking. The shy and melancholy Cecil, one of the Prime Minister's less successful younger sons, had been accompanied by his wife, Violet, who was neither shy nor melancholy. After months of spiritual isolation, of crushing anxiety alternating with crushing boredom, Milner now revelled in Lady Edward's company. Then, much to his regret, she left for Mafeking with her husband.

Her return to Government House coincided with the new peak of his personal crisis after Kruger's offer of the five-year franchise. Lady Edward was unaccompanied by her husband. It was she (the 'Godsend', he called her) who gave Milner the courage for the impassioned appeal to Chamberlain which he delivered on 30 August. He quoted Rhodes's famous belief that Kruger would 'bluff up to the cannon's mouth'. He begged for the long-overdue 'big expedition' to be sent out; this would bring Kruger 'to his knees'. And he solemnly warned Chamberlain that there would be a 'break away of our people' – the Uitlanders and Wernher-Beit – unless the troops were sent.

From a very private channel – a cable from Beit in London, 'portending a warlike turn of affairs', – Milner learnt on 5 September that his *cri de coeur* was at last to be answered.

Below Milner with his staff and his 'godsend', Violet Cecil (standing), at Government House, Cape Town, shortly before he 'precipitated' the war.

Chamberlain had swung 'back on the old right tack' with a vengeance. The Cabinet was on holiday, an incongruous moment, one might have thought, for the turning-point in the struggle. The Boers had just made that astonishing new offer. Yet quite suddenly, Chamberlain's patience began to fail. He had just received pleas from Milner and Wolseley for the extra ten thousand troops. He had also received Milner's latest cables pointing out that the new offer was qualified by impossible conditions, and demanding stiffer terms on the Uitlanders' part.

Chamberlain now accepted Milner's repeated claim that there would be no war, if they showed firmness by sending out troops. Milner's eloquence, and the impatience of the British Press, probably decided him; together they had finally shaken his confidence in negotiations with Kruger.

That Thursday, 24 August, he wrote to Lansdowne. He enclosed Milner's letter and, among much else, said that they should now give the Boers a 'week or ten days' to clarify the new offer and withdraw the unacceptable conditions. If there was no settlement within this time, they must assume that the Boers did not 'want peace'. In that case they must immediately send out the extra ten thousand troops and impose Britain's terms – at gunpoint (although words failed him at the 'hopeless' state of the War Office).

On Saturday 26 August he made, *urbi et orbi*, what his biographer was to call a 'short clanging speech'. Certainly, he showed ominous signs of strain. In his speech he said that Kruger 'procrastinates in his replies. He dribbles out reforms like water from a squeezed sponge. . . . The sands are running down in the glass.' This was not the urbane Chamberlain people knew. He seemed frankly exasperated.

For the last time he had tried the policy of bluff, of menacing Kruger without any means of enforcing his threats. The deadlock intensified. On 28 August he sent a threatening despatch to Kruger who, in reply, made an ambiguous new offer – a seven-year franchise, possibly with a joint enquiry. On 2 September Chamberlain wrote to Salisbury to call for a Cabinet meeting. The sands were reaching the end of the glass.

In the Foreign Office, the Cabinet assembled at 12.30 p.m. on 8 September in the room of Lord Salisbury, Prime Minister and Foreign Secretary: Balfour and Chamberlain, and sixteen other Cabinet members, including Lansdowne.

The political case for sending out the ten thousand troops (followed in due course by an ultimatum) was presented by Chamberlain. His argument was, at heart, simple. What was now at stake was no less than 'the position of Great Britain in South Africa – and with it 'the estimate formed of our power and influence in our colonies and throughout the world'. And, crowning all his arguments for sending troops, was the central paradox: that they would not precipitate war.

Only three ministers dissented. Lansdowne was still sceptical of the need for such a large defensive force, as was Sir Michael Hicks Beach, the Chancellor, though for quite different reasons. And Arthur Balfour, a power to be reckoned with, also expressed serious reservations about Chamberlain's policy. But then, he saw every side of the case and chose none; besides, he had been persuaded, like most of the Cabinet, that Kruger would surrender rather than fight, once the troops went out. The Cabinet therefore supported Chamberlain's plan. The first instalment of troops would be ordered to Natal as soon as possible.

Should they also send an ultimatum? The Cabinet dug in their heels. Salisbury was determined not to be rushed; British public opinion was not yet ready. Perhaps it was the Boers who could be manoeuvred into issuing the ultimatum. Besides, there was a crucial military argument for postponing hasty diplomatic action. The ten thousand troops would not be in position on the Natal borders till the first week of October. It was essential not to break the peace till then.

Half crippled by private grief (his wife lay dying of cancer), Salisbury could still show something of his old fire. He uttered a solemn warning to the Cabinet members. He did not share Chamberlain's and Balfour's optimism that Kruger would surrender rather than fight. He was afraid that the war would be the greatest war Britain had faced since the Crimea – yet they could not flinch from it. Their only alternative was to resign all pretensions to supremacy in South Africa, the strategic key to the imperial route to India. It was cruel, none the less, to be forced into a war for such a negative object: 'all for people whom we despise and for territory which will bring no power to England'.

He wrote a short comment on Milner's letter to Chamberlain that showed he had, too late, realized how Milner, with the Uitlanders and Wernher, Beit and Co., had outmanoeuvred Chamberlain and the Cabinet. 'What he has done cannot be effaced. We have to act upon a moral field prepared for us by him and his jingo supporters.'

Within ten days, the War Office could give news of the smooth embarkation of British regiments from India, all seasoned white troops, rich in stores, and with eighteen field-guns, three field hospitals, and over a thousand Indian bearers. Of other reinforcements, two battalions (about two thousand men) had been sent in late August, and Wolseley managed to scrape together a further three. The total force in Natal would come to fifteen thousand by mid-October, when all the eight thousand reinforcements (two thousand being there already) had landed, compared with the Boers' fifty-four thousand from both republics. Wolseley reckoned that these fifteen thousand men would be enough to guard all Natal – 'everything south of the Biggarsberg [range]' including the main British military depot at Ladysmith. He would 'stake his reputation on it'.

The War Office, it would soon be proved, had disastrously miscalculated the number of troops needed to defend Natal. Equally disastrous was their answer to Milner's second crucial question: who was to lead and organize the defence?

Even after agreeing to the despatch of the reinforcements, Lansdowne saw

Below left 64-year-old General Sir George White. Chamberlain believed he was too old and doddery to take command in Natal; Wolseley agreed. White was one of the 'Indians', and knew nothing of South Africa.

Below right General Sir Redvers Buller, the Commander-in-Chief in South Africa, overwhelmed by forebodings. All through that summer he had warned the War Office: 'Do not go north of the Tugela.'

no reason to send out anyone to command them. Butler had been sacked, but only a stand-in had been appointed for the Cape, while Symons remained GOC in Natal. Wolseley pressed Lansdowne, who was keen on another of Roberts's Ring, Lieutenant-General Sir George White. Chamberlain, however, thought him too old (he was sixty-four) and doddery (he still limped from a riding accident), and had proposed ever since June – very sensibly – that Buller should go himself. But White was appointed GOC in Natal (though he had served only in India, and knew nothing of war against white opponents), and chose for his staff Roberts's two keenest young partisans, Colonels Ian Hamilton and Sir Henry Rawlinson. Wolseley gave him, as his intelligence expert, the elderly Major Altham who had written *Military Notes*, with its optimistic predictions. On 16 September White, Hamilton and Rawlinson sailed for Durban via Cape Town.

Wolseley and the Army Board wanted to start buying mules, wagons, and so on, for Buller's Army Corps, so that it could be mobilized, if needed, as quickly as possible. Lansdowne refused. The fifteen thousand men would protect Natal from Boer invasion. What did it matter if their own invasion

plans were delayed by the need to economize? They could wait until it was clear Kruger wasn't bluffing.

After a stormy interview Buller sent Lansdowne a private letter of the highest importance, never published until this book first appeared. It shows that he – alone of any general – had come near to grasping the scale of the danger in which Chamberlain's policy of 'bluff' had put them. From past campaigns, Buller knew the Boers better than any other English general. (This was probably the reason, as well as Buller's links with the Liberals, why Lansdowne had dubbed him a 'pro-Boer'.) Now he begged Lansdowne to send 'a further force at once' to Natal in addition to the eight thousand: 'We have let things drift until we are in a very uncomfortable military position . . . [the Boers] have now the chance of inflicting a serious reverse upon us in Natal.' Elsewhere, he stressed that White should not push his force too far forward in Natal, but stay on the defensive behind the strong line of the Tugela River. To go nearer the Biggarsberg and garrison Ladysmith – as planned at present – would be to invite disaster.

White arrived at Cape Town on 3 October. He found Milner 'nervous and . . . overdone', and was disturbed by his news. When he left, Lansdowne was full of talk of Kruger's 'bluffing'. White himself did not believe there would be serious fighting, and told his staff that it was not their task to avenge Majuba and invade the Transvaal. They must defend Natal until the arrival of the Army Corps. His plan was to put the bulk of his forces 'just in front of Ladysmith', on the slopes of the Biggarsberg range. Thus he ignored Buller's warning (alarmist, he thought) to avoid the northern triangle and dig in behind the Tugela.

Now Milner told him that the Boer armies were in very large numbers on the frontiers of both Cape Colony and Natal. An ultimatum was expected. The first shot might be fired 'that day or the next'. The Afrikaners in the Cape were 'ripe for revolt'. At the same time, White learned that on 25 September Symons, the fire-eater, had decided on his own authority to push a brigade to Dundee, seventy miles north of Ladysmith, thus dangerously dividing the British forces.

In these alarming circumstances White decided immediately that he must cut short his journey to Natal by taking the train cross-country to East London, and then catching a boat direct to Durban. The three-day journey was a revelation. For the first time he saw the desert-like character of the South African veld. He saw, too, the armed, tough-looking Afrikaners who gathered at the wayside stations, and noted the crowds of Uitlander refugees from Johannesburg, many of them women and children.

On the voyage from East London, he was suddenly seized with the same sense of foreboding that Buller had felt for months. Belatedly, White had begun to grasp the answers to Milner's crucial three questions: he was the wrong choice as commander; Symons had pushed the troops too far forward; the reinforcements were wholly inadequate.

CHAPTER SIX

The Ultimatum

Pretoria and the Transvaal, 1–12 October 1899;
Cape Town and Ladysmith, 14–20 October 1899

'South Africa stands on the eve of a frightful blood-bath out of which our
volk shall come . . . either as . . . hewers of wood and drawers of water for
a hated race, or as victors, founders of a United South Africa, of one of
the great empires [*rijken*] of the world . . . an Afrikaner republic in South
Africa stretching from Table Bay to the Zambezi.'

Jan Smuts's secret memorandum for the
Transvaal Executive, 4 September 1899

THE OLD PRESIDENT waited in silence, outwardly as immovable as ever.
Till the final month of the crisis, Kruger had in fact struggled for a settlement.
It was his own tragedy that he understood 'Camberlen' as little as
'Camberlen' understood him.

The gap to be bridged was actually small enough. Chamberlain's terms
dating from Bloemfontein were still on the table. If Kruger gave an
unconditional five-year franchise to the Uitlanders, or a seven-year franchise,
coupled with a joint enquiry to guarantee its good faith, Chamberlain had
promised to call it a day. By the end of August, the pressures on Kruger to
make one or other of these concessions had reached a climax. Senior
politicians from both the Free State and the Cape urged him to change his
mind. If he had accepted this advice, a settlement would surely have
followed. No one – not even Milner – could have prevented it. But on 2
September Kruger, like Chamberlain, had reached breaking-point. He had
decided to make no further concessions. For three weeks more he and
Chamberlain were still to exchange messages, but the real negotiations had
ended that day.

Why did Kruger, who had, as it seems to us today, so much more than
Chamberlain to lose by war, reject the last chance of peace? Certainly not
because he was driven to it by Boer public opinion. The simple fact is that
Kruger rejected the chance of compromise because he did not realize it
existed. He thought further concessions would have been futile. Chamberlain, he believed, had set a trap to humiliate the volk before he destroyed
them: 'With God before our eyes we feel that we cannot go further without
endangering our independence.'

Kruger and Smuts had confused Milner's aims with Chamberlain's. Had

Transvaal burghers, off to the war front, leave Johannesburg by train after commandeering a tea-merchant's wagon. The women pose with the rifles; an African servant carries the luggage.

they realized Chamberlain's – and the British government's – capacity for compromise, they would have heeded the advice of their allies. But all they saw was the 'Pushful Joe' of the cartoonists, and the only voice they heard was the public one, and that hardly seemed the voice of compromise. The cycle of suspicion dating from the Raid had proved to be the Raid's most disastrous result. The one man who could have enlightened them – Milner – was set on war.

So Kruger, like Chamberlain, had decided war was inevitable. Smuts said, 'Humanly speaking a war between the Republics and England is certain.' He then launched into a feverish plan for a military offensive, its keynote a blitzkrieg against Natal before any reinforcements could arrive. By throwing all their troops against Natal, they could take Durban. They would also encourage the Cape Afrikaners to 'form themselves into a third great republic'. The international repercussions would be dramatic. Britain's enemies – France, Russia and Germany – would hasten to exploit her collapse.

The chief obstacle to this plan, however, proved to be President Steyn. On 9 September the crucial news reached South Africa: the British Cabinet had

Kit inspection at Cape Town for the reinforcements just landed from England. Before the war broke out only 10,000 British reinforcements had been sent, mainly troops from India.

decided to send out eight thousand troops to Natal. This gave the republics' combined armies barely a month before they lost the advantage of numerical superiority. Yet Steyn was still not convinced war was inevitable. On 22 September, the Cabinet pressed the second war-button, deciding to send the Army Corps. On 25 September Pretoria learned that the British were moving north to Dundee. Kruger cabled Steyn, desperately, 'If we wait longer the position may become hopeless.'

Without waiting for their allies, the Transvaal at last mobilized on 28 September. The next step was to send Britain an ultimatum. Steyn was still the stumbling-block, insisting that the ultimatum should accuse Britain of breaking the London Convention. The ultimatum was redrafted accordingly, and by the end of September was ready. Steyn's doubts were resolved: Chamberlain was bent on war. The two republics must strike first.

The Free State mobilized its forces on 2 October. A further week was lost while the burghers moved up to the frontiers. Finally, at 5 p.m. on 9 October, Francis Reitz, the Transvaal's State Secretary, called on Greene, the British Agent, and delivered the ultimatum. By then the majority of the British troop-

ships had docked at Durban. Steyn's search for peace had cost the two republics the whole of their vital four-week advantage.

The terms of the ultimatum were absolutely uncompromising. Britain had broken the London Convention of 1884 by interfering in the internal affairs of the Transvaal (that is, by taking up the Uitlanders' case) and by massing troops. It demanded immediate assurances on four crucial points. First, Britain must agree to arbitration on 'all points of mutual difference'; second, British troops 'on the borders of this Republic shall be instantly withdrawn'; third, all British reinforcements that had arrived after 1 June should be withdrawn from South Africa; fourth, troops 'which are now on the high seas shall not be landed in any port of South Africa'. Unless HMG complied within forty-eight hours, the government of the South African Republic (Transvaal) would 'with great regret be compelled to regard the action as a formal declaration of war'.

Greene was astounded. This was not the voice of the exhausted old man who had said at Bloemfontein, 'It is our country you want.' This was something much more virile and dangerous.

Transvaal burghers seen off from Pretoria Station. Before the outbreak of war 35,000 Boers had been mobilized from the Transvaal and the Orange Free State.

miss the 'row'. His Intelligence Officer reported Joubert's army at Sandspruit to consist of ten thousand men, with twenty-four guns. Yet Symons still thought Dundee was too far south for striking at the Boers.

British soldiers sharpening officers' swords in Dundee Camp in September 1899, ready to parry the expected Boer thrust into Natal.

The ultimatum had been received in London on Tuesday 10 October with derision, delight, dismay – and indifference.

Derision was the keynote of the editorials in Wednesday's newspapers, but, by and large, the British public displayed little emotion – or even tension – at the news. Wednesday's *Times* said that Britain would be at war with the republics 'at tea-time'. People took up the phrase: this was to be the tea-time war, a war in a tea-cup.

In the War Office, the ultimatum was greeted with astonishment – and delight. In September the overwhelming fear had been that the Boers might try to rush Natal before the reinforcements were in position. But by early October most of the troops had arrived. Immediately the anxieties had reversed themselves: Kruger might now try to cheat them of military victory by further diplomatic manoeuvres. And what if the Free State remained neutral? It was on the ability of Buller's force to choose the easy line of advance – over the plains of the Free State rather than through the mountains of Natal – that the invasion strategy depended. Now the ultimatum resolved this problem.

Wolseley was less pleased. He bitterly regretted the delays both in deciding to send the reinforcements and then the Army Corps, and in ordering the transport. After decades of penny-pinching, they were short of vital armaments, and mounted troops of all kinds. He had to admit, however, that the actual mobilization was a triumphant vindication of the system for which he had worked all his life. On Saturday the advance guard of the 1st Army Corps would set sail, as would Buller. Wolseley expected only a small war. Yet Britain was already committed to sending the biggest expeditionary force for nearly a century.

Chamberlain had been the first to receive the news. 'They have done it!' he is said to have exclaimed, amazed. Not only had Kruger's impertinent ultimatum resolved the strategic problems, all the interlocking political problems seemed to fall into place.

The ultimatum pulled the carpet from under the feet of the anti-imperialist Liberals, led by Harcourt. In effect, it was a declaration of independence, and an abrogation of the Conventions by which Gladstone had tried to arrange a settlement after Majuba. It was, however, the centre Liberals, led by Campbell-Bannerman, who were crucial to Chamberlain's chance of keeping the consensus: that is, by avoiding an actual division in the House.

His main political difficulty before Kruger's ultimatum had been this: to send out the Army Corps, the Cabinet had to ask Parliament for an extra £10 million. So Parliament had been summoned for 17 October. Chamberlain had to be ready then with a politically convincing answer to Campbell-Bannerman's overwhelming question: why was Britain going to war?

Painting khaki on the scabbards of British officers' swords at Dundee. Despite the camouflage, the swords were anachronisms, like many of their wearers.

Sir Redvers Buller and his ADC, Algy Trotter (left), pace the deck of the *Dunottar Castle* on their way to the Cape. Winston Churchill, who was also on board, reported that many soldiers were afraid they'd arrive too late for the fight. That was not Buller's view.

The thought of the odium that would attach to his own ultimatum had haunted Chamberlain throughout that week. The date had actually been fixed for the following day, 11 October, and the very stiff terms finally agreed by the Cabinet. Chamberlain assumed that the Boers would reject it. Its intended result was merely to justify the war to the British and to the world. Britain's basic demand remained full equality for the Uitlanders. But now they were to have a one-year franchise and proportionate representation in the Raad. It would be 'full equality' with a vengeance, for if the British Uitlander voters were in the majority, they would swiftly take political control of the Transvaal. There was also to be a new 'Great Deal' for the capitalists. And Britain demanded a new agreement to secure her own status as paramount power, and insisted that the Transvaal reduce its armaments. Finally, there was to be 'most favoured nation treatment' for the Cape Coloureds, Indians, Africans from the colonies, and other coloured British subjects. Given these concessions, the British government was generously prepared to guarantee the republic's independence and security from attack.

Having drafted this trenchant despatch, Chamberlain had still sought a way to avoid sending it. Now Kruger had sent his reckless ultimatum, and all these anxieties were forgotten. Chamberlain's own ultimatum would remain locked away in the files of the CO. Above all, the Boers had given him the perfect motive for war: to repel an enemy's invasion.

On Saturday 14 October, before a huge, cheerful, patriotic crowd gathered at Southampton Docks, General Sir Redvers Buller strode briskly up the gang-plank of the Dunottar Castle, the ship that would take him to South Africa. Few in the crowd could have guessed his feelings at that moment. It was not, as Lansdowne had claimed, that he was a Boer sympathizer. He had now come to accept the war as inevitable. But he was overwhelmed by his forebodings. All through July and August he had warned the War Office: 'Do not go north of the Tugela'. As usual, Lansdowne had ignored his advice. Now he had seen the latest War Office cables from South Africa, which left him aghast. White reported that he was allowing Symons to keep the garrison at Dundee, and Lansdowne had upheld that decision in the teeth of Buller's protests.

In public, Buller gave no hint of these bitter feelings. He was fifty-nine, yet he looked fit enough to be fifty. Bronzed, heavily moustached, the very archetype of the British warrior, he stood waving his hat as the *Dunottar Castle* steamed slowly out, to a hurricane of cheers from the quayside.

The following Tuesday, the House of Commons, recalled prematurely, voted to pay the £10 million needed for Buller's Army Corps. Chamberlain defended his South African policy, from the Raid to the Ultimatum. He spoke for three hours, his basic theme that aggressive republicanism had made war inevitable. Only a handful of members voted against the government. It had appeared, once, that South Africa would be his political graveyard. Now it seemed to have given him the greatest triumph of his career.

In Cape Town the Boer ultimatum caused little public excitement. For weeks now the war had seemed a foregone conclusion to most people in the colony, pro-British or pro-Boer. Ever since August British refugees had been flooding out of the Rand. There was a rumour (accurate enough) that the Boers

Coal trucks packed with British Uitlander refugees fleeing Johannesburg as the crisis deepened in July and August 1899.

'THE WAR SCARE'

planned to expel British subjects. Lights began to go out all over the Rand. At the great mines, boilers were let out and crushing stamps hung up – except for a few mines commandeered by the Boers for the duration. The stream of gold had now been succeeded by a stream of panic-stricken refugees heading for Johannesburg Station. Thirty thousand people, it was said, travelled in open railway trucks to the Cape and Natal in the space of those few weeks. After Johannesburg had finally emptied itself, the total number of refugees was thought to be at least sixty thousand. The Boers had become once again the majority in their own country.

Milner watched the death struggles of the Rand with apparent composure. Outwardly, he remained calm and restrained. This was the peak of the crisis. Somehow he must soldier on (a resolve in which he was much strengthened by private walks with Violet Cecil). Then, on 9 October, after a week's ominous lull, the storm had burst. Near midnight, his secretary, Ozzy Walrond, brought him the cable from Greene with the text of the Boer ultimatum. It was, it seemed, his moment of triumph. He had forced Kruger to play a card that could only lose him the game.

In that moment the overwhelming weight of anxiety he had carried so long began to slip from Milner's shoulders. He was still worried about the military situation. He did not doubt that the Transvaal was a real *military* power; he believed in the Boers' capacity for war more than any British politician or

'The War Scare': Uitlanders fleeing in cattle trucks. When the gold mines closed, the Boers were once again the majority in their own country.

Opposite General Sir George White, caricatured by 'Spy'. His job was to defend Natal until Buller's Army Corps arrived. But he found his own force dangerously divided.

soldier – except Buller. But he had had to conceal this belief from his political associates, especially Chamberlain.

It was now a relief to be able to admit his fears to Chamberlain. He was anxious about Natal, and about the strategic border towns in northern Cape Colony: Kimberley and Mafeking. He had done his level best to see them defended. Baden-Powell was now dug in at Mafeking with six hundred Rhodesian troopers, and on 7 October Schreiner had finally agreed to allow colonial troops to be used to defend Kimberley. Most of the imperial troops in the Cape (five infantry battalions, now that the reinforcements had arrived) were to be deployed holding the Orange River railway bridge and the three railway junctions south of the Orange: Stormberg, De Aar and Naauwpoort. These were the keys to the way to Bloemfontein, vital to Buller and his Army Corps. Meanwhile, Milner was 'uneasy'.

On Thursday 12 October, the telegraph line to Mafeking went dead, followed, on Saturday, by the line to Kimberley. By Sunday evening, they had lost touch with all the country down to the Orange River, and a number of minor skirmishes with Boers were reported. It was also clear that Joubert was taking the offensive in Natal. But hardly a shot had been fired, though there were 'panicky telegrams' on Sunday from Kimberley. Milner found things 'satisfactory', and kept his uneasy calm.

Milner's private feelings about Kimberley and Mafeking were unusually delicate. He knew Mafeking would be besieged, and now feared that it might be forced to surrender. Why, then, had he not opposed Baden-Powell's decision to hold it?

Part of the reason was because to have abandoned Mafeking would have outraged the Cape loyalists. But there was probably another rather more subtle reason. Milner had set his heart on the Boers invading the colony, and both towns – one the Raiders' old base, the other grabbed from the Free State for its diamonds – made excellent baits. And, on the very day before the ultimatum had expired, the *bête noire* of the Transvaal, Rhodes himself, had appeared in Kimberley.

As Milner waited for the first battles of the war, a great hymn of congratulation began to reach him from England. Chamberlain and the Tories, Grey, Haldane and the Liberals – at long last they all agreed with him. War with Kruger had always been inevitable.

Inevitable? It would have been easy, Milner later confessed to his intimates, to patch things up with Kruger, and settle those difficulties with the Uitlanders. He had resisted the temptation, and 'precipitated' a war before it was too late. He had long been determined to 'burst the mould' of Kruger's Transvaal. War was the only means. Now Britain would annex both republics, which would finally 'knock the bottom out of "the great Afrikander nation" for ever and ever Amen'.

Already he had begun to outline his vision of the great Union of South Africa he would create, 'A self-governing White Community, supported by well-treated and justly governed black labour from Cape Town to the Zambesi.' This was the imperial mission, the grand design that would follow the war (*his* war, as he boasted in private) and the Pax Milneria that would be his monument.

But he had also to admit to one striking omission. He had done nothing to help African and Coloured British subjects in the Transvaal. 'You have only to sacrifice "the nigger" absolutely,' he had told Asquith in 1897, 'and the game is easy.' He claimed two great principles in his work: to 'secure for the Natives ... protection against oppression and wrong'; and to secure the loyalty of the very men – the Uitlanders – who were determined to keep the natives oppressed. And the second principle, of course, took priority for the time being, even if the ultimate solution was to see the natives 'justly governed'.

The conflict of principle had in fact been exemplified that week in the most cruel way. In terms of human misery, the chief sufferers from the decline and fall of the Rand were not the Uitlanders, but the African mine-workers from Natal and the Cape, and the Cape Coloured population. Now their employment had gone. They had little money saved, and the Boers were quite prepared to let them starve. Should Milner intervene? What about the proud claim in Chamberlain's ultimatum that coloured British subjects would enjoy 'most favoured nation status'?

One man, an official named Marwick from the Natal Native Affairs Department on the Rand, saved seven thousand Natal Africans from starvation by leading them home in an epic march from Johannesburg. Doubtless Milner approved. But for the thousands of African refugees for whom Milner, as High Commissioner, was directly responsible, he did nothing. He had to play the game. And that, easy or not, was to 'sacrifice "the nigger" absolutely'.

Slouch hats, Lee-Metfords, brown gaiters and green-khaki uniforms: the six hundred men of the Imperial Light Horse – 'Beit's Horse' – looked uncannily like the men who had ridden with Jameson (who was himself there at Ladysmith that morning). The ILH had been raised, at Milner's suggestion, from Uitlander refugees from Johannesburg (as had a second volunteer corps, the South African Light Horse). They were becoming a new kind of Uitlander army, largely financed by Wernher-Beit, and led by the very men who had been the political leaders of the Rand since the Raid. They were already thinking, like Milner, of the new Transvaal they would build after the war. As for the next moves, their plans coincided almost exactly with Milner's, though they lacked the fine moral polish that he put on imperial ideas. Get rid of Kruger, swamp the Boers, kill off pan-Afrikaner nationalism, then 'thoroughly anglicize the country'. Otherwise 'the war is wasted'. Above all, the 'unctuous rectitude' (Rhodes's famous sneer) of the British public must not be allowed to ruin the settlement. There was only one set of laws in the Transvaal that the Uitlanders considered really 'excellent': the laws 'to keep the niggers in their place'. They were glad to think that this was a subject on which Milner was as 'healthy' as on the rest of the points.

The bugle sounded the advance. Across the Klip River, under their new imperial flag, rode the six hundred.

It was 20 October – the tenth day of the war – and still hardly a shot had been fired. Yet Milner was not reassured by the stream of code cables from Natal giving the latest military news. At 3 a.m. on the 18th, White cabled to say he was pulling Symons back to Ladysmith. At 5 a.m. he changed his mind. It was all very disquieting. Milner himself felt sure that Symons would be cut off if he stayed at Dundee.

Early that morning Milner went for a ride. He returned to find a cable. Its message was clear enough, even without decoding: 'Bookoath shelling camp.'

Symons was under attack. Milner's War had definitely begun.

Redvers Buller has gone away
In charge of a job to Table Bay;
In what direction Redvers goes
Is a matter that only Buller knows. . . .
If he's right, he'll pull us through.
If he wrong, he's better than you.

Black and White Budget, 30 December 1899

PART II
Buller's Reverse

CHAPTER SEVEN

'White Flag, *Arme Blanche*'

Dundee, North Natal, 20 October 1899;
Elandslaagte, near Ladysmith, Natal, 21 October 1899;
Dundee and Ladysmith, 22 October–2 November 1899

'I don't think the Boers will have a chance, although I expect there will be one or two stiff little shows here and there.... I think they are awful idiots to fight although we are of course very keen that they should....'

Lieutenant Reggie Kentish, Royal Irish Fusiliers, to his parents, 30 September and 12 October 1899

'We ... finished just as darkness fell over the field, & then the reactions came, I calmed down, I felt sick at the sight of the dead and dying, horrible sight, awful in their gastlesness [sic], blood to meet the eyes, groans to meet the ears, and among this we had to sleep ... but strange as it may seem I am eager to be in battle again now ...'

Private Prosper Paris, 1st Manchester Regiment, in a letter to Gerty, 24 October 1899

AT FIVE A.M. ON FRIDAY 20 OCTOBER, a curtain of mist hung low on the shoulders of Mount Impati, north of Dundee. It was from the north that Joubert's main army were known to be advancing. In the valley below, Symons's four thousand men were already on parade in full battle gear, a sombrely warlike spectacle: the 2nd Dublin Fusiliers, the 1st Royal Irish Fusiliers, the 60th Rifles and the 1st Leicesters, anonymous in khaki-brown paint over anything that might glitter, officers as drab as the men.

A sudden shout: 'There they are!' Everyone laughed. The idea of a couple of thousand Boers attacking an entire British brigade seemed comic; anyway, the expected threat was from Impati, and the north.

The whole camp was now staring across the valley at Talana Hill, a steep ridge two miles east of the town. Intermittently in the mist groups of figures appeared, crowds of riflemen with three field-guns: Lucas Meyer's eastern commandos. Officers were still staring in astonishment a quarter of an hour later when the first Creusot 75-mm shell swept high across the valley. The second splashed into the wet earth behind the Dublins' rear file.

Piet Joubert, Transvaal Commander-in-Chief, breakfasts with his staff at his *Hoofd Laager* (HQ) outside Ladysmith shortly after the beginning of the siege. His chaplain sits cross-legged in front of him.

Previous page The King's Royal Rifles retreating towards Ladysmith after a three-day march through the mud.

All three of Symons's batteries – eighteen guns – were ordered into action. They jingled off through the town, then unlimbered two miles from the enemy's position. At 6.20 a.m. the 69th Battery opened up, and at 6.30 the 13th joined in.

By 6.40, the enemy shelling had begun to slacken. The Boer guns had never had much chance. Three against eighteen, and Brother Boer had not proved himself much of a gunner. There were virtually no British casualties.

Even before the artillery duel was over, Symons had issued his orders. He was anxious to get the real battle started. His plan, like his ideas on strategy, was simple. To attack the enemy, the enemy must have first been allowed to concentrate. Yet the eastern commandos under Meyer must not be allowed to link up with the main Boer army under Joubert. Intelligence reported that the vanguard (in fact, two thousand men under General Daniel Erasmus) was now close behind Impati and might link up with Meyer's column in a few hours. There was not a moment to be lost in letting loose the infantry against Meyer.

Symons had already studied the Boer position. The ridge was, in fact, made up of twin hills – 600-foot Talana to the north, 550-foot Lennox Hill to the south. Directly below the summit of Talana was a eucalyptus wood and Smit's Farm, a group of farm buildings and stone walls. Here was the place, Symons decided, from which to launch a concentrated infantry attack. He would use conventional field-day tactics, the three-part Aldershot set-piece. First, the artillery duel and preparation of the ground. Second, the infantry attack and infantry charge. Third, the cavalry charge to cut off the enemy's

Boer scouts on Talana Hill, after the British withdrawal. In the background is Dundee; at the centre, the wood where General Symons was mortally wounded.

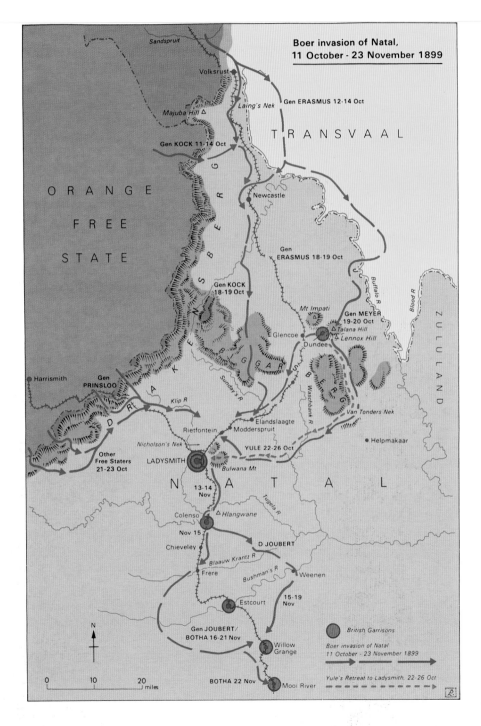

Boer invasion of Natal,
11 October - 23 November 1899

Leicesters training a Maxim machine-gun on Boers outside Ladysmith.

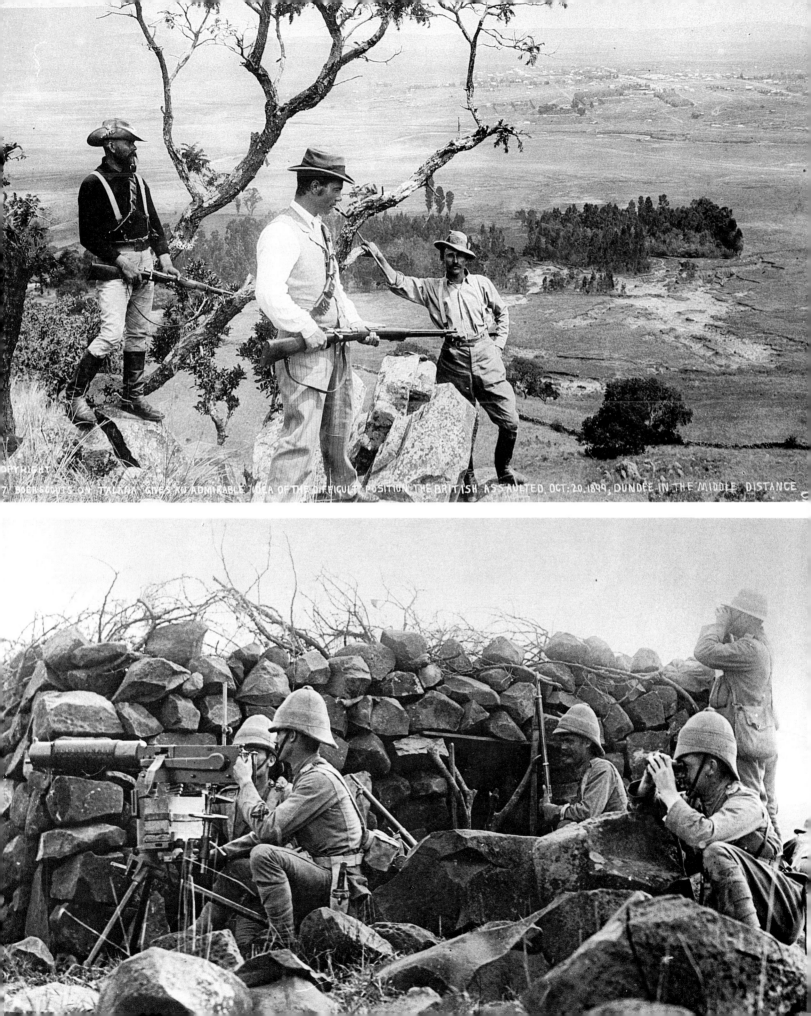

7. BOER SCOUTS ON TALANA GIVES AN ADMIRABLE IDEA OF THE DIFFICULT POSITION THE BRITISH ASSAULTED OCT. 20. 1899, DUNDEE IN THE MIDDLE DISTANCE

retreat. These were the proven tactics in which all regular armies of the period were trained.

A few of the more intelligent officers had been alarmed by Symons's belief in the well-tried virtues of close order and concentration; to them, exceptionally open order was the only tactic against magazine rifles. He had decided to leave his artillery to cope with the southern part of the ridge, Lennox Hill, concentrating his infantry in the few hundred yards covered by the stone walls and the wood directly below Talana, before storming it in overwhelming strength. He wanted to deal a knock-out blow. There was no time for manoeuvring, he believed, if he was to crush Meyer before Meyer could join hands with Joubert.

Despite his views on infantry tactics, Symons had unconventional (if not reckless) ideas on the handling of cavalry. He told Lieutenant-Colonel B. D. Möller, the cavalry commander, not to wait for the infantry but to act on his own if he saw the chance. Hence, about 7.00 a.m., Möller took his small group of cavalry and MI (Mounted Infantry) and rode to the back of Talana to cut off the enemy's line of retreat.

By 7.30 the artillery duel was well finished. Time for the set-piece's second act – the infantry attack. Symons took a calculated risk in throwing almost everything he had into the battle – three battalions of infantry, two batteries of artillery and all the cavalry and MI. This left only the Leicesters and the 67th Battery to defend the camp if Joubert launched a flank attack, which Symons was well aware might happen. But it seemed to him the only chance of giving it to the Boers straight on the jaw. It was a nervous moment for the waiting troops. In the whole of Europe there was no body of soldiers that had ever been on the receiving end of concentrated fire from magazine rifles. Then the order was taken up along the line: 'Forward, men.'

A few unlucky men dropped, hit by invisible riflemen on the misty hilltop. The casualties were scooped up by the Indian stretcher-bearers of Major Donegan's 18th Field Hospital, and carried back to the dressing-station in the town. Most of the infantry reached the wood, where they found shelter in the ditches and behind the walls of Smit's Farm. They were now less than a mile from the crest of Talana. Above their heads leaves fell in swathes, cut by Mauser bullets.

For an hour, the unfortunate infantry brigade commander, Brigadier-General James Yule, tried to organize the assault. The men were unwilling to brave the invisible curtain of bullets beyond. Then, shortly after nine, Symons rode up to the wood. He had already sent two staff officers to order the assault. What had caused the delay? Yule explained that there was still a tremendous fire coming from Talana, despite the pounding from the British field-guns. Symons refused to postpone the infantry attack until the artillery had finished its job. His strategic anxieties were too great. Everything depended on attacking Meyer before Joubert joined him. Despite the protests of his staff, he rode with his ADC through the wood, dismounted and strode to a gap in the stone wall.

There were times in the wars of the nineteenth and earlier centuries when a

The British observation balloon outside Ladysmith. But smokeless ammunition made the Boer attackers invisible.

general had to sacrifice his life to rally his men. Perhaps Symons saw himself in this noble tradition. After a few moments, he returned through the gap in the wall and, with his aide's help, stiffly remounted. When he was out of sight of the troops, he let himself be taken to the dressing station. Major Kerin, CO of the 20th Field Hospital, found him there in excruciating pain, mortally wounded in the stomach. 'Tell me, have they got the hill?' was all he could say.

In fact, some men had already begun to push forward on the west side of the wood. Despite that deafening tempest of rifle fire, the infantry began to make some ground, though with heavy casualties. By 9.30 they had reached a second wall on the main terrace below the crest-line. By 10.00 swarms of men from all three battalions could be seen firing from behind this wall, giving the rest of the infantry new heart to leave the wood.

The two artillery batteries had been having the best of the battle, and one of them now received orders to close up to fourteen hundred yards. But some of the gunners could not see the British bayonets. What happened next was described by Captain Nugent of the 60th, who was wounded three times in the final assault. Despite this, he crawled to the crest of the hill, which he found deserted by the Boers:

> I was just beginning to bandage my leg, when a shrapnel shell burst overhead. We... stared in astonishment. We could see our artillery on the plain below us 1500 yards off.... It seemed impossible that they should not have seen our advance from the wall... presently I saw another flash from a gun and then with a scream and a crash a shrapnel shell burst just behind us.... I felt rather beat then.... It seemed so hard, after escaping the Boers to be killed by our own people.

At last the shelling stopped. And fortunately for Yule's men, the Boers did not attempt to exploit the artillery's error. They crept down the reverse side of the hill and rode away.

The hill had been won. But each battalion had lost half a dozen officers killed and wounded; the total loss to the British amounted to 51 dead or dying, 203 wounded. And if the hill had been won, what else had been won with it?

Beyond the ridge, Meyer's burghers were streaming across the veld towards the Buffalo River. It was the moment for Act Three: the rout of the enemy. But Möller and the British cavalry had taken Symons at his word and vanished behind Impati – mysteriously – hours earlier. (The disastrous news of their surrender was not to reach Yule for a couple of days.) Still, the enemy were well within artillery range. After some hesitation, the gunners were ordered up the road between the crests of Talana and Lennox Hill. Here the two batteries unlimbered – and waited. Later, people said that the artillery commander had seen a white flag raised by the Boers. There was another reason for inaction: in the mist and drizzle they mistook the fleeing Boers for the 18th Hussars. At any rate, both batteries were ordered not to fire. And in a

The Raiders' revenge. Dr Jameson's field-guns, captured by the Boers in 1896, recaptured by the British at Elandslaagte on 21 October 1899.

matter of minutes, Meyer and his commando rode out of sight beyond the curtain of rain.

The Gordon Highlanders were off duty at Ladysmith camp, forty miles south of Dundee, when an officer ran down the lines shouting that they were to be out on the veld in an hour's time. The enemy, he announced, were there. Now was the moment to avenge those two white flags: at Majuba and Doornkop.

The previous evening White had learnt of Symons's tactical victory at Talana, and of part of its heavy cost: Symons's mortal wound. (The British had yet to learn of Möller's surrender.) Still understandably alarmed by the threat of superior numbers against his divided forces, that morning he had sent Major-General John French's cavalry to reconnoitre Elandslaagte, where the enemy were reported to have cut the railway and telegraph lines to Dundee. French had discovered that the Boers had occupied the station at Elandslaagte in strength of a sort. It turned out that this was the Johannesburg Commando and two hundred German and Hollander volunteers, under the overall command of General Kock. About a thousand strong, they had by-passed Dundee and ridden boldly down towards Ladysmith, ignoring Joubert's careful plans. Here was a heaven-sent opportunity for French to destroy this weak and unsupported commando, and to restore the links with Dundee. Consequently, he had despatched a message to White, asking for substantial reinforcements of infantry. It was this that sent the Gordons and the Devons scrambling into their battle kit and steaming down the line.

From the point where the men detrained, the railway line continued more or less level two miles farther to the station at Elandslaagte. On the right of the line was a stony ridge which looped round in a second ridge to form a horseshoe. Beyond the farther and steeper ridge, about a mile south-east of the station, half hidden among four kopjes, could be seen Kock's laager. The tactical problem was how to attack this natural strong-point. The hill was only three hundred feet high, but here the veld gave little cover. And, as at Talana, the Boers had three 75-mm field-guns, which outranged the British 15-pounders.

The Boers were vastly outnumbered in men and guns, however, owing to Kock's folly in advancing prematurely: 1,000 men and 3 guns compared with 1,630 infantry, 1,314 cavalry and 552 gunners with 18 guns. And by now French had, with the acting brigadier, Ian Hamilton, hammered out a plan of attack – another Aldershot set-piece. Yet there were important differences. French believed in the cavalry textbook. He had no intention of letting loose the cavalry until the infantry had succeeded. By contrast, Hamilton had his

Bringing out British soldiers for burial at Ladysmith, October 1899.

doubts about using conventional infantry tactics against magazine rifles. He now told his infantry colonels: keep exceptionally open order.

Hamilton explained his plan. The Devons would make the frontal attack, directly across the inside of the horseshoe. The other two infantry battalions – the Gordons and the Manchesters – with the ILH (dismounted) were to work round by the toe of the horseshoe and take the enemy's left flank. At 3.30 p.m. the long, regular lines of khaki began to move.

First to go were the Devons. Except for the extended order, it was exactly like a field-day. But, once down in the valley, they began to wilt under the rifle fire. As the range reduced, the acting CO told the company commanders that Hamilton had instructed him not to press home the frontal attack until the other units had worked round the flank. Thankfully, the leading three companies threw themselves down behind the stones and ant-heaps about nine hundred yards from the enemy's position, a small kopje shaped like a sugar-loaf. The men were surprised that they had had so few casualties.

Meanwhile, the main battle was raging to the right of the Devons, where the Manchesters had run up against the Boers' forward position. The Colonel gave the order to lie down and commence volley firing, which was met by a perfect storm of Mauser fire from the invisible enemy. Then, at long last, the concealed front line of Boers withdrew to the main position on a hog's-back ridge to the right of the sugar-loaf. The Manchesters pushed round the corner of the horseshoe, with the Gordons and the ILH wheeling round to the right of them. It was 3.47 p.m. So far the battle had only lasted seventeen minutes.

The Gordons were soon in worse trouble than either the Devons or the Manchesters. Despite attempts to camouflage their white webbing with khaki and cow-dung, the dark-kilted Highlanders made natural targets. As soon as the men reached the skyline at the southern end of the horseshoe, they were caught by rifle fire. The CO was hit, his arm broken. He rose and ran a few paces, shouting, 'On men, I'm coming!' Then he fainted. Men pushed forward in rushes, firing independently, stumbling over their fallen comrades. Then, at last, the forward companies found themselves in the lee of a stony hollow below the hog's-back ridge.

It was then – about 4.30 p.m. – that a full-blooded African thunderstorm swept across the veld. For the British infantry waiting below the hog's-back ridge, this was the moment. The Gordons slowly began to climb the steep, rock-strewn hillside. On their left, the Manchesters, their blood up, were going at the hill in great style. On their right, the Imperial Light Horse were strung out across the hillside, led by Colonel John Scott Chisholme, waving a Lancer's red scarf (his old regiment's) tied to a walking-stick.

Even now the attack might have faltered, had not Hamilton ridden up and pushed his way to the firing-line. He gave the order: 'Fix bayonets. Charge!' The men gave a tremendous cheer. It was answered by a bugle from the valley below – the Devons had resumed their frontal attack.

As Hamilton groped his way upwards behind the ILH he could see Chisholme's red scarf leading the race for the summit – a splendid sight, he later wrote. At last the inevitable happened: Chisholme fell, shot through

Burghers armed with Mausers. Before the war, the Transvaal government had used its revenue from the gold mines to order millions of Mauser rounds from Europe.

Symons's force were greater than the military advantages. Now he was ordering Yule to leave to the enemy not only Dundee, but all the food and stores, as well as the wounded, including Symons.

The column laboriously formed up. Only the officers knew that a retreat had been ordered. The men still believed they were going to encamp on Talana, and the townspeople were equally left in ignorance. At about 10 p.m. the troops moved off, marching in silence, with no lights. Each man took only what he could carry. Dawn found them astride the south-east shoulder of the Biggarsberg, fourteen miles from their camp. No one could doubt they were retreating now.

There was one rugged, narrow, six-mile-long pass on their route where, given a determined leader, a few men could lay ambush to an army. Yule's anxieties grew as the column approached the place. But by dawn on Tuesday 24 October the column had emerged safely. Ahead, the dusty road ran down to the plains by Elandslaagte.

In fact, the column had never been in any real danger. After it had left Dundee on Sunday evening, the Boer generals, with characteristic caution, had decided to content themselves with capturing the town and camp from the

Part of General Yule's demoralized column approaching Ladysmith after a three-day retreat from Dundee.

Safe at last? The Leicesters reach Ladysmith from Dundee, but within a week the siege had begun.

medical officers and wounded men whom Yule had abandoned there. There was no opposition.

Thousands of Boers rode down into the camp, to find it just as it had been left by the British battalions the previous morning. After taking whatever they chose, they reached the hospitals. There seemed to be no discipline of any sort. Burghers who had looted the town rode past the tents, singing and shouting from exhilaration and drink. Apart from the vast quantity of stores – forty days' supplies for five thousand men – they also discovered something else of value: Symons's code-books and other papers, including his copy of the War Office's secret handbook, *Military Notes*.

That same afternoon, while the Boers looted the tents around him, Major-General Sir Penn Symons finally expired. Despite morphia injections, he had suffered a good deal of pain. Added to this was the anguish of hearing that Yule had decided to abandon him to the enemy. He was conscious, but very weak, just before he died. He kept repeating, 'Tell everyone I died facing the enemy,' and left no one in doubt that he regarded Yule's retreat as a betrayal.

A few days later, the CO of one of the field hospitals and thirty slightly wounded men were sent north as prisoners to Pretoria, while the other hospital CO and the more seriously wounded were sent back towards

Ladysmith – though not to safety. Meanwhile, Yule and his exhausted column had marched, or rather staggered, into Ladysmith. But they found the garrison too preoccupied to give them much of a welcome. It was no time for celebrations.

Ladysmith was the third largest town in the colony; an unpretentious place of tin-roofed houses and the Africans' mud-and-wattle shanties. It was the railway junction that gave it life. Into this dusty outpost of the Empire, White had crammed thirteen thousand troops, with all the sinews of war. Every hour trains steamed into the station carrying new stores: enough to supply the whole Natal army for a siege of three months. Yet to allow himself to be besieged here was the very last thing White had in mind on 26 October, as the Dundee column straggled in. Ladysmith was hot, dusty, disease-ridden, claustrophobic, encircled by ridges and hills. Since 1897, the town had become the principal British supply base and training ground in the colony, the 'Aldershot of Natal'. But dominated as it was by those hills, there was no question of it being a suitable place to fortify and garrison in time of war.

Moreover, if White's army was besieged there, a relief force would have to be sent marching through the tangle of kopjes and ravines that White had seen from the train – the kopjes which made the north bank of the Tugela a natural fortress for the besiegers. Yet only fifteen miles south of Ladysmith, at Colenso, the veld returned. It was to these smooth plains that White could now retreat in safety and, if necessary, retire by stages farther down the railway line. At all costs he must not let himself be besieged. 'Do not go north of the Tugela', Buller had warned repeatedly. Locked up in Ladysmith, he would be a strategic liability. If he lost the initiative, he would sabotage Buller's whole plan of campaign. He would also endanger the lives of his own men if they were shut up in a town best known for its typhoid.

Such was the case against a siege. White not only acknowledged this line of reasoning; he accepted that it was on balance overwhelmingly strong. In addition, Hely-Hutchinson's political counter-arguments had proved exaggerated; indeed, the Governor was now worried that Joubert might decide to by-pass Ladysmith and strike for the coast, thus threatening both Maritzburg and Durban. Thus he would not have objected if White had quit Ladysmith. Why, then, did he stay?

The answer was simple. He hoped there would be no question of a siege. He gambled on being strong enough, though outnumbered, to destroy Joubert by a 'knock-down blow'.

It may seem odd that White, of all men, was prepared to risk everything on this bold gamble. True, the British had won their two victories. But these had only restored the strategic *status quo*, merely redeeming Symons's errors. Moreover, neither had been an unqualified tactical success. Talana had been marred by five hundred casualties (including the loss of Möller's cavalry), twice as many as the outnumbered enemy. At Elandslaagte, too, the British had had the advantage of numbers. What if the Boers had fought with equal – or superior – forces?

The lessons of the first fortnight's fighting only confirmed Buller's original advice not to advance beyond the Tugela. Yet White still clung to the hope of dealing that knock-down blow. Weak and vacillating, and fearful of appearing so, he now staked everything on a single reckess throw. It was an error of judgement that was to have the most fatal consequences: the greatest strategic mistake of the entire war.

The Boers were reported to be holding a position centred on Pepworth Hill, about four miles north-east of the town. By 29 October, they could be seen building a gun platform there, presumably for one of the Long Toms. White proposed to send his two infantry brigades to storm Pepworth. Yule had now reported sick, so Colonel Geoffrey Grimwood was to take the first brigade, consisting of men who had marched back with Yule – the Leicesters, Dublins, and 1st 60th – plus the 2nd 60th and the Liverpools. Hamilton was to take the second brigade, consisting of the three battalions he had led to victory at Elandslaagte – the Devons, Manchesters and Gordons. Each brigade was to be supported by cavalry and artillery. The plan of attack was based on the success at Elandslaagte: first an artillery barrage; then a flank attack on Pepworth by way of the hill to the east, capturing the enemy's guns; finally, the cavalry would roll up the fleeing Boers, pursuing them to the north.

The basic weakness of this rigid 'field-day' plan was that it did not allow any flexibility if the objective – the exceptionally mobile Boer force – was not where White hoped. And if the plan failed, two British brigades would be forced to improvise one – a situation for which neither officers nor men had yet shown any great aptitude.

'Horrors of war' was the caption for this picture, taken by the British war photographer, Horace Nicholls. A British gunner, his leg almost severed by a Boer shell outside Ladysmith, is taken to hospital on a gun-limber.

Yet this was not the feature of White's plan that alarmed his staff most. What gave it an air of absolute recklessness was that he proposed to send a second column on a night march through enemy lines to Nicholson's Nek, four miles behind Pepworth. Lieutenant-Colonel R.F.C. Carleton, the CO of the Royal Irish Fusiliers, selected by White to lead this expedition, had two battalions of infantry and a battery of small-calibre mountain guns carried on

'Mournful Monday' (30 October 1899) at 2.05 p.m. White's 'clubbed and broken' army retreating into Ladysmith. The ambulance cart at the rear heads for the Town Hall (with clock tower) which had been converted into a hospital.

mules, but no mounted troops. What he was supposed to do was not entirely clear, certainly not to him. But White himself had two broad objectives in mind. First, Carleton was to protect the west flank of the infantry brigades as they stormed Pepworth. Second, he was to block the enemy's line of retreat as the cavalry pursued them.

At 11 o'clock on Sunday night, 29 October, Carleton's column marched off. Soon after midnight Grimwood's brigade trundled off along the Helpmakaar road to the east, followed by Hamilton's, led by White himself.

Now for the knock-down blow.

There were no Boers to enjoy the sight of the British army in full retreat that morning; they were still hidden beyond the hills. The witnesses were British.

It was not only the fact of the retreat, but the way that it was conducted, that alarmed onlookers. The men's nerve had snapped after four hours' shelling. They did not do or die. They wandered back to the town.

There was only one bright spot to relieve this Battle of Ladysmith, alias 'Mournful Monday'. The British artillery, although outgunned by their Boer counterparts, covered the retreat. For a quarter of an hour one battery received the weight of the Boer attack. The artillerymen were joined by naval gunners using 12-pounders on improvised gun-carriages. But nothing could redeem the abject state of the infantry. Even French's cavalry came back in disorder. Among the civilians consternation turned to panic. There was a stampede at the railway station.

White was shattered by what he had seen. Nothing had gone right for him. Grimwood's main attack had spent itself against air. The Boers had changed their positions during the night and worked round Grimwood's flank. The humiliation seemed total. It was the first time in the war that two large bodies of troops had met on apparently equal terms. Man for man, general for general, the British were no match for the Boers.

Even now, White had not heard the worst. Colonel William Knox, left in charge of the reserve, told Rawlinson that earlier that day he had heard the sound of rifle fire in the direction of Nicholson's Nek. At about 2.00 p.m. the heavy firing had ceased. Later that evening, a Boer came in under a flag of truce with a message from Joubert to White. After a brisk fight, Carleton's column – 954 officers and men – had surrendered. This brought the casualties that day to 1,272. The 'knock-down blow' had fallen on White himself.

By Tuesday 31 October, Ladysmith was still not cut off. Yet White was so broken by the disaster that he would not consider the next strategic step: whether to abandon the town, burn the surplus stores and make a fighting retreat south of the Tugela.

Two days later, the Boers cut the railway line to the south, and at 2.30 p.m. the telegraph went dead. The siege had begun.

CHAPTER EIGHT

The Whale and the Fish

SS *Dunottar Castle* and the Cape,
14 October–26 November 1899

> 'My dear, the crisis – it's almost too much to be borne – how that
> marvellous Milner bears up I can't imagine, but he does and keeps his
> sense of humour that is much needed just now, until the troops come . . .'

> Lady Edward (Violet) Cecil to Lady Cranborne
> from Cape Town, autumn 1899

ON THE *DUNOTTAR CASTLE* the boyish war correspondent of the *Morning Post*, Winston Churchill, was finding the voyage 'odious'. Suppose they arrived at Cape Town to find the fighting over, as many soldiers feared?

This was not actually Churchill's own forecast. He did not think the Boers would cave in after the first defeat. He believed that Buller's Army Corps would not begin the campaign till Christmas Day, and not reach Pretoria, by way of Bloemfontein, before the end of February. So he did not himself expect to be home before the spring.

At Madeira, there were war cables from England: the Boers had launched an invasion of both colonies. In Natal they had driven south towards Dundee. In the Cape Colony they had cut off Rhodes at Kimberley. The news was not unexpected. Buller himself seemed calm and detached.

To many on the ship, even Buller's own headquarters staff, the General's aloofness seemed almost arrogance. It was a flaw in his character (though common enough as a form of shyness) that tended to make him enemies in high places. Perhaps what especially irritated such people was that towards strangers, and especially to ordinary working folk, he showed no such reserve.

So the time passed, with few diversions apart from the sight of a whale pursued by small fish – a disturbing omen for the Army Corps. Otherwise the voyage was notable for only one incident.

On Sunday 29 October a small tramp steamer heading away from the Cape altered course to pass close to the *Dunottar Castle*. As the smaller ship passed, people saw a huge blackboard hung on her ratlines, bearing the

British reinforcements just landed at East London cheerfully reading the latest newspapers. Perhaps they were reading the sports news.

words: 'BOERS DEFEATED — THREE BATTLES — PENN SYMONS KILLED'. There were no shouts in reply, just a shocked silence. For both pieces of news were bad: the death of the General, and the likelihood that, by the time they arrived, the war would be over.

On this latter score anxiety was soon removed. At 9.15 on Monday evening the *Dunottar Castle* steamed into Cape Town harbour. The secret war cables were read out to some of Buller's staff. The fiascos at Ladysmith and Nicholson's Nek had occurred a few hours earlier.

Soon after 9 o'clock next morning, Buller disembarked and drove in procession to Government House to see Milner. The strategic situation, as Milner saw it, was dominated by three things: the danger of Kimberley's surrender; the Boer invasion of the north-eastern Cape; and an Afrikaner rising all over the colony. He begged Buller to keep his Army Corps in the Cape. The War Office plan when Buller left London was for the Army Corps to land in the Cape and then push towards Bloemfontein and Pretoria. So Milner was able to say to Buller: stick to your original plan, but first, instead of launching an invasion, let your force repel one.

Yet implicit in these plausible-looking arguments was a truly abject proposal: in effect, to sacrifice Ladysmith and all Natal except Durban. For if the Army Corps were kept together in the Cape, there would be no spare reinforcements for Natal. Even if a successful advance on Bloemfontein brought in due course relief for the garrisons in Natal, it was barely conceivable that Buller could get there before January; probably he would take longer. Ladysmith had supplies to last only till the end of December. Milner was proposing to sacrifice a garrison of thirteen thousand imperial

War correspondents (Conan Doyle, right) pose for war photographer Reinhold Thiele on their way to South Africa.

Horace Nicholls, the war photographer, poses for a colleague at Estcourt, Natal.

Boer prisoners of war arriving at the Natal coast, November 1899. For the man on the right, it was his first sight of the sea.

troops, mainly regulars, to the political necessity of defending the Cape loyalists and, above all, of extricating Rhodes from Kimberley.

What was Buller to make of this extraordinary proposal? Strike for Bloemfontein, as originally planned? Take all his army to Natal? Or compromise – break up the Army Corps, and spread its battalions wherever the need was greatest?

By 4 November, he had decided: he would break up the Army Corps. It was an excruciating decision – and surely the correct one. He could not abandon Ladysmith and Natal to their fate, and the two battalions in south Natal could not save the colony. A final cable from White had confirmed that the garrison was unable to break out of Ladysmith and retreat behind the Tugela, and appealed for rescue. A few days later Buller received fuller details of the sorry state of Ladysmith, brought in person by French and his chief staff officer, Colonel Douglas Haig who, at his request, had taken one of the last trains out. Supplies of food and fodder were sufficient for two months, but the garrison was short of ammunition for the naval guns – the only guns capable of matching the Long Toms. Worse, morale among the troops was undependable after the defeats of Mournful Monday. Haig also listed in painful detail White's mixture of weakness and rashness.

Meanwhile, the authorities in London had tumbled to White's appalling strategic blunder in allowing himself to be north of the Tugela at all. Wolseley told Lansdowne that White must be sacked, and by 8 November both Buller and Lansdowne had agreed. But, of course, the siege of Ladysmith had begun; now White must first be rescued before he could be sacked.

Rescue depended on the Army Corps, and not one of the ships carrying it had yet docked in South Africa, except the *Dunottar Castle*. To the 'scandal' (Salisbury's word) of the initial delays others had been added, so that now, if War Office arithmetic was correct, the Army Corps would not be ready to move against the Boer republics till 22 December. However, nearly half the troops were now on the high seas, and would be in Cape Town before the end of the month. The leading brigade would reach Durban by 15 November, to be followed by the rest of the 2nd Infantry Division.

The problem of defending the Cape, in Milner's eyes, was bedevilled, first, by Schreiner's ministry being neutral, at best, towards the war, and second, because most of the population were Afrikaners and pro-Boer. In the event, Buller and Milner hammered out an agreed policy on most of their common problems. The worst wrangles with Schreiner concerned colonial volunteers, martial law, and natives. Both Milner and Buller wanted to arm some tribesmen for their own good; already Boers had raided and looted a number of native districts. But Schreiner insisted that this was to be exclusively a 'white man's war'. Eventually, he agreed to let these native territories be placed under the overall command of Buller, who arranged for native levies to be raised accordingly. Schreiner also agreed to the proclamation of martial law in districts that had actually gone over the the enemy.

With other delicate political questions Buller had less success. He wanted the British navy to impose a complete embargo, on food as well as arms for the Boer republics, at the Portuguese port of Delagoa Bay. Milner backed him, but the Cabinet would only agree to an – easily evaded – arms embargo. Buller was also anxious to impose news censorship in the colonies; this was blocked by Schreiner. In desperation, he devised a scheme for arresting the most notorious Afrikaner agents at the Cape. But Milner's nerve failed, and the men were released, to return to their spying.

On 9 November Milner went for a ride below Table Mountain. Behind him as he rode lay the veld, running five hundred miles north-east to the Orange River. The door was wide open to the Boers from the river to the sea. This was the nightmare that had sat on his chest throughout these harrowing days. But that day he looked down on the *Roslin Castle* anchored below him.

She was the first ship of the armada which soon crowded Table Bay. South

Africa had never seen so many liners, nor so many troops. Nor had the navy had such a task since the Crimea in 1854. Each day Milner could count the new arrivals. There were the transports bringing the 2nd Infantry Division, commanded by Lieutenant-General Sir Francis Clery and destined for Natal, and which, by 16 November, had been sent on to Durban. Still more heart-warming, from Milner's point of view, was the arrival of Lieutenant-General

Lord Methuen's 1st Infantry Division, Lieutenant-General Sir William Gatacre's 3rd Infantry Division, and a cavalry division – all destined to reinforce the Cape.

By 18 November more than a third of the Army Corps had disembarked at Cape Town, or been sent on to Durban. That day Buller decided he was strong enough to push Gatacre's division forward to Naauwpoort. Milner wrote the first cheerful entry in his diary since October; in the Cape Colony, if not yet in Natal, the Army Corps had begun to stem the tide of invasion.

There was one overwhelming – indeed, unique – feature of this war, which Buller recognized. The Boers were virtually all mounted infantry, something to which the War Office had made almost no concessions; only an eighth of the British force was mounted. Hence it would be mobile war, but of a strange, unequal sort: the war of a whale and the small fish that pursued it.

Now that disaster had come – Rhodes stranded at Kimberley, White at Ladysmith – Buller had to drop everything and speed away, leaving for Natal on 22 November – the whale to the rescue. Actually, his departure coincided with an improvement in imperial fortunes. The race to stem the tide of invasion seemed to have been virtually won. In Natal, two of the three brigades of Clery's 2nd Division were already at Estcourt and Mooi River, and should be able to shield Maritzburg. On the western borders of Cape Colony, Methuen had now crossed the Orange River; it was hoped he would be at Kimberley within a week. In the Midland and Eastern districts, it was true, the Boers were still advancing, but here, too, the imperial shield had been slipped into position in the nick of time. Gatacre's 3rd 'Division' – not yet a brigade, in fact – was holding Queenstown without difficulty, and the cavalry division, under French, was holding the line at Colesberg. The Boers might slip through the gaps; that was Milner's new source of anxiety. But only a pessimist would deny that the strategic situation had taken a dramatic turn for the better.

Milner remained a pessimist.

Foot inspection at Estcourt on the way to the Natal front.

CHAPTER NINE

Botha's Raid

South Natal, 9–30 November 1899

'Joubert stopped me from coming to Durban in 1899 to eat bananas.'

Louis Botha at a banquet in Durban, 1908

HAD MILNER HAD A SPY in Joubert's laager in those first ten days of November, it would have done wonders for his morale.

Younger burghers rightly regarded Joubert as 'weak and hesitant', because he shrank from attacking the enemy. But what the fire-eaters failed to understand was that the agreed strategy of the two republican governments was defensive. Kruger's main political objective was a new settlement, with Britain giving the Transvaal unqualified independence. Another victory in Natal could achieve this, but the first priority was to defend the land and the volk. To this end, the Boer forces had initially been disposed merely to *block* the enemy's attacks.

True, they had chosen attack as the best form of defence. But none of their pre-emptive blows was planned, as real offensive strategy demanded, to fall where the enemy was weakest. On the contrary, the aim was to find the strongest points in the opposing force and then smash them. In fact, their 'defensive-offensive' strategy involved invasion of colonial territory for two reasons. First, they had to block the immediate military threat, which they had now done in both Natal and Cape Colony, trapping forces in Ladysmith, Mafeking, and Kimberley. Second, they had to seize the best strategic positions for blocking the expected counter-attack – probably at least two relief expeditions – as well as a British invasion of the Free State from the south. Part of the second task now faced Joubert in Natal: how best to trap the expedition hurrying to rescue White?

On the afternoon of 9 November the Transvaal commandants held a council of war *(krijgsraad)* at Modderspruit, a few miles east of Ladysmith. They had been at war for a month, and from some points of view their success had been dazzling. That wild mass of irregulars who had cheered the ultimatum, had now beaten, in open warfare, the cream of the British army. The reverses at Talana and Elandslaagte had hardly affected morale, because they had involved such small numbers of burghers.

Yet Joubert had every reason to regard these first actions as disasters, for what they had cost him both in men and in opportunities lost. The Boer leaders at Talana and Elandslaagte had made serious strategic blunders,

Meyer by not waiting for the main force to come up, Kock by pushing on against orders. As a result, the Dundee garrison had escaped. And hence the exceptionally heavy cost, as Joubert saw it, of these early actions: 607 burghers killed, wounded and captured. For Joubert, these casualties represented 'a total defeat as great as has ever yet befallen the Afrikaner volk'.

Still, war is, in the last resort, a contest in blunders. Thanks to White, *all* these British troops were now trapped at Ladysmith. The question was how to frustrate the expected counter-attack. At the *krijgsraad* Joubert put the three main options to his commandants. They could try and take the town by storm before relief arrived. They could divide their own forces, and dig in along the line of the Tugela. They could drive into Natal to reconnoitre defensive positions nearer Durban. Surprisingly, Joubert inclined to the last option.

He was still intensely anxious that White might break out of the trap. Since the Battle of Ladysmith (Modderspruit, to the Boers), his own force had dwindled as men took French leave and quit the camps ringing Ladysmith to return home. Pretoria took immediate action, but these unpredictable fluctuations in the size of Joubert's army remained one of its chief sources of weakness.

Facing such difficulties, why did he propose the daring strike at south Natal? He certainly thought it less dangerous than the first option: to try to storm Ladysmith, 'a very risky business with a very doubtful outcome'. Still, there were numerous obstacles to the plan. First, the horses had not yet recovered from the strain of the fighting. Second, the Free State commandants had flatly refused to go south of the Tugela. Third, it was reported, correctly, that the British were exploiting the delay since the Battle of Ladysmith to pour reinforcements into Natal.

But Joubert for once was firm and resolute. With fifteen hundred Transvaalers – all that could be raked together without dangerously weakening the force guarding Ladysmith – and five hundred Free Staters who had ignored their leaders' decision, he reached the Tugela on Monday 13 November, and next day crossed the river, heading south beside the railway line leading to Maritzburg and Durban. At Joubert's side rode his right-hand man, Louis Botha, without doubt the driving force behind the raid. Of all the Boer leaders who were to emerge in the war, thirty-seven-year-old Botha was the prodigy. By the evening of the 14th, the raiders were some twenty miles north of Estcourt, which was reported to be garrisoned by three thousand British troops with two large field-guns and four or five smaller ones – less than Joubert had feared. (In fact, most of Buller's reinforcements were still at sea. Total British forces between Ladysmith and the coast numbered two thousand three hundred men, the bulk of them at Estcourt.) Yet neither Joubert nor Botha planned to attack Estcourt. Their primary job was to reconnoitre the country. Of course, if any plums fell into their lap, that was all to the good. And next morning, a large plum did fall to them.

It would be hard to imagine a more fatuous proceeding than that adopted

by the commander of the Estcourt garrison, Colonel Charles Long. On 3
November the British garrison, sent to guard the vital bridge over the Tugela
at Colenso, had scuttled back to Estcourt. Since then, Long had been sending
men by armoured train, unaccompanied by mounted troops, to patrol the
line as far as Colenso. It was a parody of modern mobile war: an innovation
that was already obsolete. Imprisoned on its vulnerable railway line, the train
was helpless against field-guns.

Soon after dawn on 15 November Botha saw the train – 150 men in three
armoured trucks on either side of the armoured engine, with a 7-pounder
ship's gun in one of the loop-holes – steaming north towards Chieveley. The
trap was soon sprung. Some miles south of Chieveley, just beyond a bridge
across the Blaauw Krantz River, the line swung to the right and climbed a
rise. It was here that Botha's party of about five hundred men watched (and
were actually seen by the British) as the train passed. Then they scattered
rocks on the line, and waited.

About eight o'clock that morning, the train steamed back from Chieveley.
Botha let it approach the bend close to the river, then his gunners loosed off a

Louis Botha (seated centre) under the
Transvaal *vierkleur* (national flag). Of all
the Boer generals, 37-year-old Botha was
the prodigy.

couple of shells. As expected, the engine-driver put on steam. The train swept round the corner and crashed into the rocks blocking the track. The engine remained half on the rails, but all three trucks were derailed.

From nearly a mile away, Botha's men poured shells and bullets into the stranded steel whale, soon silencing the 7-pounder. The upturned trucks gave little cover to the British. Some of the soldiers scattered across the veld, to be hunted down and captured. Only the armoured engine battered its way out of the trap, after men had struggled heroically for half an hour to free the line. The engine carried back fifty survivors, and the tale of disaster.

Botha cabled jubilantly to Pretoria: 'Loss of the enemy 4 dead, 14 wounded and 58 taken prisoner, also a mountain gun [the ship's cannon]. . . . Our loss 4 slightly wounded. . . .' (Neither he nor Joubert mentioned what would become much the most famous feature of the fight: that Winston Churchill was one of those captured.) Botha, flushed with victory, proposed striking out for Durban. Then, on 23 November, Joubert's horse threw him. He suffered internal injuries from which he was never fully to recover. His morale finally snapped, and he proposed immediate retreat, sending an extraordinary, despairing cable to Kruger, urging that they 'try to make peace with the enemy one way or the other'. This was, of course, unthinkable to Kruger; they must stick to their guns, 'dead or alive'. But when a council of war was held on 25 November, its decision was a foregone conclusion. Joubert must be escorted home, and they must all retreat to the line of the Tugela.

The raid on south Natal had been a dazzling success as a series of tactical operations. When the British attacked them at Willow Grange on 22 November, they drove them off with heavy casualties to the attackers. But the

John Bull as Gulliver: a Dutch cartoon. The caption reads: 'Help, Buller, help. The mules have run away and left me for the damn Boers.'

raid had added nothing to the defensive strength of the Boers' strategic position. For this they must now look, as Marthinus Prinsloo, the Free State's Commandant-General, had urged all along, to the extraordinary natural strength of the Tugela.

Botha threw himself into the task of fortifying the Tugela line. It was an immense undertaking, even for an army that could draw on an inexhaustible supply of forced black labour. Fifteen miles of rifle- and gun-pits, protected by dummy trenches and false gun emplacements, had to be hacked out of red, boulder-strewn terraces that rose, tier after tier, from the north bank. Five thousand riflemen, supported by ten field-guns, would man the trenches. The British would be within rifle-shot before they realized a single burgher was there.

It was the end of November. As an offensive force, the Boers had shot their bolt; now the various detachments of the Army Corps would try their hand at attack. Already, on the western front, Methuen had set out for Kimberley, where Cecil Rhodes, the Lion of the Empire, was braying like an ass.

Cecil Rhodes, besieged in Kimberley, but well supplied with champagne, according to the French satirical paper, *Le Rire*. The paper was right about that.

CHAPTER TEN

The Lights of Kimberley

The Western Frontier, Cape Colony, 20–28 November 1899

'To the indomitable will of the Chairman of this Company [Cecil Rhodes], whose pent up energies found vent in devising ways . . . of providing hungry women and children with food . . . did Kimberley owe its preservation.'

12th Annual Report of the De Beers Mining Corporation, December 1900

LIEUTENANT-GENERAL LORD METHUEN was a great English land-owner, but no one had ever claimed he was a great general. It was 20 November, and he was sitting in his HQ tent near Orange River Bridge. The pleasure he took in his job was genuine; it was all 'intensely interesting'. Buller had given him not only the 1st Division, but a field force, 'Methuen's Force'. He had eight thousand soldiers – the Guards and the 9th Brigades – here at Orange River (the Highland Brigade had been left to guard his lines of communication). He had to march the main column seventy-four miles across the sandy veld, setting out before dawn next morning, and relieve Kimberley. He was not to garrison it himself, merely throw in a few troops and guns, with full supplies, and take out the inhabitants who were reported to be giving trouble: the women and children, ten thousand Africans, and one Englishman – Rhodes.

The central problem now facing Methuen at Orange River, as, indeed, it had faced White, and was to dominate the war, was intelligence: where were the Boers? How strong was the invisible enemy blocking the path to Kimberley?

Spanning the Orange River was the bridge, which carried the single-track railway, the life-line of western Cape Colony, to Kimberley, Mafeking and on to Rhodesia. Somehow it had remained intact. Nothing showed more clearly how limited was Boer offensive strategy: the Free State commandos had never been sent to seize the vital bridge. Now it was safe, but the commandos remained, somewhere among the hills beyond the river.

Overleaf
Ammunition carts for Methuen's howitzer batteries waiting for the breakthrough at the Modder.

99

The first skirmish on Methuen's front had taken place here a couple of days before his arrival. Julian Ralph, the *Daily Mail* correspondent, climbed a kopje north of the bridge – and saw nothing except the veld. Northwards, it rolled on for fifty miles almost to Kimberley, with here and there strange funnel-shaped clouds of dust, then a galloping grey horse. A ghostly train vanished into an invisible fold of ground, as though it had sunk through a hole in the veld.

Of the actual skirmish Ralph saw only these phantoms. Yet he and the other correspondents had noted one thing that was to be the dominant theme of every battle of the war: invisibility. They began to realize that this was in the very nature of the new warfare – the warfare of the long-range, smokeless magazine rifle. The range of the rifle had spread the battlefield over five or ten miles. This, and smokeless ammunition, made conventional reconnaissance impossible. Yet the five-shot Mauser – and the ten-shot British Lee-Metford and Lee-Enfield – made the fighting doubly real.

Now Methuen had arrived, but still there was no sign of the Boers. The sketchy intelligence reports and inadequate maps had led him to believe that there were two likely positions in which the enemy would try to make a stand: first, at some kopjes at Belmont twenty miles ahead, where they had a laager of fifteen hundred to two thousand men; second, just across the Modder River, at the lines of kopjes at Magersfontein and Spytfontein, sixty miles on and about ten miles south of Kimberley. The main enemy force was expected to be at this second position. Buller had warned Methuen that nine thousand men were besieging Kimberley, some of whom would clearly move south to block his advance.

Methuen's best scouts were the 'Tigers', part of a unique corps of two hundred colonial guides raised by Major Mike Rimington, one of the special service officers sent out in July. Their nickname came from the 'tiger-skin' (actually, leopard-skin) puggaree they wore on their Boer hats. There was little else to distinguish them from Boers, for they spoke either the taal or 'Kaffir', and some knew this district as well as any trekboer. But the obstacle to all intelligence-gathering remained the Mauser; in flat ground the best scout in the world could be picked off from more than a mile away. So Methuen had only the vaguest estimate of the enemy's position and strength.

His second handicap was shortage of animal transport. For the time being everything depended on the railway, but to be fully mobile he needed draft animals. He had 190 mule wagons instead of the 367 promised. There were no oxen, and it would be nearly Christmas before any reached the front; it was only three months since the War Office had 'pressed the button'. He was also desperately short of mounted troops; of these he had less than a thousand: the 'Tigers', the 9th Lancers, and some MI. This, too, was the price of starting the expedition more than a month earlier than planned.

Weak intelligence, poor mobility, and the need to move at once, shaped Methuen's plan of attack. A wide detour cross-country was out of the question without ox transport. Instead, on Buller's advice, he planned to go bald-headed for Kimberley along the railway line, repairing the track as they went. Then the trains could follow, bringing up heavy supplies and reinforcements, and the food for Kimberley. Surprise, which had won British infantry so many victories in colonial wars, would have to carry them through. Surprise and British pluck.

At 4.00 a.m., on Wednesday 22 November, just as the sky began to lighten, Methuen's eight thousand, leaving the tents still standing and camp-fires burning to hide their departure, began to tramp northwards to Kimberley.

At the same hour, Lieutenant-Colonel Robert Kekewich, commander of the Kimberley garrison, climbed the 155-foot high 'conning-tower' and scanned the veld to the south, as he did every day. The tower was a scaffolding extension to the headgear of Kimberley's main diamond mine, the De Beers. Though it commanded a magnificent view, it also presented a magnificent target. Kekewich had strong nerves. He had been sent by Milner in August to report secretly on the defence of Kimberley, the largest and richest town in the Colony after Cape Town itself, and had telegraphed back: Kimberley was a sitting duck. So Milner, despite obstruction by Schreiner's ministry, had arranged for the place to be reinforced by British regulars. Kekewich was given a half-battalion of his own 1st Loyal North Lancashire Regiment and six semi-obsolete 2.5-inch guns. He had transformed the place. He was not happy about all aspects – and members – of the garrison. But at least the battle for Kimberley would not be a walk-over.

It was a claustrophobic place at the best of times. To this God-forsaken hillock in a sandy landscape had come diggers from all over the world, and built South Africa's first boom-town. Out of it now came 90 per cent of the world's diamonds, worth £5 million a year. Even if this was small change compared to the Rand gold mines, Kimberley was the rock on which the new self-governing Cape Colony was built. Unlike the Rand, however, Kimberley had passed into the hands of a single corporate giant, De Beers. And as managing director Rhodes behaved as though he owned the town.

The siege itself started as a light-hearted affair. On 6 November the Boers began a desultory bombardment with their 9-pounders. The shelling at first caused alarm among the civilians, but at this stage many of the shells were duds, and the mine-dumps effectively smothered most of the others. The population soon began to take the bombardment in their stride.

On the 9th, however, Kekewich received a blunt telegram from the C-in-C, Buller: 'Civilians in Kimberley representing situation there as serious. Have heard nothing about this from you. Send appreciation of the situation immediately.'

Kekewich was flabbergasted. Since mid-October, he himself had been sending, by African runner, reports that all was well. Clearly Rhodes had been sending out alarmist messages behind his back. He sent back a cautious reply: the situation was certainly *not* critical, although it might become so if the enemy brought up heavy artillery, or if the defenders ran out of ammunition for their 2.5-inch guns. Meanwhile, he could only postpone the inevitable showdown with Rhodes.

An African runner given a message for one of the besieged towns – Kimberley, Mafeking or Ladysmith – stitched into the lining of his coat. The Boers were liable to shoot African runners if they captured them.

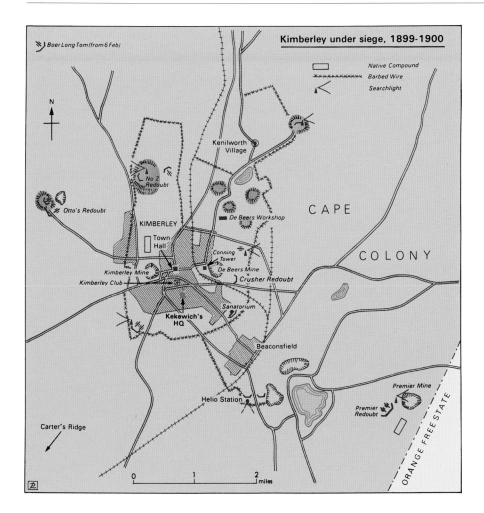

Kimberley under siege, 1899-1900

Cecil Rhodes satirized by the French paper, *L'Assiette au Beurre*. The French assumed he had pushed the British into the war.

Cecil Rhodes relaxes with the smart set in the Sanatorium Hotel during the siege of Kimberley, protected by sandbags and a machine-gun. He was less friendly to the garrison commander, Colonel Robert Kekewich.

Opposite left Cecil Rhodes and friends dispense siege soup (3d a quart) at the De Beers convict station during the siege of Kimberley.

Opposite right The 155-foot-high 'conning tower' at the De Beers Mine, Kimberley. Every morning, Colonel Kekewich climbed the ladder to scan the veld for signs of Methuen's relief expedition.

The next ten days brought mixed blessings from both Rhodes and De Beers. The ammunition problem was miraculously solved when De Beers' chief mechanical engineer, George Labram, agreed to try and cast shells in the company workshops, and succeeded brilliantly. And Rhodes's company provided weapons, food, water and volunteers.

On 23 November, the long-awaited code telegram from Buller arrived: '. . . General [Methuen] leaves here with strong force . . . and will arrive Kimberley on 26th, unless delayed at Modder River. Look for signals by searchlight. . . .' Already this news seemed to be confirmed by the enemy; large bodies of men had been seen trekking southwards. There were believed to be eight thousand Boers between Kimberley and Modder River, and it was rumoured that others, under General Piet Cronje, were on their way from Mafeking. Kekewich decided to do everything to assist the relief column but, with pitifully few mounted troops, realised that it would be reckless to try to link up with Methuen – the course Rhodes was now quick to advocate. Instead, he opted for a diversionary attack on a strong-point, 'Carter's Ridge', where the Boers had sited some 9-pounders.

The first attack on the 25th was a qualified success, killing and wounding twenty-eight Boers and capturing thirty-two, at a cost to the garrison of seven killed and twenty-five wounded. None of the guns were captured, however.

The second attack, on the 28th, was an unqualified disaster. It was then two days after the relief column had been expected to arrive, but all that Kekewich could gather from searchlight signals was that it had been checked. He decided to try to detain as many Boers as possible north of the river. But before Lieutenant-Colonel Scott-Turner (one of three special service officers sent to Kimberley in July) left for the attack, he drew him aside, and warned him not to assault Carter's Ridge 'unless it is unoccupied by the Boers, or so slightly occupied that there is every prospect of an attempt against it succeeding'.

The position *had* been heavily defended. Scott-Turner stormed it with reckless daring, and died in the attempt. Twenty-three others died with him, and thirty-two were wounded. An ugly mood seized the townspeople. Early optimism had given way to mutterings of defeat.

Rhodes, with breathtaking inconsistency, sneeringly accused Kekewich of recklessness. Kekewich did not reply; it would be disloyal to Scott-Turner to blame him for the disaster. He returned to his gloomy vigil on the conning-tower.

What had happened to Methuen?

Methuen was shattered by his successes. After leaving Orange River, he had won two minor victories – at Belmont on the 23rd, and Graspan on the 25th. He 'detested war', he told his wife. The high cost sickened him. One regiment, the Grenadier Guards, suffered thirty-six killed or mortally wounded, and a total of 137 casualties, the highest of any unit engaged. In all, Methuen's column had lost 297 men killed, wounded or missing, to the Free State Boers' loss of under 150. What had gone wrong?

As in Natal, most of the tactical errors – and thus the high casualties – could be traced to the same basic handicaps: weak intelligence and poor mobility. At Belmont Methuen had to clear the enemy from his line of communication, the railway. Yet he had no means of satisfactorily reconnoitring the enemy position. His official intelligence maps were of little use; he had to base a complex plan on a rough sketch of the Boer position made the day before the battle – a dangerous proceeding, as it proved.

Belmont, like Talana, was a short, crude, bloody affair, a 'soldiers' battle' in which all tactical refinements were submerged in the simple, overwhelming urge to seize a hill and exterminate the enemy. They seized the hills – three in turn. Then Methuen saw what the soldiers had seen at Talana: hundreds of Boers trotting away across the veld, untouched by artillery or cavalry.

Graspan, two days later, had repeated the pattern on a smaller scale. Methuen drove the enemy from the next line of ridges at heavy cost to his men. Boer losses were about a hundred, but once again, most of them got away unhindered.

It was now the night of 27 November. Methuen's army had covered fifty of the seventy-four miles to Kimberley and was only a few miles south of the Modder. His self-confidence had begun to return. He thought the Boers had withdrawn to the Spytfontein kopjes; he would turn their left flank by leaving the railway and marching in a broad arc to the east.

During that night, a mounted patrol brought news that some of the enemy, estimated at four thousand, were digging in along the banks of the Modder and Riet Rivers. Methuen decided to postpone the flank march till he had seized this position. He was confident that the report greatly exaggerated the numbers of Boers dug into the river bank; the great majority of the eight thousand were back at Spytfontein. He would strike before they expected him. He wrote to Buller that it was merely a question of pluck. Pluck and surprise. But it was the Boers who had mastered surprise.

Early next morning, 28 November, the infantry began to tramp across the open veld towards the river. They were told they would breakfast there. On the far bank, nothing moved.

'They are not here,' Methuen said to Major-General Sir Henry Colvile.

'They are sitting uncommonly tight if they are, Sir,' replied Colvile.

Less than a mile ahead, in a natural earthworks along the Modder, hidden in every hole and crevice along four miles of the river banks, three thousand Boers prepared to deliver the most concentrated rifle barrage yet fired in the war.

CHAPTER ELEVEN

Breakfast at the Island

Modder and Riet Rivers, Cape Colony,
28 November – 10 December 1899

'[The hotel] lay now calm and innocent, with its open windows looking out upon a smiling garden; but death lurked at the windows and death in the garden, and the little dark man who stood by the door, peering through his glass at the approaching column, was the minister of death, the dangerous Cronje.'

Arthur Conan Doyle, *The Great Boer War*

A COUPLE OF HOURS earlier, the Boer generals, Cronje and Koos De la Rey, had taken their own breakfast at their headquarters in the Island Hotel, close to the junction of the two rivers. Among all the Boer leaders of this period, the austere De la Rey stands out, with Steyn, as morally the most powerful and the most unyielding. It was he who was to keep alight, in its purest form, the fierce flame of Afrikaner nationalism.

Most of De La Rey's eight hundred Transvaalers were dug in on the south bank of the Riet. On his left, straddling two miles of the same side of the Riet, lay Cronje and most of the other Transvaalers, also dug in. Beyond them, in the 'island' between the two rivers, other burghers were concealed in the undergrowth, in case the British tried to turn the Boers' east flank at Bosman's Drift. Dug in beyond De la Rey to the west, and extended as far as Rosmead Drift, were Prinsloo and the Free Staters.

Whether De la Rey had agreed to the disposition of the artillery is not known. Cronje had scattered the guns on the north bank of the Riet, and along the 'island'. But not one gun was backing Prinsloo at Rosmead Drift. It was a mistake of Cronje's that was soon to have disastrous results.

It was 5.30 a.m. Already, in the first few moments of the British advance, a second mistake, equally serious, had been committed by Cronje's men along the Riet to the east. Their orders were to hold their fire as long as possible. The farther the infantry advanced, the more crushing would be the effect of the Boers' fire, and the harder it would be for Methuen to extricate his men. The nearest 'Khakis' to the angle of the Riet – the 1st Scots Guards – were at least a thousand yards from the Boer trenches when the men's nerve faltered and they opened fire. Naturally the Khakis flung themselves flat. With that wretched fusillade went all chance of a decisive victory.

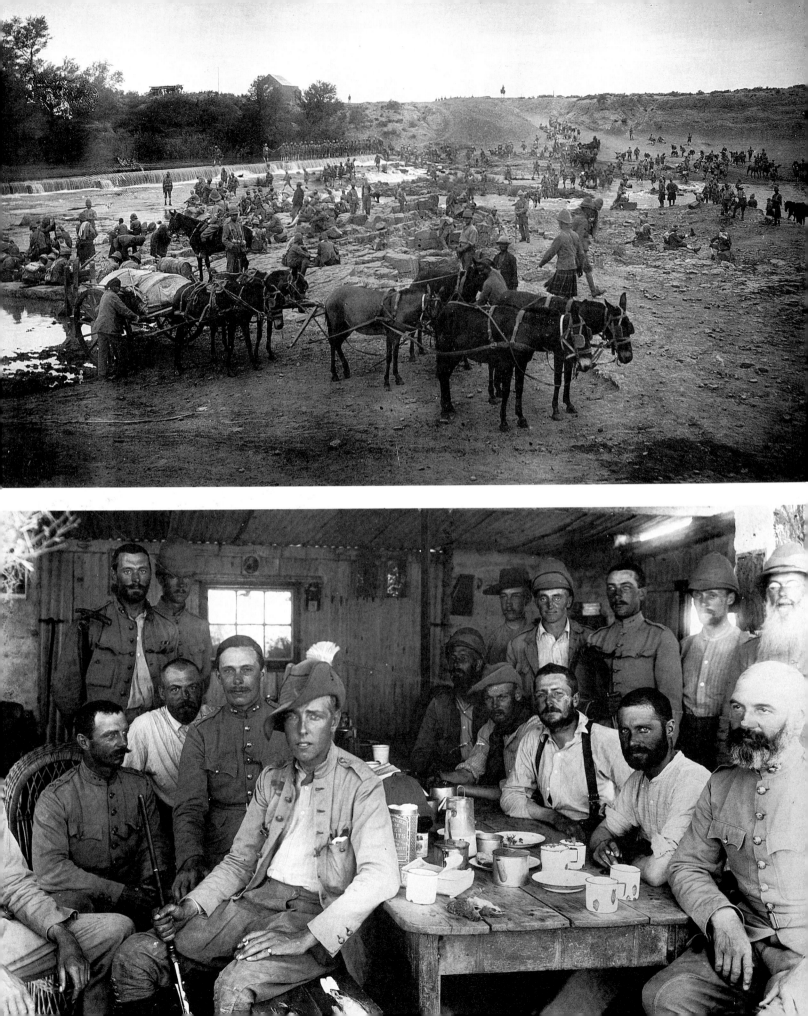

Methuen's troops fording the Modder River after the battle on 28 November 1899.

Methuen 'thought the enemy had cleared off, as did everyone else, whereas Kronje [*sic*], De La Ray [*sic*] and 9,000 men were waiting for me in an awful position. I never saw a Boer, but even at 2,000 yards when I rode a horse I had a hail of bullets around me'. He himself led a charge down towards the river, but achieved nothing. Both his brigades – east of the railway, the Guards Brigade led by Colvile; on the west, the 9th Brigade, led by Major-General Reggie Pole-Carew – were nailed down in the veld by the fire of invisible riflemen. For ten hours soldiers lay flat, hungry and thirsty, in a temperature that rose to 90°F in the shade. Despite orders to hold fast, men tried to crawl back to the water carts, and several were killed in the attempt. From sheer exhaustion – and boredom – others fell asleep where they lay.

Despite the initial blunder of firing prematurely, the advantage seemed at first to be De la Rey's. The Boers watched disaster overwhelm the two leading companies of the Scots Guards. The Coldstream Guards worked their way under fire along the bushy banks of the Riet to the east. A few waded across to the island, but Colvile ordered them back. After that the Guards gave the Boers little to worry about. It was the British artillery who took up the cudgels: twelve 15-pounders firing just over the heads of the prostrate Guardsmen; and four naval 12-pounders. One Boer wrote: 'It is simply "Hell let loose". I could never have realized, nor can one who is not here, what it is like. ... For two hours I lie on my stomach making myself as small as possible.' At first it was an unequal battle of Mauser fire against artillery.

In reply, the Boer guns performed prodigies of improvisation. Outnumbered three to one, the field-guns dodged back and forth all day between emplacements. The artillery horses suffered heavily, but the British could not knock out a single gun. From concealed positions, the Boer gunners wrought havoc on their British counterparts out in the open.

Meanwhile, alarming reports had reached De la Rey from Prinsloo on the right. Cronje had failed to put enough men there to guard Rosmead Drift, to protect it with guns, or to reinforce the place later. Now the price was paid. Opposite the drift was part of the 9th Brigade, Pole-Carew's. For about three hours they too were nailed down in the veld, but soon after eleven they could be seen creeping forward in rushes. Prinsloo's men could not hold them. The defenders were Free Staters, their morale dented by the reverses at Belmont and Graspan. By midday they had fled back to the north bank. The British followed them.

They were actually Kekewich's men, the half-battalion of Loyals he had left behind when he had taken the other half to Kimberley. Now they were first across the drift, with other men of various units following. By one o'clock, the British had dug themselves into the north bank and driven the Free Staters out of Rosmead, and were soon supported by four guns. With Pole-Carew at their head, the infantry now began to push through hedges of prickly pear towards a second hotel behind the Boers' central position.

Cronje did nothing to cope with this alarming threat, said De la Rey bitterly. It was he who organized the counter-attack, sending the Lichtenburg Commando, left in reserve on the north bank, westwards to block Pole-

Mess of the 3rd Grenadier Guards at Modder River. Times were hard when officers had to brew their own tea.

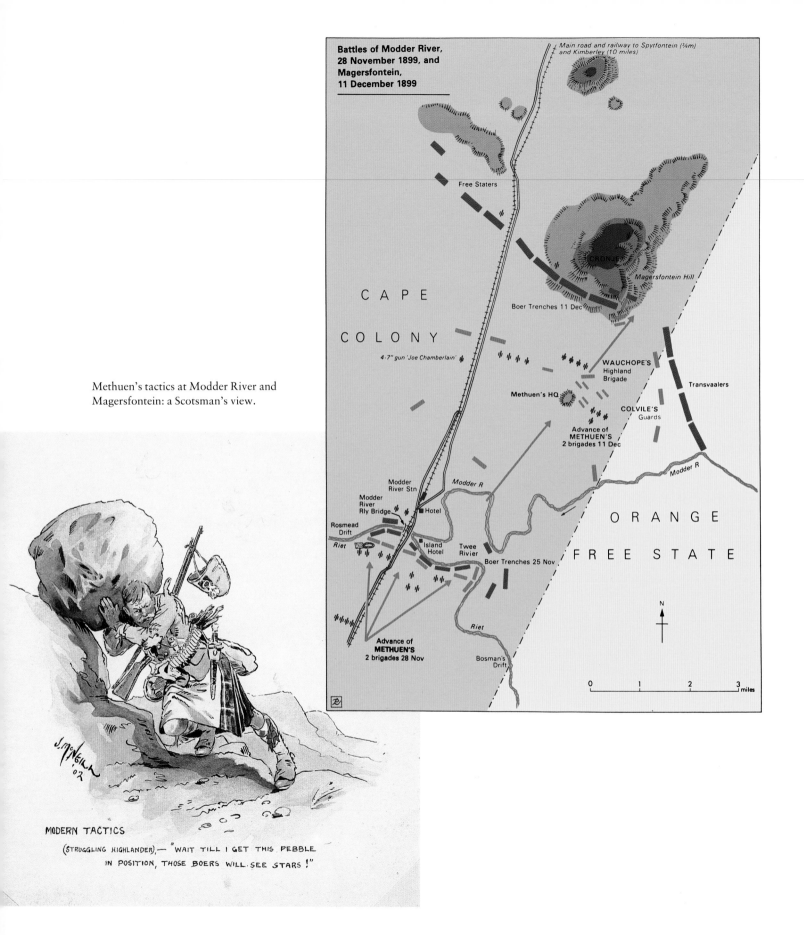

Methuen's tactics at Modder River and Magersfontein: a Scotsman's view.

MODERN TACTICS

(STRUGGLING HIGHLANDER).— "WAIT TILL I GET THIS PEBBLE IN POSITION, THOSE BOERS WILL·SEE STARS!"

Battles of Modder River, 28 November 1899, and Magersfontein, 11 December 1899

Main road and railway to Spytfontein (¾m) and Kimberley (10 miles)

Free Staters

CRONJE

Magersfontein Hill

Boer Trenches 11 Dec

CAPE

COLONY

4·7" gun 'Joe Chamberlain'

WAUCHOPE'S Highland Brigade

Methuen's HQ

Transvaalers

COLVILE'S Guards

Advance of METHUEN'S 2 brigades 11 Dec

Modder R

Modder River Stn

Modder R

Modder River Rly Bridge.

Hotel

Rosmead Drift

Island Hotel

Twee Rivier

Boer Trenches 25 Nov

ORANGE

FREE STATE

Riet

Advance of METHUEN'S 2 brigades 28 Nov

Riet

Bosman's Drift

N

0   1   2   3 miles

Carew's advance. They gave covering fire to the hard-pressed gunners, pinned down the leading British soldiers, and drove them back into Rosmead. Assisted by British shrapnel fired in error at Pole-Carew's men, the burghers then held their trenches until darkness put an end to the fighting.

It was just before this that De la Rey's eldest son, Adriaan, was wounded in the stomach. (He himself had been slightly wounded in the right shoulder by a shell fragment.) There was no ambulance. In the darkness, De la Rey's staff set out to carry him the nine miles to Jacobsdal, the Boers' base hospital. About eight o'clock they met Cronje, whose men were in full retreat. In answer to Cronje's 'How did the battle go?' De La Rey replied bitterly, 'Why did you leave us in the lurch? We saw nothing of you all day.'

The party reached Jacobsdal just after dawn. An hour later Adriaan died in his father's arms. De la Rey had earlier reached a decision almost as painful as this bereavement. Cronje and Prinsloo had betrayed them. Had the Free Staters on the west flank stayed firm, he believed Methuen would have been forced to fall back all the way to Orange River. Now he would have no difficulty in reinforcing Pole-Carew's bridgehead. De la Rey had to accept that his own men must abandon the Riet and Modder. That night, along both sides of the river, men collected up the dead and wounded: 460 British casualties and about 80 Boers. At Rosmead, British reinforcements splashed across to join Pole-Carew. Methuen lay in the field hospital. A bullet had pierced the fleshy part of his thigh a couple of hours before the end of the action; the wound was slight but painful. It was decided that both his brigades would renew the attack as soon as it was light.

At dawn, the naval guns reopened the bombardment. There was no reply. When the infantry reached De la Rey's position, they found it deserted. The trenches were knee-deep in spent cartridge cases, and there were dead bodies floating in the river. The Boers themselves had withdrawn to the north and east. Now there were only the two ridges to the north – the last natural defensive positions before Kimberley.

De la Rey stayed at Jacobsdal to bury his son, and so missed the *krijgsraad* on the day after the battle. He strenuously objected when he heard that, in his absence, Cronje and Prinsloo had decided to withdraw ten miles to Spytfontein, instead of digging in at Magersfontein, six miles back. He telegraphed to Steyn over Cronje's head, and Steyn passed on the message to Kruger.

In fact, both Presidents were already deeply disturbed by complaints – even from Prinsloo – about the behaviour of the Free State burghers at Graspan and Modder River. Kruger did not mince words. Cowardice was the cause of the flight. Officers and men must learn to do their duty. He urged Steyn to go to the front line himself, 'because this is the final moment of decision whether we are to surrender the country'.

Steyn reached the front six days after the Battle of Modder River (Twee Rivier – Two Rivers – the Boers called it). Kruger had given him a long telegram addressed to the burghers. Steyn visited each laager and read aloud

to them the old President's homely lines, which ended: 'No, no, even though we must lose almost half of our men, we must still fight to the death, in the name of the Lord.'

Next day, Steyn cabled to Kruger that the burghers were full of heart. Then he summoned the generals to a second *krijgsraad*. Here De la Rey put the case against fortifying Spytfontein, and persuaded them all to adopt his own plan.

Twee Rivier seemed to confirm his earlier ideas on tactics, formulated after the Boer defeats at Belmont and Graspen. The place to lie in wait for British infantry was the plain, not the hill. Most of the arguments for digging in at the Modder applied equally well to Magersfontein. And if the worst happened, they would still have a second line of defence – Spytfontein – before abandoning the siege of Kimberley.

Wounded Tommies in a wagon house at Klip Drift. They had run their heads against a stone wall at the Modder.

As for the Free Staters, they would fight better, since many were now unmounted, if they had no obvious means of escape. Put them in the centre, and concentrate the mounted burghers where mobility was essential – on the flanks.

The combined Boer armies had now been reinforced by the main part of Cronje's force from Mafeking. There were perhaps eight thousand two hundred burghers in all, plus camp-followers and commandeered African labourers. The latter were set to back-breaking work, digging a twelve-mile-long defence line beneath the Magersfontein ridge.

The boldness of De la Rey's plan lay not only in the way these trenches and breastworks were constructed and sited. They were also camouflaged with the skill of a man who digs a trap for an elephant. In six days the job was done. Methuen's scouts rode within a mile of the trench before they were driven away by Mauser fire. They had no inkling that the trap had been set.

CHAPTER TWELVE

Marching up in Column

Magersfontein, 9–12 December 1899

Such was the day for our regiment
  Dread the revenge we will take.
Dearly we paid for the blunder –
  A drawing-room General's mistake

Why weren't we told of the trenches?
  Why weren't we told of the wire?
Why were we marched up in column
  May Tommy Atkins enquire . . .

'The Battle of Magersfontein',
verse by Private Smith of the Black Watch
December 1899

ON SATURDAY 9 DECEMBER, Methuen issued his orders. The plan – for a night march followed by a dawn attack – was certainly risky, but less risky than the alternatives. This was his view, after nearly a fortnight since Modder River. It was his natural inclination to strike at the Boer positions immediately, before they could reorganize, but his wound, his men's exhaustion after three battles, and the need for reinforcements, supplies, and artillery, curbed his impatience. Finally, he thought it would be folly to advance before repairing the dynamited railway bridge at Modder River, a gash in his army's life-line.

Methuen had been relieved to receive a searchlight signal from Kekewich on the 4th: the Kimberley garrison still had food enough for forty days. On the night of the 10th the Highland Brigade would march off to the attack. As usual, however, his scouts could gain only a sketchy idea of the enemy's defences. The Boers appeared to be holding a line of kopjes, and the key, he believed, was the Magersfontein Kopje, six-and-a-half miles from his camp.

About three o'clock on Sunday afternoon, as a sleety rain began to fall, the five artillery batteries and the Highlanders set off across the plain. About three miles from the kopje they halted, and the brigade commander, Major-General Andrew Wauchope, rode back for Methuen's final briefing. The Highlanders would make the assault, with the Guards and the 9th Brigade

Methuen's gunners firing 'Joe Chamberlain', a converted 4.7 naval gun, to 'prepare' the ground for the British advance at Magersfontein. The bombardment certainly prepared the Boers.

115

held in reserve. Wauchope seemed satisfied with his orders (so Methuen said later) but, as the meeting broke up, he remarked to Colvile, 'Things don't always go as they are expected. You may not be in reserve for long.'

Meanwhile, the Boers were receiving their dose of British shells, delivered by twenty-four field-guns, four howitzers, and the British answer to Long Tom – 'Joe Chamberlain', the 4.7-inch naval gun. But of the enemy there was no actual evidence. Later Methuen admitted that the artillery did nothing except prepare the Boers for the British attack.

At nightfall, the fireworks faded out on the distant ridge. The wind rose and the icy rain continued. The orders were: no fires, no smoking. The Highlanders' spirits waned.

Soldiers of the Highland Brigade decorated with white stones General Wauchope's first grave at Magersfontein.

Around midnight, the four battalions – Black Watch, Seaforth Highlanders and Argyll and Sutherland Highlanders, with the Highland Light Infantry as reserve – lined up in the most compact formation in the drill-book: 3,500 men compressed into a column 45 yards wide and about 160 yards long. Even so, it was almost impossible for the files to keep in touch. At the left-hand of the leading file of the great stumbling, heaving mass marched Wauchope.

A night march by compass bearing is a delicate and dangerous manoeuvre, especially during a storm and over broken terrain. But, as the sky began to lighten, the brigade found itself about a thousand yards from the ridge. The storm had blown itself out; because of it, they were already as much as an hour behind.

There were many reasons for the disaster that now befell the British infantry. Dominating everything was Methuen's ignorance of the enemy's position, for which he cannot be altogether exonerated. He had ordered the Highland Brigade into the trap De la Rey had set, just as he had at the Modder. The Boers waited, hidden, till the leading files were about four hundred yards away. There was a single shot from the kopje, then a river of flame from the trenches. In the half-light, at a range of only four hundred yards, the massed ranks made an easy target. There was confusion, almost panic, at first, and casualties mounted frighteningly. Then discipline reasserted itself; the men scraped themselves cover behind rocks and ant-hills and began to return fire, gallantly supported by the artillery. What followed was a nine-hour duel on the same pattern as at Modder River. The sun rose to find the Highlanders pegged down, just as the Guards had been in front of the Riet.

Then the Highlanders' nerve suddenly failed.

Up to this moment, most of them had withstood their ordeal with stoicism. Now, after nine hours of terror and boredom, without water in that scorching sun, they could take no more. About one o'clock, some Boers were found working round the right flank. Two companies were ordered to trickle back a few hundred yards to deal with the threat. But the trickle became a flood, and the flood an avalanche. Officers cursed, threatening to shoot the fleeing soldiers. The men, obedient to their instincts, melted away into the veld. When the ambulance men went out next day to collect the dead and wounded – 902 British, 236 Boer – they found Wauchope, killed within two hundred yards of Cronje's trenches. But most of his brigade died with their backs to the enemy.

Methuen impassively watched the destruction of the Highlanders. He was bitter, yet stoical. Only bad luck, he believed – and Wauchope – had cost him the victory. Now 'there must be a scapegoat,' he wrote, 'so I must bear my fate like a man, holding my tongue'. Even now there was a sliver of hope: the Boers might retreat during the night, as they had after the Modder.

Soon after dawn next day, Methuen's last illusions were dispelled. The Boers, masters of the new warfare of the western front, were holding fast in their trenches.

CHAPTER THIRTEEN

'Where are the Boers?'

Tugela River, near Ladysmith, Natal, 11–15 December 1899

'I think with luck that we shall give the Boers a good hiding this side as we have a strong force in all arms . . .'

> Captain Algy Trotter, Buller's ADC, to his
> mother, Frere, 11 December 1899

'God zal voor u strijden . . . En als kop behbouden blijft, dood of levend, dan behoudt gij alles.'
('God shall thus fight for you . . . If you hold the hill, dead or alive, you hold everything.')

> President Kruger to Botha,
> 13 December 1899, telegram no.39

UNAWARE OF METHUEN'S REPULSE, the other half of Buller's army, now at Frere under his own command, were facing Colenso, twelve miles to the north. Ahead lay the Colenso position, where Botha apparently blocked the way to Ladysmith. But where were the Boers? And how many of them were lying in wait beyond the tree-lined banks of the Tugela? The Field Intelligence Department (FID) put the enemy's numbers at about seven thousand. Proper reconnaissance and surveying of the terrain were impossible, though later Buller was to be severely blamed for his ignorance of the enemy's position. He had to rely on the FID survey of the area, a blueprint inch-to-the-mile map bearing the legend: 'Vacant spaces indicate that data . . . is wanting rather than that the ground is flat.' As with the choice of generals, the lack of mounted troops and the strategy of the campaign itself, Buller had to make the best of a bad job.

He had decided first to try to force the Tugela at Potgieters Drift, a ford fifteen miles upriver. He heliographed to Ladysmith: 'I propose to march with three brigades, two regiments of cavalry, 1,000 volunteers, five batteries of field artillery, and six naval guns to Springfield on the 13th . . . I may be disappointed. . . .' It was to be the understatement of the war.

On 12 December, as he prepared to dispatch his three brigades on their fifty-mile flank march, he received news that led him to abandon this plan immediately, and to decide that the balance of risk had shifted. After all, he

must 'make a run' for Colenso, a decision that was later to bring down a storm of criticism on his head. His reasons were as follows.

The news from the Cape was shatteringly bad. On the 11th he had heard of 548 men (actually 696) missing and captured, lost by Gatacre at the Battle of Stormberg on the 10th. Gatacre, although instructed to take no risks until reinforced, had hazarded his small force in a night march to recapture a strategic railway junction. The column had lost its way; Gatacre had pressed on, and at dawn found himself at the mercy of the enemy.

Now Buller learned of the crushing reverse at Magersfontein, which Methuen reported with the conclusion: 'Possibility that further advance is questionable, but shall endeavour to hold my own and keep my communications secure.' Buller telegraphed, 'Fight or fall back' – but Methuen 'could do neither'.

For Buller, this was the last straw. Both the mobile armies in the Cape – Gatacre's and Methuen's – were now at risk. And Milner might be right about the possibility of a rising in the Cape.

Buller decided he could not hazard the only other mobile force – his own – in a long march away from the railway line. Not only would he be out of touch with Cape Town in an emergency, but his whole force, if defeated at Potgieters, could be left helpless. As he later explained, *both* plans of attack were 'forlorn hopes'. But 'Colenso was in front of me. I could attack that and control the result. . . . I could not pretend I could control [Potgieters]. I might easily have lost my whole force.'

He was ready to move on Thursday 14 December. He posted an anxious

Where are the enemy? Buller's officers scan the hillside across the Tugela at Colenso. Hidden in their trenches, Botha's men were ready to spring the trap.

despatch to the War Office, justifying his choice of Colenso because 'It will be better to lose Ladysmith altogether than to throw open Natal to the enemy'. To Lansdowne he struck a slightly more confident note: 'I fully expect to be successful but probably at heavy cost.' Then, that evening, he briefed his commanding officers for the attack, explaining his plan to storm the river and establish a 'lodgement' on the north bank.

Buller knew at least the basic topography of Colenso, and the broad lines of Botha's defence. In essence, Botha held a triangle of predominantly flat ground across the river, north of the village and railway station at Colenso. The south and east sides of the triangle were formed by the Tugela, the hypotenuse by the first tier of hills to the north-west. It was in this spot, relatively safe from artillery fire, that Buller hoped to make his lodgement. (*See map on page 123.*)

But how to cross the Tugela? Buller believed that his best chance was to ford the river by the two southernmost drifts – Old Wagon Drift and Bridle Drift – upstream of the dynamited railway bridge. But this two-pronged attack presented grave difficulties.

First, it was not certain that the river *was* fordable at these two drifts. Second, Botha would put his strongest defence line opposite the drifts. Third, a chain of low kopjes immediately north of the railway bridge commanded much of the plain, and would have to be stormed at heavy cost.

Though Buller had greatly underestimated the skill with which Botha had sited his trenches, his general appreciation of the tactical problems was sound. But with hindsight, people would later point out a weak link in the Boer defences: a hill called Hlangwane, on the *south* side of the Tugela, from which Botha's position could be enfiladed by artillery. But Buller assumed – rightly – that the Boer line would be extended across the river to include it. To seize it would thus be both complicated and costly. He was, in fact, tempted to make the capture of Hlangwane the sole objective of the first day, but decided that the 'bush-fighting' in thick scrub would be too difficult for his raw troops.

In the headquarters tent, Buller read out his orders. The cavalry commander, Lieutenant-Colonel John Burn-Murdoch, with the two regular cavalry regiments, was to protect the left flank of the infantry; Colonel Lord Dundonald, with the mounted infantry and mounted irregulars, the right flank as far as Hlangwane. Major-General Henry Hildyard's brigade would launch the main attack, storming the Old Wagon Drift; Major-General Fitzroy Hart's Irish Brigade would storm the smaller Bridle Drift three and a half miles upstream. The two other infantry brigades would be held in reserve: Major-General Neville Lyttelton's between the Irish and Hildyard's; Major-General Geoffrey Barton's between the two mounted forces. The artillery would, of course, begin the battle. Buller went up to Colonel Long – so he later gave evidence – and put his finger on the precise place on the blueprint map from where, with twelve field-guns and six naval guns, he was to prepare the ground for Hildyard's attack. The rest of the artillery was divided: Lieutenant-Colonel L.W. Parsons was to prepare the ground for

Hart's brigade; the longer-range naval guns were to bombard the position from the rear. There is no evidence that any of these officers dissented. They accepted Buller's line of reasoning; indeed, Lyttelton endorsed it. Colenso would be hard to crack, but they had to extricate White from Ladysmith.

At about 4.30 a.m. on Friday 15 December, as the sky paled, massed columns of infantry began to coil and uncoil until they found their places. At 5.30 two 4.7-inch naval guns on 'Naval Gun Hill' began firing. The lighter 12-pounders joined in. No reply from the Boers.

Then, about 6.30, Hart's Irish Brigade tramped off, and the men heard for the first time a new sound: a tremendous roar of Mauser fire.

The 'fun' had started.

Botha stood calmly by the Krupp 5-inch howitzer, watching Buller's majestic advance. He gave his final orders. They must hold their fire till the enemy reached the river bank. The signal would be a shot from the howitzer. Then, as the darkness began to drain off the valley, they could see a ghostly dust cloud at Chieveley. And out of the dust came Buller's army, 'a long, wide, brown strip', marching towards the river as though on a parade ground.

Botha had left nothing to chance, but the fact was that, as Buller had spotted, the position at Colenso was not impregnable.

There were three weaknesses. First, there was the great length of the line that would have to be held, because of the number of drifts. Second, the river's meanderings meant that the point at which Buller intended to push his main attack was barely within rifle range of the Colenso kopjes. Third, and most crucial, the Boer line would have to be extended eastwards across the river in order to control Hlangwane (Bosch Kop – 'Bush Hill' – to the Boers).

So there had been a case for retiring to a more conventional position on the hills farther back. Botha had dealt with it as De la Rey had at Magersfontein. The Boers had a secret weapon: the spade. Dig trenches in the tall grass along the river banks, camouflage them with stones, and hide the soil. Dig dummy trenches on the skyline, where the British would expect them, and arm them with dummy guns. Dig away the stones in the river to destroy the drifts. Bait the trap with the iron road bridge that had been left intact. This was the plan proposed by Botha, seconded by Joubert, and patiently carried out by the burghers in the last fortnight, with the help of reinforcements from Ladysmith, and an army of African labourers.

Then, on Wednesday 13 December, the blow had fallen. Buller's troops marched forward to Chieveley and his naval guns began their artillery 'preparation', the shells screaming harmlessly overhead. But most of the men defending Hlangwane, unnerved by the mere noise of the bombardment, rode back across the river. The tactical key to the Boer defence was now itself virtually defenceless.

Botha at once telegraphed Kruger, who rose to the occasion: 'God shall thus fight for you, so give up position under no circumstances. . . . If you hold the hill, dead or alive, you hold everything.'

Botha called a council of war that evening. He needed both tact and subtlety, for many officers were openly in favour of abandoning the entire river line. So he agreed on a temporary compromise: Hlangwane should be abandoned, but the Tugela should be held.

Next morning, a second thunderbolt arrived from Oom Paul: If you give up position . . . you give up the whole land to the enemy. Please stand fast, dead or alive. . . . And fear not the enemy but fear God. . . . If you give up position, and surrender country to England, where will you go then?

Botha read out Kruger's telegram at a second *krijgsraad*. 'Where will you go then?' This was the *cri de coeur* of the volk, the ultimate appeal to put their backs to the wall. The council of war reversed its decision. After sunset eight hundred men were sent back to reoccupy the kop.

In general, Botha's plan, like Buller's, was a rough-and-ready affair. He believed the main British attack would come at the wagon bridge, but he had had to extend his four thousand five hundred men to cover all the main crossing points: a third of them – the Free Staters, and the Middelburg and Johannesburg Commandos – on the edge of the plain opposite Robinson's Drift (a fourth drift eight miles upstream from Colenso); the Ermelo Commando in flat ground opposite the Bridle Drift (in fact, Buller's second point of attack); the Zoutpansberg and Swaziland Commandos to cover Punt Drift (between the Wagon and Bridle Drifts); the Heidelberg, Vryheid and Krugersdorp Commandos in the kopjes and along the river bank north of Colenso itself; and the Wakkerstroom and Standerton Commandos completing the line on Hlangwane. It was an excellent defence plan, given Botha's great inferiority in men and artillery, though he was especially weak at the Old Wagon Drift (Buller's first point of attack).

This was not, however, merely a defensive plan. Botha hoped to lure the leading troops across the river at the wagon bridge, then his right wing at Robinson's and his left on Hlangwane would counter-attack, and the trap would snap shut.

Now, on Friday, Botha watched the British shells futilely searching the kopjes above his trench lines, trying to draw his fire.

Then something occurred that no one – least of all Botha – had expected. The attackers had divided into three columns. The central column – Hildyard's brigade – began to march towards the wagon bridge. But at least a mile ahead of it rode Long's batteries: twelve field-guns leading, with six naval guns behind. They halted about a thousand yards from the Tugela, facing the trenches below Fort Wylie. Botha, amazed, weighed the chances. Once his men showed themselves, goodbye to the hope of luring the infantry across the wagon bridge. But if the British field-guns opened fire at such close range, they could smash his thin defence lines. The burghers begged him to give the signal.

A moment later, the British gunners unhooked the leading twelve guns from the limbers. It was enough for Botha. The howitzer boomed out high on the ridge, and an answering wave of Mauser fire swept over Long and his doomed gunners.

CHAPTER FOURTEEN

'A Devil of a Mess'

Colenso, Natal, 15 December 1899;
British Isles, 16 December 1899 – 1 February 1900

'My own plan is that about the 15th December we shall have in South
Africa a nice little Army & all the materials for a respectable war except
the enemy.'

Moberly Bell, manager of *The Times*,
to L.S. Amery, 13 October 1899

IT WAS STILL DARK when the Irish Brigade's commander, Hart, marched
off his battalions in close order. He himself rode ahead, accompanied by an
African and a Natal colonist, to help him find the Bridle Drift. Such a drill-

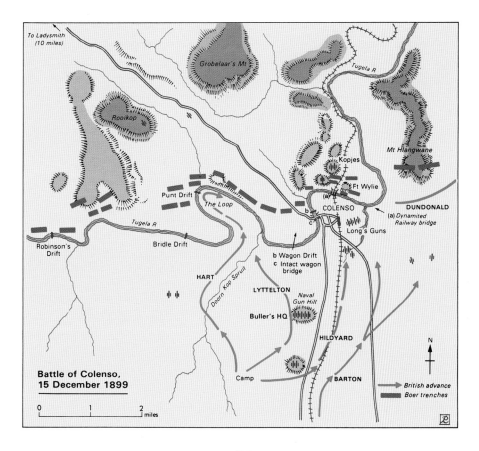

123

book advance, like Wauchope's at Magersfontein, seemed to several of
Hart's officers to be asking for trouble.

One of Buller's converted 4.7-inch naval
guns shelling Botha's defence line at
Colenso. Note the dust kicked up by the
shell leaving the barrel.

Patrols of the Royal Dragoons, sent by Buller to protect Hart's left flank,
had already ridden down to the river. Now they could actually see large
bodies of Boers on the other side, moving ahead and to the left of Hart's
column, and sent three gallopers in succession to warn him. He replied that
he intended to ignore the Boers unless they attacked him in force. The Royals
must protect his left flank. He intended to cross, as ordered, by the Bridle
Drift ahead.

About 6.15 a.m. Hart reached a point some 300 yards from the beginning
of the loop. He could see the river clearly now, running between deep banks
about 120 yards apart, swollen with Wednesday's rain. The official FID
blueprint map and another sketch-map both put Bridle Drift well to the west
of the loop. But the African guide pointed into the loop itself, a mile ahead
and to the right. The drift was up there, and it was the *only* drift.

Hart knew that there are few more dangerous places on a battlefield than a
salient. And the loop, commanded by the enemy on three sides, was a salient.
But, without any evidence, he got it into his head that both his orders and the
two maps had misplaced the Bridle Drift (in fact, they were correct). He did

not hesitate. He put himself in the hands of the guide (who spoke no English), and put his head in the noose – into the open end of the salient.

For at this moment, Botha gave the howitzer signal. His artillery began firing, and shells started to fall among Hart's battalions as the Boer gunners found the range. A storm of Mauser fire followed.

Even now, Hart could have avoided disaster. But the guide had vanished at the first burst of firing, and Hart gathered from the interpreter that the ford lay by a kraal at the end of the loop. He led his men on, fired on from three sides by an invisible enemy at a range of a few hundred yards.

The battalions became mixed at once, and so did companies. 'Come on, the Irish Brigade!' shouted the officers, and that was about as far as the orders went. There was no control, no cohesion, no system by which groups could alternately advance and provide covering fire for their neighbours.

Hart himself acted with great, even reckless, courage. Disdaining cover, he walked about calmly amidst the flying bullets and shrapnel, cheering his men on. Many simply refused to budge. They were shaken by the Boers' rifle fire, and the shells, though not very effective, made an appalling din. There was no panic – the men simply lay flat, seemingly deaf to commands.

'If I give you a lead, if your General gives you a lead – will you come on?'

'We will, sir,' came the reply.

Up they jumped, more or less cheerfully, and followed their General.

A little earlier, Hart had observed, to his great annoyance, the behaviour of his two left-hand battalions. Lieutentant-Colonel Thomas Thackeray, the CO of the Royal Inniskilling Fusiliers, had formed his men in a single rank parallel to the river, and led them to the left of the loop. In fact, they were close to Bridle Drift; even now, they might have found that way across the river. It was still probably fordable, and the high banks would have given some cover to the Inniskillings, who outnumbered the defenders and could themselves have been swiftly reinforced. Hart ordered them back into the loop. It was his final error. Now the Irish Brigade's repulse was becoming a defeat, and the defeat a disaster.

Buller stood on Naval Gun Hill, impassively watching the bombardment. It was largely ineffective. First, the Boers were not, as Buller had – with reason – assumed, on the kopjes. Second, their guns and rifles fired the new smokeless ammunition, and from concealed positions. The long-range naval guns were therefore quite unable to locate and destroy their targets, and this failure threw a larger burden on the shrapnel-firing medium-range field artillery. With this, Buller realized, things were going seriously wrong.

He had seen the Irish Brigade suddenly blunder off to the right, and sent a galloper to warn Hart to keep out of the loop. He had told Parsons, commanding the twelve guns on the left, to prepare the ground for the passage of the Bridle Drift. Parsons now did his best to help Hart in his new position, but there were no proper targets beyond the loop, and some shells fell among the leading troops. Buller watched the confusion with increasing disquiet. He sent off a second galloper, his ADC, Captain Algy Trotter.

Meanwhile, still more ominous things were happening three miles away at the centre of the plain. Buller had watched Long ride off at the head of his procession of guns. His orders to the gunner the night before were to come into action well out of rifle range from the Colenso kopjes; Buller remembered his actual words as he had put his finger on the blueprint map. Then, about 7.00 a.m., he heard Long's batteries suddenly burst into life, apparently close to the river. Astonished, he sent a staff officer to find out what the guns were doing. The officer returned soon afterwards, and said that they were under 'a little' rifle fire, but seemed 'quite comfortable'.

Buller now decided that as soon as Trotter brought news that Hart's brigade had been extricated from the loop, he would go and look at Long's position for himself. Just then there was an ominous silence. The batteries had ceased fire. Buller, certain that disaster had overtaken them, sent Stopford to order Hart to withdraw to safety, and himself rode off to see what he could do to rescue the gunner from his folly.

Long, like Hart, believed in the old vitues of close order and 'keeping the men in hand'. Despite the protests of Lieutenant Ogilvy, RN, commanding the naval guns, the Colonel had brought the 15-pounders to within a thousand yards of the river bank before he allowed a halt. Fortunately, Ogilvy's gun teams had lagged nearly six hundred yards behind, and they were still comparatively safe. True, the African drivers immediately bolted. But it was possible to cut the oxen free and bring all six 12-pounders into action against the kopjes a mile away across the river, from which most of the rifle fire appeared to be coming.

A mile was extreme range for effective rifle fire. The few Boer guns on the ridge were too dispersed to be dangerous. The naval gun detachment suffered almost no casualties. By contrast, the two 15-pounder batteries found themselves in the centre of the zone of fire.

Long himself was critically wounded; the second-in-command was also hit, as were officers from both batteries. The 15-pounders continued firing, slowly and methodically. Later, it would be said that the gunners fought on to the last man. In fact, when a third of their number had been killed or wounded, flesh and blood could stand no more. The acting commander ordered the men to take shelter in a small donga (there was also a second donga, further to the rear, where other survivors were to shelter). The ammunition wagons, nearly full, were left with the guns, abandoned in the open plain. Two officers then rode back to try to get help.

These two officers met Buller as he rode down towards the firing-line. Dazed and almost incoherent, they blurted out the news, adding (what was, in fact, quite untrue) that the gunners were all killed or wounded; also that all six naval guns, as well as the twelve field-guns, were out of action.

Buller rode on to meet Hildyard, who was still waiting to deliver the main attack, and told him about the guns. It was eight o'clock, and only one of the four infantry brigades had come into action. Buller now calculated the risks

Botha's 75-mm Creusot field-gun commanding the loop in the River Tugela at Colenso (top right), where Hart and the Irish Brigade came to grief on 15 December 1899.

coolly enough. He decided he must call off the main attack – at any rate, until he had rescued Long.

The main attack on Colenso depended on Hildyard being supported from one or more sides: on the left, by Hart forcing his way across the Bridle Drift; on the right, by Dundonald seizing enough of Hlangwane to be able to enfilade the Colenso kopjes with artillery; overhead, by Long's guns shelling the ground beyond the bridge; from behind, by the two reserve brigades. But far from supporting Hildyard, Hart, Long and Dundonald (who also seemed to be in trouble) all required help themselves, which meant drawing on both reserve brigades. So Buller decided that to attack Colenso now would be utter recklessness; besides, the worst fighting would be in those ten miles of hill country across the river. The price of failure was out of all proportion to the value of success. If he smashed and demoralized his own army, he could lose not only Ladysmith, but the whole of south Natal.

These were the reasons – not failure of nerve or morale, as his critics have long maintained – that determined him to call off the attack before Hildyard had fired a shot. They do not seem unduly alarmist. He rode on towards the small donga where Long's men were sheltering.

Buller told Lyttelton: 'Hart has got into a devil of a mess down there. Get him out of it as best you can.' Lyttelton pushed forward four companies of the Rifle Brigade and prepared to give supporting fire. At first, it seemed that the loop had swallowed up Hart's brigade. Then hundreds of stragglers and

Below The Battle of Colenso on 15 December 1899, seen from a reserve battalion waiting by an African kraal. The Tommy on the left appears to have fallen asleep. Two miles ahead, by the banks of the Tugela, there was a 'devil of a mess'.

wounded appeared, followed by Hart himself and many of his soldiers, falling back in confusion. But Lyttelton's men could not fire in support of the troops still in the loop, as the stragglers blocked their field of fire. And Parsons's two batteries, which had been unable to support Hart, now opened up inadvertently on Lyttelton.

The predicament of the men at the end of the loop was now serious, marooned in the open within easy range of the enemy's trenches, enfiladed on three sides, and under fire from two field-guns. Thackeray and his men lay beside the kraal at the end of the loop, near the ford to which Hart's African guide had sent the brigade, with such disastrous results. To cross the swirling water under such fire was out of the question.

Meanwhile, Buller's orders to evacuate the loop had at length reached the rest of the brigade. Slowly the firing diminished. Most of Hart's men marched back to their camp in tolerable order. For them, after ten hours, it was all over at last.

Thackeray's ordeal continued. About three o'clock a small party of Boers splashed across the river and cut off the loop – and his retreat. Called upon to surrender, he accused the Boers, who had crossed when they saw the British ambulance men go forward into the loop, of sneaking up behind the Red Cross flag. It would be unsporting to capture him. The victors saw the comic side. 'Well, I won't look at you while you take your men away,' came the reply.

So the story was told, at any rate, that night, after Thackeray and some of his men had staggered back. When the roll-call was taken it was found that the Irish Brigade had lost heavily enough.

In the meantime, Buller had started his attempts to rescue the guns. The only available cover from Botha's trenches to the north, apart from the two shallow dongas sheltering Long's men, was in Colenso village and in the road leading to the wagon bridge, about half a mile west of the guns. But since the smaller loop of the Tugela enclosed Colenso on two sides, both the village and the stranded guns were enfiladed from the Boer rifle pits on the river bank to the west. Buller gave Hildyard the job of neutralizing these latter positions, ordering him on 'no account to commit his men to an engagement', but to extricate the guns with the least casualties to his own brigade.

In exceptionally open order, the Queen's Regiment and the Devons successfully weathered the rifle fire. By nine o'clock the forward companies had reached the village. Intelligently handled, unlike the Irish Brigade, Hildyard's men suffered few casualties. The Queen's dug themselves in behind walls and in gardens, with some of the Devons, under Lieutenant-Colonel G.M. Bullock, on their right. All these men were under cover – sheltered in the eye of the hurricane.

But how to cross that last half-mile of open plain to the guns? About 8.30 a.m. Buller himself had ridden up to the larger of the two dongas, eight hundred yards in the rear. He arranged for artillery horses to drag Ogilvy's naval guns back to a safe position, then rode back along the firing-line to get further support. There was no lack of infantry. The problem was how to get them far enough forward to extricate Long.

As Buller and his staff rode along the firing-line, he was himself an obvious target. In fact, he had been severely bruised in the ribs by a shell fragment, but did not admit this till later. But behind the mask, his spirit was on fire. Rage

and frustration with Long's blunder ('I was sold by a d——d gunner', he later told a close friend), and Hart's, vied with the exhilaration of danger. It was fourteen years since he had last been in battle; he found he had not lost his taste for it.

He rode back to the large donga. Bullets drummed on the ground, but he stood out in the open and shouted, 'Now, my lads, this is your last chance to save the guns; will any of you volunteer to fetch them?'

One of the corporals got up, and six other gunners joined him – not enough for two teams. Buller turned to the staff (which included Prince Christian Victor, a grandson of Queen Victoria). 'Some of you go and help.' Three officers stepped forward: Captain H.N. Schofield, Captain Walter Congreve, and Lieutenant Freddy Roberts, the Field-Marshal's only son.

Congreve was never to forget that ride. They hooked the two teams into the limbers, then set off at a canter towards the guns, half a mile away. He watched his friend Freddy Roberts 'laughing, talking and slapping his leg with his stick'. Then several bullets caught Congreve and his horse, and they came down about a hundred yards from the guns. Freddy had vanished. But somehow the two teams reached the guns. After a struggle, Schofield and the corporal hooked in, and away they galloped to safety with two 15-pounders.

Botha's men beyond the river redoubled their fire. The next team was brought to a standstill. More volunteers rode out. It was hopeless. A final attempt was made with three teams. Twelve of the horses were shot, one man killed, five wounded. No one reached the guns. Buller now refused to sanction any further rescue attempts, and gave the order to retire.

Of all the accusations later levelled at Buller, the taunt that he had needlessly abandoned Long's guns probably cut him most deeply. Despite the pain of his wound, he stayed in the saddle till he had seen his own infantry companies safely home. By three o'clock, all firing had ebbed away. Out in the shimmering plain, the guns lay abandoned, encircled by dead horses. And in the small donga thirty yards behind, Colonel Long, wounded gunners, staff, and some infantrymen still lay under the midsummer sun.

The wounded Congreve later described the experiences of that interminable day, 'the most beastly day I ever spent'. He had found Freddy Roberts lying out on the veld, shot in the stomach and two other places. When the fire slackened, Congreve dragged him under shelter. He was unconscious, and there seemed little hope for him. They shaded his head, and waited.

About 4.30 p.m. some Boers crossed the river and rode over to the donga. One of them called on the British to surrender. The senior British officer there was Bullock, who had pushed forward to the east of the railway line, and taken refuge in this donga with about twenty unwounded men of his battalion. He refused to surrender, and shots were exchanged. But while more negotiations were going on, about a hundred Boers crept round the side of the donga, and emerged pointing their rifles at the Devons. One of the Boers hit Bullock in the face with a rifle butt. He and the rest of the Devons, and the unwounded gunners, were bundled off as prisoners. Congreve, Freddy Roberts, Long and the other wounded were sent back in the care of the 'bodysnatchers', the Indian and British ambulance men who now reached the donga.

In his cable for public consumption, sent that night, Buller presented his usual air of calm. He was generous to Hart. He described the heroism of the attempts to save the guns. He gave no hint of the collapse of his infantry. Only in his reference to Long did he give any real explanation for the 'serious reverse'. (This was, however, censored by the War Office.)

Had he left the matter there, the history of the war might have been different. Certainly he would have been spared deep humiliation. But by midnight, his emotions had finally got the better of him. The intense isolation of his position, the frustration of his long struggle with Lansdowne, the bitterness of his feelings towards Hart and Long, the hours under that burning sun, the pain of his wound: all were written between the lines of a midnight cypher cable to Lansdowne. There was also a crucial misunderstanding that explained the outburst.

The day before, he had received a cable from Lansdowne telling him to sack both Gatacre and Methuen. Lieutenant-General Sir Charles Warren, the commander of reinforcements he had long awaited – the 5th Division – was to take over Methuen's force at Modder River. Buller assumed from this that Lansdowne had diverted Warren *and* his new division to the Kimberley front, overriding his own judgement at the behest of Milner and the capitalists. In fact, Lansdowne's order applied only to Warren himself, not to his division, which was still at Buller's disposal.

Hence the mood of rebellious rage – what he himself called 'envy, hatred and malice for everyone'. He now cabled to Lansdowne: 'My failure today raises a serious question. I do not think I am now [that is, since the apparent diversion of the 5th Division] strong enough to relieve White. . . . My view is that I ought to let Ladysmith go, and occupy good positions for the defence of South Natal, and let time help us.'

Was Buller really proposing to abandon Ladysmith? By 'let go' he did not mean 'let fall', he claimed afterwards, and one can believe him. But what he did mean was made clear in a second, still more ill-advised outburst – a heliograph message sent early next day to Ladysmith.

White, in letting himself be besieged, had wrecked the whole strategy of the war. That was Buller's view, and there was a good deal of truth in it. Now he lashed out: 'I tried Colenso yesterday, but failed. The enemy is too strong for my force, except with siege operations, which will take one full month to prepare. Can you last so long? Stop. If not, how many days can you give me to take up defensive position, after which I suggest your firing away as much ammunition as you can, and making the best terms you can. . . .'

If only Buller could have expressed himself more plainly, and less bluntly, there would have been nothing extraordinary about either of his cables. His proposal to Lansdowne was essentially the same as that he had made, and then rejected, just after he had arrived, and was echoed by Milner. Let Ladysmith look after itself for the time being; send the bulk of the army to the western front; advance into the Free State. So, indirectly, relieve Ladysmith. Put like that, the proposal sounded statesmanlike. But his cable did not put it like that; it was a protest and a challenge – and a gift to Buller's enemies.

The message to White was still more bluntly expressed. The main questions were: how long could he hold out, and could he cut his way out? Talk of surrender was premature as well as tactless; Ladysmith still had food, though fodder and some ammunition were running short. For this error, too, Buller was to pay the price.

Buller's army marched back to Frere, and their water supply. The Boers made no attempt to attack. British losses came to 1,138: 143 killed, 755 wounded, 240 missing, mostly captured unharmed. This was about 5 per cent of the total force engaged; few of the wounded were serious cases, and after several

Below British officers recuperate in an officers' hospital in the Cape. Conditions were rougher for other ranks.

Colonel Long's 10 field-guns, captured by Botha's men at Colenso, on their way back in triumph to Pretoria.

Giving first aid to a wounded Tommy after a battle.

weeks the losses were probably reduced by a half. By military standards the battle was not a disaster; it was a 'serious reverse', as Buller had called it. The enemy did not win a yard of ground. The British only lost a small fraction of their men, and ten of their field-guns; in short, little that could not be soon replaced. And the men's morale, the key to ultimate victory, miraculously revived, for Buller was as tactful in handling his troops as he was clumsy in handling Lansdowne and White.

His own morale, too, recovered, and he began to plan a new flank march to relieve Ladysmith. Then the blow that he had half-expected, indeed, had almost courted, fell. On 18 December a telegram arrived from London: he was superseded as GOC, South Africa, and relegated to command in Natal. But the man appointed over his head was not, as he had expected, his patron, Wolseley. Instead, Lansdowne had chosen his own friend from Indian days, Roberts.

The news was painful to Buller, though he accepted that the show 'was too big for one man'. Roberts was the leader of the rival Ring to Wolseley's, and he was absolutely out of sympathy with Buller. An added twist to their tense relationship was given by the tragic news that Buller had learnt only the previous day. He had himself just drafted the cable – blunt, yet not without emotion: 'Your gallant son died today. Condolences. Buller.'

The first report of Buller's reverse at Colenso reached Lord Roberts in Ireland at breakfast time on Saturday 16 December. 'For years,' as he put it, 'I have [been] waiting for this day'. Now he must seize the chance of a lifetime. He scribbled a long, outspoken cable to Lansdowne, warning that unless a 'radical change' in both strategy and tactics was made 'we shall have to make an ignominious peace'. How to effect the radical change? Appoint himself C-in-C in South Africa. On 10 December he secretly slipped over to the War

Le Petit Journal
SUPPLÉMENT ILLUSTRÉ
Huit pages : CINQ centimes

DIMANCHE 24 DÉCEMBRE 1899   Numéro 475

A PILE OU ...
...OER. — Si c'est « pile », ce sera pou...

Then humbled Joseph crept to bed
With horrid buzzings in his head,
And visions came: he looked, O lor!
Beside his couch the horrid Boar
Whom vainly he had tried to floor!

But Joseph bides his time to smack
The stolid grinning Kruger back,
He marks the ghost with steely eye
And lips that tremble to reply:
...ill he swallows, and declares
...best for Boars and Bears!

L'État-Major

Le GÉNÉRAL en reconnaissance. — Tiens, une montagne !

LE MUSÉE DE SIRES   Nº 2

A. & Cⁱᵉ, 19, Rue de Paradis, Paris . Reproduction interdite

SIR PAUL KRUGER

Office to see Lansdowne, who had in fact already moved with uncharacteristic swiftness. The moment he received Buller's first cable after Colenso – the self-confident public one – he decided that Buller must go. But there were two solid obstacles: Wolseley and the Queen. To outwit them, Lansdowne appealed to his friend Balfour, master of the Whitehall backstairs, who that Friday was himself waiting on tenterhooks for word of what had happened at Colenso. When he heard the astonishing news – failure – he immediately resolved that he and Lansdowne would sack Buller, without informing either Wolseley or the Queen.

Buller now played straight into his hands. Early next day, Roberts was told to prepare to go to South Africa; the message crossed with his own cypher cable to Lansdowne. Later, Buller's second cable arrived, the one he had written in a mood of black rage and resentment. It was the main exhibit when the Cabinet Defence Committee met that evening. Buller had lost his nerve and proposed to leave Ladysmith to its fate. The Cabinet agreed to replace him with Roberts as C-in-C; Buller would remain in charge of the Natal army. At Salisbury's insistence, Lord Kitchener, the Sirdar of Egypt and gallant young hero of Omdurman (he was nearly eighteen years younger than Roberts), was to join Roberts as Chief of Staff.

In fact, Roberts's 'radical change' telegram was in some respects more despondent than Buller's. The text of this astonishing cable (never published before the first edition of this book) suggested, among other things, that Buller should be ordered to act 'strictly on the defensive' until Warren's 5th Division could be brought up – precisely what Buller's telegram proposed. But Roberts also proposed leaving both Kimberley and Mafeking 'to their fates', which was to out-Buller Buller.

There is no reason to believe that Salisbury and the Cabinet ever saw this 'surrender' telegram. The strategic situation improved, and Roberts, like Buller, recovered his nerve. Before he left England he agreed a compromise strategy with Balfour and Lansdowne. Buller was to relieve White and then abandon Ladysmith to the Boers. By the same token, Methuen was to relieve Kekewich and then abandon Kimberley, diamonds and all. It would be humiliating, and, of course, Milner would shriek, but the government now recognized that this was the strategy they should have followed all along. Military necessity must finally take precedence over political considerations. The alternative was the 'ignominious peace', and that, of course, no one was contemplating.

Having squared Salisbury and the Cabinet, Lansdowne and Balfour had the delicate task of tackling Wolseley and the Queen. Wolseley was 'dumbfounded', but there was nothing he could do about what what was now a *fait accompli*. The Queen, already deeply aggrieved at the Cabinet's behaviour on numerous grounds, expressed her astonishment. However, Balfour went to Windsor and found 'no great difficulty in smoothing things down'.

Meanwhile, Roberts arrived from Ireland, and went to Lansdowne House to receive confirmation of his appointment. Lansdowne had to break the

A cheerful look at British misfortunes by cartoonists in Britain, Belgium and France.

news of Freddy's death. He said later, 'The blow was almost more than he could bear, and for a moment I thought he would break down. . . . I shall never forget the courage which he showed.'

A week later, Lansdowne and many others went down to Southampton to wish Roberts godspeed on the journey to South Africa. It was two days before Christmas – a raw and cheerless day. Amidst the usual jolly scenes, Roberts and his party made up a sombre group; Lansdowne and the others wore black in deference. To his wife, Roberts wrote later that the 'rent in my heart seems to stifle all feelings. . . . I could not help thinking how different it would have been if our dear boy had been with me. Honours, rewards and congratulations have no value for me.'

Britain's 'small-war' army – the brainchild of Edward Cardwell (Gladstone's War Minister), Wolseley and Buller, starved by Lansdowne, Cabinet and country – now had a big war on its hands. It must be expanded to a size even Wolseley had never envisaged. This was the obvious lesson of 'Black Week', as the dismal week of Stormberg, Magersfontein and Colenso came to be called. The problem was how.

The public's reaction to Black Week was a spasm of astonishment, frustration and humiliation. There was no precedent in British military history for the scale of casualties suffered – not as regards those killed or wounded, but as regards the 2,000 men who had shown the white flag. This was at the root of the public's humiliation. Then the spasm of bitterness passed. Black Week had one result in which Chamberlain, the champion of imperial unity, could only take pride. All over the globe, a wave of colonial patriotism, much more astonishing than the home variety, had been set in motion. Blood was thicker than water: British Canadians, Australians and New Zealanders felt a natural solidarity with the mother country. They could also identify with the Uitlanders to a degree that the public at home could not. They were of the same class, and they had shared the experiences of the pioneer. Besides, many of the Uitlanders actually were colonials.

Hence Chamberlain's task in rallying support in the self-governing white colonies was easy enough, and the colonies replied by despatching both MI and cavalry to South Africa. The first contingents had sailed that autumn, and were already playing some part in the war. These were only token forces, but no one could now write off the self-governing Empire as an anachronism. Soon it was to bring twenty-nine thousand white colonial troops to South Africa.

A united country, a united Empire – Chamberlain's gloom might seem hard to understand. But there was a good reason: a shock-wave of anglophobia on the Continent, and especially in Germany. Two months of war had revealed to Britain that there was another side to isolationist policy. If her Continental rivals chose this moment to intervene, amicably or not, Britain would be in a splendid mess. In fact, intervention, though discussed by the other Great Powers in Europe – Germany, France and Russia – was not a practical possibility. But in the autumn of 1899, the German government had decided to double the size of the German navy. It was a new phase in the European arms race. Here were the tremors of the earthquake of 1914.

The bitter and sometimes childish feud between Lansdowne and Wolseley – and between 'Indians' and 'Africans' – was the root cause of so many of the disasters in South Africa. The fundamental strategic mistake consisted in sending out too few troops in September, under the wrong commander, and pushed too far forward into Natal. Both Lansdowne and Wolseley had to share the blame for this triple blunder. On the other hand, Lansdowne's caution was the main cause of the four-month delay in the arrival of the Army Corps. To cap it all, the War Office was to blame for the most appalling mistakes and deficiencies in vital supplies, especially ammunition, artillery and clothing. It seems not to have occurred to anyone there that a field force needed more than a field-day.

This scandal naturally strengthened Wolseley's hand. So did the three battles of Black Week. The day before Colenso, he had insisted that they must now flood South Africa with reinforcements. His proposals were far-reaching, and included plans to mobilize the 7th and 8th Divisions – and to accept civilian volunteers.

On 16 and 18 December the Army Board met, and endorsed Wolseley's proposals. On the 20th, Wolseley was astonished to hear that Lansdowne had accepted a scheme for raising civilian volunteers of a much more sensational kind.

The origin of the scheme actually lay with Buller, who cabled on the day after Colenso: 'Would it be possible for you to raise eight thousand irregulars in England. . . . equipped as mounted infantry . . . able to shoot as well as possible and ride decently.' George Wyndham, Milnerite and Lansdowne's junior minister, grasped Buller's point at once. British mobility must match Boer mobility. He agreed that seven thousand volunteers should be sent to help regular MI units. In addition, he suggested raising, as 'a matter of immediate urgency and permanent importance', a total of twenty thousand irregular MI: mainly from South Africa and other colonies, but at least five thousand from Britain.

Three days later, the formation of the 'Imperial Yeomanry' was announced. Wolseley was furious to find his own scheme so dramatically trumped. He protested officially that recruiting inexperienced civilians was a 'dangerous experiment'; they would be 'very little use in field'. Lansdowne's comment was: 'The Boers are not, I suppose, very highly drilled or disciplined.'

At the time, the most striking fact about Black Week was that it seemed to have, for everyone except the Boers, a silver lining. The new Imperial Yeomanry caught the imagination of Press and public. There was a rush to abandon the fox and pursue the Boer; large crowds formed outside the recruiting office in London; the City of London itself offered and paid for one thousand volunteers. People began to talk of the war as a 'national' war.

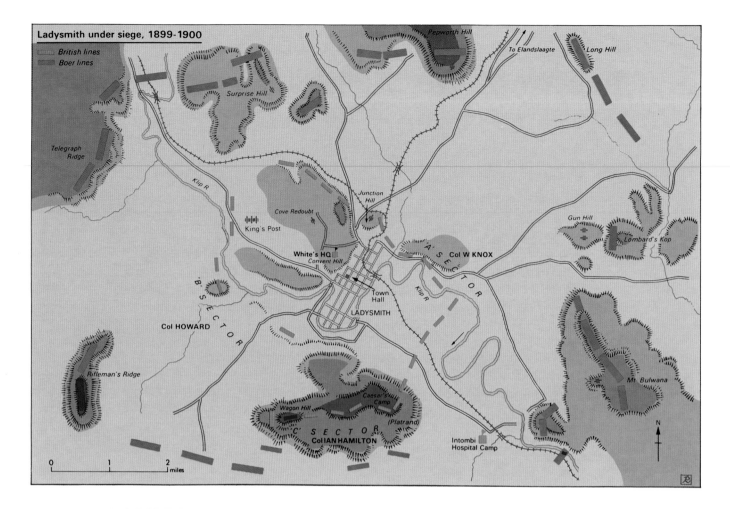

Ladysmith under siege, 1899-1900

British lines
Boer lines

Pepworth Hill
To Elandslaagte
Long Hill
Surprise Hill
Telegraph Ridge
Klip R
Junction Hill
Cove Redoubt
King's Post
Gun Hill
Lombard's Kop
White's HQ
'A' SECTOR
Col W KNOX
Convent Hill
'B' SECTOR
Town Hall
LADYSMITH
Klip R
Col HOWARD
Rifleman's Ridge
Mt. Bulwana
Wagon Hill
Caesar's Camp
(Platrand)
'C' SECTOR
Col IAN HAMILTON
Intombi Hospital Camp
N

0   1   2 miles

The sight of our men washing so infuriated the Boers that they immediately opened fire.

C·M·D

CHAPTER FIFTEEN

'Are We Rotters or Heroes?'

Pretoria, 12 December 1899–1 January 1900;
Ladysmith, 2 November 1899–6 January 1900

'We hope to be lunching at the White Hart, Pretoria, in about a month's time. . . .'

Lieutenant Reggie Kentish to his mother, near Ladysmith,
12 October 1899

'Lunch is at one o'clock & consists of Bread & Bully beef . . . vegetables, cheese, fresh meat . . . & the towns people parade in front of our cage eyeing us up and down as though we were some weird objects. . . .'

Lieutenant Kentish to his mother, Model Schools (Prisoner of War Camp), Pretoria, 9 November 1899

'THE GOD OF OUR FOREFATHERS has given us a dazzling victory. . . .' As Botha's telegram reached Pretoria, confirming the victories at Colenso, Magersfontein and Stormberg, other nations might have allowed themselves a day's public rejoicing. Kruger's people were not like that.

In the capital, always solemn and God-fearing, the church bells rang only for the dead. To the volk, victory brought a double shock: relief and delight at their achievements, bitterness at the cost. In fact, the price of victory had been heavier for them, proportionate to their numbers, than the price of defeat for the British. Besides, to the volk, surrounded by black enemies, *no* white man's death was much cause for rejoicing.

Old and half blind, his voice hoarse and frail, yet in spirit the epitome of strength and defiance, Kruger addressed his people on the day after Colenso. It was Dingaan's Day, the day when the Lord, by the destruction of Dingaan and the Zulus at the Battle of Blood River in 1838, had made a covenant with the voortrekkers. To him, there was indeed a marvellous symmetry about the pattern of his long life. Blood River, Majuba, Colenso – three times in Natal, the Lord had delivered them from their enemies. Hence the overpowering simplicity of his call: put your trust in the Lord; He will protect His people as He protected your forefathers from Dingaan.

A scene from the siege of Ladysmith, painted by Sir George White's ADC, Lieutenant Charles Dixon.

139

Simplicity, of course, was not a characteristic of Kruger's mind. A final settlement with the British Empire, giving unqualified independence to the Transvaal, was the goal of all his manoeuvring. He faced a strategic dilemma of extraordinary difficulty. How could he turn tactical successes into real strategic victories, and both into a winning seat at the conference table?

Could he make Colenso a second and better Majuba? Or must this be a war of attrition?

The first alternative, a new Majuba, seemed a tempting option. But Boer military successes had undoubtedly strengthened the jingo cause in Britain, and further reduced the slender minority who believed in a negotiated peace. The danger of Britain's being humiliated in front of the other Great Power outweighed the moral disadvantages. Kruger may not have grasped all the niceties of British politics, but he understood these sad truths well enough.

Of course, Britain might also be forced to the conference table by the pressure of public opinion in other countries – in other words, by intervention. But here again, Kruger was not so simple as to think this likely, nor did he choose to raise false hopes by pretending that it was.

Dr Leyds, the Transvaal Ambassador in Brussels, had struggled to persuade Britain's rivals – France, Germany and Russia – to make common cause against Britain. But all he achieved, despite the sympathy of most of Europe, was to inspire a couple of hundred foreign volunteers to fight on the side of the burghers, and a number of countries to send small ambulance teams.

So lack of moral support in Britain, and of military support on the Continent, meant that there was no chance of the Boer victories turning, of themselves, into new Majubas. Could they follow up their successes, then, and strike at the British in Natal and the Cape while they were still off balance? In principle, Kruger and Steyn favoured this option; still more so, the younger generation of Boers. But was it practicable? Both Cronje and Botha now refused, for excellent military reasons, to launch attacks against a vastly more numerous enemy. The truth was that the Boer governments, like the British, had failed to recognize how the new conditions of war – smokeless, long-range magazine rifles, fired by concealed infantry – had dramatically tipped the tactical balance in favour of the defence.

By default, therefore, Kruger was left with the second strategic option: a war of attrition. The two republics' military objectives were now limited to trying to block the progress of the two relief columns, meanwhile squeezing the three beleaguered garrisons. It was not a strategy that could win them a seat at the conference table – not directly, at any rate. The loss of all three garrisons, however humiliating to the British, would make their task somewhat easier. Relieved of these entanglements, they could make straight for Bloemfontein.

Kruger was soon reconciled to a war of attrition. It came naturally to the Boers, not only among the commandos in the field, but among the people as a whole. Their strength lay, above all, in self-sufficiency, which no strategic blockade could injure.

CLOSTER PIQUET WAGGON HILL LADYSMITH
BOER WAR 1899-1900

Gloucesters on picket duty at Wagon Hill, the key to the defence of Ladysmith. On 6 January 1900 the Boers attacked in strength.

There were three civilian cornerstones to Kruger's state. The first was the non-British Uitlanders, who now ran the Boer industries – especially the vital gold mines – which had been weakened by the expulsion of the British Uitlanders. The second, less visible, cornerstone, was as crucial: the vast reserve of African labour that kept the mines working. But it was chiefly in the farms, rather than on the Rand, that the third cornerstone was found: the *vrouw*, the indomitable Boer housewife. If the commandos had a secret weapon in the spade, the nation as a whole had another in the cradle. The Transvaal birth rate was phenomenal, offsetting that tidal wave of Uitlanders. Without a doubt, the volk were now in the majority.

Of course, the *vrouw* did more than rock the cradle. Already the stress of wartime had entrusted to Boer wives a mass of tasks previously done by men. Now they were overseeing the farms and the Africans, as well as supplying regular food hampers for sons and husbands at the front.

The *vrouw* was the unshakeable foundation of Kruger's state. In the last resort, if the war of attrition became a guerrilla war, the Uitlanders would be of no help, and the Africans might be a liability. On the *vrouw* everything would depend, as it had depended before the Transvaal had become an industrial state.

But guerrilla war was still far from Kruger's thoughts. He still hankered after some offensive stroke. And in the end he was rewarded. A *krijgsraad* agreed to resume the offensive on 6 January. While Botha kept Buller occupied at the Tugela, four thousand burghers would storm the Platrand at Ladysmith (known to the British as 'Wagon Hill' and 'Caesar's Camp', the flat-topped ridge that commanded the town from the south.

Sir George White's HQ, the convent at
Ladysmith, after being hit by a shell from a
'Long Tom'. No one was hurt.

Disappointment and humiliation. If Black Week sent a shudder through most
patriots in England, how much sharper the pain for the garrison of
Ladysmith – 13,745 white soldiers and 5,400 civilians (including 2,400
African servants and Indian camp-followers). The demoralizing news was
news that the relief was delayed. For six weeks the soldiers had expected
relief as soon as the Army Corps arrived. Now, on 17 December, they learned
that Buller had 'failed in his first attempt at Colenso'; relief was postponed
until after Christmas, at least.

The inertia and apathy of the defenders, coupled with the increasing toll of
disease, worried the more intelligent officers. This was at the root of their
bitter feelings towards White and his staff. Why, asked Captain John Gough
of the Rifle Brigade, are we not allowed to raid the enemy's lines? It was a
question that was echoed by many of the Natal refugees inside Ladysmith.
They had embarked on the siege already bitterly resentful of the imperial
authorities; Milner's splendid promise to defend Natal 'with the whole might
of the Empire' contrasted with the absurdly small number of troops sent
there on the outbreak of war. They were loyal, but they blamed White for
most of their trouble. In early December, one civilian pressed the authorities
to try a raid on Bulwana to silence the Long Tom there. He was refused. A
few days later a fiercely worded poster appeared in the town, denouncing
White's pusillanimity. Indeed, at Ladysmith – unlike Kimberley – it was the
civilians who were most eager for an active defence.

In the small hours of 8 December, six hundred men of the garrison –
appropriately, the Uitlanders of the ILH and the colonials of the Natal
Carbineers, led by imperial officers – were sent out to raid Gun Hill, the

forward slope of Lombard's Kop. At 3.17 a.m. came the rumble of three explosions.

All had gone exactly as Rawlinson, one of the ablest men on White's staff, had planned. There were two big guns on the lower slope – a 4·5-inch howitzer and one of the Long Toms. The Boer picket bolted, and the raiding party were back inside the lines by dawn, after disabling both guns with gun-cotton charges. A second raid, by regulars, on the night of 11 December, was equally successful, destroying a 4·5-inch howitzer on Surprise Hill. This time, however, British casualties were heavy – nine killed and fifty-four wounded. But Rawlinson was satisfied. Their own losses might be heavy, but the moral effect 'would not be lost on the Boers'.

A further week passed, full of conflicting plans for offensives. Poor White could still not reach any firm conclusion how best to help Buller. Came the news of Colenso, with its dispiriting effect on the Ladysmith garrison, which relapsed into apparent helplessness. Above all, there were the nagging fears of what the British public thought of them. As a subaltern of the 60th wrote home, 'Are we rotters or heroes?'

One uncertainty, at least, was settled on Saturday 6 January – the night the Boer leaders had agreed with Kruger to make that decisive stroke against the Platrand.

Something was up, Rawlinson had decided. An eerie silence prevailed in the Boer lines. White still could not make up his mind how or when to help Buller. But he had decided to relocate two naval 12-pounders and the 4·7-inch 'Lady Anne' (one of the only two guns with the range to answer the Long Toms) on Wagon Hill, in case he should summon up courage for the long-delayed plan to break out to the south.

At 2.40 a.m. a party of naval gunners and some sappers, with an escort of Gordons, were lowering Lady Anne's gun platform into the emplacement at Wagon Point, the extreme south-west point of Wagon Hill. The gun itself was still at the bottom of the hill.

Suddenly, there came a new noise: rifle bullets splashing on the stones around them. Wagon Hill now became a confused mass of shouting men. The pickets, less than a hundred men of the ILH, wore the same slouch hats as the Boers, which added to the confusion. Against the glare of a Boer searchlight several hundred Free Staters poured on to the ridge, beating down the pickets. Fortunately for the garrison, the ILH had built one small 'fort': a loop-holed ring of stones, about twenty feet around, into which rushed Lieutenant Digby-Jones and some of the sappers. Others took refuge in one of the gun emplacements. Here the naval gunner, Sims, added to the incongruity of the scene by numbering his men as though on parade. Perhaps it steadied them.

Meanwhile, at Caesar's Camp, the pickets had a quarter of an hour's warning before a force of Transvaalers stormed over the ridge. But, owing to the extreme feebleness of Hamilton's defences at 'C' sector, there was no real obstacle here to the Boers' seizing the vital crest line. The Transvaalers not only established a foothold on the crest, they also took the picket line of the Manchesters in the rear, cutting them down in swathes. When dawn came, the whole hillside was seen to be swarming with Boers.

Two miles away, Rawlinson and Major-General Sir Archibald Hunter were woken by the firing. The HQ was connected to each section of the defences by telephone, and before long, astonishing messages reached them. Discarding their conventional tactics, the Boers were storming all sides of the perimeter, supported by every gun they had. The attacks on 'A' and 'B' sectors, better fortified than Hamilton's, were beaten off almost without loss to the defenders. It was the situation at Wagon Hill and Caesar's Camp that was critical. White, weak with fever, was hardly able to stir from his house. The main burden of saving Ladysmith rested on Hunter and Rawlinson.

The first step was to send field-guns to attack from below what a properly sited fort would have prevented the Boers ever establishing: a position on the south-east slopes of Caesar's Camp. In the early morning sunshine, Major Abdy's 53rd Battery trotted out towards Intombi Camp, unlimbered, and began to splash the south-east slopes of Caesar's Camp with shrapnel. Soon after 6.00 a.m., these slopes were cleared of the enemy, except for dead and wounded. But the field-guns could not reach the southern crest line, nor the slopes beyond. To drive the enemy from these positions, infantry was needed. About 8.00 a.m., six companies of the Rifle Brigade reached the scene, more than doubling the strength of the garrison there, composed of Manchesters and Gordons. One of the company commanders was Gough. His battalion took terrible casualties, especially among the officers; soon Gough found himself the senior Rifle Brigade officer under fire. But they could find no one in command; no one who 'knew in the least what was going on'; or even whether the Boers were on the ridge or not.

The man responsible for the whole débâcle was Hamilton. He had galloped off to Wagon Hill as soon as he was woken by the firing, leaving no one in command at Caesar's Camp. However, he now did his best to redeem himself by personal gallantry. The situation at Wagon Hill was equally confused, but much more critical, as the 'forts' were still flimsier here, and no help could be given by field-guns firing from the flank. Soon after dawn, the first reinforcements, the remainder of the ILH, reached the hilltop, followed by two reserve companies of Gordons under Major Miller-Wallnut. At 7.00 a.m. eight companies of the 1st and 2nd 60th joined them. There were now more than two thousand men lying flat in the firing-line – 250 Free Staters, and eight times that number of British infantry. In places, the combatants were separated by only a few yards of grassy hillside. And never was the firepower of the new magazine rifle – and the inability of British officers to recognize it – better displayed. Three times a small party of men, led by an officer, charged towards the hidden enemy, and each time they were annihilated. At last, Hamilton called off these suicidal counter-attacks. And, miraculously, the firing melted away. By 11.00 a.m., Hamilton felt confident enough to order some men down the hill. It was fiercely hot, and it was time for lunch.

At about one o'clock, for the second time that astonishing day, the Boers broke all the rules of their own tactics. Digby-Jones and Miller-Wallnut were sitting close to Lady Anne's gun emplacement at Wagon Point; Hamilton had just joined them. A party of Boers stormed over the crest, sending the British line streaming back in a panic. The first that Hamilton knew of this was when a rifle was thrust over the emplacement. Digby-Jones sprang up and shot one of the leaders of this gallant attack; someone else shot the other from inside the emplacement. Lower down, Gunner Sims heard shots and yelling as the mass of men rushed helter-skelter towards him. 'Naval Brigade,' he roared, 'extend in skirmishing order . . . forward-d-d!' Once again Sims and Digby-Jones saved the day. The thirteen naval gunners charged back with the bayonet. The panic subsided, and the handful of Boers who had made the attack were shot down or driven off, although both Digby-Jones and Miller-Wallnut were killed.

The news of the fighting in 'C' sector had been continuously reported to the HQ by telephone. They were nerve-racking hours for everyone. White sent a half-despairing telegram to Buller, begging him to create a diversion at Colenso. Virtually all the reserves had been committed. Hunter and Rawlinson kept calm.

By 4.00 p.m., it was obvious to Hamilton that both Boer assaults had failed. And then White intervened, overreacting violently, as only weak men can. The crest line must be cleared of Boers *before* darkness. The final infantry reserves, three companies of Devons, must drive them off with the bayonet.

Now – just as at Elandslaagte – a furious thunderstorm burst over the ground. Fifteen miles away, Buller's signallers watched the flash of the heliograph fade in the blackness: 'Attack renewed, very hard pressed. . . .' So the message ended, leaving Buller in suspense for more than a day.

At Wagon Hill, the storm was already passing when, with a rattle of bayonets and a wild cheer, the Devons set off across that 130-yard-wide strip of slippery grass. An answering crash of Mausers from the crest line; they hardly faltered. They reached the crest, but there was no chance to use the bayonet. The Boers had merely taken a new position among some rocks further back. So the fight went on till darkness, as confused and bloody as it had begun.

Next morning, there was an armistice to collect up the dead and wounded. On top of Caesar's Camp Gough counted fifty-two dead burghers, many of them terribly mangled by shrapnel. The total number of Boer dead was believed to be a good deal higher.

British losses were 424: seventeen officers dead or dying, 28 wounded; 158 men killed (more than at Colenso), 221 wounded. Captain Steavenson, Adjutant of the Liverpools, wrote in his diary, 'Civilized war is awful.'

CHAPTER SIXTEEN

An Acre of Massacre

Spion Kop, Natal, 24–25 January 1900

'We waded through the Tugela, up to our breasts like, to get across, and we climbed up this 'ere hill – cor, God it was a climb – you climbed up so far and you came to a big flat rock and you had to go all the way round . . . cor it was stinkin' 'ot it was . . . and we laid out there firing at one another, us and the Boers – the Boers was up *above* us, see – they'd got us in a trap like . . . I couldn't see all round but I could 'ear blokes shoutin' you know, blokes that was getting 'it and all that . . .'

Private Joe Packer, 2nd Middlesex, describing the Battle of
Spion Kop to the author in June 1970

BULLER, OUTWARDLY AS SOLID and reassuring as ever, had never doubted the danger of the Boers attacking Ladysmith. Now their near-success made it all the more urgent for him to resume operations. Besides, Roberts was expected at Cape Town on 11 January. Despite a cable from him, urging caution, Buller had no wish to stay on the defensive a day longer than necessary. Warren's division was now at Estcourt. In a couple of days extra horse artillery would have arrived. On the 10th, the day before Roberts superseded him as GOC, South Africa, the army at Frere would leave the railway and set off on a flank march to Ladysmith by way of Springfield, twenty-five miles to the west.

Buller now believed he had found a way round. Despite all his handicaps, he hoped it would carry him across those 'beastly mountains' to Ladysmith.

The troops crossed the Tugela on 16 January. Buller was now convinced that to attack Potgieters directly would invite another Colenso. He had decided to divide his force and tell Warren to take the larger part and cross the Tugela at Trichardt's Drift, five miles up river from Potgieters. Warren was told to break the enemy's line west of a strange, hog-backed hill that would soon be famous in a sombre fashion: 'Look-out Hill' – in Dutch, Spion Kop (*see map on page 147.*) In the event Warren dithered, then decided to attack Spion Kop itself, as it was so precipitous that it was the last place the Boers would expect the British to attack. It commanded the wagon road which he needed if he was to march north. If it could be seized and held, if heavy guns could be installed there, the Boers would be driven back to the plain.

Buller agreed. As soon as Warren's attack had succeeded, he would push forward his own force from Potgieters. But he blamed Warren for not cutting

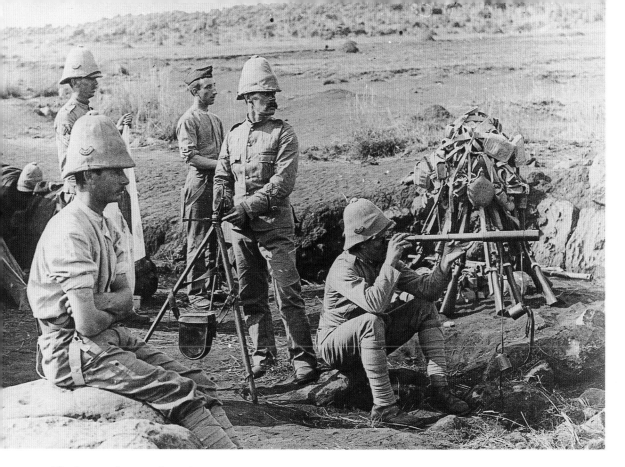

The Devons during a skirmish.

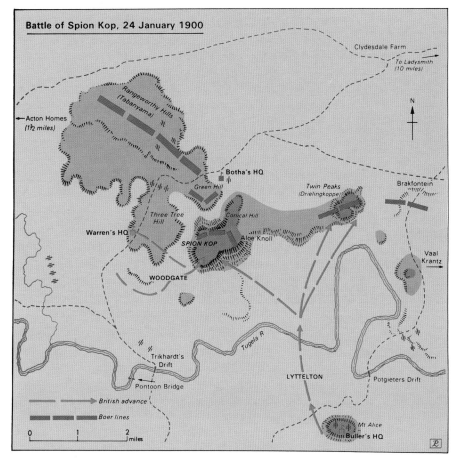

Battle of Spion Kop, 24 January 1900

Clydesdale Farm

To Ladysmith
(10 miles)

Rangeworthy Hills
(Tabanyama)

←Acton Homes
(1½ miles)

N

Botha's HQ

Green Hill

Twin Peaks
(Drielingkoppe)

Brakfontein

Three Tree
Hill

Conical Hill

Warren's HQ

SPION KOP

Aloe Knoll

Vaal
Krantz

WOODGATE

Tugela R

Trikhardt's
Drift

LYTTELTON

Potgieters Drift

Pontoon Bridge

→ British advance

Boer lines

0   1   2
                miles

Mt Alice
Buller's HQ

his way through earlier, at Tabanyama west of Spion Kop, before Botha was ready to parry the thrust.

There are few excitements like a night attack. Major-General E. R. P. Woodgate's column of two thousand men – soldiers from three battalions of his own Lancashire Brigade, plus two hundred MI and a half-company of sappers – reached the crest line in safety. Then suddenly, out of the pre-dawn mist, came a sentry's challenge, followed by rifle flashes. Lieutenant-Colonel Alec Thorneycroft, the MI commander and leader of the column, waited until he judged the Mauser magazines were empty, then gave the order: fix bayonets and charge. With a hoarse yell of 'Majuba!', his men vanished into the mist. So did the small Boer picket. Spion Kop, the key to Ladysmith, was now ready to turn in the lock.

Manoeuvring a naval long-range 12-pounder, converted to be drawn by oxen, into a firing position outside Ladysmith.

It was just after 4.00 a.m. Major Massey of the sappers began methodically to tape out a curved, 300-yard line of trenches on what seemed, in the mist, to be the forward crest of the summit. His half-company began work, while the rest of the officers and men – even Woodgate – relaxed after the night's tensions.

The mist had given the column three hours' grace. Everything had gone according to plan, despite delays. It was too misty to heliograph, so Woodgate decided to send Colonel Charles à Court, Buller's staff officer attached to the column, back down the hill to ask for naval guns to be brought up and to brief Warren and Buller. He pencilled a curt note to Warren: 'We are entrenched . . . and are, I hope, secure; but fog is too thick to see. . . .'

Botha did not flinch at the news brought by the fleeing picket. The Khakis had taken the Kop. Well, the burghers must take it back; he made it sound as simple as that.

Meanwhile, the news had reached Schalk Burger, laagered roughly two miles away, behind the twin eastern summits of Spion Kop. Burger was nominally Botha's superior, and Joubert's second-in-command; in effect, Botha and he jointly commanded this sector, and Botha, much the stronger character, called the tune. Together, they now fixed the plans for the counter-attack. Its essence was speed.

Provided that the British did not drag heavy guns up to the main peak, the situation was dangerous, but not desperate. The fire of their own heavy guns could be brought to converge on the hub of the hilltop like the spokes of a wheel, and there were perfect positions for riflemen not only on surrounding hills, but on parts of Spion Kop itself still unoccupied by the British.

Botha therefore ordered three field-guns and two pom-poms into action at close range, and two more guns to give supporting fire at about three miles' range. But there was no question of knocking the British off the Kop from a safe distance with artillery. They would have to storm it, and how many of the burghers had that kind of courage to spare?

Henrik Prinsloo, Commandant of the Carolina Commando, rose immediately to the occasion. 'Burghers,' he said, 'we're now going in to attack the enemy and we shan't all be coming back. Do your duty and trust in the Lord.' Then the commando, barely ninety strong, began to climb through the mist, fanning out towards two unoccupied kopjes on the kop itself, Conical Hill and Aloe Knoll. Botha had called up all the reinforcements he could spare: in all, less than a quarter of his force of four thousand. But would they respond to his call? And meanwhile, could the Carolina Commando hold out alone? If the British struck vigorously at Conical Hill and Aloe Knoll, the whole of Spion Kop would soon be theirs.

Outwardly Botha, like Buller, was quite unflustered in battle. But the last six weeks had been intensely depressing. He believed passionately that the republic must adopt an offensive strategy. The failure at the Platrand put paid to all his hopes of taking Ladysmith and wresting the initiative from Buller.

Since then, he had been forced back to the blocking strategy he despised.

The last ten days had been a far more severe ordeal than Colenso. He had to anticipate and parry a second attack by Buller, whose movements were by no means obvious to Botha, the most brilliant of the Boer commanders. Buller was right: if the slow and over-cautious Warren had struck hard and swiftly, he might have cut his way through Tabanyama (Rangeworthy Hills) on 17 January. As it was, Botha and his staff had worn themselves out in repeated manoeuvring.

Yet now, at the supreme moment, he found new reserves of moral and physical strength. He saw his chance and seized it.

About eight o'clock on 24 January the mist, the forerunner of a cloudless, hot morning, cleared. During the night, Deneys Reitz had been woken by the sputter of gunfire on Spion Kop. At daybreak, the British began to pound Tabanyama once more. Then someone rode up with orders: Khakis on Spion Kop. They must take it back. Now. Reitz and his friends galloped off to the northern foot of the hill, where hundreds of saddled horses stood in long rows. Above them was one of the most arresting sights of the entire war.

Three or four hundred men – mainly from the Carolina and Pretoria Commandos – were clambering up the grassy slope. The ascent itself, though steep, was not difficult for men carrying only rifles and bandoliers, but the British manned the crest line. Many burghers dropped, shot by invisible marksmen. Others reached the crest, and Reitz saw British soldiers suddenly rise up from behind the rocks to meet the rush. Then the struggling figures surged over the rim of the plateau and were lost to view. Reitz started to clamber up. The hillside and the rocks on the crest were strewn with Boer dead, but the burghers had succeeded in seizing this northern edge of the summit, supported by Mauser fire from Conical Hill and Green Hill.

The main British line was that long, shallow, crescent-shaped trench dug in the misty dawn. Some of the Pretoria men took up a position four hundred yards beyond the trench, at Aloe Knoll. Reitz tried to follow, but was driven back to the main firing-line. By nine o'clock, the enemy's rifle fire began to slacken as Boer shrapnel started to crash into the tableland ahead. But the sun was growing hotter, and the burghers had neither food nor water. Nothing could be seen of the British, for the trench was screened by a breastwork of rocks. The Boer casualties were hideously evident.

The few hundred burghers on the summit became increasingly demoralized. At a terrible cost, their attack had only half succeeded. Large bodies of Boer horsemen could now be seen in the plain below them. They shirked the battle, though their leaders – Opperman, the Pretoria Commandant, and Prinsloo, the Carolina Commandant – tried promises and threats. On the hill, a sense of betrayal, anger and hopelessness began to sweep over the burghers. Hunger and thirst and indiscipline did their work – and a belief that the British were easily holding their own. By midday, they were stealthily abandoning the positions they had seized with such heroism a short while before.

Below Spion Kop: the morning after. The main trench choked with British dead after the battle on 24 January 1900. It was made to serve as their grave.

Woodgate was mortally wounded. Soon after 8.30 a.m. he had been struck by a shell splinter above the right eye. Then Colonel Blomfield, CO of the Lancashire Fusiliers, fell, severely injured; Massey, the sappers' CO, was killed, and so was Woodgate's Brigade Major. The column had suddenly lost its leaders.

The next senior officer was now Colonel Malby Crofton of the Royal Lancasters. He was appalled by the situation. Woodgate had made a series of blunders in preparing the summit as a strong-point. The fact was that the defensive perimeter was too small, and the trenches in the wrong place and too shallow.

Had the mist allowed him to realize their importance, Woodgate should have seized Conical Hill and – above all – Aloe Knoll. As it was, the main trench should have been two hundred yards farther forwards, on the crest-line commanding the valley below. When the mist began to clear, the sappers tried to dig a new trench in the right place. But it was too late: the Boers on Conical Hill and Aloe Knoll could enfilade the east side of the main trench. Moreover, the trench itself was too shallow to shield the occupants. It had

been dug by a few sappers, while over a thousand soldiers lay idle. The British had still not understood the new rule of war – dig your own trench now, or they'll dig you a grave later.

Nor could they reply to the Boer guns. 'The most awful scene of carnage,' wrote one of Thorneycroft's Uitlanders. 'Everything was confusion, officers were killed or mixed up in other regiments, the men had no one to rally them and became demoralized. . . .'

Demoralization and confusion: above all, confusion. By nine o'clock, Crofton had already decided, understandably, that they needed reinforcements. And it was essential to get accurate information about their situation, and the Boer positions, to Warren. Crofton, however, was an ordinary, unimaginative regimental officer. He should have written a proper report to be taken to Warren's HQ, only an hour's ride away. Instead, he merely dictated a brief SOS to an officer who was signalling with a flag, before himself retiring from the scene.

It was Thorneycroft who did most to rally the men. By ten o'clock the battle, ebbing and flowing between the main trench and the new forward trench on the crest-line, had reached a crisis. One of his young officers dashed out with twenty men towards some rocks on the right front. But they were soon beaten back to the main trench, losing half their number.

Then Thorneycroft himself led a charge of forty men. He found three officers surrounded by the bodies of their men – wounded, dying, dead. All three died in the hail of bullets. He was only saved because he tripped and crashed to the ground, twisting his ankle. Almost all the forty men were shot down. Three officers tried to lead further charges, and were felled too.

Thorneycroft lay on the stony ground, under the grid-mesh of bullets. How long would it take Warren to send reinforcements, he wondered? And how long could his own men stick this inferno?

Warren, who claimed he 'knew the Boer', had been absolutely unprepared for the speed and ferocity of Botha's counter-attack. Now this message came from Crofton: 'Reinforce at once or all is lost. General dead.' He replied brusquely: 'I am sending two battalions, and the Imperial Light Infantry are on their way up. You must hold on to the last. No surrender.'

Warren had already told Major-General Talbot Coke, commanding 10th Brigade, to take up the Imperial Light Infantry (the infantry counterpart of the ILH), the 2nd Middlesex and the 2nd Dorsets. But he simply could not understand this panicky message. À Court had just ridden up with Woodgate's note, written only two hours earlier: 'We have entrenched . . . and are, I hope, secure.' Warren, however, now bestirred himself to send some of the vital equipment Woodgate had left behind. And he agreed with à Court: it was vital to get heavy guns on the summit as soon as possible. What about a diversion on the left? Hart and many of his officers were keener than ever to launch the long-delayed attack on Tabanyama, now that the burghers had thinned down this section of their line in order to reinforce Spion Kop.

But Warren was unshakeable. His tactic remained to force the enemy to attack *them* at Spion Kop.

One new idea did occur now to him, however, which was to have a dramatic effect on events, though not in the way he anticipated. He heliographed to Lyttelton, whose brigade was dug in north of the river at Potgieters, five miles to the east. 'Give every assistance you can on your side; this side is clear, but the enemy are too strong on your side, and ... if assistance is not given at once all is lost.'

'This side is clear' was a strange way to describe the beleaguered force on Spion Kop. The fact was that Warren had only the haziest idea of what was going on. The result was a confused optimism in his own mind about the extent and strength of the British position. He had sent off his weakest brigade commander, Coke, to lead the reinforcements. Still more disastrous, he stopped Lyttelton's long-range guns from shelling Aloe Knoll from the east; apparently he thought the knoll was part of the British position.

At Mount Alice, Buller's HQ, it was impossible to have the illusion that the battle was going well. One war correspondent wrote: 'I shall always have it in my memory – that acre of massacre, that complete shambles.' Buller stood watching the scene, apparently impassive. In fact, he was burning with resentment. Once again, a good plan had been thrown away by subordinates. He had been sold by 'a damned gunner' at Colenso; now it was a damned sapper. Warren had failed to strike at Tabanyama on the 17th, when it was almost undefended. He had funked attacking it on the 21st, when to attack needed courage, yet was practicable. Today his obstinacy had wrecked Buller's plan for a two-pronged assault. For his own attack at Potgieters was now in jeopardy. Warren had asked Lyttelton for reinforcements, instead of drawing on the eleven battalions he had on his left flank. Without consulting Buller, Lyttelton had sent two infantry battalions and most of his few mounted troops. When Buller discovered this, it was too late either to recall them, or to divert men from the left flank.

The blow to his plans only stiffened his determination to press on, however. À Court had galloped on to his HQ after reporting to Warren: above all, they must get naval guns onto the main summit. Buller arranged for two to be sent up at once. Equally vital, he sent his own Intelligence Officer, Lieutenant-Colonel Arthur Sandbach, to report back to him personally on the situation on the summit.

He intervened only once more that morning, though it was to be of crucial importance. He had heard from à Court that Thorneycroft had been the soul of the defence; indeed, he could now see him through the telescope, literally a tower of strength in that acre of massacre. At 11.40 a.m. he wired to Warren, who agreed that Thorneycroft should take command on the summit. Ten minutes later, the heliographists on Spion Kop received a curt message. Thorneycroft had superseded Crofton in command.

Thorneycroft heard of his promotion well after midday. The situation was more critical than ever. The main trench was now the forward line, and he was the only officer there. Unknown to his men, the reinforcements led by Coke were now hurrying up the hill. But five hours without food and water had brought the men to the limit of endurance.

Soon after one o'clock, Thorneycroft heard a commotion in the main trench on his right. Some men, chiefly Lancashire Fusiliers, dropped their rifles and put up their hands. Three or four Boers came out, and were greeted by a burst of ineffective fire – and then by a fluttering of white handkerchiefs. A Transvaaler described the next moment: 'The English were about to surrender . . . when a great big, angry, red-faced soldier ran out of the trench on our right and shouted, "I'm the Commandant here; take your men back to hell, sir! I allow no surrenders."'

It was Thorneycroft, of course. He shouted to his men to follow him to a line of rocks behind the trench, from which they opened fire. Some of the Boers flung themselves flat, others managed to hustle back the prisoners they had already seized (nearly 170 according to their accounts). There was a deafening fire at point-blank range.

At this desperate moment, Thorneycroft looked back and saw, at long last, the reinforcements. A company of the Middlesex was advancing with fixed bayonets. He ordered them to charge. The sudden reversal knocked the Boers off balance. They fled, dragging their exhausted prisoners with them. Thorneycroft's men reoccupied the main trench, and pushed forward once more to within yards of the crest. Despite the Boer artillery, in the next hour fresh British troops continued to stream on to the summit. Thorneycroft positioned the reinforcements, then crawled back into shelter and scribbled a note, which he gave to the newly arrived Sandbach to take down to Warren. The heliograph had long since been smashed by a shell.

It was 2.30 p.m. For the first time since dawn, Thorneycroft had a respite, of a sort. The note, somewhat desperate in tone, asked what reinforcements Warren could send, explaining that his force was still inadequate, and that they were badly in need of water. He added that to make certain of the hill that night, Warren must send more infantry, and attack the Boer guns.

The confusion in Warren's own mind was not dispelled by the brief note, which reached him at about four o'clock. But he was only partly to blame for the optimism he felt. The note had passed through the hands of Thorneycroft's immediate superior, Coke, who was to take overall charge of the defence of the summit. Warren could not know that Coke had not even reached the plateau, but had contented himself with reassuring Warren about the situation from the safety of the track below. He endorsed Thorneycroft's message, adding that he had ordered two battalions to reinforce, and that 'We appear to be holding our own.' According to one report, he then took a nap.

One thing *was* clear to Warren: Spion Kop must be made secure against artillery. They must drag the mountain and naval guns to the summit, and deepen and improve the British trenches. Warren was a sapper. Spion Kop was less than an hour's ride from his HQ. Why did he not go there himself?

Arguably, Warren's overriding error that day was that he did not order a diversion to the west, striking at Tabanyama. What is certain is that where Lyttelton did make a diversion – to the east – it had the most dramatic effect.

The eastern ridge of Spion Kop is marked by twin peaks, two thousand yards and three thousand yards respectively from the main summit. These made a formidable defensive position; still more formidable would they be as an offensive position for the British. Once astride them, they would command not only Aloe Knoll, but two Boer gun positions and Burger's laager.

Burger learned late that day that the Khakis were storming the 'Drielingkoppe' ('Triplets'), as the Boers called the Twin Peaks. Lyttelton's reinforcements had divided: the head turning west to reinforce Thorneycroft, the tail striking due north and dividing into two again, each group tackling one of the peaks. The burghers were so thinly stretched they could not hold back even these few Khakis, and by 5.00 p.m. had been forced from their hastily dug trenches. It was too late to affect the battle for the main summit that day. But next morning the burghers would have a simple choice. Either storm the Drielingkoppe, or gallop back to Ladysmith. Schalk Burger became utterly demoralized.

The situation on the Boer side of the main summit was also desperate. At seven, darkness came at last, and with it silence, apart from odd bursts of rifle fire, and the ghastly sounds of wounded, delirious men crying out in the dark.

Reitz found himself with hardly two dozen men left to defend the crestline. By ten o'clock, even his own leader, Opperman, had decided they must abandon the position, at least for the time being. They scrambled down to the foot of the hill. The long lines of horses tethered there earlier had gone, apart from their own; supplies and ammunition were strewn everywhere.

Just as the first wagons were leaving, someone galloped up and shouted to the burghers to halt. It was Botha. From the saddle, he told them to think of the dishonour of deserting their posts in the hour of danger. Shamed, some burghers returned to their positions east and west of Spion Kop. But no one returned to the main summit.

If ever Botha's extraordinary optimism was needed, it was now. To Burger he wrote, bluntly and desperately: 'Let us struggle and die together. But, brother, let us not give way an inch more to the English.' He promised to send reinforcements as soon as the moon rose. Meanwhile, Burger must take one hundred Free Staters from his own left wing to reinforce the line behind the Drielingkoppe.

The appeal fell on deaf ears. In panic, Burger had taken part of the Carolina and Lydenburg Commandos, with their field-gun and pom-pom, and fled northwards to Ladysmith.

Only a handful of burghers remained. Nothing, it seemed, could now prevent the British from streaming through the two breaches in the Boer position, and rolling up the whole of their line along the Tugela.

But one man did have this power – poor, plodding General Warren.

Now that darkness had fallen, who can blame Thorneycroft for not recognizing his unseen victory? But he was equally ignorant of Warren's own plans, for which only Warren can be blamed. This lay at the root of the extraordinary blunder which now brought tragedy to the verge of farce.

All around Spion Kop, the British were at long last preparing to exploit the advantage they had gained. Although, after 7.00 p.m., the battalion that had so brilliantly captured Twin Peaks withdrew under cover of darkness, due to a misunderstanding of Lyttelton's, they had achieved far more than he could have guessed. Indeed, their withdrawal made little difference to events. The thought of them there (though their Colonel had been killed, and they had a hundred other casualties) had been enough to send Burger scurrying back to Ladysmith, leaving that second great breach in the Boer line.

But Warren's ponderous time-table cannot seriously be defended. It was not until two hours after darkness that he even ordered Lieutenant-Colonel G. H. Sim, the sappers' commander, to proceed to Spion Kop with a fatigue party of fourteen hundred men. These were to build emplacements for the artillery, as well as digging proper trenches. The rest of Warren's preparations showed no greater urgency. Stretcher-bearers, water, ammunition, fresh troops, above all, heavy guns, were still missing five hours after dark.

It was not Warren's failure to remedy these deficiencies, however, that arguably proved his worst error. It was his failure to tell Thorneycroft of his plans.

Astonishingly, he had sent no direct instructions to Thorneycroft since promoting him at midday. He had left it to Coke to reassure him, although (by another astonishing blunder) he had not actually told Coke that he had put Thorneycroft in charge. Then, to compound these blunders, at 9.00 p.m. Warren had ordered Coke to return to the HQ for consultation.

Midnight. The scales still quivered in the balance, each army weighed down with the sense of disaster. Then, out of the darkness and confusion, appeared one man who might have turned the balance in favour of the British. It was Churchill, who, not content with his double job as *Morning Post* correspondent and lieutenant in the South African Light Horse, was instinctively taking over the role of general.

Churchill was back at the front after a daring escape from Pretoria gaol. His troop of the SALH, in keeping with Warren's distrust of cavalry, had been confined to camp. At four o'clock, Churchill could bear it no more. Without permission, he rode off to Spion Kop, left his horse by the village of ambulances at the foot, and began to climb the narrow track to the summit.

What he saw profoundly shocked him, especially the wounded, and the small numbers of unwounded creeping away to safety. He rode back to Warren's HQ and told him what he had seen. Then he volunteered to take a note to Thorneycroft, and the news that the guns and the working party were on their way.

His second visit to Spion Kop was, if less macabre, more unnerving. Night, which hid the horrors, had also doubled the confusion. Only one solid battalion now remained, the Dorsets, which Coke had kept in reserve. The

One of the Boer commandos which defended Spion Kop, posing against the background of the mountain in January 1900.

Opposite 26-year-old Winston Churchill, fresh from the prison camp at Pretoria, returns triumphantly to Durban.

others were all intermingled; as battalions they had ceased to exist. 'The darkness and the broken ground', Churchill said, 'paralysed everyone.'

He found Thorneycroft surrounded by the remnants of the regiment he had raised. Churchill gave him Warren's note and told him the good news. But Thorneycroft was in a state of shock, of complete physical and moral breakdown. Twelve hours in the firing-line had finished him. They must retire; he had already decided it.

Even now, withdrawal – and disaster – were not inevitable. Thorneycroft had called a brief council of war before making his decision. Two of the COs agreed, somewhat hesitantly. But Lieutenant-Colonel Hill of the Middlesex had insisted he was the senior officer present, refusing to believe that Thorneycroft was now a brigadier, and Coke (not having been told by Warren) upheld the claim. But no one listened to Hill.

As Thorneycroft led the rearguard down the track, leaving the dead and

many seriously wounded on the summit, they were met by another obstacle. When he had been recalled to see Warren, Coke had left his staff officer, Captain Phillips, at his HQ on the shelf half-way up the hillside. Phillips woke too late to challenge Thorneycroft, and he therefore wrote a formal memorandum addressed to all commanding officers. 'This withdrawal is absolutely without the authority of either Major-General Coke or Sir Charles Warren. . . . Were the General here he would order an instant reoccupation of the heights.'

If only Phillips could have signalled to Warren's HQ. But there was no oil in the signalling lamp. The battle was lost for want of a pennyworth of oil. No one listened to Phillips, either. The withdrawal continued.

Spion Kop was left to the dead and the dying of both armies: on the British side, 243 had died; bodies were piled three-deep in the scanty shelter of the main trench.

A still from Dickson's pioneering newsreel of the Battle of Spion Kop. Buller's second throw has failed. His shattered columns retreat over the Tugela by the pontoon bridge, protected by the troops entrenched in the foreground.

Soon after dawn, the small party of burghers with Reitz and Opperman looked up at Spion Kop and saw an amazing, unbelievable sight. Two figures stood on the summit, triumphantly waving their rifles and bush hats. Burghers. The hill was theirs.

Buller was spared the knowledge of the ultimate irony: that Burger and his Boers had abandoned their positions. He did not blame Thorneycroft, who had exercised 'a wise discretion'. He blamed Warren. 'If at sundown the defence of the summit had been taken regularly in hand . . . in fact the whole place brought under regular military command . . . the hills would have been held I am sure.'

Buller also blamed himself. He should have obeyed his instincts and superseded Warren six days earlier. Both his – unchallengeable – verdicts were to be echoed by Roberts.

Buller took charge of the retreat in person, at last 'gripping the whole business', as Churchill wrote with relief, 'in his strong hands'. It was accomplished without the loss of a man or a pound of stores. But then, the Boers had lost 335 men; though their line was now reinforced, they were too exhausted to follow up their success.

In ten days the British had lost fifteen hundred men killed, wounded or captured, and were back where they started. It would have been odd if there had not been recriminations. Humiliation was still a novelty. Among the generals, a whispering campaign, led by Lyttelton, gathered momentum. People began to talk of 'Sir Reverse', and 'The Ferryman of the Tugela'. Even the NCOs, who had previously shown blind faith in old Buller, began to grumble about him.

Old Buller addressed his army, praising their courage, and thanking them 'from the bottom of his heart' for their great sacrifices. There was something about his ill-suppressed emotion that disarmed most opposition. He told the men that they had given him 'the key to Ladysmith', and promised that they would be there within a week.

Poor Buller, he was doomed, ten days later, to retreat yet again across the river: the Ferryman of the Tugela with a new load, 333 casualties suffered at the Battle of Vaal Krantz. Yet, in a sense, Spion Kop *had* given him the key to Ladysmith. From their mistakes, humiliating as they were, the officers and men of Buller's nineteenth-century army were all learning how to fight a twentieth-century war.

Winston Churchill, from a watercolour painted by Mortimer Menpes at the war-front.

What 'e does not know o' war,
            Gen'ral Bobs,
You can arst the shop next door –
            Can't they, Bobs?
Oh 'e's little but 'e's wise,
'E's terror for 'is size,
An' – 'e – does – not – advertise
            Do yer, Bobs?

Rudyard Kipling, 'Bobs', 1898

PART III
Roberts's Advance

CHAPTER SEVENTEEN

The Steam-Roller

The Western Front, 11–15 February 1900

'It was the worst run war ever – no transport, no grub, nothing . . .'

One of Roberts's old soldiers, describing
Roberts's great flank march to the author
in June 1970

ROBERTS'S ADVANCE on Bloemfontein, launched on 11 February, had a majestic momentum. Its sheer scale took away the breath: five divisions – about forty thousand men with one hundred guns, and a whole division of cavalry.

For the first time in the war, a real flying column was available – five thousand cavalry and MI. Before they left their base camp at Modder River, Kitchener summoned French and his Chief of Staff, Haig. It was their job to relieve Kimberley. They must outflank Cronje's line at Magersfontein. Everything depended on 'surprise'. Kitchener added, somewhat ominously, 'If it fails neither I nor the Field-Marshal can tell what the result on the empire may be.'

No doubt French understood the nuances. Rhodes was locked up in Kimberley. He had given Roberts a characteristically reckless ultimatum: make the relief the first priority or he would surrender. So the cavalry's task was to ride like the wind to save the town from the Boers, and Rhodes from his own worst enemy, himself.

French had serious misgivings about the transport arrangements, the key to success. Roberts and Kitchener had dismantled the regimental system of transport and supply, taking it under their central control. French wisely kept his divisional transport intact, safe from Kitchener's grasp. To make matters worse, he knew that his dash to Kimberley would exact a heavy price from the cavalry. In the regular units, some of the horses were green after a long voyage, and all of them had suffered gruelling train journeys. The state of the irregular horse – which included British regulars whom Roberts had turned into makeshift MI – was still more alarming. Yet they could hardly fail to break through the enemy's line. The Boers were outnumbered four to one. Methuen had attacked the line at Magersfontein with three brigades and nearly broken through; Roberts had five divisions.

By the 11th they had reached Ramdam in the Free State – the first halting-place in enemy territory. Thirty-four thousand white troops supported by

Previous page
Bringing in a Boer emissary to discuss surrender at Modder River Camp early in 1900.

Opposite left Field-Marshal Lord Roberts and his generals, portrayed in *Vanity Fair*. Standing, from left to right: Methuen, Hector MacDonald, Buller, Baden-Powell, Dundonald, Lord Kitchener, Pole-Carew. Sitting, from left to right: Lord Roberts, White, French.

four thousand African drivers rolled through the place. After French's cavalry, plodded Major-General Charles Tucker's 7th Division, followed by Lieutenant-General Thomas Kelly-Kenny's 6th Division (the two new infantry divisions ordered out to the Cape after Black Week). Finally, there was a newly constituted 9th Division, under Colvile, consisting of the 19th Brigade, just arrived and led by Major-General Horace Smith-Dorrien, and the original Highland Brigade, now under Major-General Hector MacDonald. (The balance of Roberts's forty thousand guarded the rear.)

French's cavalry trotted out at 2 a.m. on Monday the 12th. Ahead lay the only two obstacles in the veld; the Riet and Modder Rivers. Cronje had a force at Magersfontein estimated to be larger than their own, but they were the cream of Britain's cavalry – six regular regiments, two MI corps and seven horse artillery batteries. Speed should carry them safely through their eighty-mile detour to the east.

The obstacle proved to be the infantry's transport arrangements. On Monday, the cavalry halted at the Riet, after fording it almost without opposition. But their baggage column kept becoming trapped behind the slower-moving infantry transport, with the result that it was not until 9.30 a.m. on Thursday that French was free to go. His scouts reported that up to two thousand Boers were holding two ridges at Abon Dam, about four miles north of the Modder. French gave the order to charge through the lightly held gap between the ridges. The cavalry division galloped forward and vanished in a great fog of dust.

The same morning found Roberts twenty miles to the south, at Waterval Drift on the Riet. He was both confident and anxious. The invasion of the Free State had been greatly complicated by the need to advance by way of

Lord Kitchener of Khartoum ('K of K').

Lord Roberts.

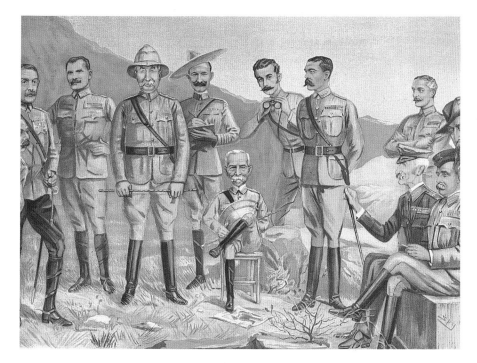

Kimberley. But the great flank march to by-pass Magersfontein seemed to be working; Cronje's army was reported to be still pinned down by Methuen at Modder River Station.

The flank march was not, however, working smoothly. Roberts had anticipated that transport and supply would be the main difficulty, and arrangements were indeed chaotic. He was upset by the news from Natal, where Buller's third attempt to relieve White – the attack on Vaal Krantz – had ended in a third reverse. Roberts had now ordered him to act 'strictly on the defensive', even if this meant abandoning Ladysmith to its fate, until his own advance on Bloemfontein forced the withdrawal of the Free State commandos in Natal. And in the Cape, the Boers had taken advantage of his weakening the garrison at Colesberg in order to strengthen his invasion force. They were now attacking again in that sector; Milner, as usual, expected the worst.

Still, Roberts was scarcely overwhelmed by worries. He was usually level-headed, even unemotional. Only once had he collapsed, almost in public, under the weight of grief at Freddy's death. Kitchener would never have allowed himself such a moment of weakness. 'K of K' liked to behave as though he had no human emotions. The new imperialism owed much to him. He was to be the right-hand man and partner; the troubleshooter, cutting War Office red tape. His demonic energy in organization, coupled with Roberts's nimble strategy, would sweep them both to victory.

Or such, at least, had been Roberts's plan. The reality had proved somewhat different. Ironically, he had more than once denounced Buller for weakness in abandoning his own strategic plans. Now he found himself acting in much the same way when feeling the same squeeze of circumstances.

Roberts's preferred strategy was to postpone the relief of Kimberley until after the capture of Bloemfontein. He had originally planned a great flank march from north of Orange River Bridge across the veld to strike the railway at Springfontein, just a hundred miles south of Bloemfontein. He had assembled a mass of transport, enough to keep him independent of the railway for weeks. Thus his force would take the Free State capital virtually by surprise, trapping the Boer raiding parties south of the Orange (after cutting off their main line of supply), as well as helping to relieve Kimberley and Ladysmith.

Then, for various reasons, principally Rhodes's begging and bullying, Roberts had changed his mind. What tipped the balance was the news of Spion Kop. In addition, he was anxious about his lines of communication while Cronje remained at Magersfontein, and about getting water in the open veld. And Milner was quaking about a Cape rising.

It was in his decision not to reinforce Buller in Natal that Roberts took the greatest risk. Buller had double the number of Boers to cope with, yet Roberts had given himself a fighting force larger and much more mobile than Buller's.

Buller protested too late. Not that protests would have helped. Roberts was ruthless and formidable. He curtly ordered Buller to stay on the defensive, if he had too few troops to relieve Ladysmith. And *pour*

General De Wet, first of the Boer leaders to take to guerrilla war. When his men disobeyed him he disciplined them with his sjambok.

encourager les autres, he proceeded to sack or demote a number of generals.

Arguably, Roberts kept too many troops for himself and starved Buller in Natal, who faced the harder task. Arguably, he was hasty in sacking subordinates. But there can be no argument about his shortcomings as a general caused by his impatience. His sweeping changes in the system of transport and supply constituted one of the great blunders of the war.

Strange to say, neither he nor Kitchener understood the War Office system of transport and supply adopted in South Africa: the so-called 'regimental', or decentralized, system. They believed, wrongly, that the system must be extremely wasteful of transport; nor had they grasped the existence of non-regimental transport, the brigades' supply columns. Except for the 'first-line' regimental transport (with ammunition and fighting materiél), they swept away the system completely, instead creating a 'general transport' system, meant to supply all the different needs of the army.

When a highly technical, long-established logistical system is suddenly replaced mid-war, there is bound to be trouble. Kitchener became known as 'K of Chaos'. Professional transport officers prophesied disaster. They did not have to wait long.

At Waterval Drift on the 15th, Roberts waited on tenterhooks for news of French's dash to Kimberley. Delays in crossing the Riet had been so appalling that a convoy of two hundred ox wagons was left behind on the north bank for the three thousand oxen to graze and recuperate. About 9.00 a.m., Roberts received news that threatened the whole expedition. A Boer raiding party under Christiaan De Wet had ambushed the convoy and stampeded most of the oxen. Now the wagons, nearly a third of the entire transport available for the advance to Bloemfontein, were stranded, their precious loads, without which the army could not fight, at the Boers' mercy. To save time, Roberts abandoned them. Nor did he react to the disaster with the unflinching spirit of a great general, as his admirers later claimed.

Fortunately, French had managed to keep his transport safe from Kitchener, and his divisional supply park now came to the rescue, mule carts making up for part of the disabled convoy.

And fortune smiled on Roberts once again. A few hours after the news of the disaster to the convoys came word that French was sweeping across the veld towards Kimberley.

Lord Roberts, Commander-in-Chief in South Africa, on the steps of his HQ.

CHAPTER EIGHTEEN

The Siege within the Siege

Kimberley, 9–17 February 1900;
Paardeberg, 17–27 February 1900

'You low, damned, mean cur, Kekewich, you deny me at your peril.'

Cecil Rhodes to Colonel Kekewich,
10 February 1900

'We then had a regular fusillade all day and were doing splendidly when Lord K. getting impatient ordered ½ the Cornwalls . . . over the river to charge with the Canadians. I was horrified when I saw them moving forward to charge about 3.30 p.m. as I could see they had not a ghost of a chance . . .'

Major-General Horace Smith-Dorrien's diary,
18 February 1900

EVENTS HAD MOVED swiftly inside as well as outside Kimberley. On 9 February Kekewich had sent a desperate telegram to Roberts, suggesting that Rhodes was threatening to surrender the town. This was the climax of the siege within the siege, the four-month struggle between the Colonel and the Colossus.

It was all very well for Roberts to answer by telling him to clap Rhodes in irons if he defied him. As Kekewich replied, Rhodes and the resources and employees of De Beers (the majority of the volunteer forces) were the key to the military situation. Rhodes was De Beers and De Beers was Kimberley. How could a handful of imperial troops arrest half a town? Besides, Rhodes, despite his general recklessness, had been careful never to make his threat of surrender explicit.

What had happened was this. On 9 February, the Mayor had warned Kekewich that Rhodes was planning to hold a public meeting to protest against the delays in relieving the town. Kekewich warned in turn that it would be suicidal. There was the actual danger of shellfire. There were also a dangerously large number of Afrikaners among the population, and it was reported that some of these were said to have started a movement to

Opposite 'Shrapnel Hotel': a dug-out for four Kimberley residents during the siege.

Colonel Robert Kekewich and staff.

stampede the town into surrender. Rhodes's public meeting would play into the enemy's hands.

Rhodes himself called on Kekewich later that morning. Kekewich told him (as was true enough) that he had already most strongly impressed the townspeople's views on the C-in-C, and officially banned the meeting. Rhodes became violent, threatening to defy the ban unless Kekewich revealed within forty-eight hours 'full and definite' information about Roberts's plans.

Next day he returned to the attack with a long, bombastic editorial in the the local newspaper (which he owned).

It was a characteristic production – and a flagrant breach of the military censorship. Kekewich ordered the editor to be arrested, only to be told that Rhodes had hidden him. Instead, Rhodes himself stormed the HQ and taunted the unfortunate Kekewich with the news: 'You forbade a public meeting, but I have held the meeting all the same; it was attended by the twelve leading citizens of Kimberley.' Rhodes was then shown Roberts's latest tactful messages for him, but still insisted that a long petition, drawn up by the twelve good men, be sent to Roberts. Kekewich undertook to send a précis. At this, Rhodes lost his temper completely. He accused Kekewich, among other things, of keeping him in the dark about the relief; finally, clenching his fist, he rushed towards the other man, shouting 'You low, damned, mean cur, Kekewich, you deny me at your peril.' Kekewich rose – perhaps he would have knocked Rhodes down. But Rhodes suddenly turned tail and made for the door.

Ludicrous as this all was, it only confirmed Kekewich's feeling that Rhodes had put the whole town in peril. Characteristically, Rhodes took the top-secret cable with the news that Roberts was marching directly to the rescue, and read it aloud to passers-by.

There was a real reason for a collapse of the townspeople's morale, which partly explained Rhodes's antics, and why a reported postponement of the relief had caused such despondency. At 11.00 a.m. on Wednesday 7 February, a sinister new sound was heard in the town.

People had got used to ordinary bombardment – that is, by field-guns, which did little or no damage. True, it was depressing not to be able to fire back; the garrison's own artillery was completely outranged. Then Labram had improvised a 4-inch gun of his own design in the De Beers workshops. On 19 January, 'Long Cecil' first opened his mouth, flinging a 28-pound shell accurately enough for five miles, smack into a Boer laager.

Now, that Wednesday, came the Boers' reply – Long Tom. Heavy shells began to smash into the town. The effect was almost all the Boers could have hoped: panic in Kekewich's HQ, several buildings set on fire, casualties.

Kekewich acted at once to minimize the blitz, but Long Tom achieved more in three days than the field-guns had in four months. Casualties mounted. Labram was among those killed. His funeral was held at night to avoid the bombardment. But still the shells crashed down, hitting, indiscriminately, private houses, the railway and the hospital. For many, this night blitz proved the last straw.

Below 'Long Cecil' in action at Kimberley. The gun was commissioned by Cecil Rhodes and built by De Beers during the siege.

As at Ladysmith, most destructive of all were the classic weapons of a siege: starvation and disease. Soon after Christmas, Kimberley began to 'feel the nip'. For most townspeople the diet became increasingly poor and monotonous. Predictably, the scale of rations was highest for the garrison and lowest for the blacks – and the siege pinched the Africans worst. Infant mortality, 50 per cent among the whites, was catastrophic among the black and brown populations; between October and mid-February coloured children died at a rate of 93.5 per cent. And scurvy began to kill the ten thousand mine 'boys' in the compounds.

To say that Rhodes deliberately starved his African workers to death would be absurd: the mine boys were De Beers' most important asset, after the diamonds themselves. Still, businesslike principles left little room for sentiment. Recruited for the diamond mines, the Africans were now temporarily redundant. A bare handful managed to escape; the rest were allowed only a few ounces of mealies. Down in the compounds there were fifteen hundred cases of scurvy, of which a third proved fatal. Starving people lay about under the wire netting, waiting to die.

Meanwhile, Rhodes realised that the two great diamond mines, although out of use at the moment, could provide shelter against Long Tom. Notices recommending that women and children should take shelter in the Kimberley and De Beers Mines were posted up that Sunday, 11 February.

It was a typical *coup de théâtre*. There had been rumours about more Long Toms; Monday would surely be a black day. It was assumed that Rhodes had

Below George Labram, De Beers's American chief engineer, with 'Long Cecil', his answer to the Boers' Long Tom. But Long Tom had the last word. A shell killed Labram just before the siege ended.

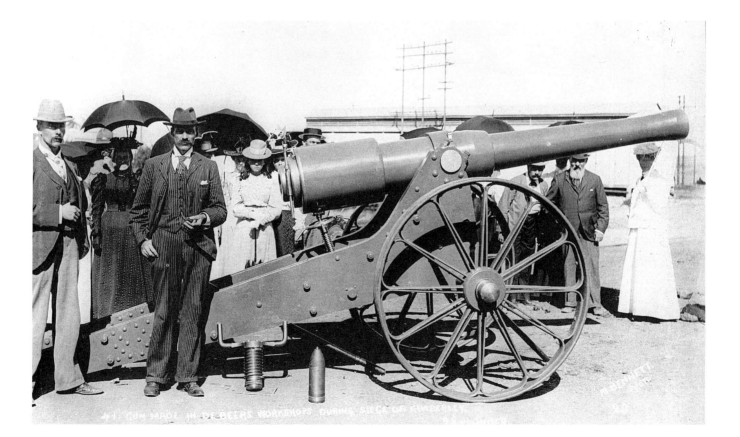

had definite information, and a regular panic ensued. (Though if Rhodes had told Kekewich of his scheme, the panic could have been avoided.) Two and a half thousand women and children fled to the mine-heads as though their last hour had come.

Up at the Sanatorium Hotel, Rhodes savoured his triumph. He was now setting the stage for the final scene in the great drama: the relief, in which, naturally, he cast himself as hero.

The great cavalry charge at Abon Dam on Thursday 15 February did almost no damage to Cronje's troops. Of course, damage to the enemy had not been Roberts's first aim. French's instructions (thanks to Rhodes) were simply to ride like the wind to save Kimberley. But this was Britain's only large mobile force in South Africa, a unique instrument for hunting down a mobile enemy and their not-so-mobile siege guns. Instead, the five thousand had to expend themselves in a magnificent, but quite unnecessary, dash to self-destruction. For the extraordinary fact was that the mere effort of galloping a few miles killed hundreds of horses, not just because many were still unacclimatised, but through the heavy-handedness of their riders. Trained cavalry mounts were impossible to replace. Now the division was virtually destroyed as an effective fighting force.

Meanwhile, Kimberley waited agog for the end of the 124-day ordeal. On the afternoon of the 15th, Long Tom fired his last shell. When the vanguard of the relief column finally appeared – the Tigers and some Scots Greys – there were uninhibited scenes.

Kimberley was relieved. The strategic situation was utterly transformed. For Cronje, now that the static blocking campaign had failed, the strategic options were hazardous, yet full of opportunities. Since the collapse of the British cavalry, he could safely withdraw northwards along the railway towards Mafeking. Alternatively, he could wage guerrilla war against Roberts's communications. Or he could retreat eastwards across the open veld to help block the expected advance on Bloemfontein. But whatever he did, there was one iron law of Boer strategy: the answer to superior numbers is superior mobility. And it was this that Piet Cronje, the fox, forgot.

He chose the third, more risky, strategic option, beginning his retreat on the night of 15 February, when some five thousand Transvaalers and Free Staters at last uprooted themselves from Magersfontein. Luck stayed with him at first. He was able to evade Kelly-Kenny's 6th Division and, when they did catch up, to shake them off, though he was forced to abandon seventy-eight loaded supply wagons. But on the 17th French's surviving cavalry at last overtook the van of his column near Paardeberg Drift, about twenty miles north-east of Ramdam.

Cronje was still not in any great danger, provided he kept moving. He could have brushed aside French's pitifully small force. Instead, in a mood of self-destructive inertia, he halted. Two nights after leaving the defences at Magersfontein, Cronje's men were once again burrowing into the earth – digging trenches in the banks of the Modder at Paardeberg.

Major-General Hector MacDonald, sketched by Mortimer Menpes. Known as 'Fighting Mac', he had risen from the ranks – and had knocked down a Boer with his bare fists at Majuba.

French's great cavalry charge at Abon Dam on 15 February, sketched by Captain St Leger, who took part in it. The charge relieved Kimberley but destroyed the cavalry.

Roberts's mounted infantry under shell fire, sketched by Captain St Leger.

Kimberley siege scenes. *Right* A well-to-do family with their black servant outside their dug-out ('Madam Cordita's Retreat').

Opposite Better-off Africans queuing outside the station.

But the old fox had not found a new earth. He had found a steel noose and put his head in it.

By midnight on Sunday 17 February, De Wet had already made the decision to leave his hiding-place at Koffyfontein. They must do what they could to rescue Cronje and the main force of Boers, which was thirty miles away to the north.

A Boer commando travelled light and fast. An hour after dawn on the 18th they heard heavy guns, though they were still fifteen miles to the south. The worst had happened – or was about to. They rode on, and at 4.30 p.m. halted at 'Horse Hill', a kopje six miles east of Paardeberg. Through field-glasses, De Wet could see, on the opposite bank of the Modder, 'Khaki-coloured groups dotted everywhere about. . . . All around the laager were the guns of

Right 'Dulce domum' ('Sweet Home'): Messrs Johnson and Howie parade by their tent.

Opposite Local defence forces man a gun at one of Kekewich's outposts.

the English, belching forth death and destruction. . . . We decided to make an immediate attack . . . and to seize some ridges . . . about two and a half miles south-east of the laager.'

So, while Cronje was attacked on every side, De Wet's gallant little band rode into action: three hundred against fifteen thousand.

Eleven hours earlier, Kitchener, too, had gazed out across the river at Cronje's laager, from a kopje two miles to the west. Beside him stood General Kelly-Kenny. Though no genius, he had a sensible plan and, if Kitchener had not interfered, it would probably have succeeded at very small cost. His instinct was sound: use the infantry to seal off Cronje (especially from De

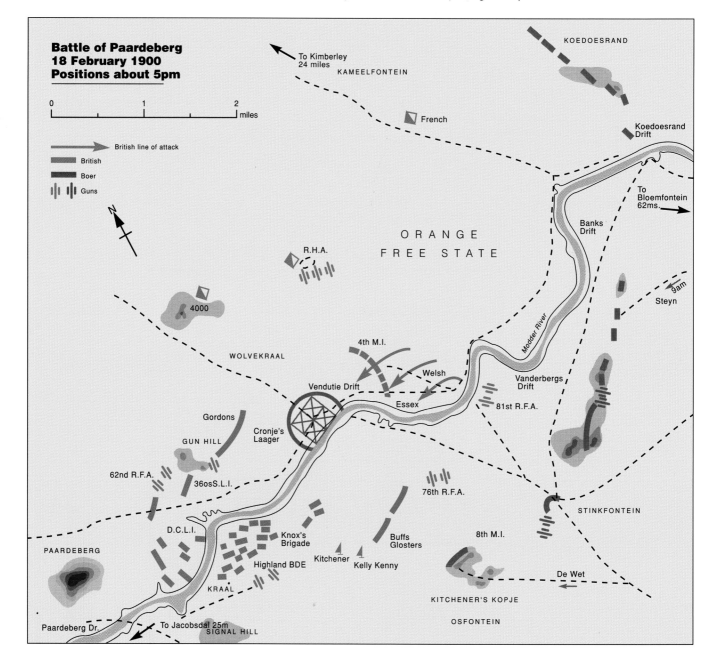

Battle of Paardeberg
18 February 1900
Positions about 5pm

Wet's and F.S. Ferreiras's commandos, known to be hurrying to the rescue); rely on the artillery to bombard him into surrender. But relations between the two men were poor, and Kitchener brusquely countermanded him. The infantry must storm the laager immediately.

Kitchener's plan, like his attitude to tactics in general, was aggressive and brutally simple. He would throw all his infantry into the battle before Cronje could bolt – or help could reach him. Kelly-Kenny and most of the 6th Division must launch a frontal attack from the south bank. Meanwhile, Colvile would divide his 9th Division, with MacDonald's Highland Brigade attacking upstream from the south bank, and Smith-Dorrien's 19th Brigade fording the Modder at Paardeberg Drift and attacking upstream along the north (Boer) bank. To complete the encircling movement, a small force – Lieutenant-Colonel O.C. Hannay's MI (part of the 6th Division), supported by two battalions from Brigadier-General T.E. Stephenson's 18th Brigade, the 1st Welsh and the 1st Essex – would attack downstream along the north bank.

Hold the Boers down with a frontal attack from the plain to the south. Then simultaneously fling a right hook from upstream and a left hook from downstream. This was Kitchener's simple tactical plan. And simply disastrous it was to prove.

At eight o'clock, he sent a brief, confident cable to Roberts, detailing his plan of attack, and predicting, 'I think it must be a case of complete surrender.' An hour earlier, he had told a staff officer that they would be in the Boer laager by half-past ten.

Kelly-Kenny's frontal attack could already be seen to be developing: brown dots, strung out across two miles of absolutely exposed plain, approaching the enemy invisible in the trees and scrub across the river. Ahead of them, shells from twenty heavy guns pounded the laager. Soon the covered wagons began to catch fire, the ammunition carts exploding. Old Cronje. He was now completely cornered. Even though they had been on the march for a week, and on half rations, a shiver of excitement passed through the exhausted British columns.

First into the attack were the 1st Welsh and 1st Essex. Both units suffered heavy casualties, pinned down in the plain with only occasional glimpses of the enemy. Behind them came four more battalions from 6th Division, charging straight across the plain from the south-west towards the line of trees marking the Modder. The Yorkshire Regiment, which was advancing by rushes of alternate sections, managed to get within two hundred yards of the river bank, but lost their CO and many others in the process. A party from this battalion then tried to ford the river, but found it in flood, and were driven back by a storm of bullets. To their left, two other battalions fared a little better. The West Riding were in more extended order and found some cover in broken ground. With the Oxfordshire Light Infantry, they succeeded in charging up to the Modder itself, where they captured some outlying trenches on the south bank. But the 13th Brigade commander, Major-General Charles Knox, was himself wounded. And shortly before noon a

'Canadians seizing a Kopje', according to the original caption. It looks more like a reconstruction.

message came from Kelly-Kenny: on no account attempt to cross the river and storm the laager.

Meanwhile, the Highland Brigade closed up on the 6th Division's left. No one was more surprised to see their advance than their own divisional commander, Colvile. His instinct had been to concentrate both his brigades on Cronje's side of the river and then attack upstream from the west. But Kitchener had ordered the brigade off for some purpose of his own. Colvile watched, astonished, as they wheeled into a frontal attack. But it was too late to recall them. Anyway, it was out of his hands. Presumably Kitchener had ordered this reckless attack.

The Highlanders who had survived Magersfontein did not this time lose their heads. But their thin line grew 'thinner and thinner, and thicker and thicker the brown patches on the grass behind it. What men are able to do, the Highlanders did. . . .' By midday, the attack had petered out, the brigade nailed down along the south bank below Knox's; and MacDonald, too, had been wounded.

At one o'clock, Kitchener left the kopje and rode over to Colvile's HQ. What about Colvile's men, making a 'more determined assault'? Colvile replied that he had only a handful of fresh troops: a half-battalion of the Cornwall Light Infantry. They must go at once, said Kitchener. They must ford the river and rush the position with the other 9th Division brigade – Smith-Dorrien's 19th. This was the long-delayed left hook.

Kitchener rode off, but returned about an hour later to tell Kelly-Kenny that the 6th Division must renew the attack. Relations between the two men had reached a nadir. Kelly-Kenny successfully resisted this attempt to renew the frontal attack, but failed to prevent Kitchener continuing the flank attack – the equally long-delayed right hook. He also failed to prevent him making a new blunder by weakening the British hold on the kopje on his right flank (soon ironically called 'Kitchener's Kopje'). This kopje, near Stinkfontein Farm, proved to be the tactical key to the whole position. By taking troops from it, Kitchener had offered it to the enemy on a plate.

Kitchener now ordered Hannay to launch the right hook at once: 'All troops have been warned that the laager must be rushed at all costs. Try and carry Stephenson's brigade on with you. But if they cannot go the mounted infantry should do it.'

It would be hard to beat this extraordinary note either for its callous tone or for its reckless misstatement of facts. Kelly-Kenny had, of course, refused to renew the attack. Nor had any of the brigadiers been 'warned that the laager must be rushed at all costs'. They seemed the orders of a madman, and in this spirit Hannay received them. He assumed that he had no time to co-ordinate with Stephenson, two miles away. He sent away his staff on various pretexts, then gathered a few men, perhaps fifty. 'We are going to charge the laager,' he said, simply. Then he galloped forward. For some time he survived the Mauser fire, though many of his men were struck down behind him. His horse fell. Somehow he staggered on, till he, too, fell at last, far out

Roberts's gunners and infantry, clinging to a steel cable, crossing the Modder River in February 1900. This time they were getting somewhere.

ahead of the firing-line, two hundred yards short of the Boer trenches. The left hook had failed. Hannay had died just as he intended: as a supreme act of protest against the way Kitchener had sacrificed his army.

Three miles away, on the north-west side of the laager, Smith-Dorrien heard the storm of fire in which Hannay cast away his life. It was just before 3.30 p.m. Since early morning, when his brigade had forded the Modder at Paardeberg, he had been waiting for orders from Kitchener or his staff. None came. 'I was in a complete fog as to what was happening.' Apart from the detachment of Cornwalls with the baggage, his 19th Brigade had been extended along the north bank as far as Gun Hill, a kopje from which the 82nd Field Battery had a perfect field of fire into the laager a mile and a half away.

At 5.15 p.m. he was amazed to see the troops on the right of his line rise up and charge. He knew nothing of Kitchener's orders to Colvile to send the half-battalion of Cornwalls across the river. All he could see was that the 1st Royal Canadians had suddenly advanced without his orders. He had not time to recall them – nor to co-ordinate the attack with the Shropshires (another of his battalions) and the 82nd Battery. The wave of attackers rolled forward. Then, like all the attacks all day, the line wavered, paused and vanished. The

gallant charge was gallantly led, Smith-Dorrien noted, but its futility was clear: the right hook had failed, without getting within three hundred yards of the Boer trenches.

It was now an hour from sunset. Even Kitchener thought the battle over. It was the most severe reverse, judged by British losses, of the war: 24 officers and 279 men killed, 59 officers and 847 men wounded, and 2 officers and 59 men missing. Characteristically, Kitchener reported it to Roberts as though it was a minor victory.

But was the battle over? Among the bitter wrangles between Kitchener and Kelly-Kenny was the defence of 'Kitchener's Kopje'. It was this vital point, stripped of troops by Kitchener, that De Wet, with uncanny instinct, attacked shortly after five o'clock. The timing proved perfect. Kitchener's attention was concentrated on trying – and failing – to co-ordinate the left and right hooks. A handful of irregulars held the kopje. Utterly unprepared, they surrendered almost without opposition.

Before dusk De Wet, outnumbered fifty to one, had snatched the whole south-east line from under the noses of the British. Not only could he now make their position south of the river untenable, he might also rescue Cronje. Kelly-Kenny watched the ineffective attempts to dislodge the Boers with infantry and artillery. He had told Kitchener not to remove the troops holding the kopje. Now it was open for Cronje to escape.

With darkness, Kitchener decided that the troops should entrench where they were. But few units received these orders, and, anyway, the exhausted and confused men were desperate after twenty-four hours without food or water. They trickled back to camp.

The night was even worse for Cronje's men. Comparatively few had been killed or injured by the infantry or the day-long bombardment: 100 dead and

250 wounded. The Modder's canyon walls, into which they had dug a honeycomb of trenches, had protected most of them. Still, the moral destruction was devastating. They had been retreating for three days, hunted by a vastly superior force. They were exhausted and demoralized before the battle began. The bombardment had smashed and burnt their wagons – and with them all that many burghers possessed. Worst of all, Kitchener's guns had destroyed most of their horses, the foundation of their fighting strength.

The supreme irony was that De Wet had now restored their life-line. But all that night, and all Monday, his guns flashed from Kitchener's Kopje, and less than a hundred burghers seized the chance. The rest stayed amid the stench of the battlefield. Cronje asked for a truce to bury the dead. He was refused. He sent a final message of defiance: 'If you are so uncharitable as to refuse me a truce as requested, then you may do as you please. I shall not surrender alive. Therefore bombard as you please.'

Roberts reached the battlefield at 10 a.m. on 19 February. His first impulse was to renew the infantry attack. Fortunately for the troops, Cronje's request for an armistice intervened. The exchange of messages took a better part of the day. On Tuesday, Roberts decided to attack again, as Kitchener demanded. But the other generals, though taunted by Kitchener, were firmly opposed. After inspecting the position himself, Roberts decided to cancel the attack.

He then swung to the opposite extreme. Perhaps he was shaken by the sight of the wounded. It was they who paid the price of the new transport system, since he had cut the number of regimental ambulance wagons by three-quarters. No doubt he was also alarmed by the general strategic situation. Milner, as usual, was fretting about the Cape; indeed, a small rising had taken place at Prieska. There were also other problems – bad water, the chaotic transport, the army's disorganization – that now seemed quite overwhelming. And, of course, there was the shadow cast by Kitchener's Kopje. At any rate, Roberts's nerve failed him.

On Wednesday, he 'strongly urged' retirement during a confidential talk with Kelly-Kenny, who disagreed. To retreat then, and so let Cronje escape, would have been one of the great mistakes of the war. Fortunately for Roberts, he was again saved by a sudden twist of events.

For three days, Cronje's men had stubbornly rejected rescue, while Kitchener had tried to re-take that ridge. But even De Wet's insights had their limits – not even he could guess at Roberts's loss of nerve. On Wednesday, an hour or two before Roberts was to abandon the hunt, De Wet himself abandoned the kopje. The British army breathed again. All talk of retirement was over.

The following Tuesday, 27 February 1900, the nineteenth anniversary of Majuba, General Piet Cronje, with 4,069 Transvaalers and Free Staters (including 150 wounded and 50 women), surrendered. Cronje's blunders had outmatched those of Kitchener and Roberts after all. It was the first great British victory of the war.

Cronje, carrying a sjambok, poses at Paardeberg with Roberts's ADC, Captain Watermeier.

Some of Cronje's 4,000 men who surrendered at Paardeberg. They seemed in reasonably good spirits, despite the 10-day bombardment.

CHAPTER NINETEEN

The Key Turns

The Tugela Line and Ladysmith, 12–28 February 1900

There once was a general who said:
'If to Ladysmith you would be led
The key's in my pocket
The door I'll unlock it.'
– But he went back to Chieveley instead.

From the diary of Lieutenant Alford,
February 1900

BULLER'S ARMY had recrossed the Tugela. They were back to Chieveley, back to wretched, sweltering Frere. Two months of bloody fighting, and they were back at the beginning – or worse.

There are few short cuts in war. What was needed now was an answer to the complicated problems posed by Botha's brilliant defensive tactics and strategy. And Buller, for all his fumbling, was beginning to find the answer. He had cabled Roberts for reinforcements, and had been rebuffed. But he believed that to 'act strictly on the defensive' (as Roberts urged) could be fatal for the Ladysmith garrison. He decided to press on.

Buller realized that the old three-act, one-day battle had been killed by the combination of trench and magazine rifle. Modern battle required a series of interlocking engagements, spread not only over many miles, but over many days, even weeks. New infantry tactics had begun to emerge: open order, better use of ground, more individual initiative, creeping barrages fired ahead of the advancing infantry. Buller was not alone in recognizing the significance of these dramatic innovations; indeed, some of his senior commanders complained of his caution in putting them into practice. What they all agreed was that the real 'key' to Ladysmith was the tenacity of the British infantry.

In the simple geographical sense, there was not so much a 'key' as a double combination lock, whose first sequence of positions centred on a hill nicknamed 'Monte Cristo', on the British side of the Tugela.

Hlangwane had long seemed to offer tempting possibilities, for its continued occupation isolated the Boers' left flank on the south bank of the river. Buller had originally rejected the idea of making a serious attack on it for two main reasons. First, the hill was pitted with ravines and covered with thorns. Second, it was only five hundred feet high, and was itself commanded by a series of wooded ridges to the east, culminating in the thousand-foot Monte Cristo. Now they had to trust to their immense superiority in heavy guns, and to the new tactical skills of both gunners and infantry, hammering and squeezing out the Boers, hill by hill; crumpling their line from Hussar Hill, by way of Cingolo, to Monte Cristo. It was a ponderous style of fighting. But it was indisputably correct: the painful prototype of modern warfare.

In seven days from 12 February, the advance resumed, faltered, resumed. The men grumbled about the exceptional heat, the officers about the delays. Buller, as usual, seemed deaf to his critics: he would go at his own pace. On 14 February, Dundonald's men occupied Hussar Hill. Next day, Buller pushed up Lyttelton's division crabwise onto Green Hill, the ridge linking Hussar Hill and Cingolo. Heavy guns were dragged on to Hussar Hill, and soon shell-bursts marked the infantry's way forwards. By the 17th, the original fingerhold on Hussar Hill had become a firm grip on four miles of tangled ridges east of Colenso.

Two days, later, Buller himself stood on the summit of Monte Cristo. Taking these ridges had made him master of the south bank of the Tugela. Overnight, the Boers had fled across the river. The capture of Monte Cristo had turned the trench lines at Hlangwane; the capture of Hlangwane, on the 19th, and the installation of heavy guns on its summit, opened the way to Colenso. It was a sound tactical victory – even if Buller, perhaps mistakenly, did not risk sending troops forward to cut off the fleeing Boers. Morale – boosted by news, on the 16th, of Kimberley's relief – soared. The first part of that combination lock had sprung open.

The problem was how to open the second part – from the Tugela to Ladysmith. On 19 February, Colenso was occupied. Of the Boers there was now no sign, except for occasional ineffective shelling. But both roads from Colenso to Ladysmith – the new road to the north-west, the old road to the north-east alongside the railway line – were dominated by high hills which presented tiers of natural defence lines.

Buller's plan, when he left Chieveley on the 14th, had been to try to by-pass Colenso. À Court urged him to press on northwards, either by swinging north-east of Monte Cristo or by cutting a way through to the north-west. Buller himself was keen to follow one or other of these routes. But Sandbach, an engineer by training, reconnoitred them and reported both to be out of the question. Buller saw no choice but to double back to Colenso.

On the 22nd, the advance resumed. Major-General Arthur Wynne was ordered to take the Lancashire (11th) Brigade and seize the kopjes three miles north of Colenso, and a mile above the falls (*see map on page 123*). The main Boer position was reported by White to be at Pieters Hill, two miles farther north; beyond, it was downhill all the way to Ladysmith.'

À Court remained unconvinced, confiding to Churchill the cheerful view that 'It will be like being in the Coliseum and shot at by every row of seats.' But most people believed that Buller, assisted by Roberts's sweeping success in the Free State, had at last got Botha on the run. Sandbach confidently

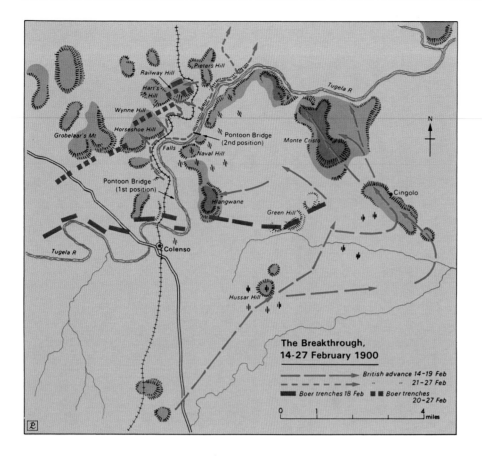

The Breakthrough,
14-27 February 1900

A suitable case for
'Chevril' – horse-
meat Bovril –
painted by Sir
George White's
ADC, Lieutenant
Charles Dixon.

predicted on the 22nd: 'We shall have one more big battle before we get to Ladysmith.'

Despite all the encouraging news that had reached them from both fronts since mid-February, there was a stagnant, exhausted air about the Ladysmith garrison. At its heart lay the low spirits of the GOC, 'Invisible White'.

For four months they had lived a 'pendulum existence' (Violet Cecil's phrase), swinging between hope and disappointment during each of Buller's attempts to rescue them. The officers, many of whom could afford expensive luxuries like eggs and potatoes, had only recently begun to feel the pangs of hunger. But they had long felt the pangs of humiliation. Towards Buller, and his army, there was a corresponding bitterness that ebbed and flowed with each reverse. 'Buller is a myth,' wrote Gough.

It was Spion Kop that had set the pendulum swinging most violently. The chief vantage points of the town commanded a tantalizing view over the shoulders of the surrounding hills. At first Buller's army was audible but invisible. Then, in the afternoon of 24 January, observers on Wagon Hill saw what they realized were British soldiers creeping up to the summit of Spion Kop. There were still more heart-warming sights: Boers, wounded and whole, fleeing for their lives.

Next day there was a strange calm on Spion Kop. But there was no reassuring flash of the heliograph. And a day later no one could deny what it all meant. The Boer tents were back on Spion Kop.

Buller's reverses, and White's own pessimism, did, however, have one unexpectedly good result. He decided to abandon the pretence that Ladysmith was a 'field force' – a mobile striking force – and accept that it was a beleaguered garrison. He had clung to the idea that he could redeem the disasters of Mournful Monday by some great feat of arms. Hence all the underlying mistakes before the siege, and the blunders during it: above all, an extraordinary decision to go on feeding cavalry horses with mealies, potentially the largest single source of foodstuff for the garrison.

Rawlinson and Hunter had always believed that to abandon their sick and wounded and try to cut their way out would be a reckless and futile act. Now, six days after Spion Kop, White told Rawlinson that the garrison must rely upon their food and defences, and 'stick to their sick and wounded', until relief came. Psychologically and strategically, it was the turning-point of the whole siege.

The new policy had two immediate and dramatic effects on the food supply. The remaining stock of mealies would be used for the men's rations. And most of the horses could also be turned into rations. No one could deny the compelling arithmetic of these new arrangements. Keep the cavalry brigade, and the garrison would have had to surrender by mid-February. Dismount it, and they could hang on till at least mid-March, perhaps even April. The garrison munched their tough new rations with enthusiasm.

Unfortunately, however, White had also decided to cut the men's rations. By doing so, he could spin out food supplies into April. This cast a gloom on everyone, and morale reached bottom ten days later, after Vaal Krantz, when the ration was reduced still further. And there were other privations besides starvation: above all disease.

Typhoid and dysentery now did the Boers' work for them. The death-toll from the disease had risen every week since November. At Intombi, the large British-run hospital in no-man's land, outside the perimeter, ten to twenty were dying every day by January.

Besides Intombi, there were three field hospitals inside the town. From November to the end of February these handled a total of 10,688 cases (out of 13,500 soldiers): 551 died. Conditions were bound to be bad at the height of the typhoid epidemic in January and February, but they were much worse than they need have been. Poor diet and worse hygiene greatly exacerbated the diseases' effects. All typhoid patients – except the Press, who might see too much – were meant to go to Intombi, yet it was deliberately starved of medicines and medical comforts.

Even in the field hospitals in Ladysmith itself, conditions were needlessly bad. At the centre of this scandal was Lieutenant-Colonel Richard Exham, the Principal Medical Officer. In January he had ordered that *all* medical comforts for the sick men in the 18th Field Hospital should be stopped. When the hospital CO asked for the orders in writing, Exham told him he would be removed from his command if he did so again.

Exham's motives were decidedly odd: 'All he cares about is to have some medicines and medical comforts when the relief column comes in & then pretend he made a most splendid [defence] . . . he is leaving the men to starve . . . & does not care.' At the same time, by keeping supplies from the soldiers, he was able to divert them to civilian cronies, although they appeared in official records as having gone to the field hospitals. 'Why can't the HQ staff intervene?', wrote the 18th's CO.

But White did not even visit the hospitals, and accused his staff of usurping his authority if they did so. He had retreated into a world that grew more distant from reality as the siege progressed. He was still talking of the flying column a month after his order that the horses should be eaten. The garrison would march out with colours flying – no matter that his men were in no fit state for marching. If he died, his death would help redeem the siege's humiliations. He would never be taken prisoner.

Each day, that last week of February, Buller's guns sounded closer. White, however, remained deeply pessimistic. On 27 February – actually the day of Buller's culminating battle – he put the men on half-rations once again. He was girding himself for the Last Stand.

CHAPTER TWENTY

The Handshake

Across the Tugela, 27 February–15 March 1900

'However even sinners are allowed their relaxation, and I must confess I did enjoy the getting in here [after] 15 days fighting with only one check, and 72 hours without a break was indeed excitement for a combative man, and the beauty of it was that I felt all through I had got them this time and was going to win . . .'

Buller to Sir Arthur Bigge,
15 March 1900

IT WAS 27 FEBRUARY – Majuba Day. A triumphant telegram from Roberts to Buller, announcing Cronje's capture. Now for the double.

But how wretchedly slow was Buller's advance. By the night of the 22nd, Wynne's Lancashire Brigade had won positions on the first pair of hills, 'Horse-Shoe Hill' and 'Wynne's Hill'. Next day, the Irish Brigade established a precarious foothold at 'Hart's Hill', a mile farther on. But the last two miles of the corridor to the great Ladysmith plain were barred. Somehow there was never enough room for the British to exploit their four-to-one superiority in numbers, and ten-to-one in artillery.

Hart's Hill had given the bloodiest lesson of this sort. About an hour before dusk on the 23rd, Hart's Irish battalions had clambered up to storm the ridge, finally closing with the enemy. 'And now followed the most frantic battle-piece that I have ever seen,' wrote John Atkins, a war correspondent. 'Night soon snatched it away, but for the time it lasted it was a frenzy.' And it failed.

The failure was not only due to the usual cause – topography that frustrated the British artillery – but also to the usual delays, and to Hart's still more characteristic impatience. The Irishman had shown his usual fearless-ness, but, as at Colenso, his men had to march up in column of fours in full view of the enemy on the hills. He had flung his battalions piecemeal into the firing-line, just as they arrived. The result was, inevitably, a weak attack on a narrow front, and it was then too dark for proper artillery support.

Next morning, the Irish Brigade had drifted back to the valley, leaving the wounded to their fate. Their gallant but futile charges had cost them nearly five hundred casualties in less than twenty-four hours.

Unlike Spion Kop, however, Hart's Hill did not prove a tactical dead-end. Two missing battalions arrived in the morning, in time to prevent a rout.

185

Perhaps the Irish Brigade were only holding on to the lower ridges by their eyelids, but they were holding on.

Hart's aim, predictably, was to keep battering on down the corridor. Buller was convinced there must be a way round, and sent Sandbach to reconnoitre the beginning of the gorge of the Tugela. He returned with the advice that he thought the pontoon bridge could be re-laid there and a path for the guns hacked out along the line of a narrow track. At last, the topography suited the British. The shelter of the deep gorge could be used to push up new brigades to the end of the corridor, without running the gauntlet of the Boers on the ramparts.

By the 27th, Buller's arrangements were complete. The plan was an ingenious, two-handed manoeuvre. While Botha's main forces were kept pinned down on the hills at the lower part of the corridor, the three hills commanding the upper part – Hart's, Railway, and Pieters – were now to be attacked in reverse order, from the east, thus outflanking the Boer line.

Meanwhile, on Sunday the 25th, a cease-fire had at last put an end to the nightmare of the wounded British soldiers trapped in no-man's-land on the flat plateaux above the corridor. On Wynne's Hill they had been lying there for three nights and two days without food or water; on Hart's Hill, for two nights and a day.

To abandon white men to such a fate went against the grain for both Boers and British. Buller had first learnt of the men's plight on the night of the 24th, and had arranged an armistice with Botha. On the disputed hills, a strange silence prevailed, the first for five days and nights. Then, about 11 a.m. on the 25th, white flags rose shakily above both lines of trenches, and an eerie day of fraternization began. For the British, the truce had an extra depth. For four months, they had been fighting an enemy so invisible that many had never yet seen a Boer, alive or dead.

Johnny Boer at last – Brother Boer. Out of the shell-torn earth the burghers came, straightening their backs and glancing warily from side to side. They were a 'rum-looking lot': old, middle aged, young, bearded and clean shaven, their clothes a homely peasant muddle. At first they maintained a sullen reserve, but offers of tobacco loosened the burghers' tongues. Soon the scene became animated, the British officers characteristically adopting the part of hosts. At length an officer popped the overwhelming question: 'Aren't you fellows sick of this?' Bluntly came the reply: 'Of course, we don't like it any more than you do, but three years, yes! three years we will stay out and fight!' Meanwhile, the mutilated bodies of the dead, and a few survivors, were carried off.

A handshake across the gulf, but no meeting of minds. At sunset, the truce ended.

Majuba Day, and the supreme effort. Victory. It was hard to believe – not least for Buller. As at Cingolo and Monte Cristo, he had outmanoeuvred Botha, who had left his flank at Pieters hardly defended, apparently believing the country was too rugged for the British. Moreover, from a high platform

The original British caption says, bluntly: 'Dead, Boer, a sniper'.

The 'key' to Ladysmith turns in the lock. On 27 February, Buller's long-suffering infantry attack the Boer trenches on the skyline of Hart's Hill.

across the river, Buller's artillery could cover the attack with converging fire. For the first time, Parsons's gunners could fully exploit Buller's revolutionary new tactic for co-ordinating artillery and infantry: to send a creeping curtain of fire over the heads of the infantry, the shells pitching only a hundred yards ahead of them.

But once Barton's Fusilier Brigade – the first of the three brigades ordered to attack in turn from east to west – were actually astride the Pieters plateau, the guns were too far away and too low to cover them. The Boers began to recover. Botha, recognizing the danger to the whole line if the British turned his flank at Pieters, had desperately thrown reinforcements into the breach. At 2.30 p.m., Barton sent forward a company of Scots Fusiliers and two companies of the Dublins to storm the strong-point on the northern kopje of Pieters. They were beaten back with severe casualties. Meanwhile, a mile away to the west, the Boers on Railway Hill poured a violent cross-fire into them with impunity.

But not for long. At about three o'clock, small brown dots began to appear

on Railway Hill. It was the 5th Brigade, under Kitchener's young brother, Walter. It was also the turning-point. Now these men, the West Yorkshires and South Lancashires (previously commanded by Wynne), attacking from the Pieters side, gradually squirmed their way up the series of terraces. To Atkins, watching from below, it seemed the critical moment. 'And then came the most extraordinary revolution, sudden, astounding, brilliant, almost incomprehensible. Across the railway the South Lancashires suddenly rose up out of the ground . . . and all began to run, not in stiff lines, but with the graceful spreading of a bird's wings straight up the hill. . . . I watched, stricken with admiration and suspense.'

Closer to, it was a stabbing, jabbing, flailing bayonet charge that won the neck of ground between Railway Hill and Hart's Hill. It also made the novel acquisition of some Boer prisoners.

Meanwhile, Major-General Norcott's 4th Brigade had fanned out in the third and final phase of the attack. The eastern positions in the Boer line had fallen in turn like skittles. Now for Hart's Hill. From across the river, the HQ staff and correspondents saw the last gallant moments of Botha's four-month-long defence of his trench lines. The 4.7-inch naval guns redoubled their efforts. Many of the Boers fought on, but nothing could live under such fire. At last, with a tremendous cheer, the British troops ran forward, charging with the bayonet.

As the Boers melted away, British cheers echoed back and forth. Pieters Hill (enough of it, at any rate), Railway Hill, Hart's Hill – the three last notches of the combination lock had dropped into place. Something extraordinary had happened – something, Churchill wrote, 'which had been thrice forbidden us, and which was all the more splendid since it had been so long delayed – victory'. The wave of cheering lapped against Buller's staff. They had done it at last.

Buller stood there, paradise regained. 'It has all seemed like a dream.'

In Ladysmith, boredom lay like lead on everyone's backs. No one dreamt that this, the 118th day of the siege, was to be the last.

But there was something odd about the view to the east that morning. A war correspondent half-curiously picked up the binoculars. 'Look there! What do you make of it?' 'It's a trek . . . a great trek. They're retreating at last.'

Plainly visible through the glasses was a long snake of retreating wagons, unquestionably Boer. There was no doubt. It *was* the great trek – a five-mile train of wagons. And not wagons only, but riders as well.

Of course, it was frustrating to see the Boers go free – under the noses of the Ladysmith guns. If only the gun teams or the cavalry could have galloped out to try and stop them. But most of the horses had been eaten, and the men were too exhausted. The 12-pounder naval guns did their best, but their shells fell hundreds of yards short.

At White's HQ, the news of the sudden Boer flight was greeted with the same mixture of nervous enthusiasm and frustration. At 1.00 p.m. they received a triumphant message from Buller: 'I beat the enemy thoroughly yesterday.' If only they could have joined in themselves.

On Bulwana, a giant wooden derrick appeared in the sand-bagged gun emplacement. The naval gunners had hoarded the last of their ammunition for this moment, and let fly with their 4.7s. The derrick vanished in smoke. But no one could say if the Long Tom had been hit. Then one of those operatic African thunderstorms struck and Bulwana disappeared behind the curtain of rain.

Soon after the rain had stopped, the relief column itself came in sight: two squadrons of mounted infantry, about 120 men, plodding along on tired horses. The Natal Volunteers were sent out to meet them, and White prepared himself for the ordeal of the relief.

Meanwhile, the incredible news was spreading. People – black, brown, white – began to run through the streets, shouting and pushing, forgetting caste and colour. Ladysmith had gone wild. Already the pavements were lined with soldiers off duty, officers, townsfolk, Zulus and doolie-bearers – all yelling and cheering like lunatics. The two strange-looking squadrons clattered up the street, and paused opposite the gaol. General White and his staff appeared. Then the junction of the two armies was sealed in a handshake.

It was about six o'clock when White met his rescuers, who were led by Lieutenant-Colonel Hubert Gough (brother of John of the Rifle Brigade, one of the besieged). The meeting had a quality of pathos: White now looked ten years older, a stooped, almost pathetic figure, walking with a cane. He had known that many of the garrison mocked him and protested at his inertia and feebleness. Now his emotions were too much to bear.

He began almost inaudibly, his voice breaking; then, in firmer tones: 'Thank God we kept the flag flying'. He faltered again: 'It cut me to the heart . . . to reduce your rations as I did.' Another long, agonizing silence; it looked as though he would break down completely. He squeezed out a wan smile. 'I promise you, though, that I'll never do it again.' Everyone laughed and cheered. Relief was, in every sense, the word. The crowd melted away into the night; by eight o'clock, 'There was nothing to show how great a change had befallen us.'

The ordeal of the relief was still not complete. Three days later, it was arranged that Buller should lead a ceremonial march-past through the town. He had agreed reluctantly, perhaps because he sensed the curiously mixed reactions to the first meeting. Some of White's force did not conceal their resentment at the slowness of the relief. For their part, some of the relief column regarded the victory parade as a cheap stunt, and an insult to both relieved and relievers. Paradoxically, others were surprised at – and even resentful of – how *fit* the garrison looked. To suggest that Ladysmith was not, after all, at its last gasp, though true, was hardly tactful. And it was on this issue – and others – that all the submerged mutual resentment between White and Buller finally broke surface.

Sir George White gives three cheers for the Queen after the relief of Ladysmith. Sketch by Melton Prior, a war artist trapped in the town during the siege.

White's bitterness towards Buller, and the furious resentment of his confidant, Ian Hamilton, were fanned by the anti-Buller faction in the latter's own army. Lyttelton, whom Buller himself trusted, arrived at White's HQ on 6 March 'full of abuse', according to Rawlinson. And it was not only Lyttelton. One of Buller's own staff – presumably à Court, his feelings clearly wounded by the rejection of his advice after Monte Cristo – launched into a tirade against his chief's errors. Rawlinson, though no supporter, was at least fair: 'The Divl. leaders [Lyttelton, Warren, and Clery] all crab each other . . . the fact is that they are all at loggerheads.'

Now, with the enemy beaten, the real battle began: among Buller's generals. He himself was partly to blame. His *grand seigneurial* manner, his brusqueness, his habit of not explaining himself to the outer circle of his staff: these were dangerous flaws in a commander-in-chief, though their source was a kind of shyness. But those he knew well, especially his personal staff, were all devoted to him. Regimental officers admired him, and the rank-and-file revelled in old Buller's success.

As for Buller himself, it was his poor bloody infantry's moment of triumph, and he delighted in it, writing, 'I am filled with admiration for the

British soldier, really the manner in which the men have worked, fought and endured has been something more than human. . . .' To the men themselves he paid the compliment of a Special Army Order, thanking and congratulating them. And a shower of telegrams echoed the congratulations: from the Queen, Lansdowne, Roberts, from friends and enemies alike. It was indeed like a dream. And with what depth of feeling Buller looked back on his ordeal: 'However it is all over and well over thank God.'

For the moment, it seemed that he was right. The squabbles among his generals seemed to fizzle out. The Roberts clique in the Ladysmith garrison – Hamilton, Rawlinson, and so on – were called away to serve with the C-in-C on the western front. White went down with fever a few days after the relief.

The most humiliating defeat of his life was still ahead of Buller, however. The Boers were no longer to give him great trouble. But the campaign against him was only beginning. It was led by a vindictive Hamilton, burning from his own humiliations in Ladysmith. He wrote to Roberts, 'Buller was very rude to Sir George and spoke to him in the vilest way of you and Kitchener, whom he appears to dislike and to attribute dishonest motives to, almost as much as he does you. . . .' He denounced Buller in an almost ludicrously violent tone to Spenser Wilkinson, the military correspondent of the *Morning Post*, and a leading imperialist writer on military questions (and, significantly, an intimate of both Milner and Roberts). He gave a grossly distorted text of Buller's telegram to White after Colenso, and continued with the remarkable statements that '*Buller is no use*. He is indeed *far* worse than useless'; that 'generally officers and men have lost all confidence in Sir Reverse'; and that 'everyone is confident' that in every case, except Colenso, the infantry could have won through 'if they had been given their heads'. And he begged Wilkinson to use all his influence to get Buller recalled 'before he does more mischief'.

This was heaven-sent ammunition for the young imperialists, like Amery, who sought one simple explanation for Britain's humiliations. Amery, tacitly encouraged by Roberts and Lansdowne, orchestrated a whispering campaign in the imperialist Press, which would culminate in Buller's dismissal from the army. And the idea that he was the main cause of defeat has passed into permanent currency through Amery's *Times History*.

At the time, however, it was White whose reputation seemed to have found the proverbial graveyard in South Africa. Refused another command by his friend, Roberts, his illness came as a relief to everyone. He went to Durban with Rawlinson, and was invalided home.

As the two men passed in the train all Buller's battlefields, a sudden, astonishing change of heart occurred in Rawlinson. Now he saw the extraordinary natural strength of Botha's Tugela line. Perhaps he was ashamed at the way Buller was being made the scapegoat for the setbacks. He wrote that night, 'It was marvellous they got through at all.'

CHAPTER TWENTY-ONE

The Plague of Bloemfontein

The Orange Free State, 13–28 March 1900;
Northern and Eastern Free State, 17 March–April 1900

Who recalls the noontide and the funerals through the
  market,
  (Blanket-hidden bodies, flagless, followed by the flies?)
And the footsore firing-party, and the dust and stench and
  staleness,
  And the faces of the Sisters and the glory in their eyes?

Rudyard Kipling 'Dirge of Dead Sisters'

Why do the Boojers go to bed with their boots on?
To keep De Wet from defeat.

Story told to the author by one of
Roberts's veterans in 1970

THE FALL OF BLOEMFONTEIN on the morning of 13 March took everyone – not least Lord Roberts – by surprise. The Boer armies had fled. Those men, who fought so stubbornly to hold their trenches in British territory, abandoned the trenches around their own capital without even an apology for a fight.

The previous evening, President Steyn had fled northwards by one of the last trains to get away before the British blew up the line. At about eight the following morning one of the Press corps rode up to Roberts with the news that in reply to a threat to bombard the city, the Mayor, the *Landrost* (magistrate) and other worthies had already surrendered. In due course, the Field-Marshal and the Flag followed the Press into the town. As a triumphal procession, the column of battle-stained khaki presented an austere, almost drab, impression, though it did have its moments.

But success, like defeat, magnifies the inner strains of a campaign. Roberts and his generals were no different in kind from Buller and his generals. Roberts blamed French and Kelly-Kenny for losing him one of the great

Royal Munster Fusiliers cheering the news that they were to advance to the front.

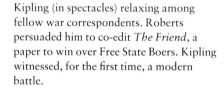

Kipling (in spectacles) relaxing among fellow war correspondents. Roberts persuaded him to co-edit *The Friend*, a paper to win over Free State Boers. Kipling witnessed, for the first time, a modern battle.

opportunities of the war. In return, they claimed that his reckless rearrangement of the transport had starved men and horses, thus crippling the army, especially the cavalry and artillery.

It is hard to apportion responsibility for what went wrong at Poplar Grove on the morning of 7 March. Certainly there was a chance of making a sensational capture, far outweighing Paardeberg. Though Roberts did not know it, Oom Paul himself was there, helping the Almighty to put new heart in His people.

The Boers held a ten-mile line of kopjes on either side of the Modder, some thirty miles east of Kimberley. Roberts ordered French's cavalry to make a wide detour to the east and take the laagers in the rear, cutting the escape route to Bloemfontein. After this, Kelly-Kenny's infantry were to attack the Boer trenches, supported by an artillery barrage.

The Boers, however, started to run the moment they saw the cavalry outflanking them. In itself, this need not have wrecked the plan – the purpose of cavalry was to hunt down a panic-stricken enemy. But to Roberts's disgust, French never gave chase. The cavalry advanced at a walk; indeed, they fought dismounted, several thousand troops checked by De Wet with absurdly few riflemen. Roberts blamed French for the fiasco.

He also accused him of wretched horse-mastership. If the cavalry had treated their mounts better, they would not have collapsed. French bitterly resented this accusation, and blamed Roberts's hopeless transport system for the breakdown of his division. But in truth, the cavalry charge had been rendered obsolete by the Mauser; the 'white arm' had become a white elephant.

Kelly-Kenny's slowness and caution in attack also came in for blame. He, in turn, blamed Roberts for the collapse of his own men and horses. De Wet's capture of the food convoy at Waterval Drift had left the 6th Division 'starving', and it was also very short of water.

Whoever was at fault, the effects of the Battle of Poplar Grove were disastrous for the British. Not only did Roberts fail to catch Kruger and the rest, he also made the crucial deduction that Boer morale was broken, and the war nearly over. This, apparently confirmed by an action at Driefontein on 10 March, and by the Boers giving up Bloemfontein, was the greatest strategic miscalculation of his career.

On 15 March, Roberts sent a reassuring letter to the Queen. It was weeks since he had had the opportunity. How dramatically the pattern of the war had changed since then! No wonder he enjoyed the respite at Bloemfontein, though impatient to resupply the army and be off. His army also enjoyed it: there were new boots and uniforms, pretty women in the streets, and for them, too, the chance to write home. Above all, there was a blessed respite from the veld.

Roberts prided himself on the level-headed way he looked fortune in the face. But now, with the astonishingly sudden collapse of the Boer armies, he made the great miscalculation: the Free State, he forecast to the Queen, was unlikely to 'give much more trouble'. The amnesty he had just proclaimed was having the desired effect. The Transvaalers would probably hold out; however, 'their numbers must be greatly reduced'. It would 'not be very' long before the war was 'brought to a satisfactory conclusion'. And he would only have to rest his army at Bloemfontein 'for a short time'.

'Not very long' till the end of the war. To rest 'for a short time'. Both these crucial strategic estimates – of Boer weakness and British strength – were to prove disastrously optimistic. Roberts knew nothing of the complexity of colonialism, of the tenacity of Afrikaner nationalism, of the extraordinary resilience of the Boer.

Significantly it was Buller, who knew the Boers, who accurately predicted the peculiar difficulty of a war against them. He believed that military strategy based on the 'single blow' would not bring conquest much closer. It was no good capturing capitals, unless they could subdue the territory between. He forecast a guerrilla war, and advised Roberts not to march on Pretoria before he had thoroughly crushed the Free State armies.

Roberts, by contrast, stuck to the conventional idea of surrender, of capturing the capitals. And he had long intended to use political means to smooth his march to Pretoria. On 15 March he offered an amnesty for every

Above Sorting mail for the troops at Modder River early in 1900. Often months late, every soldier received a box of Christmas chocolates from the Queen.

The new literacy at the war front. In the camp near Colesberg, an NCO reads a book, and the drummer boy writes a letter home.

British soldiers' graves at Bloemfontein. Though 22,000 died in South Africa, far more perished from preventable diseases, like typhoid, than from Boer bullets.

Free State burgher, except the leaders, who returned home, took the oath of neutrality, and surrendered their arms.

The Boer forces in the field, according to Intelligence, had been reduced to a total of about thirty-seven thousand in mid-March. The largest single concentration was still believed to be the invasion force in Natal: thirteen thousand. In Cape Colony, a raiding party, led by General Steenkamp, about a thousand strong, had started a local Afrikaner rebellion around Prieska.

The other Boer forces had, by 17 March, abandoned their posts south of the Orange River. The strength of the enemy still occupying British territory was thus estimated at 15,500; 21,500 other burghers were believed to be scattered about the Free State, including 5,000 to 6,000 under De Wet and De la Rey, who had fled north from Bloemfontein. There was another large force north of Kimberley. And 4,000 men under General J.H. Olivier were known to have retreated from Colesberg at the end of February.

Olivier's force, trapped a hundred miles behind British lines, would have been a prime target, if Roberts's priority had been to crush the Boer armies in the Free State. But Roberts had decided to halt at Bloemfontein until he could build up a still larger army ready for the next 'tiger-spring', the march on Pretoria. His strategy was for the moment defensive: to protect Bloemfontein from a raid by De Wet from the north, to reopen the town's water-works twenty miles to the east, and to reopen the railway line to the south. He ordered Buller to remain on the defensive in Natal, too: Buller protested violently. Roberts's only initiatives were political. He sent out small parties of troops to proclaim the amnesty and collect surrendered arms.

On 15 March he heard that Olivier was advancing north up the road that passes some forty miles east of Bloemfontein. But Roberts, with an army of over 34,000 in the Free State, waited till 20 March before he sent French with a small force to Thabanchu, astride Olivier's route. This was hardly more than a gesture, and Olivier side-stepped French, the ponderous wagon train passing safely through the British lines.

Roberts's first miscalculation was his belief that the Free Staters would accept his amnesty and disperse – hence his letting Olivier escape. His second miscalculation was that his own army would be ready to move 'in a short time'. In fact his army had broken down. By the end of March his force was little nearer being ready to move.

The underlying reason was that, by temperament and background, Roberts was not interested in the dull grind of military administration. But he had failed to create a competent staff to whom he could delegate. The result was chaos in his HQ, and thus in his transport. And the transport problem bedevilled everything.

A British garrison in the Free State suffered a peculiar and dangerous isolation, kept alive by the single-track railway that ran due south from Bloemfontein for the first hundred miles before diverting at Springfontein towards the three Cape ports. Congestion was now acute, and Roberts had delayed cabling to England for extra rolling stock, but all supplies had to run up that wretched single-track railway. Horses, too, by the thousand, had to come up that line, battered and bruised after travelling half-way across the world. Roberts's army swallowed horses as a modern army swallows petrol. Now, however, he planned to mount fifteen thousand men as MI. Where were the horses to come from? Whatever the War Office's failures, Roberts had grossly underestimated the scale and complexity of the problem.

In fact the breakdown of Roberts's army – men and horses – was due to their being put on half-rations, largely because of the loss of the virtually unguarded convoy at Waterval Drift, itself the result of Roberts's abolition of 'regimental' transport. A little less impatience, and the men that Roberts had marched into Bloemfontein might have been in no worse condition than the men Buller marched into Ladysmith.

The worst symptom of the defects in Roberts's military system was the death-rate from typhoid. The disease feeds on poor hygiene and overcrowding. Preventing it needed careful sanitation; treating it needed careful nursing and a careful diet. During the siege of Ladysmith, none of these had been provided. And Bloemfontein soon began to outstrip Ladysmith's grim record.

The basic cause of the typhoid epidemic at Bloemfontein was obvious enough); it was endemic. Many soldiers, unsatisfied by Roberts's ration of

Below The Palace of Justice at Pretoria, converted for use as a hospital during the great typhoid epidemic of April–June 1900.

half a water-bottle a day, had drunk water wherever they found it. But why had typhoid *spread* so rapidly? Negligence, was the simple answer. Neglect of elementary sanitary precautions in the army camps, as Bloemfontein's population soared from four thousand to forty thousand in a month; above all, neglect of the patients in hospitals, which turned a crisis into a disaster. The truth was that Roberts knew little of the workings of his army, and paid too little interest in the health of his men. His Surgeon-General, Wilson, was out of his depth, and the fearsome Colonel Exham had been transferred to Bloemfontein as sanitary officer. The army hospitals were bad *because* they were run by the army. Roberts at first failed to realize this; when he did, he failed to act quickly enough to deal with the crisis.

Late in March, Sir Alfred Milner arrived in Bloemfontein. He had serious political matters to concert with Roberts. The generous terms of the amnesty proclamation of 15 March were originally inspired by Milner. He now stood firmly behind Roberts as he held out the olive branch.

It might seem out of character that Milner, who had precipitated the war, was now prepared to gamble on this short-cut to peace. After all, *he* had

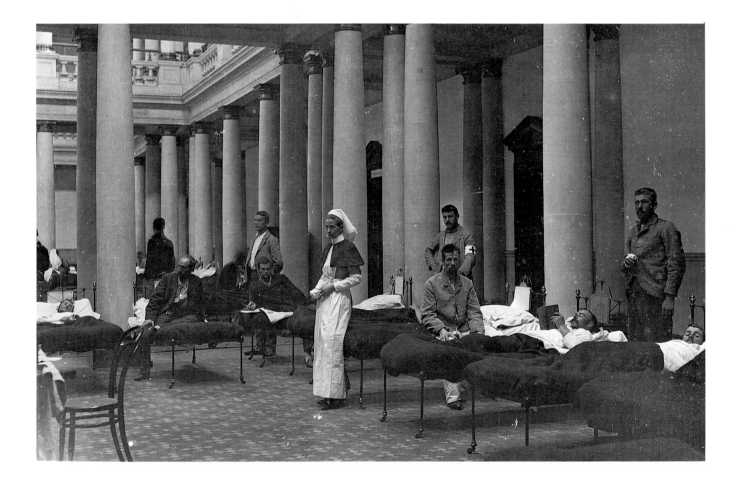

Below The Palace of Justice at Pretoria, converted for use as a hospital during the great typhoid epidemic of April–June 1900.

never underrated Afrikaner nationalism, and he was bent on crushing the 'Afrikaner idea' for ever. But he was prepared to risk the gamble for two reasons. First, although he shared the current hero-worship 'Bobs' (Roberts), the continuation of the war left him bitter and frustrated. The dream of his life could not even begin with this blundering army in occupation. Meanwhile, the enemy were forging a new nationalism in the crucible of the war.

Milner's second reason was equally fundamental. His secret alliance with Beit and Wernher depended on the profitability of the gold mines. Now he had learned that the Boer authorities planned to dynamite the Rand mines. So he was prepared to lean over backwards to be conciliatory to the Boers – at least, until the British army had seized the Rand.

Milner kept these anxieties to himself. Meanwhile, Roberts's praises were on every lip. 'This wonderful little man [wrote Churchill] . . . had suddenly appeared on the scene . . . and the sun shone once again brightly on the British armies. . . .'

But the weather in South Africa runs to extremes, and the storm-clouds were gathering fast.

Four days after the fall of Bloemfontein, the Free State and Transvaal leaders had held a *krijgsraad* at Kroonstad in the Free State, 130 miles north of the capital. The problem facing them was no less than how to find a new way of pursuing the war. Both deputations decided to prosecute the war 'more energetically than ever'. But what could a war council achieve if the Free Staters decided to accept the amnesty?

De Wet, now Commandant-General of the Free State army, claimed to have the answer: already the basic guerrilla war principles of the new phase of the war were taking shape in his mind. First, weed out the unreliable men, and so make the commandos an élite striking force. Second, increase their mobility by abolishing the wagon trains that endangered every Boer expedition, as Cronje had learned. Third, give up the conventional defensive strategy of trying to block or delay an invasion. It was hopeless against the enormous numerical superiority of the British. Instead, they should develop the strategy of raiding behind enemy lines that had proved so successful at Waterval Drift. Apart from the military value of attacking lines of communication – and De Wet recognized the vulnerability of that single-track railway – there was also the vital question of the burghers' morale. Give him one day's 'good work', and he'd have the burghers flocking back – even those who were now taking Roberts's amnesty.

In principle, the *krijgsraad* accepted De Wet's ideas, which coincided with those of De la Rey. But the two Presidents, while they agreed to the plan, did not abandon conventional defensive strategy. They also decided to use political methods to stiffen the burghers' shattered morale, and prevent the Free State men from accepting Roberts's amnesty. On 5 March, they addressed a joint appeal to Salisbury, repudiating the claim that they had gone to war with aggressive intentions. This was not an olive branch, of course, but a challenge to Britain to state her intentions, thus exposing her as an aggressor both to the world and to their own burghers. Salisbury's reply, on 11 March, was, as expected, quite uncompromising. Britain would not 'acknowledge the independence' of either republic. Kruger also made capital out of that captured copy of *Military Notes on the Dutch Republics*, which proved that Britain's aim had always been annexation. Surrender would thus destroy the volk as a political nation – the perpetual fear that was central to the voortrekkers' very existence.

Fear and shame were powerful moral propellants, but something more was needed: hope. Kruger did not, like Steyn, hold out the hope of intervention by one or more of the Powers, nor did he have much faith in Afrikaner risings in the two colonies. The volk must trust in themselves and in the Lord. Whatever calamities had befallen them, they must not doubt the Lord's purpose – *they* were the chosen people.

Kruger, the prophet, probably stirred more hearts than Steyn, the statesman, for all the latter's talk of foreign intervention. The Bible remained more familiar to the volk than European and imperial politics. At any rate, Boer morale, always mercurial, soared. And De Wet, above all, saw himself as the Lord's chosen instrument.

The *krijgsraad* had unanimously agreed that the commandos would be divided into flying columns. One large column, led by De la Rey and Philip Botha, would drive south towards Bloemfontein, 'to entice the enemy out of it'. Meanwhile, De Wet's Free Staters would swoop to the south-east, join hands with Olivier (then withdrawing from the Orange River), and attack the British lines of communication.

Roberts took De la Rey's bait, and moved troops north to screen the capital. De Wet therefore decided that his first target would be the water-works at Sannah's Post, twenty-three miles east of Bloemfontein. He gathered that the place was only lightly defended, so the main danger was from Roberts's enormous army. Well, he would rely on speed and its counterpart, secrecy. But even he was overwhelmed by the sight of the great fish that he found flapping in the Modder.

Brigadier-General Robert Broadwood was a favourite of both Roberts and Kitchener. But the lapse that sent him straight into De Wet's arms suggests that he was no military genius. He had failed to send out scouts ahead of his column.

The trap was sprung soon after dawn on 31 March, as Broadwood was withdrawing from an amnesty 'bill-posting' expedition in the Thabanchu district. Olivier's commando had forced him to seek safety at the water-works. His relatively small force numbered 1,700: some of the Tigers, two under-strength cavalry regiments, 830 MI, and Q and U Batteries, Royal Horse Artillery. He also had a convoy of ninety-two wagons, many of which belonged to civilian refugees seeking Roberts's protection.

Sannah's Post stood astride the western bank of the Modder, by a drift (ford) carrying the main Bloemfontein–Thabanchu road. There was a second drift, two and a half miles to the west, where the road crossed the tributary, the Korn Spruit, which joined the main river a couple of miles below. South of the road and about five miles west of Korn Spruit was a kopje, Bushman's Kop, where there was a British outpost with both telegraph and heliograph.

It was midnight on 30 March before the first of Broadwood's straggling column reached the pumping station. Everyone was exhausted after the long slog from Thabanchu, and a running fight with Olivier's commandos the previous day. Broadwood, ignorant of De Wet's force, gave no special orders to guard the bivouac. The commander of the water-works garrison had already sent four men to patrol the road westwards as far as Bushman's Kop, as they did every night. Before dawn, other patrols would be sent out to the north and east.

Soon after dawn, these patrols returned, followed, to everyone's astonishment, by rifle fire and shelling from some kopjes on the far bank of the Modder. Broadwood then made his fatal lapse. He decided to withdraw his whole force to Bushman's Kop – without sending scouts ahead. The wagons rumbled off, followed by some dismounted men and the two batteries, straight into De Wet's hands at Korn Spruit; the Boer leader had split his force between there and the pumping station. In minutes the burghers had captured two hundred soldiers and were all set to take twelve guns, more than were captured at Colenso.

Broadwood, two miles away at Sannah's Post, at last realized his predicament. He was trapped between two forces, with a third, Olivier's, somewhere to the east. A hussar officer was ordered to ride like the wind to Bloemfontein. The 'little man' must get them out of the mess.

The little man was not at his best in a crisis. Roberts, unlike Buller, tended to overreact, unable for once to control the nervous and impatient side of his character.

Sannah's Post was a mere twenty miles from his HQ. His new staff officer, Rawlinson, actually heard the distant rumble of guns. Roberts did nothing. Two hours later, Broadwood's first SOS, relayed from Bushman's Kop, reached the HQ. It was followed, about half an hour later, by the breathless report of the hussar officer.

It should have been Roberts's opportunity. Since Poplar Grove, the problem of fighting Boers had been to find them. Here was De Wet's forward line – less than five hundred men at Korn Spruit – isolated between Broadwood and Bloemfontein; Roberts had thirty thousand men within twenty miles. But he now swung from over-confidence to near-panic. Somehow he got it into his head that Bloemfontein itself was in danger. The best mobile force – part of French's cavalry division – was not despatched at once to help Broadwood, but wasted the whole morning and afternoon hunting for Boers around Bloemfontein. Colvile's infantry division was sent instead. In the meantime, Broadwood was left to cut his way out as best he could.

Mounted Infantry watering horses. Water was always scarce. During the war over 400,000 horses and mules were officially 'expended'.

If the root cause of the disaster went deeper than Broadwood's blunder, the reason that it was not still more serious can largely be ascribed to one man.

By the Korn Spruit, the battle had now resolved itself into a struggle to save – or capture – the British guns. Commanding Q Battery was Major Edward Phipps-Hornby, whose guns had gone into action at Sannah's Post about 5.30 a.m., when the Boer firing started. But the two British batteries found that the Boer guns outranged them by nearly a thousand yards. Broadwood ordered a retirement: U Battery, to lead, followed by Q Battery. Ahead of them the convoy's wagons and the refugees galloped pell-mell towards the Korn Spruit.

After about a mile, Phipps-Hornby watched the confused mass halt and spread out along the tributary's deep, crumbling banks. He thought the convoy had halted to let the batteries cross by the drift. Suddenly a gunner ran up: 'We are all prisoners! The Boers are *there* [pointing to the river-bank]. They are in among the convoy and among the guns.'

Phipps-Hornby did not believe the gunner, but realized there was some kind of ambush. He ordered Q Battery to retire by the way they had come. As the leading horses wheeled, a wave of bullets caught them. Horses and men went down. One of the guns overturned and had to be abandoned. But somehow he got the other five back and into action on a ridge 1,150 yards from the ford.

Q Battery was soon silenced. Of the original fifty officers and men, only one officer (Phipps-Hornby), two NCOs and eight men were still in action. Broadwood's ADC then appeared with orders to retire with the guns. The question was how?

About seventy yards behind the firing-line were some station buildings. Phipps-Hornby found some of his missing gunners and a crowd of infantry cringing against the lee side of the station. 'I called them cowards,' he said later, '. . . and said I would shoot any man who didn't go out. . . . They went somewhere but I never saw them again.'

Meanwhile, the ten NCOs and men and some of the Essex Regiment had begun to bring in the five guns and the limbers – manhandling them, as it was impossible to hook in the limbers in that blizzard of fire. Eventually, all except one gun and one limber were safely brought under cover. Then the surviving men galloped the four guns back across the Korn Spruit by another drift and joined the rest of Broadwood's column.

So there were no more captures for De Wet. His nimble column easily eluded Colvile's lumbering infantry and French's shattered cavalry, belatedly sent in pursuit. Colvile was later blamed for the fiasco. Broadwood was privately censured, officially exonerated. The seven captured guns (five of U Battery's and the two that Phipps-Hornby had been forced to abandon), 117 wagons and 428 prisoners were sent back northwards. Meanwhile, De Wet's column continued their raiding expedition to the south. With only eight hundred men, he attacked a British garrison near Reddersburg on 3 April. After a day and a night, the entire garrison surrendered, losing 45 officers and men killed and wounded, and 546 taken prisoner. Next, he laid siege to nineteen hundred men of Brabant's Horse at Wepener. However, the garrison skilfully dug themselves in, while Roberts's infantry divisions plodded to the rescue. After sixteen days, De Wet gave up and headed back north.

With a handful of men, De Wet had opened a new front; more, he had opened a new dimension in the war. He had failed, however, to cut the railway line. And Steyn and Kruger and the rest were not yet convinced of the need for such a revolution in their strategy. They still clung to the hope of somehow halting Roberts's force as it marched to the Transvaal.

From Roberts's point of view, De Wet's raid postponed, but did not prevent, his advance. And, on 3 May, he was finally ready for a double 'tiger-spring': the advance on Pretoria with his main army, while Colonel Bryan Mahon's flying column struck out far to the north-west to relieve Mafeking.

CHAPTER TWENTY-TWO

'The White Man's War'

Mafeking (Cape Colony border), 30 April-May 1900

'It is understood that you have armed Bastards, Fingos and Baralongs
against us – in this you have committed an enormous act of wickedness
... reconsider the matter, even if it cost you the loss of Mafeking ...
disarm your blacks and thereby act the part of a white man in a white
man's war.'

General Piet Cronje's message to Colonel
Baden-Powell, 29 October 1899

Opposite above
Colonel Baden-
Powell (seated
second left) and
staff outside their
'bomb-proof' at
Mafeking during
the siege. Perhaps
his antics saved
South Africa.

Opposite below
The opening score:
one train. On 13
October 1899,
Baden-Powell's
armoured train,
despatched from
Mafeking, was
ambushed and
captured by a party
of Boers at
Kraaipan.

COLONEL ROBERT STEPHENSON SMYTH BADEN-POWELL would not
have been human if he had survived the six and a half months locked up at
Mafeking without feeling the strain, though his messages from Mafeking
portrayed the stereotype of the stiff-upper-lip Englishman to perfection. It
was exactly what the other BP, the British Public, wanted to hear.
Throughout the siege he remained (unlike poor General White) the life
and soul of his garrison.

B-P's secret instructions (curiously, never published before the first edition
of this book) were to *raid* the Transvaal the moment war broke out. The idea
seems almost incredible now: two regiments of colonial irregulars to be
raised in Bulawayo and other colonial towns, and then sent to attack the
Transvaal 'à la Jameson', as B-P rightly described it. The object, however,
was of great strategic importance: to draw off large numbers of Transvaal
burghers and so protect the vulnerable parts of Cape Colony and Natal in the
first weeks before the reinforcements arrived.

In the event, the raiding strategy was abandoned. B-P had successfully
raised two regiments of MI – 'loafers', he called them – a Rhodesian corps
and a Bechuanaland Protectorate corps. But, by September, Milner had
proposed that the Mafeking force was needed to garrison the town against
Boer attacks from across the frontier. B-P acquiesced, put the Rhodesian
force at Tuli under Lieutenant-Colonel Herbert Plumer, and himself took
command of the Bechuanaland force at Mafeking. He now planned to
provoke the Boers, but without risking a raid. Mafeking was not only the

Colonel 'Bathing-Towel', as he was nicknamed. (In fact, Baden-Powell pronounced his name to rhyme with 'Noel'.)

most vulnerable town in Cape Colony, it was also the exposed nerve of the Boers' political consciousness: from here, and nearby Pitsani, Jameson and his Raiders had set off.

The Boers swallowed the bait whole. During the first agonizing month of the war, the whole of Cape Colony south of Kimberley, and the whole of Natal south of Ladysmith, had been guarded by wholly inadequate forces. Here was the Boers' greatest strategic opportunity of the war. It was largely thanks to B-P that they had not taken it. His two regiments had actually drawn off Cronje and 7,700 burghers, nearly a fifth of the two Boer armies. Historians (unaware of B-P's secret War Office instructions) have tended to deride his claims to have played a crucial part in the strategy of the first phase of the war. The figures speak for themselves. Arguably, his antics saved South Africa for the British.

Once the Army Corps arrived, however, Mafeking became a side-show. Cronje went south, and an even more stolid general, Snyman, with a much smaller force of fifteen hundred burghers, took over. Hence the second, and most depressing, phase. Now holding on to the town meant little more than denying it as a base for the Boers – to whom it had little practical value. Arguably, if it had surrendered in December 1899, it would have made no direct difference to the war. That Mafeking had not surrendered was largely due to B-P's remarkable professionalism – the will to win, hidden behind the mask of good clean fun.

To keep a proper field of fire, Mafeking needed a perimeter of some five to six miles. How were twenty imperial officers, 680 men of the Protectorate Regiment, and police, to defend this? Add another three hundred – every able-bodied white man in the town – and the garrison were still at a massive

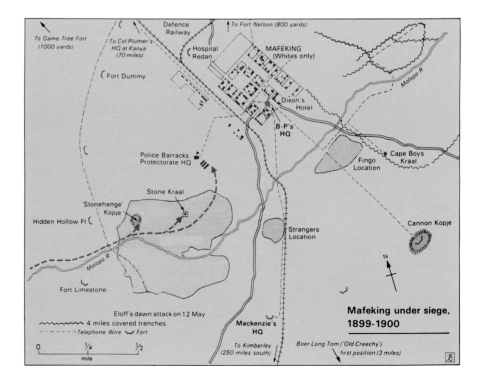

Mafeking under siege, 1899-1900

Long Tom (alias 'Creechy') preparing to bombard Mafeking. Later this gun was moved south to bombard Kimberley.

disadvantage (and proportionately far weaker than either Ladysmith or Kimberley). Add the guns – the best of which were two muzzle-loading 7-pounders – and set them against Cronje's nine modern field-guns and a Long Tom, and there was no avoiding the conclusion: the Mafeking garrison was a paper tiger.

B-P had survived the first two months partly owing to his own audacity, partly to the good fortune of having Cronje for an enemy, whom he bluffed into believing that the tiger had sharp claws. On seven different occasions in October and November, he sent out raiding parties to make what he called 'kicks' at the Boers, although these were expensive in casualties. He improvised dummy forts, guns and armoured trains to draw the enemy fire, the kind of military prank that was good for British morale.

Like Kimberley, Mafeking improvised heavy artillery. The counterpart of 'Long Cecil' was the 'Wolf'. The gun was a piece of 4-inch steel pipe, part of a threshing machine, and a breech cast in the railway foundry, but it could throw an 18-pound shell four thousand yards. Still more heart-warming was the way a gun called 'Lord Nelson', a brass ship's cannon dated 1770, rose to the occasion. B-P spoke most highly of the effects of its 10-pound solid cannon-ball. Other 'specialities' of the garrison included dynamite grenades made up in potted meat tins. A miniature railway was constructed within the precincts of the town, and a patent fuel – cow dung and coal dust in equal parts – helped mitigate the coal shortage.

B-P's flair for improvisation, and his ability to bend the rules, were most evident in his policy towards the Africans. It had so far been axiomatic, for both sides, that it was to be a 'white man's war'. In practice, this had meant that fighting was limited to white men (apart from a raid by Africans under their chief, Linchwe, on the Boers at Deerdepoort on 26 November). But each army had enrolled thousands of brown men and black men as unarmed scouts, grooms, drivers, and (principally on the Boer side) the all-important diggers of trenches. B-P took a daring step towards making it a black man's war.

Beyond the neat lines of bungalows lay the other Mafeking: a picturesque native town sprawling along the Molopo River. Within this 'Stadt' lived seven to eight thousand Africans: five thousand regular inhabitants, Baràlongs; the rest various African refugees, Fingoes whose villages had been burnt by the Boers, and Shangans expelled from the Rand gold mines, their savings taken by the Boer authorities.

Now B-P knew how to handle Kaffirs. You had to be fair but firm. By hanging some for stealing food, and flogging others, he persuaded the Africans to play the important part he had designed for them. Some were set to work digging trenches, others were roped in as scouts, spies, runners, and

Below Baden-Powell's officers (including Lord Edward Cecil, with black arm band) sentence to death a starving African for stealing a goat. He was executed by firing squad *pour encourager les autres*.

cattle herds. But B-P also *armed* three hundred Africans. Christened the 'Black Watch', they were set to guard part of the perimeter. He took this remarkable step for two reasons. First, he had increased the garrison by a third. And second, if the Boers attacked the Stadt, the natives must pull their weight in repelling them.

Mafeking had one great advantage, apart from a resourceful commander: there were relatively few civilians to make trouble. Then the twenty imperial officers, hand-picked for the abandoned raid, were an élite. Two in particular, both Irish, he relied on: Major Alick Godley, Adjutant of the Protectorate Regiment, and Captain FitzClarence, commanding B Squadron. But he found his second-in-command, Lieutenant-Colonel C.O. Hore, CO of the Protectorate Regiment, and his Chief of Staff, Major Lord Edward Cecil, a considerable strain. Fortunately, B-P was able to give the latter a task in which he could do no great harm – looking after an improvised cadet corps (ironically, the most famous product of the siege, the prototype of the Boy Scout movement).

B-P also found himself at loggerheads with some civilians. The leading local doctor, Hayes, had been made PMO; B-P told him to resign 'before I have to order you out'. The Press Corps was at first a thorn in B-P's side: 'all with very incorrect views of the situation – some alarmist, others incautious'. In November, some of them had asked B-P's permission to leave. He refused it. Later, however, their relations mellowed.

For the first couple of months, B-P coped well enough with the civilians'

Below Women and children drawing water at the women's laager during the siege.

tensions. The second part of the siege saw morale fluctuating dangerously. There was little physical danger from 'Old Creechy', the Long Tom; the place was so open, and the white inhabitants so few and so dispersed, that the shelling killed few except natives. He realized that the most serious threat from shellfire was to morale, and took counter-measures. But, as in the other besieged towns, nothing could altogether dispel the pervading boredom. And in trying to counter that B-P made his only serious tactical error of the siege.

On 'Black Boxing Day' B-P decided to try to capture Game Tree Fort, a Boer strong-point three thousand yards north of the town. There was little to be gained by the attack, apart from giving the enemy a 'kick'. But B-P was keen to have a go at the Boers before they strengthened the fort. It was already too late. Since the last reconnaissance, the Boers had roofed in the strong-point; it was impregnable without proper artillery support. With the gallantry of regulars, C and D Squadrons of the Protectorate Regiment had charged the parapet and been shot down at point-blank range. Twenty-four (including three officers) were killed. B-P took the disaster with his usual air of mastery. And with perhaps unconscious irony, he wrote to Roberts that it would be a lesson to the enemy not to make frontal attacks.

By January, food was at last running short. B-P's calculation before the start of the siege was that he had food for the white garrison to last till the end of February. Supplies for the Africans, meaning their staple diet of mealies, were not expected to last beyond December. That the white garrison was relatively well off was a lucky chance: the firm of Weil had recently stockpiled thousands of tons of supplies at Mafeking, and B-P had snapped them up. Still, even this was near exhaustion in January. How, then, was the garrison – at least, the white garrison – still fat and well as *April* ended?

The answer was hidden for seventy-eight years in B-P's confidential staff diary of the siege. The whites took part of the rations of the black garrison. And some of the blacks were accordingly given the choice of starving to death or running the gauntlet of the Boers.

That this *was* B-P's policy is made chillingly clear in his diary. The entry for 14 November shows the number of whites to be 1,074 men, 229 women, and 405 children, and the natives to be '7,500 all told'. He next listed the main food stocks – excluding the horses' rations – by weight, and calculated that he required 1,340 daily rations for whites, and 7,000 for natives. His last figure shows that he therefore had white rations for 134 days, but only 15 days' worth for natives.

This was very serious. B-P therefore rationed all the meal and flour in the town – private, official or commercial – and forbade Africans to buy bread. He was determined not to allow 'white' rations (flour or meal) to be used to eke out the proportionately far smaller supplies of 'black' rations. But he could prevent the Africans from starving by feeding them part of the 362,000 pounds of *horses'* rations of grain and oats. This levelled up the 'white' and 'black' rations exactly at '60 days for both white and natives if my present system . . . is strictly adhered to'.

At the beginning of January, he decided slightly to reduce the horses' rations of grain (though they were still ten times the men's). But the rationing of the Africans presented a new source of economy. Whites who could not afford to buy rations were provided with them anyway. The Africans were all made to pay, even for food commandeered from their own stocks.

By 8 February, he had decided, astonishingly, that he could stretch the 'white' rations, after all, right up to the third week of May. The 'black' rations, on the other hand, would only last thirty-four days. Whatever had happened now?

It turned out that the white merchants and their cronies had been hoarding grain. Weil, the main army supplier, had deliberately understated his supplies in the hope of raising his prices. And the sergeant-major in charge of rations was running a black market for whites who could pay. But, as well as finding that there was more food than had at first appeared, B-P had also discovered that 'mealie meal set aside for natives will be available for . . . whites'. As a result, he came to a very remarkable decision: to expel part of the garrison.

In effect, B-P was saying to the part of the garrison that was militarily (and politically) expendable, the 'refugee and foreign [i.e. not Mafeking] natives': leave here or starve here. These two thousand outsiders were to have no food at all. Banned from all employment, they hunted for bones on rubbish heaps, and dug up the corpses of dogs. Just how many of these wretched black 'Uitlanders', the real helots of the Rand, died of starvation in Mafeking, or in attempting to break through the Boer lines and reach Plumer's food-depot seventy miles away at Kanya, will never be known.

Early in April, B-P adopted the final and most drastic solution for survival. He decided to try to reduce the native garrison by a further two thousand, by forcing the Baralongs to abandon their homes and go to Kanya.

The reason for this drastic new twist of policy was that, at the beginning of April, he had received bad news from his subordinate and would-be rescuer, Plumer. B-P himself had doubted whether Plumer's Rhodesian Regiment – less than seven hundred strong, and with no proper guns – could cut its way into Mafeking. On 31 March, Plumer had made his run for it. He came within five miles, but was driven back. The disappointment was heavy – as were his losses.

B-P was now, for many weeks more, doomed to sit tight. He had already warned Roberts that if he (Roberts) heard no news of Plumer's success by mid-April, he must himself send a larger relief column. Then, on 20 April, B-P heard that owing to 'unexpected difficulties' (Sannah's Post), the relief might not arrive till the end of May.

Meanwhile, attempts to run more food into Mafeking, and more Africans out, had both run into trouble. On several occasions the Boers caught and shot some of the Africans who tried to drive cattle into the town, and Snyman sent a letter protesting against the use of natives in the war. Replying, B-P claimed, untruthfully, that he knew nothing about it.

The most savage incidents, however, involved the Baralong women. On the night of 7 April, seven hundred of them were persuaded to attempt a mass exodus. Only ten got away; the rest returned, many having been stripped and flogged by the Boers. On the night of 13 April, two hundred got away undetected. Then on the 15th, thirteen women were caught and nine were shot and killed. B-P protested to the Boers in his turn, and no doubt he was genuinely shocked. However, his tactic of expelling the surplus native garrison had certainly succeeded in its aim. By the end of April, he hoped to be able to *increase* white rations: 'By forcing natives away from Mafeking we can get their share . . . for whites. . . .'

It was, indeed, a 'white man's war', as both British and Boers were so fond of saying.

The finale to the siege was more dashing and melodramatic than even B-P could have hoped.

It began just before four o'clock on the morning of 12 May. Sarel Eloff, Commandant of the Johanesburg Commando, already knew that Mahon's relief column was now only a few days' ride away to the south, so it was now or never. His plan was so daring that Snyman was only half-convinced that it was worth attempting. As soon as the moon had set, Snyman's men would make a feint against the eastern lines of trenches and the artillery redoubts. Meanwhile, Eloff would break into the Stadt with seven hundred men, guided by friendly Kaffirs and a turncoat British trooper called Hay.

The Stadt was, in military as well as human terms, B-P's blind spot. With care, a raiding party could approach it unseen; once inside there was only a small police barracks between the attackers and B-P's HQ. However, success in actually capturing the town depended on Eloff's small party being reinforced once daylight had come. And for this they relied absolutely on Snyman, the most stolid of all the Boer generals.

Sarel Eloff was, however, an enthusiast: he meant to capture Mafeking, whatever the odds. With characteristic swagger, he boasted that they would breakfast at Dixon's Hotel the following morning. But few burghers took up his invitation. When he counted his party, he found it numbered only 240 men (and some of them were French and German volunteers) – not 700, as proposed.

Still, the first phase succeeded brilliantly. Snyman launched the feint, and Eloff's small force, assisted by Hay, slipped unobserved into the Stadt. To signal to Snyman, and to strike terror into the Baralongs, they set fire to the densely packed huts. The fire sent a useful screen of smoke and sparks, and a mob of panic-striken natives, flying ahead of them. However, it also warned B-P.

Before Eloff had got far, the garrison awoke. The burghers rushed on, without opposition, beyond the Stadt. Mistaken in the smoky half-light for British troops, they surrounded the Protectorate Regiment's HQ in the police barracks and, with hardly a shot, captured the occupants, including Hore. It was about 5.25 a.m. With a final piece of swagger, Eloff telephoned B-P's HQ. Hore and the barracks were theirs: and they were only eight hundred yards away.

It can have been no great surprise to B-P. He had little confidence in Hore, and was already aware that the position was critical. He soon identified the shape of Eloff's attack. The most successful of all his 'specialities' – the web of telephones connecting forts and outposts with HQ – did sterling work that morning, their messages confirmed by the flames sweeping towards the town. B-P reacted calmly and quickly. He could not risk reducing the eastern defence lines, which Snyman might attack in force at any moment. To deal with Eloff, the main responsibility rested with Godley. B-P telephoned him after 5.30. Things were 'rather serious'. He must do his best with A and B Squadrons.

Godley, his two squadrons, and his natives, had all risen to the occasion. In fact, it was the Africans who bore the brunt of the fighting and saved the day. When Eloff's fire-raisers stormed through the Stadt, the armed Baralongs had stood aside until they had passed, then re-formed, waving their muskets and shouting war cries. It was the turning-point. Now was the moment for Snyman to pour in reinforcements. But the Baralongs barred the way – and cut off Eloff's retreat.

When FitzClarence rode up with D Squadron, the worst was already over. Godley could be seen rallying his two squadrons after strengthening the outposts. Eloff's men were taken piecemeal: one party huddled behind the stone kraal six hundred yards beyond the police barracks; another on a kopje covered with a Stonehenge of limestone boulders; the third with He in the barracks itself. The stone kraal was surrendered first. The Baralongs rushed forward, and if an officer had not raced them to the kraal, there would not have been many Boers left to surrender. Later, the second group of Boers in the Stonehenge were driven off, assisted by the ancient muzzle-loader, Lord Nelson, though for some reason B-P, who directed the attack by telephone, let most of them escape.

In the police barracks Eloff's fiery dream was fast turning to ashes. He treated his thirty-two prisoners chivalrously, but there were unpleasant moments, especially from Trooper Hay. Eloff then put the captives, for their own safety, in the store-house.

From time to time, Eloff visited his prisoners. No British officer could have kept a stiffer upper lip. But as the shadows lengthened, so did the odds against him. After dark, the prisoners became extremely demoralized. Outside, there were deafening sounds; British bullets smashed through the wall, roof, and door. The strain became almost unendurable. One of the captives was convinced that they were about to be executed.

Then Eloff reappeared and, to their amazement, offered to surrender if Hore could arrange a cease-fire. Hore bellowed out, 'Cease fire, cease fire!' until his voice was recognized and the firing ceased. The Boers had lost some 60 men killed or wounded, and 108 prisoners; the garrison 12 killed and 8 wounded, most of them Africans.

Next morning, Eloff, accompanied by a French and a German officer, sat down to the delayed breakfast at Dixon's Hotel. B-P played host.

John Bull celebrating
Mafeking Night in
London. 'A man'sh ash
young ash 'e feelsh, an'
ash dignified.' Cartoon by
Max Beerbohm.

The relief itself seemed almost an anticlimax after the melodrama of
Saturday's battle. Early on 17 May, after 217 days, rescue was at last at hand.
The relief column, 1,149 strong, largely consisted of rough-and-ready South
African mounted irregulars. The great majority were Uitlanders, the men of
the ILH; indeed, apart from Mahon himself, the column was dominated by
those would-be revolutionaries of the Rand, the Reformers, and at least three
of the leading ex-Raiders also rode with the expedition. In 1895 the Raiders
had ridden from Mafeking to Johannesburg; now Johannesburg had ridden
to Mafeking. And it was in this sense – an inverted victory – that the news of
the relief was received with hysterical acclaim all over the British world.

The hysteria may look ludicrous in retrospect. Yet there was much, in the
short term, to celebrate. The relief proved to be only the first of a new run of

victories for the British. And Mafeking was not only a new English word (*OED*: 'maffick: extravagant behaviour'). It was a symbol of the new imperial unity forged by the war. B-P's garrison had been raised in the Cape; Plumer's column in Rhodesia (and Plumer could not have succeeded without his Canadian gunners and Australian infantry); and the Rand had come riding to the rescue.

In Britain, Mafeking meant, in every sense, relief: hysterical, euphoric relief. Relief from that nightmare of national humiliation, from the series of confused disasters that had characterized the first part of the war. It was a story the sporting British public took immediately to their hearts (where it was to remain for two generations). How one man and some loafers, against fearful odds, had, by English pluck and ingenuity, turned a forlorn hope into a triumph. In short, B-P had given back the British Public its faith in itself.

But myth and counter-myth were already beginning to overlay the siege, as the sand began to drift over the graves of the 354 Africans officially recorded as having died of shell and shot, and of countless others who died of hunger or disease. Apart from a brisk mention of some of the Baralongs in B-P's despatches, no thanks were given to the majority of the garrison – the Africans. £29,000 was raised in England to put Mafeking back on its feet. None of this went to the thousands of Africans whose farms had been looted, towns burnt, and families expelled or died of starvation. The Stadt represented the plight of all black South Africa in microcosm. This was 'white man's country'. The Africans were there to be useful to white men. When no longer useful, they must go back to wherever they belonged. In the 'white man's war', they had to pay a terrible price. In Milner's lapidary phrase: 'You have only to sacrifice "the nigger" absolutely, and the game is easy.'

'Well done, Gallant Little Mafeking'. A postcard produced by an enterprising publisher. (The siege ended on 17 May.)

CHAPTER TWENTY-THREE

Across the Vaal

The Orange River Colony and the Transvaal, 31 May-June 1900

Cook's son – Duke's son – son of belted Earl –
Son of a Lambeth publican – it's all the same today!

Rudyard Kipling,
'The Absent-Minded Beggar'

THE TIGERS had ridden 260 miles in twenty-six days. They were the head of a triumphant, undulating centipede – the forty-three thousand men of Roberts's 'Grand Army'. It was 31 May, and victory now seemed as close as the mine dumps of the Rand. British Johannesburg was only ten miles away, awaiting relief. And beyond was Kruger's Pretoria, awaiting her conquerors.

No one had expected the Boers to give much of a 'show', but the speed and momentum had surprised even Roberts. Exit the old Orange Free State; thus Roberts's official proclamation on 28 May.* Enter the new 'Orange River Colony'. And the Transvaal would follow.

There was, however, one thing about this war Roberts could not explain, even to himself. His own army had marched at prodigious speed, but the enemy had marched faster. Theirs was a retreat, chaotic and demoralized, yet never a rout. His main column had hardly a skirmish, and the Boers always saved even their wagons and heavy guns without paying the price in casualties. Botha's army, in full flight, marched like victors.

So the great question still remained open. Roberts could save the gold mines, perhaps. He could rescue the three thousand British prisoners held at Pretoria, probably. He could capture Pretoria, certainly, and proclaim the Transvaal, like the Free State, a British colony. But would this end the war?

The Director of Military Intelligence, Colonel C. J. McKenzie, forecast that Kruger would retreat north, and only defend Pretoria lightly. The war would go on, a view echoed by Rawlinson, who also forecast guerrilla war, 'which will entail much time and blood'.

Roberts disagreed, as did his favourite, Hamilton. Instead, he pinned his faith on the psychological effect of a blow to the heart – striking at Pretoria.

---

* Standard history books give the wrong date for the annexation. It was formally proclaimed on 28 May – not 26 May (as in Lord Roberts's official despatch), nor 24 May, when it was issued in Army Orders.

Exit the Orange Free State. Enter the Orange River Colony. Saluting the Union Jack in Bloemfontein, capital of the Free State, 28 May 1900, after the reading of Roberts's proclamation annexing the Free State in the name of the Queen.

Not that he ignored the fact that about seven thousand of De Wet's Free Staters would be left behind his own lines. On the contrary, he had detached nearly half the Transvaal invasion force to protect the Free State, and the all-important railway to the Cape ports, from raids. These twenty thousand men had another task: to disarm and unhorse the Boer population, so as to deny the guerrillas any further support. But he had set his face against trying to crush De Wet *before* marching out of the Free State. He was impatient to end the war, anxious to keep his losses down, as demanded by the British public. De Wet's and Steyn's re-emergence as the centre of the Boer resistance was a 'risk he had to run', he told Lansdowne. He did not expect it.

Thus on 3 May he had started the push northwards. On 10 May, Buller had at last agreed to bestir himself with the two remaining Natal divisions from his bases south of the Biggarsberg. So, on this broad front of 330 miles, (despite the troops left in the Free State) Roberts still retained crushing numerical superiority of numbers: eight thousand with Hunter along the Vaal; thirty thousand with himself and Hamilton in the centre; twenty thousand with Buller in Natal.

Roberts soon had to reconcile himself to his failure to make any 'bag'.

Roberts's grand army 'on the tramp' near Kroonstad, Orange Free State, with ox carts on the horizon.

Despite attacks on the railway line, and the dynamiting of most railway bridges, Roberts's advance continued inexorably.

After driving the Boers out of Kroonstad, he halted ten days (to Rawlinson's disgust) in order to allow the railway to be repaired behind him. Despite the improvement made by largely restoring the old transport system, the troops still went hungry when they stepped far from the railway; and repairs to the line were desperately slow. Meanwhile, the Boers consolidated their flight.

The worst aspect of the disruption of the railway was that it exacerbated the crisis in the field hospitals. Typhoid caused more British casualties that month than all the battles of Black Week. Belatedly, Roberts was coming to recognize the disaster and its causes – although he did not admit it to Lansdowne. He told the Surgeon-General, Wilson, to replace the notorious Exham, and gave him a stiff reprimand for failing to send doctors and nurses with the army.

Since the great advance had begun, Roberts and Buller had both been fighting on roughly comparable terms against relatively weak and demoralized Boer forces. Both were triumphant. But the reverses that blighted the triumphs changed the whole character of the war and, above all, trebled its length. These reverses were all on Roberts's side.

Ian Hamilton was in his element. The little man had made him acting Lieutenant-General. His division, created specially for him, formed the right flank of Roberts's double column: two mounted brigades (Broadwood's cavalry and Colonel C.P. Ridley's MI) and two infantry brigades (Smith-Dorrien's 19th and Major-General Bruce Hamilton's 21st) – fifteen thousand men and thirty-eight guns. His job was to smooth the path of the main column, and smooth it he would.

To say that his force had thus seen some brisk fighting was not to say much. There had been a stiff action at Houtnek on 7 May; and, in turning the flank of the Boers at Zand River on 10 May, he had suffered rather less than a hundred casualties. But the pattern of his lumbering advance was hardly less monotonous than Bobs's.

On 18 May the column approached Lindley, which the Boers had proclaimed the new provisional capital of the Free State after the fall of Kroonstad. It had already been abandoned by Steyn and his government when Hamilton's vanguard rumbled into the town. But an encouraging message reached Broadwood from De Wet's brother, Piet: he was contemplating surrender, and would bring in a thousand burghers; could Broadwood guarantee he would not be sent as a prisoner to Cape Town? Broadwood guaranteed it, and Hamilton agreed. But Roberts told Broadwood he had no authority to make these terms. The surrender offer lapsed.

The column left Lindley with Piet De Wet's men snapping at their heels. There was an unfortunate incident when Hamilton lost fifty-nine of his rearguard, though this was partly offset by Broadwood capturing fifteen Boer wagons. Colvile and the Highland Brigade, whose job was to sweep up behind Hamilton, would be able to deal with Piet De Wet – and Lindley – in a few days. So it was fondly imagined.

Hamilton's force crossed the Vaal on 26 May, having been switched from

The Guards pause in the veld on their way to Pretoria.

Roberts (hatless) writes despatches on the step of a commandeered house on the march to Pretoria.

the east flank to west of the railway. Roberts's plan for taking Johannesburg was straightforward enough. The two most mobile columns – twenty thousand men, under French and Hamilton – were to swing round to the west of the city and cut the main road from the townships along the Rand. Meanwhile, the main force, of about the same size, would go straight up the railway line to the east and so outflank Johannesburg from the other side. Hamilton now saw his way to the honours of a real battle. The Boers were entrenched at Doornkop, on the actual kopje where Jameson had raised the white flag five years before. On 29 May, therefore, he launched his two infantry brigades in a frontal attack on the ridge.

The assault that followed – the City Imperial Volunteers and the Gordon Highlanders charging up a hillside without covering fire or proper artillery support – was to provide one of the last set-piece battles of the war. It was, in a way, magnificent, but it was conducted with the same drill-book tactics Hamilton had used at Elandslaagte.

Before the front line of Gordons had reached the floor of the valley, Hamilton and other watchers could hear the Mausers. (The Boers were a few hundred Johannesburgers, led by Viljoen, and the Lichtenburgers, led by De la Rey.) Still the lines advanced, despite taking casualties. Then, sparkling in the sun, the ripple of steel as bayonets were fixed. Figures gained the skyline, a few at first, then more. There was a sharp, exchange of shots, then the firing died away. The Gordons had the hill. They had lost a hundred men in ten minutes, but they had done the trick.

By contrast, the CIV, being an amateur battalion, had little of the Balaclava mentality to unlearn. They had made their charge, against the western end of the ridge, in short rushes, one group giving covering fire to another, taking care to offer as small targets as possible. They, too, took their hill. But they suffered few casualties, compared to the Gordons' eighteen killed and eighty wounded.

But was any charge necessary at all? Hamilton later gave his reasons for risking a frontal attack, none of them very convincing. For the most likely explanation for his decision to fight the Battle of Doornkop, rather than go round, was that he could not resist the chance to redeem the two white flags of Majuba and Doornkop. He received nothing but praise from Roberts and Roberts's admirers.

Meanwhile, Roberts's central column – Colonel St G. Henry's MI, Tucker's 7th and Pole-Carew's 11th Divisions – had plodded on to Elandsfontein, a strategic railway junction eight miles east of Johannesburg. But apart from a small skirmish with some Boers concealed in spoil-heaps near the station, which cost the MI some casualties, there was nothing further to check the army here, and they pushed on a few miles before dark.

Their Chief was in high spirits. True, Colvile and the Highland Brigade had got themselves into a 'tight corner' somewhere north of Lindley, in the Free State. Otherwise, the news seemed, in every sense, golden. Commandant Krause, the Boer official now in charge of Johannesburg, had promised that the mines would all be left intact. The city would be surrendered next morning, at eleven o'clock. There was one vital condition imposed by the Boers: they must be given twenty-four hours to withdraw their army from the town. Roberts had been perfectly willing to agree.

It was probably the most serious strategic mistake of his career, though it was in keeping with his 'velvet-glove' strategy of trying to bring the war to a speedy and humane conclusion, and of giving priority to saving the gold mines. Now the mines were virtually safe – as were Wernher-Beit's millions, and the grand design that depended on them, the idea of a Federation of British South Africa. The war was nearly over, so Roberts believed. Why waste British lives attacking the Boers now?

All that day, Botha's army trundled north in utter confusion. Next day, Thursday 31 May, the conquerors marched in, watched by 'mainly friendly' crowds, chiefly of Africans.

After the briefest of ceremonial – Roberts presiding over the formal raising of the Union Jack, three cheers for the Queen, a march-past – the humdrum life of the big city began to return, especially the life of those Africans. There were fourteen thousand mine boys still employed on the Rand; they had kept the vats full in enough of the commandeered gold mines to pay for the whole Boer war effort, with a balance of £1,294,000 still on hand.

Now they found that their celebrations of Roberts's victory had been premature. The conquerors had no intention of changing the Transvaal's laws affecting the natives; indeed, these laws were now to be applied with an efficiency exceeding anything the Boers had managed.

The Naval Brigade welcomed to Johannesburg after the town's surrender, 31 May 1900.

Fortunately for the British, Chamberlain's ultimatum, with its brave words of 'most favoured nation status' for coloured British subjects in the Transvaal, was still in the Colonial Office files. At any rate, the men who were now to administer British Johannesburg were not interested in such reforms. They were Uitlanders. Their aim was to take political control of the country in which they had such vast wealth at risk. But one reform, they had always said, was absolutely vital: to cut the absurdly high level of African wages. It was no coincidence that the two principal civilian Commissioners – for Mines, and Finance – whom Roberts appointed to administer the Rand under the military governor, were not only Uitlanders, but also employees of the mining firms.

In due course, Milner, who had sent them, would follow, to begin clearing out the 'Augean stables' at Pretoria.

Botha's burghers streamed back from the Rand and vanished into Pretoria. Smuts was to remember 'that awful moment' all his life. He, with Botha, De la Rey, and all the stoutest hearts and strongest wills in the Transvaal army, had become convinced of the 'utter hopelessness' of continuing the struggle.

Kruger himself had given way to despair. He had been smuggled out of Pretoria on 29 May, after a last farewell to his invalid wife. They were never to meet again. Then he had taken the train eastwards to Machadodorp, 140 miles to the east. With him went most of the Transvaal government.

When it became known that the last guns were being removed from the

British officers, with African servant, well supplied with champagne in a commandeered house at Pretoria.

Major McGrigor, 1st Scots Guards, taking his bath.

elephantine forts, utter misery seized the volk. With a cry of '*Huis-toe!*' ('Off home!') the burghers began to pour out of Pretoria, after looting anything they could find. Others prepared to hand over the city to Roberts.

The nadir was reached on 1 June, when a *krijgsraad* was held at which the senior officers, led by Botha and Smuts, drafted a telegram to Kruger suggesting immediate surrender. Kruger replied with an equally despairing telegram to Steyn.

In fact, the spasm of despair quickly passed. Already a new spirit was stirring in the burghers – and a new phase beginning in both republics. How had this miracle been achieved?

The first vital breathing-space had been won by Krause's Johannesburg armistice. It allowed Botha to extricate his best men and all his heavy guns, and Smuts to remove all the reserve ammunition from the Magazine, and all the gold and coin, totalling £400,000–£500,000, from the Mint and the Standard bank. Krause had bluffed that the gold-mines would be dynamited unless the Boer armies were allowed to withdraw. But in fact it had already been decided that destroying the mines would antagonize foreign opinion; many of the Rand companies' shareholders were French, German, and American.

The man who inspired Botha and Smuts, however, was Steyn. He had seen his own capital occupied, and had realized that the true symbol of the volk was not a city, but the illimitable veld. His reply to Kruger's despairing telegram of 1 June was characteristically blunt: Smuts said later that Steyn 'practically accused the Transvaalers of cowardice'. Having involved their allies in ruin, said Steyn, they were now ready to conclude a selfish and disgraceful peace.

It was the most important telegram of the war.

To the wavering generals at the *krijgsraad*, it came like a slap in the face. Talk of surrender was forgotten; instead, they would make a fighting retreat. Even then, however, precious time was needed to rebuild morale. They decided on a ruse – in order to buy that time, they would negotiate the disposal of Pretoria, and put out peace feelers to Roberts.

Roberts received the proposal of peace talks, and took the bait, as expected. Pretoria was his. How could it not be the end of the war, and the climax of his career?

The triumphal entry took place on 2 June. The usual crowds of 'niggers' cheered; down came the vierkleur, up went the Union Jack. To some of the war correspondents, however, this was the climax of anti-climaxes. The British Press felt cheated; instead of Armageddon, they witnessed another dull march-past. Roberts's mistaken talk of civilized warfare had left the Boers to fight again. As one correspondent said: 'There is nothing civilised in war and never could be.'

It was not until 10 June that Roberts realized he had been duped, and sent his army back into battle. His own fighting force had by now been reduced to sixteen thousand; Botha, meanwhile, had managed to gather five thousand

Transvaalers. The ensuing Battle of Diamond Hill ('Donkerhoek' to the
Boers) was another anti-climax. Roberts achieved his limited aim of driving
Botha from his east flank, at a cost of 180 men. But Botha had done more.
Thanks to those two breathing-spaces, he had restored the volk's hope. They
fled from the battlefield, but it was '*vlug in vol moed*', 'flight in good spirits'.
The defeat, said Smuts, had an inspiring effect.

Meanwhile, something extraordinary had happened in the Free State which
explained both the relative weakness of Roberts's force at Diamond Hill, and
Botha's new self-confidence. Christiaan and Piet De Wet, masters of guerrilla
strategy, had lashed out against the lines of communication in the south.

The entire Free State forces had now been reduced to a mere eight
thousand men by the combined effect of Cronje's surrender and the partial
success of the amnesty. How could the Boer armies make a stand,
outnumbered by twelve to one?

Already, a new defensive plan had been agreed between the two Boer
governments. Their two armies should now separate. Christian De Wet was
thus free to resume guerrilla strategy, the policy he had always recommended, though he had only eight hundred men and three guns. On 4 June he

ambushed a convoy carrying supplies from the railway to Colvile and the Highland Brigade at Heilbron. Without a shot, he captured fifty-six food wagons and 160 prisoners, mainly Highlanders.

He was after bigger game, however. At Roodewal railway station, roughly half-way between Kroonstad and the Vaal, was a mountain of ammunition and other supplies. It was a part of the country that De Wet knew well; four miles away was his own farm. On 6 June he attacked, and despite finding that there were many more British troops in the area than he had been led to believe, quickly secured their surrender. His bag of prisoners was 486 officers and men; 38 British soldiers were killed and 104 wounded; his own losses were negligible. His only regret was that he could carry off only a small part of the booty. He seized all the ammunition he needed and buried several spare wagon-loads near his farm. Then he put a torch to the rest.

The 13th Battalion, Imperial Yeomanry, was the show-piece of the new volunteer army: a company of Irish MFHs, known as the Irish Hunt Contingent, including the Earl of Longford and Viscount Ennismore; two companies of Ulster Protestant Unionists, including the Earl of Leitrim, a whisky baronet (Sir John Power), and the future Lord Craigavon; and a company of English and Irish men-about-town raised by Lord Donoughmore. Commanded by a British regular, Lieutenant-Colonel Basil Spragge, who proved himself a regular ass, they were supposed to join Colvile. When they arrived at Lindley on 27 May, they found the town had slipped back under Boer control. Instead of making a fighting retreat, Spragge sent an SOS to Colvile and then sat down astride some kopjes to await rescue. Unfortunately, Colvile had been ordered to be at Heilbron by 29 May and, not fully aware of Spragge's dangerous situation, decided not to delay his brigade by returning to rescue him. On 1 June, when a rescue column did reach Lindley, they found the hills strewn with Spragge's dead. The rest of the yeomen had surrendered to Piet De Wet on the previous day.

In fact, there had been a gallant Last Stand. Lord Longford, blood streaming from several wounds, ordered his men to fight to the end. In general, raw Irish yeomen fought no worse than British regulars. A respectable total of eighty were killed or wounded.

Piet De Wet's bag totalled about 530, including Spragge, Lords Longford, Ennismore, Leitrim and Donoughmore (and the future Lord Craigavon) all captured, and Power killed. The wounded were left at Lindley; the other prisoners were marched away to the eastern Transvaal.

By mid-June, Christiaan De Wet had vanished again in the direction of Lindley. The war would never be the same again. He had amply demonstrated that the guerrilla tactics he had so long urged could achieve successes impossible in conventional warfare. Roberts's main advance had now become secondary to the task of hunting down the twin leaders and symbols of Boer resistance, Steyn and De Wet.

CHAPTER TWENTY-FOUR

'Practically Over'

The Ex-Republics, 8 July – September 1900

'We sat down and had a nice song round the piano. Then we just piled up
the furniture and set fire to the farm. All columns were doing it . . . The
idea was to starve the Boojers out.'

Private Bowers, tape-recorded by the author in 1970,
describing Roberts's farm-burning in October 1900

ON 8 JULY, Lieutenant-General Sir Archibald Hunter's two-thousand-
strong column plodded into Bethlehem, in the east of the new-born 'Orange
River Colony'. Hunter was overall commander of all five columns converging on De Wet. The strategic task Roberts had given him was to bring De Wet
to action and so force him to surrender. The method proposed was to corner
him and the other eight thousand survivors of the Free State army within the
basin of the Brandwater River – that is, to use the horseshoe of mountains
ringing the basin (Roodebergen on the east, Wittebergen on the west) to pin
the guerrillas against the Basuto frontier. His main anxiety was that De Wet's
columns would break back through the mountains and creep through the net.

Hunter, the unfaltering prop of Ladysmith's defence, had proved himself
one of Roberts's few really able senior generals. When, after Diamond Hill,
Ian Hamilton had broken his collar-bone, Hunter had been given Roberts's
main mobile force of three divisions to hunt out De Wet. The total seemed
large: Lieutenant-General Sir Leslie Rundle's 8th and Colonial Divisions;
four more infantry brigades – MacDonald's Highland Brigade, Major-
General R. A. P. Clement's 12th, Major-General Arthur Paget's 20th and
Bruce Hamilton's 21st; and two mounted brigades, Broadwood's 2nd
Cavalry and Ridley's MI. But many detachments had to be left behind to
guard the convoy route, and he knew that even this force was not large
enough to do all that was required.

Already about a third of the enemy had escaped. On the night of 15 July,
while he was stuck at Bethlehem waiting for ox convoys, one of the Boer
columns had slipped through the central pass, Slabbert's Nek. Hunter
blamed himself. If only he had a proper system of field intelligence; he could
get nothing out of the Boer farmers in this country. And if only his own
mounted troops had been as mobile as the Boers who, though hampered by a
great train of wagons, still outdistanced the pursuing cavalry.

Hunter might have blamed himself still more if he knew who were the Boer

De Wet was a hero in France. From *L'Assiette au Beurre*.

leaders who had escaped. Like Buller, Hunter had that rare gift of making ordinary people feel that he cared. But in one respect, his goodness of heart was not unlimited. There had been official changes in Roberts's 'kid-glove' policy. Nothing was yet said publicly, but as Roberts himself explained privately, 'More stringent measures than hitherto are being taken as punishment for wrecking trains, destroying telegraph lines, etc'. Now the generals were ordered to burn certain selected farms. So Hunter's columns left their signature behind them, a pillar of black smoke.

Meanwhile, Hunter had at last begun to gather some idea of what was going on in the Brandwater Basin, behind the screen of mountains. Then, on the 19th, scouts reported that the eastern pass, Naauwpoort, was held in force. Excellent news: the enemy were still inside the basin. Their HQ was apparently Fouriesburg, where Steyn had set up his latest provisional government.

There were six wagon roads into and out of the mountains. Rundle and four battalions, with ten guns and sixteen hundred mounted troops, would block the two most westerly passes: Commando Nek and Witnek. Clement's and Paget's brigades would attack Slabbert's Nek in the centre, while Hunter's own force of three battalions attacked Retief's Nek. Bruce Hamilton would take a battalion of infantry and five hundred MI and make for Naauwpoort. This left no troops to block the most easterly pass – Golden Gate – until reinforcements could be sent. But Hunter had a hunch that the enemy were not trying to break out to the east. He was right.

The concerted attacks on the two northern passes were launched a few hours after dawn on 23 July. On the summit of Slabbert's Nek, the wagon road passed close to an African kraal where the Boers had dug well-concealed rifle pits. These were engaged by some Imperial Yeomanry scouts until two infantry companies – Royal Irish Rifles – came up, and were ordered to advance with the bayonet. Within fifty yards they had lost four killed and twelve wounded, but they carried an almost impregnable position.

At Retief's Nek there was a battle of a sort; indeed, that dangerous little hollow kept Hunter's entire column occupied for the next day and a half, and cost him eighty-six men. Then the Boers melted away into the mist. Once across, Hunter's column joined hands with Clements's and Paget's brigades, and the Highland Brigade was sent ahead to support Bruce Hamilton in blocking Naauwpoort Nek and the Golden Gate. The main body then almost sauntered on down the valley towards Fouriesburg, giving time for the trap to be closed.

Everyone was on tenterhooks. Roberts had failed so often in the last six months to inflict a really decisive defeat on the enemy. Now, after only a few skirmishes, they were cornered. Or were they?

About 7 a.m. on 29 July, Hunter's vanguard heard the deep baying of one of Bruce Hamilton's heavy guns. The way was blocked.

The main body of some five thousand Free Staters prepared to meet their fate with an odd sense of resignation. Even now, if they were prepared to abandon their wagons, they could have escaped over the mountains. But they had been hunted and harried long enough. A sense of hopelessness came over them at the prospect of an extended guerrilla war. 'Huis-toe' now became their *cri de coeur*. All they wanted was to take their wagons and go home.

Below Boers handing in their rifles at Slap Kranz on 30 July 1900. General Hunter's hunting bag topped 4,000.

Only De Wet and Steyn could have prevented a moral collapse of this sort. But it was their column that had escaped on the night of 15 July. With them gone, the morale of the burghers evaporated.

On the morning of 29 July, as soon as Golden Gate was finally sealed off, Prinsloo sent a message under a white flag to Hunter. As the commander-in-chief he was prepared to surrender the whole force, on condition that all except leaders would be free to go home. Only Olivier escaped, fleeing barely in time with fifteen hundred men.

The terms offered by Hunter were stiff, but not, in the circumstances, too stiff. Roberts, at Milner's insistence, demanded unconditional surrender. Hunter, off his own bat, offered a concession: although he refused Prinsloo's principal demand – not to treat the burghers as POWs, but to let them go home – he was prepared to let them keep their wagons. There were sensible reasons for this concession. The pursuit of De Wet was now in full swing; Pretoria was crying out for Hunter's divisions to go north. And his long supply line was stretched dangerously thin.

By 10 August, the total of surrenders had already reached 4,314 men – including three generals and half-a-dozen commandants. Hunter had made the greatest haul of prisoners in the war, at astonishingly little cost: 33 dead and 242 wounded, for a fortnight's campaign in some of the wildest terrain in South Africa. In scale and cheapness, his victory outstripped all others.

Yet the surrender of one lot of Boers only seemed to encourage the others to fight. De Wet was now roaming the veld, unhampered by faint-hearts, eager to grip, once again, the jugular of Roberts's main army.

Below Following Lord Roberts's proclamation of July 1900, the families of Boers who refused to surrender were deported in cattle trucks to join their menfolk. Later Kitchener was to take tougher measures against them.

Below Farm-burning was supposed to punish the guerrillas, but it seemed only to stiffen their morale. Belatedly, Roberts banned it.

To the British public, De Wet's exploits had earned him the reputation of a magician. But in the eyes of his own men, and of his British prisoners, there was little mystery about him. On the contrary, he seemed intensely painstaking, one of the few really professional commanders on either side. He had none of the charisma of Botha. De Wet was blunt, charmless, even brutal; 'he rules his mob by the strength of his right arm and character,' wrote one captured British officer admiringly.

In fact, De Wet's strong right arm was hardly tested after Prinsloo's surrender. 'It was impossible to think of fighting,' he wrote, 'the enemy's numbers were far too great – our only safety lay in flight.' In early August, there were twenty thousand men pursuing him. His own column was a mere 2,500, including Steyn, his entourage – and four hundred wagons and carts. Against his orders, the burghers clung to their wretched possessions, though their part in Prinsloo's surrender was obvious enough. So De Wet could only flee at the pace of an ox; and even his oxen could barely do thirty miles a day. How, then, could he elude the British?

The secret lay in his professional scouts (unlike the British, who used ordinary mounted troops, he had trained two special corps). Through them he now discovered that, though the cordon was pulled tight behind him, Roberts had failed to block one route into the Transvaal. He crossed the Vaal on 6 August by the regular crossing at Schoeman's Drift. His situation was still critical, however. He was no longer campaigning on home ground, and the mountainous country ahead suited his pursuers better than the open plains of the Free State. His route lay across the western flank of the Rand to a higher chain, the Magaliesberg, which he must cross if he was to shake off his pursuers. But all the passes were likely to be blocked by the English.

They reached the Magalies valley on the morning of 14 August, and set off towards Olifant's Nek, the main south-western pass over the Magaliesberg. It had been occupied by Methuen's column a few days earlier. De Wet's men had marched two hundred miles in the last month, only to be trapped, it seemed, more completely than Prinsloo.

Two days earlier, Roberts had sent a jaunty cable to Lansdowne, predicting the imminent doom of Steyn and De Wet. Three columns – about twelve thousand men, led by Kitchener, Methuen, and Smith-Dorrien – on their heels; Ian Hamilton and a further eight thousand hurrying across to block Olifant's Nek. There had, however, been a spate of new 'unfortunate affairs' in July: the most recent, disaster to the Scots Greys and Lincolns at Zilikat's Nek on 11 July; 189 had surrendered to De la Rey when he struck out from his lair north of the Magaliesberg. Roberts struck out, too, sacking the COs of both units.

Six weeks ago, Roberts had been convinced that the war was virtually over. Now he was not so sure. Should he give priority to rounding up the guerrilla leaders, De Wet and De la Rey? Or press on with regular warfare: march against the last real Boer army in the field, Botha's, now at Machadodorp?

Lord Roberts satirized by the French.

There was also the overwhelming political question: what terms to offer the Boers. Ian Hamilton, on whom Roberts relied above all, was strongly against demanding unconditional surrender, and also against a new Proclamation of 31 May, which, while largely offering amnesty to the rank-and-file, made it clear that the leaders would be deported. But Milner had changed his 'velvet-glove' strategy, now that the Rand mines were safe. They must stick to unconditional surrender for the governments, and change the Proclamation so that all the rank-and-file, as well as the leaders, would be made prisoners of war.

In the event, Roberts had compromised. He had decided to attempt both to round up De Wet *and* to march against Botha. He resisted Milner's attempts to revise the official Proclamation, although privately the generals were ordered to extend farm-burning.

How could 20,000 men fail to hunt down De Wet's mere 2,500? But fail they did, and in a way peculiarly humiliating for the two generals whom Roberts thought the brightest stars in his army.

The first failure was Kitchener's. By moving troops on the Vaal, he had let De Wet cross on 6 August by the one unguarded drift. Then, equally mistakenly, he sent his cavalry *away* from De Wet's line of march. Methuen, redeeming his earlier failures, dogged the Boers so closely that De Wet was forced to abandon a gun and all his prisoners. But on the night of 10 August, the commando swung westward, side-stepping another column. Now Ian Hamilton joined the chase, only to prove still more incompetent than Kitchener. He knew the crucial importance of his task, which was to block Olifant's Nek. Yet instead he tried to intercept thee Boers on the Rand, and his troops dawdled. The guerrillas escaped, and with them hopes of ending the war at a stroke. Kitchener was predictably furious. But Roberts's official despatches – so vocal on the failures of men like Buller – were silent about Hamilton's blunder.

Having lost one dazzling opportunity, Roberts now turned to grasp the other: to beat Botha in regular warfare and destroy the last of the Transvaal army. And here, despite himself, he was soon to be grateful to Buller.

Buller's army joined up with Roberts's on 20 August at Twyfelaar, south of Belfast. There was some sly self-congratulation among Buller's men; they noted that Roberts's ragged soldiers seemed half-starved. The combined forces were to advance next day against the Boer strong-point west of Machadodorp, where Botha was reported to have seven thousand men and fifteen guns. Lyttelton, whose 4th Infantry Division was to make the attack, did not expect much of a 'show'.

This final phase of the advance of the Natal army had begun on 7 August, when Buller pushed up twelve thousand men – Lyttelton's infantry and Dundonald's mounted brigade, with forty guns – leaving the rest of his force as a garrison in the rear.

But Buller disagreed profoundly with Roberts's overall strategy, believing that the priority was to destroy the Boer armies in the field, not occupy their towns and burn their farms (indeed, he refused to sanction farm-burning by his army). Hence he had wanted to pursue Botha when he had had him on the run after the relief of Ladysmith.

Instead, Roberts clung to the psychological effects of capturing Pretoria. So he postponed both Buller's objectives – clearing Natal and crushing De Wet and the Free Staters. He ordered Hunter's division to join him, which reduced Buller's mobile force to three infantry divisions and two cavalry brigades. And he told Buller in March and April to stay 'strictly on the defensive'. The wrangle between the two men continued throughout April and early May. Roberts proposed that Buller then join him on the Vaal for a converging thrust on Pretoria. Buller insisted on the need to cross the Biggarsberg and clear the main railway northwards; eventually he had got his way, and took his three divisions scrambling over the Natal passes, and so into the Transvaal and up to Standerton.

Buller showed no great tact (or tactics) in the wrangles with Roberts. What he enjoyed was success in the field. Between 10–15 May he outflanked an estimated seven thousand Boers dug into the Biggarsberg, for the loss of only five wounded, one of the neatest tactical feats of the war.

On 6–12 June, he repeated the trick, in the spectacularly difficult country around Majuba, when he outflanked a large, well-entrenched Boer force at Laing's Nek. To take such a famous strong-point – the Gibraltar of Natal – without a shot delighted him. It seemed to him 'the hardest knock the Boers have had in this war'. And what pleased him most was the telegram that arrived from Roberts four hours *after* the nek had been captured, ordering him not to attempt to take the strong-point. 'I had already turned them out. That was rather pleasant.'

The Natal army had spent the next six weeks by turns advancing then consolidating their hold on the south-east Transvaal. On 4 July, units of Buller's and Roberts's armies first met. The linking of the Natal railway with Pretoria, brought about by Buller, transformed Roberts's supply situation. Prinsloo's surrender removed the main threat to Buller's lines of communication from the commandos in the Free State. So, by early August, the way was at last clear for the combined armies – Roberts's from the west, Buller's from the south – to strike at Botha.

The Battle of Belfast (alias Bergendal), the last set-piece battle of any size in the war, began on 27 August with a cavalry strike and then the usual artillery barrage. Buller had spotted the tactical key to Botha's position, a big kopje near a farm called Bergendal, a three-acre jumble of fantastic boulders whose great natural strength belied its fatal weakness in relation to Botha's defence line. It jutted out in a salient from the centre of Botha's twenty-mile front, but it could not be supported from sides or rear. So Botha had entrusted the crucial kopje to sixty men of his élite: the Zarps, the Johannesburg Police. They were given a pom-pom and ordered to hold out to the end. They did exactly that.

How ironic that the notorious 'bully-boys' of Johannesburg, the epitome of the brutal Boer, who had helped precipitate the war by shooting Tom Edgar, should now come to be regarded by the British as heroes cast in their own mould. A three-hour bombardment by forty guns hammered the strongpoint to powder. And the Zarps took it on the jaw like Tommies. 'No ordinary Dutchman would have held on like that,' said Lyttelton admiringly.

About 2.30 p.m., Buller gave the nod to Lyttelton, who let loose four battalions of infantry. By now, Lyttelton thought that the Zarps' resistance had been crushed. Yet, though the artillery still hammered the kopje ahead of the advancing infantry, the surviving Zarps had only held their fire. As the infantry went over the skyline, Lyttelton saw his riflemen 'falling pretty thick, but there was little flinching'. Their losses were severe; three officers dead and seven wounded; twelve men dead and a hundred wounded or missing. But in the smoking remains of the kopje they found that, for once, the enemy had suffered severely, too: fourteen dead (including a police lieutenant) lay beside their posts; nineteen prisoners were taken (of whom eight, including the commander, were wounded); other wounded had been removed by the Boers. As a force, the Zarps had been annihilated.

The storming of the kopje achieved much more. Buller had smashed open the weak joint in Botha's armour. At once, the Boer lines caved in along the whole front (pursued, with the usual lack of success, by the over-weighted and under-armed British cavalry). But it was a crushing victory, and Buller was understandably delighted, especially because he had won with Roberts looking on. Not the least of his pleasure was 'That I defeated the army and opened the road to Machadodorp, while Lord Roberts's army, which had got there before me, had missed the chance and had to sit looking on'. Three days after the battle, his continuing advance secured the release of the last British POWs – 2,000, held at Nooitgedacht.

'Ladysmith Street' at Waterval Onder, the Transvaal's main prisoner of war camp for British soldiers after the fall of Pretoria. The British complained of the bad food and conditions.

House at Yassfontein, in the Free State, looted by Colonel Rimington's notorious scouts, the 'Tigers' (note the 'tiger skin' puggaree on their hats).

In September and October, Buller's two divisions plodded northwards among the gorges and precipices of the Mauchberg that culminate in the great eastern escarpment of the Transvaal. It was God-given country for Boer tactics. Buller's veterans manoeuvred the commandos out of a series of Spion Kops with less than a hundred casualties. Botha's northern army, now only 2,500 strong, concentrated on flight. Then, at the end of October, Buller sailed for Southampton and a hero's welcome – from the crowds, at least. The government's welcome was to be less rapturous. Despite eight months of unbroken success in an independent command, at the head of a third of the British fighting force, he was to be given no official honour of any kind. (Roberts himself would be given an earldom and £100,000, and was appointed to succeed Wolseley as C-in-C in December 1900, as soon as he returned.) Buller was packed off to his pre-war job, training the Army Corps at Aldershot.

It seemed a quiet ending to the long feud between 'Africans' and 'Indians'.

In January 1901 Roberts and the 'Indians' returned to claim their kingdom from Wolseley. The old wounds reopened; the feud with Buller was resumed. St John Brodrick, the new War Minister, did his best, he claimed, to keep the peace; but Buller was 'impracticable'. In October 1901, Roberts and Brodrick concerted a plan for a 'coup' (Roberts's word) against Buller. Roberts's clever young protégé, Leo Amery, wrote an anonymous letter to *The Times*, taunting Buller with the so-called 'surrender telegram' in which he was supposed to have ordered White to give up Ladysmith. The government refused Buller permission to publish the true text, and he had then blurted it out at an official lunch at which Amery was present. Roberts threatened to resign if the Cabinet would not allow him to sack Buller for indiscipline. He was given Buller's head on a plate.

The war was 'practically' over, so Roberts told an audience in Durban at the beginning of December. President Kruger, after weeks as a fugitive in a railway carriage, had finally crossed into Mozambique on 11 September and taken ship for Europe. Routed at Belfast, Botha's army split into fragments, pursued by three British forces: Buller's in the north; French's at the centre; while Pole-Carew and Ian Hamilton plodded east, sweeping three thousand Boers before them down the railway line to Komati Poort and the Mozambique frontier. The British inflicted few casualties. About two thousand Boers and foreign volunteers surrendered to the Portuguese colonial authorities. On 25 October – six weeks after publishing it in Army Orders – Roberts jauntily proclaimed the annexation of the Transvaal. He proposed to hand over command to Kitchener early in November, and return to England after a sombre visit to Natal to see Freddy's grave.

What of the thirty thousand Boers still at large in the Free State and the Western Transvaal, including De Wet, Botha and De la Rey? Characteristically, Roberts gave the public the impression that he opposed harsh measures. In fact, he ordered his generals to extend farm-burning as a means of denying food to the guerrillas and punishing their civilian supporters. To one of his admirers, he confessed that he had perhaps erred on the side of weakness in the past. He would 'starve into submission' the last of these 'banditti'. He would be home for Christmas.

Painful events, as it turned out, delayed his departure. The Queen's soldier grandson, Prince Christian Victor, one of Roberts's ADCs, died of typhoid in Pretoria. So he did not reach England till January 1901.

By then, the whole strategic map had changed once again. Roberts was partially right: the war of set-piece battles was 'practically over'. But a new war – just as costly in time and money and lives, and far more bitter, because it directly involved civilians – had just begun.

'I do not want any incentive to do what is possible to finish. . . . I think I hate the country, the people, the whole thing more every day.'

Lord Kitchener to St John Brodrick,
the new War Minister, 1901

PART IV

Kitchener's Peace

CHAPTER TWENTY-FIVE

The Worm Turns

South Africa, 30 October–16 December 1900

'Low types of animal organism will survive injuries which would kill organisms of a higher type outright. They die, too . . . but it takes time. For the moment the severed pieces wriggle very vigorously . . .'

Milner to Richard Haldane, 21 January 1901

TO THE BRITISH PUBLIC, the government's conduct of the war – especially the hospital scandals – had confirmed its reputation for incompetence. But the war had also knocked the Liberals flat, divided into three warring factions – radicals, moderates, imperialists – with Campbell-Bannerman quite unable to unite them. With victory apparently in sight, the government needed to spring a general election before either war – in South Africa, and among the Opposition – was over.

For weeks, an early election had been anxiously debated by the government and whispered in the Press. Chamberlain originally plumped for June, a post-Mafeking election. Salisbury, as usual, refused to be hustled, and eventually settled on September. They would seek a double mandate: to confirm that the war could not, this time, be ended by a compromise over Boer independence, and that the newly annexed states were to be governed as Crown Colonies. The Opposition would be trapped; an election would force them to swallow both these distasteful propositions, yet still leave them in danger of being labelled 'pro-Boer'. On 17 September, the Queen duly dissolved Parliament. Polling for the 'Khaki election', as people called it, would start in a fortnight.

In fact, 'Khaki' played little direct part in the election. Of course, the war was popular in a negative sense. There was no outburst of pacifism – but there was no evidence of war-fever, either. The public had run the gamut of emotions in the last few months. The decisive election issue was not particularly emotive. It was, simply, how could a divided opposition govern?

The Tories' tactics were obvious enough: to impale the Opposition on the issue which above all divided them – South Africa; and to tar all Liberals, except the Liberal imperialists, with the 'pro-Boer' brush. The methods they used recoiled on them – at any rate, on Chamberlain.

Chamberlain was thought to have taken to extremes the use of 'pro-Boer' taunts, choosing as a kind of slogan a remark said to have been made by the loyalist Mayor of Mafeking: 'Every seat lost to the government was a seat

Previous page
A 12-span mule cart in De Wet's commando crossing the Orange River. Even De Wet, nimblest of the guerrilla leaders, was restricted to the pace of his slowest wagon.

gained by the Boers.' In fact, other Conservatives and Unionists all took the theme that to vote Liberal was to support the Boers.

The response was equally obvious, equally crude: to 'go for Joe'. The Liberals were trapped, unable to broaden the election to include everyday issues on which they could win seats and unite the party. So why not narrow the issue down to 'Pushful Joe'? And one aspect of Chamberlain's life had been skilfully, even venomously, exploited by David Lloyd George. His charge was quite simply that Joe was a profiteer, exploiting the war to swell the profits of his family's armaments firms, one of which was the principal private supplier of small-arms ammunition to the army. (Ironically, it had actually fallen foul of the War Office, because of late delivery and poor quality.) The charge was, in fact, just rhetoric. But it was enough to poison the election for Chamberlain. His outrage at Lloyd George's tactics surprised even those who knew him well.

It was notable, however, that the Liberals made almost no reference to the drastic methods which Roberts had begun to adopt in an effort to end the war. They were acutely aware of the political danger, in a Khaki election, of attacking the gentlemen in khaki, although their meek acceptance of the farm-burning policy is odd, in the light of the political storm it would soon raise.

In the event, the 'Khaki election' certainly looked conclusive. The government gained an even more copper-bottomed majority: 134 seats more than the Liberals and Irish Nationalists combined. Another term for an unpopular administration was a bonus that no one could have dared predict

Milner in Johannesburg exults in a parade of the Rand Rifles in 1901. But he was afraid Kitchener would throw away the game.

Imperial Yeomanry looting and burning in the Free State.

a year earlier. Salisbury was satisfied, and set about reshaping his Cabinet. Among other changes, he decided he could no longer himself carry the double burden as Foreign Secretary and Prime Minister, so he gave Lansdowne the Foreign Office, and handed the War Office to St John Brodrick.

Early in November, Brodrick received a long, emotional and disheartening letter from Milner. It predicted disaster in South Africa unless they adopted a more systematic military strategy. The war was not, as Roberts still claimed, 'practically over'; it had taken a more virulent form: guerrilla war. Milner put the blame fairly and squarely on Roberts, but he had little more confidence in Kitchener, who was shortly to replace him.

An increasingly bitter guerrilla war, an increasingly bitter rift between Milner and Kitchener: these were indeed serious matters. But Brodrick's instructions from Salisbury and the Cabinet were based on Roberts's opposite advice: the war was 'practically' over. There were already plans for bringing back some of the troops. At any rate, Brodrick did not raise the alarm at Milner's warnings.

Milner was not exaggerating. Valley after valley of the rugged south-western Transvaal had slipped back under De la Rey's control. In the plains either side of the Vaal, De Wet was back, snapping up convoys and prisoners.

A Transvaal farm called Cypherfontein, about seventy-five miles west of Pretoria, was at the centre of this resurgence. To this secluded lair, for a few days in late October, came the leaders of both governments, Botha and Steyn. De la Rey and Smuts (now the former's second-in-command) played host, and De Wet was expected. Their task was a heavy one. Roberts's policy of large-scale farm-burning had changed the war utterly. They must now hammer out a *joint* offensive strategy to counter it. But from before the beginning of the war relations between the two allies had been dangerously variable. The two republics were, of course, fundamentally different: the one rooted in farming, the other in gold. Hence the divergent attitudes to war and peace. There was also the clash of personalities between Steyn and Botha.

The case for continuing the struggle depended on whether guerrilla war was – at present – practicable. De Wet and De la Rey had proved this in the Free State, at Sannah's Post, Reddersburg, and Zilikat's Nek. Since then, the guerrillas' techniques, and the areas they controlled, had been dramatically extended. But, however practicable, was a guerrilla war a 'civilized war'? The question obviously troubled the Transvaal leaders, especially Botha, and explains why they clung so long to the strategy of regular warfare on the eastern front. They knew what a guerrilla war inevitably entails for civilians. And such a war in South Africa threatened to have uncivilized elements. The spectre of a black peril, however exaggerated in Boer propaganda, was real enough in Boer minds.

In short, here was a daunting moral problem. Was it fair to the volk – including women and children – to involve them in this savage kind of war?

There were also doubts about the practical aspects. How long would guerrilla war be possible, assuming that Roberts continued to ravage the

Jan Smuts (seated centre) and his guerrilla band, posing for the photographer after successfully raiding Cape Colony. Some of the men are carrying captured British .303 rifles.

countryside? Drastic as farm-burning was, it did get burghers back in the field – how better to demonstrate Roberts's ill-faith? But it was designed to make guerrilla war impossible, and in certain areas had already begun to achieve this, forcing the Boers to retire to other districts. In such an arid country, once the commandos let themselves be squeezed off the farm land they would wither away.

So it was vital from both points of view – humanitarian and military – to find an answer to farm-burning. The answer was simple: invade Cape Colony and Natal, British territories where farm-burning would be politically impossible.

This was the policy agreed by Botha and Steyn at Cypherfontein. Had it been carried into effect as a joint offensive, it might possibly have changed the whole course of the war. But the divisions between the two allies ran too deep. Besides, it was learned that the British were planning to raid the area. The leaders and their various commandos dispersed.

Near-fatal disaster overtook Steyn's and De Wet's Free State Commando at Bothaville soon after dawn on 6 November. Only the speed of their flight, the heroism of their rearguard, and the slowness of the main British column, commanded by Charles Knox, saved De Wet and Steyn from death or capture. As it was, De Wet lost all his artillery. Worse, the Khakis trapped the rearguard: 155 men, 25 of whom were killed and 30 wounded. And of those who escaped, others, too, were wounded. Marked by the heroism of both sides, Bothaville was one of the most ferocious and gruesome little actions of the war, made more so by the Boers using 'dum-dum' (soft-nosed bullets, contrary to the as-yet unsigned Hague Convention). It was also the most shattering defeat De Wet had yet suffered himself. What made it doubly humiliating was that the British had exchanged roles with the Boers. The men of De Wet's main outpost had simply gone to sleep, and the small British advance guard – only six hundred, to De Wet's eight hundred – routed the burghers. If Knox (who did not come up with the main body of troops till the evening) had displayed the same dash as the storming party, he would undoubtedly have captured the whole Boer force.

Characteristically, Knox made little attempt to follow up this victory, and the guerrillas recovered their self-confidence. Within a few days De Wet was back, plundering and burning with apparent impunity.

Major-General Clements had first burnt his way up the Moot (the nickname for this once fertile valley of the Magalies) three months before, forcing the burghers on to the defensive. Smuts himself bore the brunt of the campaign, both as a member of Kruger's old government and as the newly created Assistant Commandant-General. He had to regroup and revitalize the commandos of the Western Transvaal: appointing new leaders, expelling burghers whose loyalty was suspect, even condemning and executing those found guilty of treason. He was admirably suited for such work. To the tactical demands of the guerrilla war, an endless series of humiliating retreats, he was less well-suited. Hence his delight when the British, careless after weeks when the guerrillas had lain low, gave him and De la Rey a golden chance to seize the initiative.

On 3 December, Smuts and De la Rey pounced on a supply convoy at Buffelshoek, and got a fine haul of 118 wagons and fifty-four prisoners. The British lost sixty-four other casualties. Smuts released the prisoners, kept fifteen wagons, and made a bonfire of the rest.

This success naturally whetted his and De la Rey's appetite for bigger game. A week later they found it: Clements, the destroyer of the Moot, caught in the gorge at Nooitgedacht ('Never Expected') inside the Moot. 'I do not think', Smuts wrote, 'it was possible to have selected a more fatal spot for a camp and one which gave better scope for Boer dash and ingenuity.' Moreover, Clements's intelligence was so poor that he had no notion that Smuts and De la Rey were intending to attack him with superior numbers; indeed, had been spying out the land for days. General Christiaan Beyers, with fifteen hundred more burghers, was hurrying to join them. The three leaders jointly agreed that half Beyers's men would wait behind, in case Broadwood, twenty miles away at Rustenburg, tried to come to the rescue. All the others – about fifteen hundred, to Clements's twelve hundred – would storm the camp next day – 13 December – at dawn.

On the Boer side, it was the boldest assault since the attack on the Platrand at Ladysmith. Still, that had been a forlorn hope; here, the position was very different. The fatal defect of Clements's camp-site was that the mountain, held only by a line of pickets, commanded it. The plan was for Beyers's men to roll up the pickets, while Commandant Badenhorst, detached from De la

Rey's force, attacked the camp from the west. Smuts and De la Rey were to seize the kopjes to the south, and so block the only escape route.

Despite some blunders in the pre-dawn darkness, by daylight Beyers and Badenhorst had inflicted a hundred casualties on the pickets and driven them to surrender. Soon after, a fusillade fired downwards on the camp announced to the astonished Clements that the key to his position – and the heliograph – were in enemy hands.

Clements had lost half his force, and all chance of signalling to Broadwood. The camp was doomed. By all the rules, a general fool enough to get into such a mess should have found it impossible to extricate himself. But Clements not only spotted the one theoretical chance, he acted with dash and resolution. Somehow, 350 riflemen, horse-guns, transport animals, and all, crawled back to Yeomanry Hill, out of range of Beyers's riflemen on the mountain. Only the largest gun was left behind, a six-ton 4·7-inch naval piece, and even that was dragged, under fire, to safety.

The way that Clements now concentrated on Yeomanry Hill, his 'insight and soldierly qualities', aroused even Smuts's admiration. Whether he was still doomed depended on the insight and soldierly qualities of Smuts, De la Rey and Beyers. Clements had no proper water supply, little cover, and no time to dig trenches. Rescue could not come until next day, at the earliest. All the Boers had to do was bombard the place, killing the transport animals. Even if Clements did cut his way out, most of his equipment, including the guns, would be captured. More likely, his whole force would be driven to surrender: the greatest blow to British prestige, in prisoners, of the whole war. Instead, Smuts watched wretchedly as Clements's survivors rode off at 4 p.m., almost unopposed. At the last moment, the victors had flinched.

The loosely organized Boer armies, ill-disciplined and ill-coordinated, had always been unsuited to large-scale offensive strategy. The fragmented character of guerrilla warfare only intensified this defect. A major strategic offensive involving a cumulative series of operations could have been the next step, if Clements had been crushed. Broadwood could then have been dealt with. Then they could have launched a combined offensive to blow up the Rand mines, a *volte-face* that Smuts had advocated at Cypherfontein, and still passionately believed in. But perhaps, given the nature of the Boer armies, it was like crying for the moon.

For the moment Smuts had to accept that the initiative had passed back to the British. Kruger was in exile. Three thousand Boers had been killed or crippled; fifteen thousand were in prisoner-of-war camps. Both capitals, all the main towns, and all the main railways, were in enemy hands. Guerrilla warfare had long been De Wet's preferred strategy. It was now their only remaining option. In due course he would carry the war into the enemy's country: into Cape Colony, his own homeland, where the volk, away from the towns, were still in the majority. It might even precipitate a great Afrikaner rising.

CHAPTER TWENTY-SIX

Disregarding the Screamers

Cape Town and Beyond, 17 December 1900–28 May 1901;
London and South Africa, 1901

'If we are to build up anything in South Africa, we *must disregard* and absolutely disregard the screamers.'

Milner to Haldane, 7 June 1901

'*Ons mans, kinders, vaders, broers, susters, huis, alles ja alles moet ons agterlaat, en ons – wat sal van ons word?*'
('We must leave our menfolk, children, fathers, brothers, sisters, house, everything, yes everything, and us – what shall become of us?')

Maria Fischer's diary for 29 May 1901, the day she was taken off to a British concentration camp

SIR ALFRED MILNER was dog-tired. Worse than the physical strain, however, was the moral exhaustion. He had described Roberts and Kitchener as 'stale' in that *cri de coeur* to Brodrick. Secretly, he confessed it was true of himself.

Of course, these black moods soon blew themselves out. But he needed a break, a run home to England. He would go in May, if the war could spare him. Besides, he had an exciting task: to recruit imperially minded young men, his 'Kindergarten', for the much bigger task of building modern South Africa. Provided always that K of K and his blundering generals allowed the process to begin.

Bobs had been given a triumphant send-off on 10 December, to Milner's vast relief. By his misplaced optimism, by claiming the war was practically over, Milner believed – and events were to prove him right – that Roberts had done great damage both at home and in South Africa.

But Kitchener, his successor, was no more susceptible to Milner's advice. Milner was now, in theory, civilian administrator of the Transvaal and the Orange River Colony, but was pointedly kept ignorant about plans for the war. And, he felt, the month since K had taken over had seen rapid progress in the wrong direction. Yet the soldiers ignored Milner's own plan for

bringing the war to a swift end. Then, on 17 December, the news had worsened.

Telegrams reported the invasion of Cape Colony by three thousand Boers (actually two thousand) led by General P. H. Kritzinger and Judge Barry Hertzog. Although De Wet had been foiled in his own attempts to lead them across the Orange River, Kitchener in turn had failed to trap De Wet. So he could break loose again, follow Kritzinger, and raise the Cape.

The political consequences were what terrified Milner most; like Smuts, he believed that the colony, outside the main towns where the British were in the majority, was still ripe for revolution. And he had absolutely no doubt what should be done. First, if he was not allowed to suspend the self-governing constitution of the Cape, at least the loyalists should be armed in their own defence, and martial law proclaimed to help deal with Afrikaner 'traitors'. Second, Kitchener should adopt his – Milner's – military plan in the two new colonies.

In fact, the Boer invasion helped Milner to achieve the first of these aims. By 17 January, the Cape government had brought in martial law for virtually all the colony and formed a loyalist militia that was soon to comprise ten thousand men. And, as if by magic, Kritzinger's invasion began to fizzle out.

Milner's military plan for the two new colonies called for the 'gradual securing of each district before tackling the next, and slowly occupying the country, bit by bit, rather than rapidly and repeatedly scouring it'. As well as being the most efficient way of ending the war, there were two other vital

Kritzinger's commando, their wagons laagered in a circle, ready to saddle up and slip away. Guerrilla tactics came naturally to the Boers, trained in war with African peoples. The British learnt the hard way how to make an ally of the veld.

advantages. First, it would avoid the need further to devastate the country, with all the bitterness that would create. Second, the moment Johannesburg was made a protected area, the gold mines – the key to the Transvaal – could begin to reopen and the Uitlanders could be allowed back.

Of course, he did not doubt that sheer numbers would wear down the guerrillas in the end *whatever* policy they adopted. 'But I fear that on present lines we shall be at it for another 12 months, and that the amount of destruction will be enormous.' It was this unnecessary devastation (his plan was simply to remove *horses*) that sickened Milner. The policy would only give them 'a greater number of roving blackguards to deal with,' he said, adding (prophetically, though he scratched it out) 'besides tens of thousands of homeless women and children to keep and feed'.

In February, however, he turned to a prospect he regarded with still more horror than that of a protracted and destructive war: the prospect, offered by a plan for Kitchener to parley with Botha at Middelburg, of an immediate negotiated peace. Privately, he felt 'totally opposed' to any peace terms for these 'banditti'. They must shut their ears to the 'pro-Boers' and 'screamers'. His aim was *total* victory, 'to knock the bottom out of the "great Afrikander nation" for ever and ever Amen'.

Kitchener was baffled as to how to persuade the Boer leaders that, on very reasonable terms, peace was there for the asking. Twice he had sent intermediaries to Botha, with appeals from prominent Boers urging him to give up, and stressing the price paid by Boer women and children. The replies were somewhat puzzling. Botha accused the intermediaries of being traitors (surrendered Boers who had sought to persuade the burghers to give up had, with uncharacteristic ruthlessness, been sentenced as traitors, and some were shot). A. H. Malan, one of his aides, stressed the paradox that most Boers 'still defending their rights belong to the party that opposed the war most strenuously and also everything that could lead to it.' However, what was promising was that he added that if the British wanted peace it was they who must make the first move.

So, in late January, Kitchener renewed his efforts to get the talks started. But his envoy returned with the gloomy report that Botha and Schalk Burger (now the Transvaal's acting President) 'would not discuss any question of peace', and meant to fight to the bitter end.

The breakthrough came in late February after Botha's own wife was asked to mediate. Kitchener had assured her that, provided the Boers understood that the annexation of the twin republics was not negotiable, he would discuss anything else. In fact, he had already informed London of the main points he anticipated discussing at the peace talks. First, he wanted to confirm the legal position of (and, of course, discrimination against) the native majority. Second, he wanted to compensate the Boers for war damage. Third, he would like to reassure the Boer politicians that they would not be ruled by the capitalists and would have a voice in their own affairs. Finally – and here Kitchener sought the biggest concession – he wished to offer an amnesty not only to the Boers of the republics, but to the Cape and Natal Afrikaners who had taken up arms against the British.

The conference duly took place on the last day of February at Middelburg. Botha's principal points were exactly as Kitchener had forecast. But K did not get his 'free hand' to deal with them in a conciliatory manner. For Milner insisted on vetting the proposed terms before Kitchener cabled them to London for Cabinet approval.

Although the two men *openly* disagreed only on the amnesty for colonial rebels, Milner was prepared to seize on any pretext to make the peace talks fail. However, Kitchener, not to be outflanked, tried to frighten Milner into agreeing to the terms, claiming that 'disaster is not even now impossible if the Boers stick to it'. Milner therefore decided to compromise. Kitchener's proposed concessions were endorsed, if somewhat toned down, by Milner, with one important qualification: he publicly dissented from the proposed amnesty for the colonial rebels.

Kitchener's original four points had thus become a ten-point peace plan: (1) Amnesty for all bona fide acts of war (with disfranchisement for the colonial rebels). (2) Prisoners of war to be brought home. (3) The two new colonies to be governed at first by a governor and executive (that is, as Crown Colonies) but to be given self-government 'as soon as circumstances permit'. (4) Both the English and Dutch languages to be used in schools and in courts. (5) Property of the Dutch Reformed Church to be respected. (6) Legal debts of the State, even if contracted during the war, to be paid, with a limit of one million pounds. (7) Farmers to be compensated for horses lost during the war. (8) No war indemnity for farmers. (9) Certain burghers to be licensed to keep rifles. (10) 'As regards the extension of the franchise to Kaffirs in the Transvaal and Orange River Colony, it is not the intention of His Majesty's Government to give such a franchise before a representative government is granted to those colonies.'

The Cabinet's reply, on 6 March, a week later, made it clear that the first and last two points had aroused serious objections. Kitchener was rebuffed on the amnesty, and Milner's opposition endorsed. Both men were rebuffed on the question of the civil rights of Africans. Chamberlain insisted on tacking on to the native franchise clause: 'And if then given it will be so limited as to secure the just predominance of the white races, but the legal position of Kaffirs will be similar to that which they hold in the Cape Colony.' He added, privately, that one of the war aims was to protect the natives. If they failed to do so, they would be consenting 'to purchase a *shameful peace*'.

The revised text was duly forwarded to Botha on 7 March. Kitchener, fearing that Milner, by toning down the concessions, had tilted the balance disastrously against peace, threw himself with his usual demonic energy into prosecuting the war.

Yet to Brodrick (and even Milner) he openly confessed his distaste for the business. And he was fearful that it might cost him the prize on which he had set his heart: the post of Commander-in-Chief in India. Then, a week

Kitchener and his staff (wearing black arm bands for Queen Victoria's death) meet Botha and his guerrilla leaders at Middelburg on 28 February 1901. Negotiations proved abortive – to Milner's delight.

Boer prisoners of war hunting the enemy – fleas – at Main Street, Broad Bottom Camp, St Helena.

after Middelburg, Brodrick cabled him that, once the war was over, India would be his. A quick end remained his overwhelming objective. Hence he now proposed to London a policy for progressively adopting more drastic methods of forcing the enemy either to give battle or throw in the sponge.

In early March, Kitchener decided to flush out the guerrillas in a series of systematic 'drives', with success defined in a weekly 'bag' of killed, captured and wounded; and to clear the country of everything that might sustain the guerrillas – horses, cattle, sheep, women, and children.

Administrative problems involving civilians always bored Kitchener. He had to prevent the guerrillas receiving help from civilians; and he had to protect the families of surrendered Boers from official Boer wrath. The two sorts of 'refugees' should therefore be concentrated in huge 'laagers', close to railways and be run on military lines, with reduced-scale army rations. He left the details to administrators, who in turn arranged for tents and mattresses, plus roughly one superintendent, one doctor, and a few nurses for each of the twenty-four camps.

Ladies playing lawn tennis at Norvals Pont concentration camp. This was a scene that favourably surprised the Fawcett Commission. But Norvals Pont was one of the better-run camps.

A Boer *vrouw* gives a tea party in one of the better-run concentration camps.

Below Boer families in one of the British concentration camps. Kitchener's neglect of elementary precautions led to epidemics of typhoid and dysentery.

The French accused the British of genocide in South Africa. Cartoon from *L'Assiette au Beurre*, November 1901.

Below Kitchener the mass murderer: a French view. He promised tougher measures still after September 1901.

Thus, the plan had all the hallmarks of one of Kitchener's famous short-cuts. It was big, ambitious, simple – and extremely cheap. Kitchener does not appear to have been alarmed at the prospect of what might happen in his new 'laagers'. In March, Brodrick indicated that the camps might be about to cause a row, and asked to be told 'all that will help the defence'. Kitchener blandly replied that no defence was needed.

In South Africa today, the 'concentration camp' is, to Afrikaners, a symbol of deliberate genocide. In fact, K did not desire the death of women and children in the camps. He was simply not interested. What he wanted, passionately, was to win the war quickly. To that he was prepared to sacrifice most things and most people.

But when would the war be over? In February, Field Intelligence informed Kitchener that there were about twenty thousand Boers still in arms, and he estimated that they reduced them by 'about 1000 a month'. By May he had already settled in his own mind that 'hustling' the enemy was not enough. True, the monthly bag for the whole country had risen by this time. But at this rate the war could still drag on for months. The answer, for Kitchener, was to be found in two new weapons: barbed wire and the blockhouse, specifically a gigantic grid-mesh of blockhouse lines. Each blockhouse would be within rifle range of the next, and linked to it by barbed wire, so forming a steel net into which the columns could drive their quarry. The miniature forts could be made more or less impregnable, provided the Boers had no field-guns.

It was not, of course, an ideal short-cut to ending the war. Nor was it going to be cheap. Then, on 16 March, he received the bad news he had been expecting: Botha had turned down the Middelburg terms, apparently because of the refusal to allow amnesty for the colonial rebels. The news hardened Kitchener's heart. He would press on with his blockhouse lines.

He regarded Milner as the villain of the peace talks, however, and could not resist expressing to Brodrick his own blunt feelings about Milner's policy of disbarring the colonial rebels from amnesty. Furious, he began to make provocative new suggestions of his own for dealing with recalcitrant Boers and their dependants. But between despatching wild proposals, he gave the British Cabinet an astonishingly sound piece of political advice. They could prolong the war by condoning Milner's 'vindictive' insistence on unconditional surrender. But in the end, South Africa was a 'white man's country', and the British colonials would have to share it with the Boers. In due course, Britain would have to give self-government back to – white – South Africa, just as she had given it to all the other white nations of the Empire.

A few weeks after the collapse of the Middelburg talks, Milner temporarily handed over the keys of his new kingdom, making Kitchener acting High Commissioner for the two new colonies. On 8 May, he boarded the *Saxon* to take his 'holiday' in England. He was exhausted after weeks of wrangling with Kitchener, but victorious. He shed no tears over the collapse of the peace talks. He was content that the war would have no 'definite end' at all, but merely fade away. But there must be no 'wobbles' at home – either in the Cabinet, or among his allies in the Opposition. Hence the need to go back for a spell at 'Headquarters' himself, to prepare for the first moves of the new game: reconstruction under arms.

In the last two months, Milner had begun some of the groundwork in the Transvaal. Now that the origins of the war were forgotten, and the war itself was fading away, the capitalists' alliance with the imperial government would become eminently respectable. Already, the mines were beginning to work once more, and a trickle of gold had begun to flow. It might be only a fraction of what was needed to reshape South Africa, but it was a beginning.

One of the passengers on board the *Saxon* was a dumpy, middle-aged English spinster called Emily Hobhouse. Milner had helped arrange for her to tour the burgher refugee camps, and now regretted his generosity. There had been numerous protests about her trouble-making.

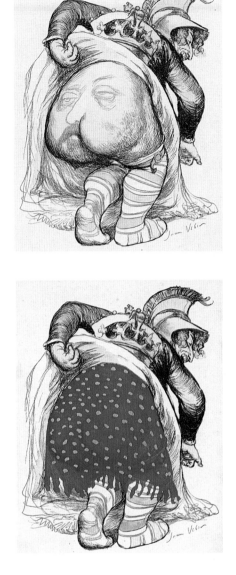

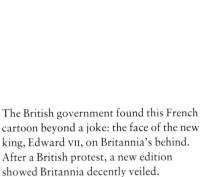

The British government found this French cartoon beyond a joke: the face of the new king, Edward VII, on Britannia's behind. After a British protest, a new edition showed Britannia decently veiled.

On 24 May, the *Saxon* docked at Southampton. In 1898, he had slipped into England almost unknown, a man of the shadows, sustained by a private dream of 'big things'. Now he belonged to the public. He was the Empire made flesh.

Milner found that most of the government had come to celebrate his apotheosis on the platform at Waterloo: Salisbury, Balfour, Chamberlain, Lansdowne, even Roberts. Impatient to honour him, Salisbury and Chamberlain whisked him off immediately in an open landau, driving through cheering crowds to be received by the new King at Marlborough House. Milner arrived back at his lodgings under the heady title of Baron Milner of St James's and Cape Town.

How he was later to regret his own fatal blunder at this moment of triumph. He still dismissed Emily Hobhouse as a 'pro-Boer' and a 'screamer'. In fact, the story she told was only too true. As congratulations flooded Milner, she set off on her self-appointed mission to waken the conscience of England. Epidemics had broken out in the camps and were spreading fast.

Emily Hobhouse was an odd figure for the leader of a great moral crusade. A forty-one-year-old spinster, she was passionate in public, yet inwardly reserved and lonely. When the war-clouds gathered, she had flung herself into the work of the 'pro-Boer' South African Women and Children Distress Fund. Humour, tact, organizational power, common prudence: these were not her gifts. But she was aglow with moral indignation. And she alone had seen the camps. In the first week of June, Brodrick gave her a long hearing. He listened to her recommendations politely, but did not commit himself. A week later, she saw Campbell-Bannerman. He listened aghast, and began to murmur, 'Methods of barbarism . . . methods of barbarism.' It was a phrase that would soon echo round the world.

The radical MP John Ellis sent his relation, Joshua Rowntree, to report on the camps; when he was refused entry into the two new colonies by Kitchener, Ellis's instincts were aroused. Brodrick continued to insist that these were 'voluntary camps'; the inmates went there, of their own free will, as refugees. Ellis charged – correctly, of course – that most were effectively prisoners. How many lived in them, he asked in March; indeed, how many had already died in them? Although he and Lloyd George had little enough information of their own, they succeeded in exposing Brodrick as apparently having still less. It was not till April that the House was given the first statistics of the numbers in the Transvaal camps (21,105); not till May, those of the Orange River Colony (ORC) and Natal (19,680 and 2,524 respectively). Even then, the facts remained extremely obscure. For example, Brodrick claimed – erroneously – that many of these 'refugees' were coloured people. As for the death-rate in the camps, all he could say was that there had been several hundred deaths in the early months of the year; high, but not outrageously high, rates for the period. Less reassuring were the reports of Rowntree and others. But they, of course, had not visited the camps. In this lay the overwhelming importance of Emily Hobhouse.

What she said – not only to politicians, but at public meetings all over the country – was that conditions in the camps were bad, and they were *deteriorating*. At Bloemfontein she found the bare necessities lacking, the tents overcrowded and the whole place insanitary. At her request the officials agreed to supply soap and to build brick boilers; but forage was 'too precious' and tap-water impossible as 'the price was prohibitive'. The most striking fact about the camps, however, was not the discomforts and deprivation, but the appalling rate at which people were dying. The whole system was a gigantic, lethal blunder.

The report Emily Hobhouse made to the Committee of the Distress Fund, coupled with her personal testimony, sent a shock-wave through the 'pro-Boers'. Lloyd George and Ellis intensified their attacks on the government. Still more important, CB was dislodged from the tight-rope between the two Liberal factions. He told a Liberal dinner party on 14 June that he was sickened by the policy of sweeping the women and children into camps: 'A phrase often used is that "war is war". But when one comes to ask about it, one is told that no war is going on – that it is not war. When is a war not a war? When it is carried on by methods of barbarism in South Africa.' And in the camps themselves, crisis was becoming catastrophe.

By persisting so unexpectedly, the war united the government as effectively as it divided the Opposition. But it did not give the Cabinet a clear-cut policy. For months they had been uncertain *whose* policy to pursue: Milner's or Kitchener's; the 'policy of protection' (of gently phasing out the war), or the policy of devastation (of trying to end it by some sudden, violent stroke). It was natural that, after meeting Milner, they should screw up their courage to try his 'protection policy'.

The most telling argument against Kitchener's policy was not a moral one – that to make war on women and children was barbarous. It was that it was not working: in short, worse than a crime, a blunder. The other main argument was financial – this was the most ruinously expensive war in British history since 1815.

On 2 July, the Cabinet made its wishes clear to Kitchener in what amounted to an ultimatum: he must end the war by September or adopt Milner's policy. It also spelt out the 'protection policy': protecting the Rand and the other parts of the country that were potentially revenue-producing or populous or otherwise important; then gradually pushing the lines outwards from these protected areas. This should enable him to reduce his army from 250,000 men to 140,000.

First round, victory for Milner.

Kitchener stalled. For weeks, he argued about reducing the army, but did nothing, while British successes and reverses both came conveniently to hand as arguments on his side.

The column war was formless by nature, its effects consequently difficult to judge. On the credit side, for the British, was the 'bag'. Even so, the war could drag on for months, unless there was a sudden collapse of the

Overleaf Emily Hobhouse's strained relations with the British army in 1901 – illustrated by one of Milner's *kindergarten*, Lord Basil Blackwood (he later illustrated Belloc's *Cautionary Tales*). But the Fawcett Commission vindicated Emily Hobhouse's claims about the terrible death toll in the camps.

guerrillas' morale. But at the end of June the British learnt just how firm was at least the Free State's will to fight on.

Botha made a new peace overture, and was allowed by Kitchener to consult Kruger by cypher cable about peace terms. There followed much the same pattern as at Middelburg, culminating in a devil-may-care challenge stating that neither so-called government would accept terms that did not preserve their independence.

In mid-July, British Intelligence broke the cypher used in the cables to Kruger. They showed how confident Steyn felt of his ability to continue the struggle, though they also confirmed that Botha and the Transvaal were genuinely anxious for peace. But Steyn appeared to be able to paralyse Botha's peace efforts indefinitely. Ironically, Steyn himself had a hair's-breadth escape from his laager at Reitz that same week. Broadwood surrounded it, capturing twenty-nine other members of the 'government', £11,500, and all the government papers, which confirmed that the Transvaal was in dire straits, but also that Steyn was determined to prevent a surrender.

Kitchener seized on such successes to show the danger of abandoning the sweep-and-scour policy, neatly reversing the argument when pointing to the enemy's own occasional flashes of success. It was foolish to reduce his forces when they triumphed; and dangerous to do so when the Boers did.

In general, the commandos in the last few months had dealt only pin-pricks to Kitchener's army. True, they regularly blew up railway lines and trains, causing general irritation, and sometimes casualties. They even dynamited one of the Rand mines. But the latter was a unique incident, and attacks on the railway declined as the year wore on. Occasionally, however, Kitchener's hunting columns were savaged. On 29 May, Brigadier-General H. G. Dixon, combing the south-west Transvaal, was attacked near his camp at Vlakfontein by General Kemp and 1,500 Boers, who snapped up Dixon's rearguard, and captured two guns. The guns were recaptured, but the action cost Dixon 49 men killed and 130 wounded. The direct strategic result of Vlakfontein was nil. Yet the psychological effect – the capacity to prolong the war – of this and similar actions seemed to Kitchener serious enough.

Most serious of all was the effect of Kritzinger's 'invasion' of Cape Colony, which had now been in progress for seven months. In itself, this seemed a small enough affair: about two thousand burghers (half of whom were believed to be Cape rebels), without much food or ammunition or the means to concentrate and deal an effective blow. Provided they were kept hustled, they could be kept weak and dispersed. Yet as a symbol of the unbroken spirit of the two republics, this Lilliputian commando had to be destroyed as a matter of urgency.

Hence Kitchener's second line of argument: to reduce my army is out of the question until I have cleared the Cape.

The full weight of Kitchener's counter-attack on the Cabinet developed in July and August. He proposed a new stick-and-carrot policy of his own: mild punishment for Boers or Cape rebels who surrendered voluntarily, savage treatment for those who did not.

The Cabinet, forced back on to the defensive, blocked Kitchener's wildest ideas, and protested at the brutal public executions of some captured Cape rebels. When Kitchener rounded on Brodrick – a 'strong line' would finish the war quickly – he was quietly reminded that 'severity' had not proved a great success so far. On the major issues, the bitter wrangle continued. Kitchener was forced to accept a much-diluted version of a proposed new proclamation, issued on 7 August, warning the Boers to expect tougher measures after 15 September. The Cabinet had to accept that if the proclamation failed (as it did) there would be no troop reductions after all. They would have to go crawling to Parliament for extra money.

The Fawcett Commisson was a daring experiment, a ladies-only commission to report on the concentration camps. They had one important political qualification: they all believed, unlike Emily Hobhouse and her supporters, that the war was just. That in turn justified certain unpleasant measures against the civilian population. Their criticisms, however, confirmed in all essentials the accuracy of Emily Hobhouse's account, and their chief recommendations went further: (1) Forty trained nurses to be sent out immediately. (2) A 'strong effort' to be made to improve rail transport to camps. (3) Rations to be raised by $\frac{1}{2}$ lb rice per week. (4) Where no other fuel was available, coal rations to be at least $1\frac{1}{2}$ lb a day. (5) Wood to be provided for bedsteads, so no internees had to sleep on the ground. (6) Every camp to have proper apparatus for sterilizing linen used by typhoid patients. (7) A travelling inspector of camps to be appointed. (8) Water boilers to be provided, enough to boil all drinking water. (9) Vegetables to be added to the rations. (10) Camp matrons to be appointed as rapidly as possible. In all, they visited thirty-three white concentration camps during August and September (though a characteristic flaw in their philanthropy was their failure to visit a single camp for Africans; there were thirty-one such camps in the ORC alone).

The Commission formally reported its conclusions in December, to the government's discomfiture. But Chamberlain at last recognized the ultimate causes of the catastrophe: the main decisions (or their absence) had been left to the soldiers, to whom the life or death of the 154,000 Boer and African civilians in the camps was an abysmally low priority. He ordered Milner, now in 'full control of the arrangements for all camps', to take 'all possible steps . . . to reduce the rate of mortality, especially among children'.

In fact, the common sense of the Fawcett Commission had a magical effect on the annual death-rate, which was to fall by February to 6·9 per cent and soon to 2 per cent, less than the average in Glasgow. But at least twenty thousand whites and twelve thousand coloured people had died in the concentration camps, the majority from avoidable epidemics of measles and typhoid.

CHAPTER TWENTY-SEVEN

Raiding the Colonies

Cape Colony and Natal, 3 September–December 1901

'Dams everwhere full of rotting animals; water undrinkable. Veld covered with slaughtered herds of sheep and goats, cattle and horses. The horror passes description ... Surely such outrages on man and nature will lead to certain doom.'

Smuts's diary, 7 August 1901, while he and his
200 men were trekking through the Free State

SMUTS DECIDED to make for Kiba Drift with his 250 men. It was 3 September. Ahead of them in the failing light lay the great canyon cut by the Orange River. For several days, his men had been hunting for a suitable drift. But every path down to the water seemed to be blocked by files of white tents. Except the bridle path to Kiba Drift. It was still open – that night. But they must go at once. The Khakis were sweeping down from the north.

A few men wore uniforms captured from the British (a dangerous blessing, it would soon prove), but most – apart from the dapper Smuts – were in rags. Some carried Lee-Metfords. Otherwise the commando was short of nearly everything: there were no medical supplies, little ammunition. They had plenty of horses, as well as pack animals. But forage was scarce.

As the sun came up, Smuts's band crossed into Cape Colony, into British territory.

Was this mission of Oom Jannie's a forlorn hope, or a perfectly feasible strategic stroke that might well change the whole course of the war? In the last ten months, all the most famous 'invaders' of the colony had been hunted back into the Free State, with heavy losses: De Wet, Hertzog, Kritzinger. The scattered guerrilla bands still operating there were able to survive only at the cost of their effectiveness as striking forces. As for the precise purpose of Smuts's mission, its leader remained distinctly uncommunicative, although he did not by any means regard it as a forlorn hope.

Since Cypherfontein, he had believed passionately in the need for carrying the war into the enemy's country: into the Cape where, outside the towns, the volk were still the overwhelming majority. The advantages were, he claimed, obvious: friends everywhere to supply and hide the guerrillas, friends whose farms could not be burnt. Successive Free State missions by De Wet, Kritzinger and Hertzog had failed, he said, because there had been no joint strategy between them, let alone with the Transvaal.

In June, Botha had asked a war council at Standerton what hope remained; in fact, he conceded the success of Kitchener's sweep-and-scour strategy. In the republics, their bases were destroyed, hundreds of their men were surrendering each month, there were no new recruits, and the blockhouse lines along the railways were beginning to criss-cross the country. Smuts repeated his plan for a Cape offensive. He would join forces with Kritzinger, and help him reorganize the surviving Free State bands holed up in the mountains of the Eastern Cape. Then he would cut his way through to the Western Cape, to prepare the ground for a large-scale invasion by Transvaalers under De la Rey. Even this pilot expedition should have a disproportionate effect in relieving Botha's and De Wet's hard-pressed forces. At best, it would start a great Cape Afrikaner rising, the last positive hope of winning the war by force of arms.

Of course, there was a less spectacular alternative, the classic of guerrilla warfare: to preserve their countries' independence by forcing a stalemate. Smuts was far too intelligent and politically astute to despise this negative strategy. He had noted that Chamberlain was weakening. Allies in England had stirred up a wave of outrage about the concentration camps, a wave that might propel the Liberals back into power. But would they come to power in time? And would they then wish to repeat the conciliatory policy pursued after Majuba? Here the Cape invasion, however militarily weak, could tip the balance in the political war.

By 15 September Smuts's commando was on its last legs: many horses dead, little ammunition, starving. It was the spring rains, not the British, that had nearly finished them. All that terrible night they floundered in the mud. Near daybreak, they found a deserted farm, where they came back to life. But fourteen men were found to be missing, and the survivors were too exhausted to send out a search party. Outside, the bodies of fifty or sixty ponies lay in heaps where they had fallen. That ordeal – the 'Night of the Great Rain', as it came to be called – brought Smuts' young protégé, Deneys Reitz, closer to despair than any other experience in the war.

On the 17th, still heading south, they came to a long gorge leading to the Elands River valley. Smuts ordered Reitz and his section, the 'Dandy Fifth', to scout foward. At the place where the gorge began to widen, a farmer excitedly told them of two hundred Khakis laagered on the pass at the end of the gorge, Elands River Poort. Smuts decided to attack at once.

The battle that followed was brief, bloody, and decisive. The burghers' shooting was deadly – they were, after all, De la Rey's veterans, honed by two years' grind in the Transvaal. Their opponents, Captain Sandeman and Lord Vivian, with 130 men of the famous 17th Lancers (the 'Death or Glory Boys'), were relative amateurs. Moreover, the weather had suddenly sided with the commando. The morning was foggy, and when Reitz's scouts were sighted by a British patrol, they were mistaken for irregulars from another column. The Boers made no such mistaké, and a desperate duel followed, 'almost at handshake distance', as Reitz put it. In all, his party claimed to have killed twelve or thirteen, without loss to themselves, though three of their men were wounded.

Meanwhile, the main commando had worked up to the British camp from the rear. Many Boers were dressed in captured khaki, which let them approach within a few hundred yards, a crucial advantage. When the confused butchery was over – twenty-nine British killed and forty-one wounded, to one Boer killed and six wounded – the victors found the camp to be stocked beyond their dreams. 'We were like giants refreshed,' wrote Reitz. 'We had ridden into action that morning at our last gasp, and we emerged refitted from head to heel. We all had fresh horses, fresh rifles, clothing, saddlery, boots and more ammunition than we could carry away, as well as supplies for every man.'

Smuts told the men to set fire to the surplus, including a field-gun, too immobile to be any use. Then, leaving the prisoners and their African retinue to shift for themselves, the new race of giants rode in triumph into the open plain, their confidence in Smuts reborn.

Haig, the commander directly responsible, under French, for this section of the cordon, galloped to Elands River Poort the moment the news reached him. He did not regard Smuts or his commando as giants, but as 'brutes' and 'ruffians'. He was appalled by what he saw ('The brutes had used explosive bullets'). Four of the six officers were dead, and Sandeman and Vivian (whose sister Haig was to marry) were wounded. He looked at the smashed and mangled bodies, and renewed his orders (they were French's and Kitchener's, too): all Boers caught wearing British uniforms were to be shot on the spot.

French had given Haig three columns totalling roughly two thousand men,

Christiaan De Wet, as seen by the cartoonist of *Vanity Fair*.

'Stiggins (mounted on Toastrack): I prefer trekking.' An unromantic British officer's view of guerrilla war.

but both men had trouble with interference from Kitchener. On the night of 3 September, K had ordered away the troops guarding Kiba Drift, and Smuts had slipped over the river unchallenged.

This fiasco was all the more galling because much of the information now pouring out of French's FID was surprisingly accurate. Smuts's commando was the most important, but not the only, needle in the haystack. The FID identified six smaller enemy fragments in Cape Colony south of the Orange. Add Smuts and his two hundred and fifty and the total of guerrillas south of the river was reckoned, rightly, at about a thousand. (Roughly the same number of Boers were thought to have invaded the western Cape Colony, north of the Orange.) The counter-strategy comprised three basic aims. First, they must prevent these severed fragments from combining; second, hustle them, so that they were unable to recruit followers or effectively raid the countryside; third, wear them out, so that they could eventually be hunted down.

Of course, 'invasions' by a total of two thousand men could hardly be compared to the military threat posed by the main guerrilla armies in the Free State and the Transvaal. But the colony was huge, and its topography often favoured the guerrillas. The weather, however, had favoured the British. It played a crucial tactical role in French's operations and helped bring the first real British success in the guerrilla war in the Cape. On the night of 4-5 September, Commandant Lotter, with a commando of 130 rebels (Cape Afrikaners), was run to earth by Colonel Harry Scobell's column.

Scobell was perhaps the most dashing of all the column commanders in the Cape, a 'rattling good man' in the eyes of the troopers. The speed at which his force travelled put it in the Boer class. He had hunted Malan and Kritzinger and Scheepers up and down these same mountains ever since May. And it was largely his work that eventually drove Kritzinger back in despair. Since then, Scobell had refined his counter-commando tactics still further by adopting Boer supply methods. He had discarded his wagons in favour of pack mules, carrying three days' rations for a six-day Boer hunt. The gain was not only in speed. The column could climb like goats up steep mountainsides.

On the night of 4–5 September, a storm was raging in the Tandjesberg, the tangle of mountains between Cradock and Graaf Reinet. After a night march, Scobell's eleven hundred men surrounded Lotter's commando as they slept in a sheep-house in a mountain gorge called Groenkloof. The Boers leapt to action, but after a savage fire-fight were beaten down by weight of numbers. The British lost ten men killed, the Boers thirteen, with forty-six wounded and sixty-one other prisoners, including Lotter (he and seven other Cape rebels were in due course executed). In losing Lotter, the Boers had lost more than a tenth of the guerrillas in the Cape north of the Orange, and their élite commando at that. The British Empire was a bottomless well when it came to replacing troops. The Boer wells were virtually dry.

By the day of Smuts's victory, Botha was poised to invade Natal. This was the other half of the grand strategy agreed with Smuts at Standerton: its military

Below The Boer guerrillas were chivalrous enough to return their British prisoners after stripping them of their trousers – as correctly shown in this French cartoon.

aim, to divert pressure from the occupied republics; its political aim, to prove that the war was by no means over. It was also a direct challenge to Kitchener's proclamation of 7 August.

Botha's commandos had set out from the remote eastern border of the Transvaal a week earlier. They marched light and fast, the old ox wagons replaced by pack mules and pack horses. The pace was too hot for the British columns. It was also too hot for their own horses, which were weak after the winter. And spring here also turned cruelly pro-British. The cold rain made roads into rivers; the horses shivered and starved. By 14 September, the transport problem was critical, and Botha had to halt for several days to let the animals recover. And, if the rain also hampered the Khakis, the Buffalo River, which marked the Natal frontier, was now in spate. The commando splashed on towards Zululand, hoping to dodge the British patrols and cross the Buffalo somewhere to the south.

Major Hubert Gough had plenty of 'dash', the quality Kitchener liked to see (but seldom did) in his cavalry COs. When Intelligence learned of Botha's plan to invade Natal, Gough's MI were ordered 'to entrain without delay for the north'. Having reached Dundee, he marched his men off in pouring rain to De Jager's Drift, a depressing little camp guarding the main crossing-point of the Buffalo River, astride the old Natal–Transvaal frontier; Botha and up to seven hundred men were reported to be threatening an attack. Next day, 17 September, Gough was delighted to find that the Boers were indeed at Blood River Poort.

Botha had no field-guns, and only a thousand men. He had set no trap. But he saw his chance. The Khakis were still outnumbered, but soon the main British army would be brought up. He must turn the Khakis' chosen weapon – surprise – back against them. Three hundred of his burghers off-saddled at a farm. Meanwhile, his main force, seven hundred men under his own command, galloped round Gough's right-hand company, who were holding a ridge. In twenty minutes, they had cut through them. Gough watched, aghast, as hundreds of Boers swarmed all over the ridge. He threw himself off his horse and tried to use it as a shield. But Botha's men had overrun them completely.

The nightmare soon turned to farce. Gough, stripped of his boots and equipment, played hide-and-seek with his captors under cover of darkness. Later, when it grew pitch-dark, he made good his escape, groping his way on blistered feet to the nearest British patrol.

Next day, the telegraph lines hummed with the news of Gough's disaster: an officer and 19 men killed, 5 officers and 19 men wounded (3 officers mortally), 6 officers and 235 men taken prisoner. It was the most humiliating reverse since Nooitgedacht. But, for Botha, it was less than enough. He had captured rifles, ammunition, two hundred horses, and two field-guns, as well as the Khakis. What he desperately needed was fresh horses, food and fodder, and a smooth path into Natal. He decided to raid two British camps – 'Fort Itala' and 'Fort Prospect' – astride the Zulu frontier.

Now, on 26 September, he succumbed to a fit of over-confidence quite as serious as Gough's – worse, in fact. He had been told by local burghers that the two forts had no trenches. Actually, they had not only good trenches, but good men to man them, too. To cap it all, the burghers threw themselves with British-style recklessness against the trenches at Fort Itala, losing at least fifty-eight men killed and wounded. The attack on Fort Prospect was equally brave and equally futile. Botha's demoralized men scampered back into the Transvaal, just as fifteen thousand Khakis lumbered up to overwhelm them. The invaders were fugitives once more.

The Natal invasion could never have been more than a forlorn hope. The raid had cost Botha some of his best men and brought the others into a cul-de-sac. The Zulus stood grimly on this south-east borderland, instructed by the British to repel invasion of their own territory.

The fiasco must only have confirmed what Botha had soberly recognized ever since Middelburg. There *were* no other options: only to fight to the end, or accept Kitchener's peace.

By the standards he had set himself, Smuts failed more completely than Botha. He himself put the best gloss, understandably, on his epic march. But in his secret report he admitted failing in the main task: paving the way for the arrival of De la Rey with a large Transvaal army, and the official establishment of a Cape Afrikaner government as a third belligerent. The colonial Afrikaners had decided not to join the commandos. The underlying reason, which Smuts did not admit, was that most of them believed that the republics were now too weak to achieve anything by prolonging the struggle.

He must now have recognized that no diversions outside the two republics could alter the grim logic of Kitchener's 'bag'. K had ground down the Boer forces to about twenty-five thousand – roughly half their number when Roberts had left. If this process went on, the end would be bitter indeed.

Headquarters S.A.C. Zuurfontein Transvaal S.

CHAPTER TWENTY-EIGHT

Blockhouse or Blockhead?

The New Colonies, November 1901 – March 1902

'This war is fast degenerating into the same kind of dacoit hunt we used to have in Burmah. The Boer is becoming just as cold-blooded a ruffian as the dacoit was and his wholesale slaughter of Kaffirs ... has I think forfeited his right to be considered a belligerent. I found the bodies of four Kaffir boys none of them over 12 years of age with their heads broken in by the Boers and left in the Kraal of their fathers. Strong measures will be required to stop this slaughter.'

Colonel Rawlinson to Lord Roberts,
28 August 1901

Opposite above
Blockhouse or blockhead? At first the Boers laughed at Kitchener's tin and concrete blockhouse lines. By May 1902, there were over 8,000 blockhouses covering 3,700 miles. Gradually the guerrillas became trapped like flies in a web.

Opposite below
Inside a British army blockhouse during the guerrilla war.

KITCHENER, AT LONG LAST, saw light at the end of the tunnel. The war should be over by April, he forecast to Brodrick on 13 December. It would be winter then; the grass would be dead. Now that the blockhouse system was working well, and the guerrillas were almost completely dependent on grass to feed their ponies (the hay had vanished in smoke), winter must surely freeze them to immobility. For once, his forecast was almost correct, though there were to be reasons other than blockhouses and no grass that would bring the Boers to their knees. The turning-point of the guerrilla war had begun in late November. It followed a period of intense frustration.

It was soon after Kitchener read the news of Buller's downfall. Not that this event depressed him; however, the Press campaign against Buller had whetted its appetite. In early November, Kitchener learnt that an article had appeared denouncing him for incompetence, and calling for his removal.

These attacks in the *Spectator*, confirmed K's fears that the government had lost patience with him. He had more or less invited this fate. Ever since the collapse of the Middelburg peace talks, he had been conducting the war under protest.

There was ill-concealed resentment in every line of his reports to Brodrick in mid-October. The Cabinet's overriding priority was to cut the cost of the war by cutting the number of troops in South Africa. Kitchener wanted *more* troops. On 1 November, he sent an SOS: '... It would be admirable to send any troops you can spare.' A few days later, he cabled Roberts secretly about: '... the strong rumours ... that I am to be relieved of my command. ...

Perhaps a new commander might be able to . . . hasten the end of the war.'

Roberts's swift reassurance was followed by a list of promised reinforcements, but it soon emerged that most of them had to be exchanged for troops already in South Africa. Nor was Kitchener so foolish as to doubt that the Cabinet was considering whether to sack him.

The final blow to his self-confidence was the 'smash-up' on 30 October of Lieutenant-Colonel G.E. Benson and his column at Bakenlaagte, in the Eastern Transvaal. He had found this news much more disheartening than the recent disasters. Benson was virtually his best commander, his column led by the best Intelligence Officer.

Fortunately, this spasm of near-despair had passed by the time Ian Hamilton, to his delight, arrived in Pretoria as his Chief of Staff. By then, the facts about Benson's death at Bakenlaagte were clearer, and they were not, after all, so discouraging to the British, nor so cheering to the Boers. The rearguard had fought heroically, losing 66 men killed and 165 wounded,

British irregulars camped on the veld. To win, they had to out-Boer the Boers.

sacrificing themselves to save the main column. On their part, the Boers, led by Botha himself, had suffered a heavy loss in the death of Opperman.

The grand strategy to which Kitchener had now reluctantly applied himself was, in effect, Milner's: to establish 'protected areas', centred on Bloemfontein, Pretoria, and the Rand, then progressively work outwards, clearing the country of all guerrillas and restoring civilian life within it.

This new policy was Milner's, the weapons Kitchener's: lines of barbed-wire fence, guarded at intervals by earth-and-iron blockhouses. By May 1902, there would be over eight thousand blockhouses covering 3,700 miles, guarded by at least fifty thousand white troops and sixteen thousand African scouts. Already, by the end of October 1901, the system had dramatically improved the strategic map of the war. The 'bag' had increased, averaging two thousand a month since March. Natal was clear. In Cape Colony, the two thousand-odd guerrillas had been hustled into the two least important areas. In the Transvaal and the Orange River Colony, the guerrillas were fragmented and powerless. Most of the central parts of both new colonies were clear.

There were three main centres of resistance: the north-east corner of the ORC, where Steyn and De Wet had gathered 2,000–2,500 men; the semi-deserts of the western Transvaal, where De la Rey had 2,200 men; and the plains of the Eastern Transvaal, to which Botha had returned after his abortive raid on Natal.

Obviously, it was to crush these leaders and their men that Kitchener attached the highest priority. In November, the cleared areas were more than doubled. Beyond this cordon, the hunted Boers would have only three choices: to try to break through the blockhouse lines, to break back through the mounted infantry pursuing them, or to give up the hopeless struggle and voluntarily add themselves to the 'bag'.

Frustration, the keynote of most wars, took a thousand forms: from Kitchener's inability to give the *coup de grâce* to the guerrillas, to the excruciating boredom of life in the blockhouse. Among the scattered mounted columns, the isolation intensified the sense of bitterness against an enemy who would not fight, or broke the rules when he did.

In December came good news, however. The second and third weeks of the month brought a 'bag' totalling 756 Boers, some 300 of these falling to Rawlinson and his new Intelligence Officer, Woolls-Sampson. Woolls-Sampson had proved himself the finest of all the Intelligence Officers, and the columns' successes depended almost wholly on such officers. In turn, an Intelligence Officer's success depended upon how well he organized and ran his black scouts, guides and spies. Botha's commandos in the Eastern Transvaal were so crippled by these raids that Kitchener decided to transfer Rawlinson and Woolls-Sampson to a still more important sector: the north-east corner of the Orange River Colony, where Steyn and De Wet had baffled their pursuers for months.

The blockhouse system, De Wet claimed, did not worry him. He called it the

Below Lord K and the 'Brat', his ADC, Captain Maxwell. 'K. made a vile fuss about my appearance,' Maxwell wrote about this photograph.

'*blockhead*' system, and reckoned it had prolonged the war by three months.

It was the Khakis' excellent African Intelligence and their new raiding tactic, the dawn tiger-spring on the laager, that alarmed him. His reply was to borrow the tactic for his own purposes. He needed what guerrillas traditionally needed: fresh horses, food, and clothing. The network of ox-wagon convoys and protecting columns supporting the blockhouses seemed to provide a heaven-sent opportunity.

On 28 November, he called a *krijgsraad* near Reitz for his commando leaders. They decided to launch a concentrated attack, De Wet's first serious attempt to take the offensive since early in 1901. The strength of his own main force numbered seven hundred. Pitted against him were at least twenty thousand men, including his brother, Piet, now fighting for the British as one of General Andries Cronje's National Scouts. But the columns were scattered all over the north-eastern Free State. De Wet waited, watching for his chance.

He found it near Bethlehem, grimly apposite, on Christmas Day.

Clearly, the most vulnerable point of an incomplete blockhouse line was the head, the unsupported end on which the engineers were still working. Just before Christmas, General Rundle had half completed the eastern half of the great line, 160 miles long, being pushed from Harrismith to join the line from Kroonstad. The blockhouse head on the eastern side had reached Tweefontein, a farm about twenty-five miles east of Bethlehem. Rundle had been allocated a weak covering force, mixed in quality as well as type. He had further weakened it by dividing it into four groups: the main force (four hundred yeomanry and two guns, commanded by Major Williams) at Groenkop, a two hundred-foot knob of a hill commanding the convoy road from the south; the other three all at points some distance away.

It was the supplies in the yeomanry camp at Groenkop that drew De Wet's hungry and thirsty burghers. It should have been a natural strong-point, for the craggy west face of the hill seemed insurmountable, but in fact a gully led up to the summit. The British had failed to station pickets below this face. At 2.00 a.m. on Christmas morning, De Wet sprang.

He described what followed: 'When we had gone up about half-way we heard the challenge of a sentry. . . . My command rang out through the night – "Burghers, storm." The word was taken up by the burghers. . . . Amidst the bullets . . . whistling above and around us, the burghers advanced to the top calling out, "Storm, Storm".'

The British rushed from their tents, to find the Boers already upon them. The result was little short of a massacre. Many soldiers were shot down where they lay or as they rushed to arms, many more were made prisoner. Sixty-nine years later, Trooper Bowers, who somehow survived unscathed, recalled the moment of his capture: 'Somebody had ripped off my bandolier of cartridges and snatched my rifle out of my hand. . . . [The Boers] said get in that tent . . . and don't move. . . . And presently a black-bearded chap with a *sjambok* in his hand . . . put his head in the tent and said, "Don't move or we'll shoot you!" And when he'd gone, the sentry said "Don't you know who that was? . . . That was General Christiaan De Wet".'

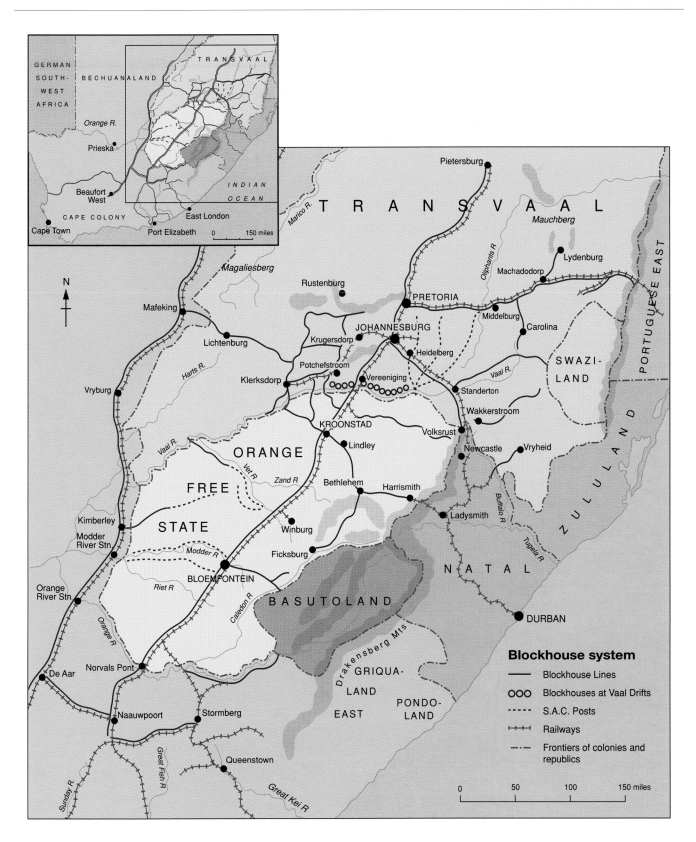

Blockhouse system

——	Blockhouse Lines
OOO	Blockhouses at Vaal Drifts
----	S.A.C. Posts
+++	Railways
-·-·-	Frontiers of colonies and republics

Flogging an African at the wagon wheel, an everyday sight in both the British and Boer camps.

By daylight, the camp was a terrible sight. The Boers had once again used expanding bullets. Bowers, who helped carry the wounded to a makeshift hospital, was soon caked in blood from head to foot. The British prisoners were struck by the incongruous dress of De Wet's men: they were so short of clothes that many were wearing the poke bonnets and black dresses of the Boer *vrouw*. Bowers himself was sent back naked to Rundle's camp.

The Tweefontein disaster depressed Kitchener, who feared it might give the Boers new heart. Then it became clear that De Wet's coup had only marginally impeded British progress. The January bag of 1,386 seemed conclusive evidence: below the December average, yet still reasonable.

Tweefontein only increased Kitchener's desire to put his steam-roller strategy into practice, as soon as the blockhouse lines were completed. By 5 February, he was ready. The FID reported De Wet and Steyn to be based at Elandskop, near Reitz, a commanding hill to the east of the centre of an open rectangle roughly fifty miles square: the west side formed by the Kroonstad-Wolvehoek line of railway and blockhouses; the south side, by the Kroonstad-Lindley-Bethlehem blockhouse line; the north side, by the Wolvehoek-Heilbron-Frankfort blockhouse line. It was from the open side – from east to west – that the columns would advance, squeezing the enemy against the blockhouse lines. Kitchener had welded together his best MI columns under four top commanders: Rawlinson, Lieutenant-Colonel Julian Byng, Rimington, and Major-General E. L. Elliot. Although all mounted, none of their extra-mobile units was cavalry, and many were colonial irregulars. They were the élite of the army.

On the night of 5 February, these four super-columns, about nine thousand strong, lined out across the fifty-four miles of the open end of the rectangle. Meanwhile, other columns, backed up by armoured trains, were sent to reinforce the blockhouses on the three other sides. At dawn on the 6th, the commanders received Kitchener's orders to march west.

To Kitchener, the next two days passed in ill-suppressed frustration, for his columns were virtually incommunicado. He left Pretoria on the 7th to see for himself the climax of his drive. The results he pronounced 'considerable', if 'disappointing'. By dawn on 8 February, only 285 out of 2,500-odd Boers had been accounted for, though cattle were captured in huge numbers. For the first time, a great many exhausted saddle-horses were also brought in, proof of the extent to which the Boers had been hustled. But the blockhouse lines had not held firm. And Steyn and De Wet, whose capture now transcended all other objectives, for Kitchener believed it might end the war at a stroke, still eluded him. De Wet had sensed where the net was weakest: along the Kroonstad–Lindley blockhouse line. With an ordinary pair of wire-clippers, he and Steyn broke the line at 1.00 a.m. on the 7th and trotted out of the trap, losing only three men out of seven hundred.

Kitchener grimly thrust the steam-roller into reverse. A few days spent strengthening the south-west corner, then back eastwards towards the starting-point, and beyond it, up to the Drakensberg. Kitchener, meanwhile, set off for Cape Colony to hustle French.

Chanting Africans repairing railway lines at Chieveley, Natal. Both sides depended on African muscles for much of the heavy work in the war.

Was the blockhouse system in fact a 'blockhead system', as De Wet claimed? The answer is uncertain, even today. Certainly the new arrangements still left much to be desired. On the other hand, it was a great improvement on the aimless sweep-and-scour policy; even K of Chaos had had to accept the discipline of a co-ordinated plan of attack. There were other inbuilt advantages: the grid-mesh of blockhouses served as lines of communication and of supply, increasing the columns' mobility and intelligence.

Yet the system was not in itself a short-cut to the war's end. There were two other innovations, both forced upon Kitchener by circumstances, and perhaps even more decisive as moral weapons.

The first was the large-scale use of native troops. In all the myths that have accumulated around the war, none has been as misleading as the idea that it was, as both sides claimed, exclusively a 'white man's war'. From the beginning, Africans had played a central role as non-combatants serving both armies. At a conservative estimate, there were forty thousand labourers on each side. At any rate, there were never enough to serve either army willingly; many were forced labourers. Behind every white man with a rifle was a black man, digging trenches, driving wagons, guarding cattle; ubiquitous and docile as the cattle themselves – and (to most white men) as invisible.

Black fingers on the trigger. Both British and Boers armed their African supporters, though publicly denying it.

When an African had a gun in his hand, however, he became suddenly very visible indeed. And Kitchener, despite his protestations to the contrary, *did* arm the Africans. The total to which he finally confessed in answer to questions in Parliament came to over ten thousand, of which a good proportion served on the blockhouse lines. Kitchener claimed that these men were only armed for their own defence, but intelligence reports give the reality. They were the key to the blockhouse line; they took an offensive role; and in certain areas they certainly accounted for more of the bag (occasionally, and inadvertently, of British soldiers) than white troops.

Not included in Kitchener's totals were the Africans who were a large minority in every mobile column. No doubt the proportion varied, but the total number serving with Kitchener's ninety-odd columns must have been enormous: twenty thousand, perhaps. African scouts were the main source of each column's intelligence, and it was Kitchener's policy to arm them. In the Transvaal, this did more than protect the scouts. It struck terror into the Boers.

In Kitchener's second innovation, political and military interests coincided better. At the end of 1901, he reversed his concentration camp policy. No doubt the continued 'hullabaloo' at the death-rate helped change his mind. By mid-December, at any rate, he was instructing column commanders *not* to bring in women and children, but to leave them with the guerrillas.

As a gesture to the Liberals, it was a shrewd political move. It also made excellent military sense, as it greatly handicapped the guerrillas, now that the drives were in full swing. Indeed, this was perhaps the most effective of all the anti-guerrilla weapons, precisely because, contrary to the Liberals' convictions, it was less humane than the camps, though this was of no great concern to Kitchener.

Opposite above A pair of steam traction engines bringing up supplies for the British army. Like their commanders, they often got bogged down in the veld.

Opposite below Away from the railway, British columns still depended on ox wagons to bring up heavy supplies.

A week after the four super-columns had made their first drive westwards, they began to roll back in the opposite direction; Kitchener had, he hoped, corrected the obvious weaknesses. But the drive of 16–28 February also failed in its principal object: once again De Wet sidled out of the trap. His men were harried and abandoned most of their cattle, their mobile food supply. Otherwise, the bag seemed even thinner than usual. With one exception, every organized commando made good its escape. Then, on 27 February (Majuba Day), one column achieved the greatest single coup, in number of prisoners taken, since Hunter's capture of Prinsloo. Rawlinson had surrounded a laager at Lang Riet, only a few miles from Tweefontein. The commando, Meyer's, was physically intact, but demoralized by the drive. It surrendered on condition that the burghers could keep their personal property. The total bag for the drive came to 25,000 cattle, 2,000 horses, 200 wagons and 778 prisoners. It was sweet revenge after Tweefontein.

Kitchener's thunderous third drive, westwards for the second time, on 4–11 March, was a thunderous flop. The bag was a mere hundred. De Wet and Steyn flew to safety once again. Worse, they broke clean out of the Orange River Colony (across no less than three blockhouse lines) and by mid-March had touched hands with De la Rey in the Western Transvaal.

By then Kitchener's eyes, too, were turned to that wild and inhospitable region. There was little in the way of a blockhouse system there; water was too short. Instead, Kitchener had given 'extra-mobile' columns to nine separate column commanders, the most important of whom was Methuen. Their job was to hunt down De la Rey in his lair between the Mafeking railway and the Magaliesberg.

After two months of desultory manoeuvring, the hunters at last made contact. For the British the results were utterly disastrous. On 24 February, at Yzer Spruit, De la Rey swooped on a convoy, captured its 150 wagons, and killed, wounded, or took prisoner 12 officers and 369 men, at a loss to his own force of 51. Emboldened, he then attacked Methuen himself, and crushed his force at Tweebosch on 7 March in circumstances that could hardly have been more humiliating. Most of the soldiers were freshly recruited irregulars. They panicked and fled. Methuen, wounded in the thigh (again), was forced to surrender, the only British general to be captured by the Boers since Symons.

News of Tweebosch was telegraphed to Kitchener next day, and knocked him flat. A column of twelve hundred men virtually wiped out, and six 15-pounders captured: it was the biggest disaster for two years. His elastic morale, frayed by months of alternating hope and disappointment, finally snapped. He shut himself in his bedroom and refused to see anyone or eat anything for two days.

However, it turned out that the Boers, as usual, were unable to turn a tactical victory to any strategic account. De la Rey was driven back onto the defensive. A fortnight later, Kitchener heard that a Boer delegation, led by Schalk Burger, were on their way to Pretoria to talk about ending the war.

CHAPTER TWENTY-NINE

Peace 'Betrayed'

Pretoria, 11 April – June 1902

> Not by lust of praise or show,
>   Not by Peace herself betrayed –
> Peace herself must they forgo
>   Till that peace be fitly made . . .
>
> Rudyard Kipling, 'The Pro-Consuls'

MILNER WAITED, heart in mouth. Was this the clear-cut military victory that he had yearned for ever since 1897, that would give him a free hand to 'break the mould' and recast South Africa? In other words, had the Boers come to discuss surrender? Or to bargain about peace?

The idea of peace, on political terms negotiated between governments, filled Milner with a kind of disgust. Peace terms meant compromise, anathema to his plans. Yet now, if this was the beginning of peace negotiations, everything depended on him. He must save British South Africa from a disastrous peace. Above all, he must stop Kitchener from throwing away their own trump card – that *they* had no need to end the war.

The Boers had indeed come to bargain for peace, and Milner was not invited to the first meeting. Even Kitchener had to admit that the Boer proposals were somewhat unreal: a plan for a 'perpetual treaty of friendship and peace' which would settle all the points of difference between the governments, including the franchise. The proposal explicitly stated, however, that the Boers did not recognize the annexation of the republics. The offer was, of course, rejected out of hand.

It was not until 14 April that Milner, now permitted to negotiate jointly alongside Kitchener, first met his adversaries. He found the proceedings 'farcical'. Kitchener, to his disgust, was 'extremely adroit in his management of the negotiations, but he does not care what he gives away'. Milner cabled his protests to Chamberlain: they must at all costs try to nail down the Boers – and Kitchener – to the terms of the abortive Middelburg peace conference. Above all, they must not go beyond the Middelburg terms regarding the length of time the ex-republics would be governed directly as Crown Colonies; they must avoid fixing a date for the restoration of self-government.

Two days later, Milner and Kitchener received the Cabinet's instructions. The cable was almost exactly what Milner had asked for: Middelburg was to be the guiding principle of the conference, and only on the subject of amnesty was there to be any substantial concession. This news was given to the Boers on 17 April. They asked for a general armistice and a safe conduct for their deputies in Europe. Kitchener refused both requests, but agreed to a sort of local armistice so that they could consult their own followers. (The Boer negotiatiors had no right to discuss surrender without first consulting the burghers still out on commando.) Then the meeting broke up, without commitment on either side. The Boers rode back into the veld.

For Milner, the supreme irony was that the blundering British army had at last found out how to beat the Boers – and win the great game for South Africa. Yet here was Kitchener, 'dead set on chucking it away', conceding an armistice 'in substance if not in name'.

The Boers still under arms had their own conflicting answers to Milner's claim that Britain held the trump card. But despite Methuen's disaster at Tweebosch, the civilian side of the see-saw had come down with a bump on the side of the British. Reconstruction was becoming a fact. Milner's own élite corps – his 'crèche' or 'Kindergarten' – had already got their noses to the grindstone. Patrick Duncan, Geoffrey Robinson, John Buchan: these were South Africa's new guardians, intellectual blues recruited by Milner from 'Headquarters'.

True, at present, their hands were full enough with the task of clearing up the mess left by Kitchener. Buchan, Milner's personal assistant since November, struggled to *de*concentrate the camps, though transport was still critically short. Schools were set up in the camps themselves; and under proper civilian management the tide of deaths subsided as rapidly as it had risen. The statistics for the twin annual death-rates, white and black, in both colonies combined, astonished everyone: from the appalling peak of 34 per cent for whites and 20 per cent for Africans in October 1901, to 3 per cent and 6 per cent, respectively, the following April.

Milner's achievements in other fields – especially in making the gold mines hum – were less dramatic. On the credit side, he claimed to have abolished the corrupt administrative practices long denounced by mine owners. As for black labour, new 'pass laws', better enforced, had tightened up things. And Milner's new Native Commissioner argued unblushingly the case for cutting African wages. Of course, there was nothing unusual about this; the view that the Kaffir was underworked and overpaid had long been held throughout white South Africa. Hence Milner's reassuring hints that Downing Street was sound enough on the native question: a message later confirmed at the peace talks. For the moment, however, competition from the army had pushed up African wages alarmingly.

Demand still far outstripped supply. Before the war, mine owners had recruited 80 per cent of their labour from outside. Now the first train-loads from Mozambique had begun to arrive. By November 1901, the black labour force on the Rand had already reached sixteen thousand. At the same time, white miners had flooded back from Natal and the Cape; by April 1902, thirty-nine thousand Uitlanders had returned. The return of the work-force explained the encouraging gold output figures, the counterpart of Kitchener's 'bag': from 150 mine stamps working in May 1901 (there were 6,000 before the war), producing 7,400 ounces of gold (the pre-war monthly peak was 300,000 ounces), to 2,095 mine stamps and 120,000 ounces of gold in April 1902.

Everything depended on the Rand, the rock on which Milner would build the new British South Africa. These gold figures were thus the measure of his achievement in putting the Transvaal back on to its feet. By April, production had still only reached a third of its pre-war level, but with only a third of the mines back in production, the two new colonies were still actually self-sufficient. Only get Kitchener off the country's back, restore the railways to civilian use, and introduce a flood of (low-paid) African labour, and this new 'estate' would be magnificent indeed.

Meanwhile, the news from the veld was at least enough to wipe out the humiliation of Tweebosch – perhaps even to tip the balance towards peace.

On 11 April (the day that the Boer delegation had reached Pretoria) Ian Hamilton's columns had dealt a stinging blow to De la Rey's commandos at Rooiwal, two hundred miles to the west. At long last Hamilton had forced the enemy to stand and fight. And a fight it was: a real 'soldiers' battle' – a final, reassuring echo from the nineteenth century.

The problem for the British in the western Transvaal, apart from the terrain, had always been how to track down De la Rey's large and well-supplied commando. And De la Rey had perfected the tactic that best ensured the guerrillas' survival: to remain hidden until it was the moment to strike. The attacks at Yzer Spruit and Tweebosch had proved that he led the largest and fittest concentration of Boer commandos left in the war; out of the twenty thousand 'bitter-enders', about three thousand were his. Of course, Kitchener still had overwhelming superiority in men and guns. But De la Rey's men were veterans; many of the British were half-trained yeomanry, like Methuen's men.

To crush De la Rey, Kitchener had predictably decided to let loose his ponderous steam-roller again. He ordered up Rawlinson, with Woolls-Sampson as Intelligence Officer. Klerksdorp, the western railhead on the Vaal, became the base of operations; on it converged sixteen thousand mounted troops – thirteen columns arranged in four super-columns commanded by Rawlinson, Kekewich, Colonel A. N. Rochfort, and Walter Kitchener. The steam-roller lumbered off for the first drive on 23 March. The result, like the last drive in the ORC, was disappointing: only 8 Boers killed and 165 captured. Worse, De la Rey slipped through the net, after mauling part of Walter Kitchener's force at Boschbult on 31 March, which cost the British 178 men killed and wounded.

To succeed, the steam-roller demanded, above all, that someone should be on the spot to co-ordinate the super-columns. Kitchener's dislike of delegating anything to subordinates had blinded him to this defect, although it had already begun to show in the mixed success of the system in the ORC. Now it was embarrassingly obvious in this inhospitable region, where the net had to be cast so wide. The crisis prompted the generals to ask K to appoint Ian Hamilton as overlord. It was thus that Hamilton became overall commander of all thirteen columns. He raced down to Klerksdorp on the afternoon of 6 April, and set the steam-roller in motion again.

The new plan was not particularly subtle, though competent. Hamilton now planned to march three of the four super-columns for two days south-westwards from the blockhouse line. Then they would swing south at the point where two small rivers, the Brakspruit and the Little Hart's River, flowed into the main western tributary of the Vaal, the Great Hart's River. It was this relatively fertile valley at the centre of the 'box' formed by the western blockhouse lines that had proved De la Rey's main lair and hunting-ground. Here were Boschbult and Tweebosch; Hamilton assumed that the Boers were still somewhere beyond the valley, and would themselves break away to the south. In fact, he had arranged for the columns to double back, instead of squeezing the Boers against the Klerksdorp blockhouse line.

The steam-roller lumbered off on 10 April. The advantage of having someone in overall charge was immediately apparent. A signal to Kekewich to push on to a farm called Rooiwal miscarried, and he halted his column. Hamilton, since he was nearby, was able to order Kekewich to resume his march. By dusk, the British lines extended for twenty miles, from close to the Great Hart's River to east of Boschbult.

By virtue of being on the spot, Hamilton had been able to prevent a serious blunder; indeed, unknown to anyone, he had achieved a great deal more. The confusion of Kekewich's move westwards, late on the evening of the 10th, served to mislead the enemy better than any ruse. Early next morning, Kekewich concentrated three thousand men at Rooiwal to prepare for the drive. So the western part of the British line, which had been the weakest when reconnoitred by the enemy, was now the strongest.

About 7.15 a.m. next morning, an advanced screen of MI witnessed one of the eeriest sights of the war. A great wave of slouch-hatted horsemen swept knee-to-knee towards them, opened fire from the saddle and, still firing, cantered up the hillside. Then the wave broke over the MI, killing and wounding half the small party.

But the Boers had overreached themselves. To succeed, their revolutionary new version of the cavalry charge not only demanded courage, good luck and bad weather; the terrain too, must favour them. Here there was no cover. By contrast, the stony hillside of Rooiwal, half a mile to the north, hid Kekewich's two columns like a curtain. Led by Kemp and Potgieter, the horsemen galloped on towards destruction.

When they were about a mile and a half from Rooiwal, they breasted a rise and saw the overwhelming odds: their own force numbered seventeen hundred in all, without field-guns; opposite them, in close order, were Kekewich's three thousand dismounted MI, with six guns and two pom-poms. Yet Kemp and Potgieter, in their desire to outdo De la Rey, threw his tactics to the wind. They cantered on in mass, two, three, and four deep, gambling everything on the chance that the British would turn and run.

Below Commandant Potgieter sprawled in the grass thirty yards from the British line, after the Battle of Rooiwal on 11 April 1902. He and 50 of his men died gallantly charging the British line on horseback.

If fortune always favoured the brave, Kemp and Potgieter would have won the most spectacular victory of the war. As it was, they were assisted by the dismal shooting of the MI. Some of the raw yeomen turned and fled. But no Boers followed. Potgieter lay sprawled thirty yards from the British line. Beside him lay fifty other dead Boers, and those too seriously wounded for their comrades to carry back on their horses.

The Boer charge had failed, and now it was Hamilton's turn. If ever there was a chance to display those dashing qualities which Roberts and Kitchener so admired in him, it was surely now. There were twelve thousand troops within twenty miles, more than half of them within seven miles. But it was an hour and a half before Hamilton, fearful of a counter-attack on Kekewich's transport, let loose any of his troops. The enemy went to ground, and all that his men captured after a fourteen-mile gallop were fifty stragglers and two of Methuen's guns. Kekewich thought bitterly of his MI's bad shooting. With one good company of infantry, he could have killed three hundred of Potgieter's line.

So ended the last formal battle of the war. Hamilton led the columns backwards and forwards for a further four weeks, flattening De la Rey's old hunting-ground. His opposite number, Bruce Hamilton, played a similar game with Botha in the Eastern Transvaal. Neither caught much.

But all eyes were now turning to Pretoria, where, on 19 May, the peace talks resumed. The 'interminable' war was fizzling out at last, it appeared. A new battle, not only between Briton and Boer, but between Kitchener and Milner, was to be fought out over the peace terms.

Boer delegates from the commandos relaxing at Vereeniging – like men who have won a moral victory.

The clash of personality and principle between the two proconsuls had now reached a climax.

Milner of course did not admit to Kitchener, any more than to the Boers, that he hoped to see the peace talks fail. But there was something in his sarcastic manner that alerted Kitchener and his staff – especially Ian Hamilton – to the danger. When the Pretoria talks began, Hamilton found his insights dramatically confirmed. Now he saw why the Bloemfontein conference had failed three years before – because of Milner. The inevitable result had been 'this bloody war'. Rawlinson was equally hostile to Milner's policy. No doubt both men's views reflected, to a great extent, their Chief's. At the same time, a subtle change had recently come over Kitchener and his staff in their attitude to the Boers. It is this that accounts for the deep gulf between their views of the peace talks, and Milner's.

It was only a few months since Rawlinson had recommended executing such 'cold blooded ruffians' out of hand. Kitchener himself had, without compunction, executed Cape rebels like Scheepers and Lotter as war criminals. His executions now totalled fifty-one. Yet now a sense of solidarity immediately sprang up between the soldiers on either side. Hamilton found the Boer leaders the 'best men in South Africa', and was in ecstasies when they invited him to a birthday party for Smuts on 24 May.

The 'best men in South Africa' was a sneer at the loyalists – especially the non-British variety. Hamilton had not only grasped that Milner was trying to block the peace talks. He realized why: Milner wished to 'destroy the Boers as a political force and tip the balance in favour of the loyalists'. And he agreed with Churchill that the Boers, not the loyalists, must be 'the rock' on which the British position was founded.

Meanwhile, Milner had managed to block the first dangerous offers of peace.

By 15 May, sixty national delegates, elected by the commandos, had safely reached Vereeniging, fifty miles south of Pretoria. These duly chose the negotiating team: Botha, De la Rey and Smuts for the Transvaal; Hertzog and De Wet for the Free State. The team had still not been given plenary powers, so the peace terms, if agreed, had to be ratified by the delegates at Vereeniging; equally, they had to be ratified by the British Cabinet in London. Negotiations resumed at noon on 19 May.

The new peace offer seemed to Milner as farcical as the old. The Boers proposed a protectorate, offering to surrender independence in foreign relations, preserve internal self-government under British supervision, and hand over part of the Rand and Swaziland. In effect, this meant that part of the two countries would be a Crown Colony, part a protectorate. Kitchener agreed that the proposals were unworkable, even in military terms. After several hours' manoeuvring, the Boers suggested that Smuts had an informal talk with Kitchener and Milner. This gave Milner the chance to restore the talks to the Middelburg line. The three men worked out the draft of a preamble to the surrender terms, in which the Boer leaders were recognized to be 'acting as' the governments of 'the South African Republic', and 'the Orange Free State' (both officially abolished by the British nearly two years earlier). In return, they were to agree that the burghers would recognize King Edward VII 'as their lawful sovereign'. It was then proposed that a sub-committee would begin to draw up the details of the agreement to add to this preamble.

At this point, De Wet exploded. He and Steyn had long been recognized as the main obstacles to a peace conference (and thus Milner's principal remaining hope of a breakdown). Steyn was now too ill to come to Pretoria, but clearly De Wet spoke for him, saying that 'Whatever conditions may be added . . . I cannot get over the difficulty of the preamble.' Milner replied that it was therefore clear that they could go no further.

But Kitchener and Smuts were equally intent on keeping the talks going, both offering to draft a document for De Wet to see before he expressed an opinion. The draft agreement was duly put to the full committee and, with one long addendum, the text was cabled to London.

There were only three significant changes – all to the benefit of the Boers. First, the amnesty: all Cape rebels, except leaders, would be exempted from imprisonment, and let off with permanent disfranchisement. (Natal rebels, however, would have to take their chance under the ordinary law.)

Second, native rights in the two new colonies. At Middelburg, it had been proposed to exclude the grant of the franchise to 'Kaffirs' (there was no mention of Indians or Coloureds) '*before*' representative government was granted. Now it was proposed to exclude the consideration of the question of granting the vote to 'natives . . . *until after*' its introduction. This subtle change meant, in effect, that Milner was proposing that they should make the exclusion permanent. Once given self-government, no Boer state would give the vote to Africans. So much for Chamberlain's determination not 'to purchase a shameful peace'.

Third, financial help for the shattered ex-republics. According to the Middelburg terms, Britain was to pay her enemies' pre-war debts up to £1 million. The new Clause 11 and its addendum increased this figure to £3 million, and the new Clause 12 offered generous loans to burghers, in addition to assisting loyalists.

The growing chance of agreement naturally increased Milner's sense of frustration. He had sent a last 'over-my-dead-body' cable to Chamberlain on the 21st, but recognized that he could not hope for much from that quarter, given 'public feeling' in Britain, and abroad. Chamberlain had made it clear in January that the Middelburg terms still lay on the table. Milner's hopes of fighting to the bitter end all depended on Steyn and De Wet.

The proposed peace terms astonished the Colonial Office officials when they received the text on 22 May. It did not strike them as 'preposterous' (Milner's word) at all; indeed, it seemed practically the same as the Middelburg terms, although there was some worry about the 'native franchise' point, and about the financial help.

Chamberlain had received private cables from Milner denouncing the new terms, especially the 'detestable' Clause 11. He cabled back, acidly, 'There should be some argument more cogent than the money cost to justify risking failure on this point. Can you supply it, and would you go so far as to wreck agreement at this stage upon this question.'

The Cabinet discussed the new terms on the 23rd, and were pleased with them; they were an 'improvement' on Middelburg. Chamberlain raised two main objections. What about Clause 9 and native political rights? Why not strike out the crucial word 'after'? Otherwise, the natives would be permanently disfranchised.

Back came Milner's reply: 'That was the object of the clause. Clause suggested by you would defeat that object. It would be better to leave out clause altogether than propose such a change. While averse in principle to all pledges, there is much to be said for leaving question of political rights of natives to be settled by colonists themselves.' Chamberlain, and the Cabinet, gave way. The crucial 'after' remained, mocking Chamberlain's claim that one of Britain's war aims was to improve the status of Africans.

On Clause 11 and its addendum the Cabinet compromised with Milner. The clause was amalgamated with Clause 12 (loans to cover war losses), and so avoided the objection that the £3 million would be paid as a gift. Otherwise, Milner failed to change the terms, and Salisbury's Cabinet left them much as they had found them. On 27 May, the text was cabled back to South Africa, to be put at once before the Boer delegates at Vereeniging. One slim chance of blocking agreement had been gained by Milner. The Cabinet had agreed to allow the Boers only time for a simple 'yes' or 'no'.

Should they fight on to the bitter end? The Boers had debated that question repeatedly, ever since Roberts's peace offer of June 1900. There was not a single leader who had set his face unequivocally against coming to terms with the British. Even the most tenacious champion of independence, Steyn and De Wet, had now agreed that the volk must swallow their pride, and accept terms far more humiliating than those rejected by Kruger at Bloemfontein. But Milner and Kitchener had rejected those terms – the protectorate plan – on 19 May. Peace was to cost still more, nothing short of annexation. Could they say 'yes' to this?

What if they said 'no'? The military answers were given in detail at Vereeniging, and broadly confirmed Kitchener's and Milner's claims. Despite all his set-backs, Kitchener had claimed he was on the verge of victory, and he was right – in the Transvaal at any rate.

When the sixty delegates had first gathered in the great marquee at Vereeniging on 15 May, there were recognised to be three main military obstacles to continuing guerrilla war: shortages of horses, shortages of food, and the miserable condition of those of the women and children who had remained with the commandos in the veld. The Transvaal delegates confirmed Kitchener's claims that the burghers were at the end of their tether. One-third of the men had no horses. Food was critically short. Some fourteen Transvaal districts would have to be abandoned, allowing the enemy to concentrate against the rest.

Above all, it was the sufferings of their women and children on commando that had demoralized the Transvaal burghers – not those in the concentration camps. Indeed, under Kitchener's latest policy, dependants were refused admittance to the camps. And their plight was now exacerbated by another ominous new development; the African menace, real or imaginary.

One of the most striking features of the war had been the meekness of the African majority. This was all the more surprising given the way they had been treated by the Boers, who had looted their cattle, flogged and murdered those who helped the British, and even massacred the whole civilian population of one Transvaal village, Modderfontein.

However, it was now apparent that the natives were stirring. At Zoutpansberg, in the north, they were 'getting out of hand'. Much the same was said at Bethel and Carolina. And, in May, a most alarming episode occurred at Holkrantz, near Vryheid, when a Zulu tribe attacked a Boer laager in reprisal for the theft of their cattle, killing fifty-six burghers and wounding three. So far, Boer women and children in the district had not been molested, but the Zulus had been restrained with difficulty.

Thus the Transvaal was now threatened from two sides: the natives were stirring, and the women and children were correspondingly vulnerable, just when their menfolk were least able to protect them. These commandos – 'bitter-einders', they called themselves – were a dwindling band, facing extinction as a military force. So Botha had summed up the situation in the Transvaal in early May; Acting President Burger, and even De la Rey, agreed. 'Fight to the bitter end?' asked the latter. 'But has the bitter end not come?'

In the Free State, no. That was De Wet's blunt answer, echoed by most of the Free State leaders. Grain was scarce, and so were horses, naturally. But morale was still reasonably good, largely because the womenfolk were either safely in concentration camps, or could fend for themselves on the veld; and the Free State Kaffirs were generally prepared to collaborate. However, the blockhouses were a 'source of constant annoyance'.

What of the third front, the 3,300-strong invasion force in the far west and north-west of Cape Colony? Smuts answered equally bluntly that nothing much could be expected from this quarter. And there would be no general Afrikaner rising. The Boer cause must stand or fall by what could be achieved in the republics.

Eloquently supported by Smuts, the Transvaal generals continued to press the case for peace, and the Free State counter-arguments began to falter. The argument, at its simplest, was that the war was ending anyway. They must now win the peace. Negotiate now, said Botha and De la Rey and Smuts, while we still have control of our destiny, and can keep the volk together as a nation. Fight on, and the volk will die. The threat was not only to the lives of individuals, but to the continued existence of the nation. And, most ominously of all, Botha added, 'There are men of our own kith and kin who are helping to bring us to ruin. If we continue the war, it may be that the Afrikaners against us will outnumber our own men.'

Botha was not exaggerating. There were already 5,464 'handsuppers' – Boers recruited to the British army as National Scouts, guides, transport drivers and so on (De Wet's own brother, Piet, led the 'handsuppers' in the Free State). It was not difficult to imagine the new politics if the volk were thus left divided. But they could retain their political supremacy, at least in the long term, by reasserting Afrikaner unity, by keeping their political majority intact for the day when, according to the terms now offered, Milner's new Crown Colonies lapsed, and white South Africans were free to govern themselves.

De Wet and his generals clutched at the counter-arguments. They were convinced that military resistance was still possible, though they could not say how. But even De Wet recognized that the Free State could not – and must not – struggle on alone.

Probably, even before these long-drawn-out and anguished debates, the outcome had been a foregone conclusion, once the meeting at Vereeniging had been arranged. What made the hard-liners finally realize that the collapse of resistance was inevitable was that all the scattered commandos had come together and exchanged information, and heard Botha himself declare the condition of the whole country 'hopeless'.

The vote was taken at Vereeniging, soon after 2.00 p.m. on Saturday 31 May. Botha and De la Rey asked De Wet and the Free State leaders to accept the resolution of the Transvaal. De Wet and most of the others agreed. The delegates voted for Kitchener's peace by an overwhelming majority: fifty-four to six. It was the bitter end. But the alliance stood firm.

The members of the two governments were rushed back by train to

Piet De Wet, brother of General Christiaan De Wet, who changed sides and led the 'handsuppers' in the Free State. By the end of the war over 5,000 'handsuppers' were fighting for the British.

Christiaan De Wet (centre right) signing the peace terms at Pretoria on 31 May 1902, encouraged by Kitchener (centre left). Once De Wet agreed to sign, it was all over.

Pretoria, to sign the death-warrants – technically 'terms of surrender' – of the republics. It was now eleven o'clock on Saturday night. They were driven to GHQ, where they were met by Kitchener and Milner, the latter looking grey and ill. Burger signed first for the Transvaal, De Wet for the Free State. Kitchener and Milner signed last. It was all over in five minutes; the republics finally dead and buried. There was an embarrassed silence, broken by Kitchener's well-meant 'We are good friends now'.

In his heart, Milner must have known he had lost the 'great game for mastery' in South Africa. To have the game thrown away by Kitchener, with victory in sight – that was hard to bear. All that he could say was that he had prevented a disastrous peace, stopping Kitchener from putting a date to the restoration of self-government. He had bought time for himself, and his crèche. They must now build up the gold industry, and thus bring new blood into the Transvaal: united, loyal, imperial-minded British settlers, drawing on loans offered by Wernher-Beit.

Peace. Apart from the Uitlanders (who shared Milner's forebodings), the hundred-odd British columns in the field took the news with the same mixture of delight and incredulity with which the army had greeted the Boer

Opposite above On 8 June 1902 massed choirs sing a Te Deum for Kitchener and 5,000 troops outside Government Buildings, Pretoria.

Opposite below Kitchener (right) and his Chief of Staff, Ian Hamilton, at the victory parade at Pretoria on 8 June 1902.

Above Fleet Street, London, celebrating the news that the war was finally over.

Below British Uitlanders returning home after two and a half years in exile.

ultimatum in 1899. Then, a few days later, the trek to the ports began: all but 20,000 of the 250,000 British troops were being sent home or disbanded.

The commandos, too, seemed glad the struggle was over. Twenty-one thousand *bitter-einders* emerged from their hiding-places (over twice as many as British Intelligence had bargained for). There were brief surrender rituals, then they trekked off to the concentration camps, to look for their families. Their discipline and morale were conspicuous. They held their heads high, like men who have won a moral victory. Their time would come. Equally conspicuous was the hang-dog look of the 'handsuppers'. Politically, they were to be outcasts – skeletons well hidden in the cupboard. The fact that a fifth of the Afrikaners in arms at the end of the war fought for the British was a secret that remained hidden for many decades.

As the British officers marched their men down to the docks, their own mythology was also being born. 'A very pleasant time for a young fellow. . . . A regular sort of picnic. . . . A gentleman's war. . . . The happiest years of my life.' The easy phrases covered the crudities of war, like the sand blowing in over the graves of their comrades. Yet this mythology did not extend far into the ranks. 'It was a cruel war, it was. . . . We were half-starved all the time. . . . I never saw the point of it. . . . It was the worst war ever. . . . Johnny Boer, he used to shoot niggers like you'd shoot a dog. . . . It was all for the gold-mines.' So the majority of the veterans whose voices I recorded, seventy years later.

But, whatever it was, and whatever it was for, it was over.

A French view of the British victory.

'Winners and Losers'

They took the hill (Whose hill? What for?)
But what a climb they left to do!
Out of that bungled, unwise war
An alp of unforgiveness grew.

William Plomer

No BRITISH WAR since 1815 had been so prodigal of money and lives. Milner's little 'Armageddon' had cost the British taxpayer more than £200 million. The cost in blood was equally high. The War Office reckoned that 400,346 horses, mules and donkeys were 'expended' in the war. There were over a hundred thousand casualties of all kinds among the 364,693 imperial and 82,742 colonial soldiers who had fought. Twenty-two thousand died: 5,774 killed by enemy action (or accident) and shovelled into the veld where they fell; 16,168 died of wounds or killed by disease (or poor medical care).

On the Boer side, the cost, measured in suffering, was relatively much higher. It was estimated that there were over 7,000 deaths among the 87,365 Boers (including 2,120 foreign volunteers and 13,300 Afrikaners from the Cape and Natal) who fought for the two republics. No one knows how many Boers died in the concentration camps. Official estimates vary between 18,000 and 28,000. The survivors returned to homesteads devastated almost beyond recognition. Several million cattle, horses and sheep, their chief capital, had been killed or looted. The imperial government received 63,000 separate claims for compensation for war losses, and paid out more than the £3 million promised at Vereeniging, though a disproportionate amount went to 'handsuppers'. In addition, Uitlanders and other loyalists received compensation totalling £2 million.

Most severe were the losses borne by the Africans. The damage to their property may not seem large: yet they filed compensation claims of £661,000 in the Transvaal. But few Africans owned much property in the ex-republics, and they were compensated at a lower rate than the Boers received. No one bothered to keep full records of the deaths among the 107,000 'black Boers' (as one of them described himself) in the Africans' concentration camps. The incomplete records give the total as 7,000, but it probably exceeded 12,000. The number of deaths among the 50,000 or so Africans on the British side is not known. The Boers openly admitted killing armed Africans when they captured them, but there is much unpublished evidence that they killed unarmed ones too.

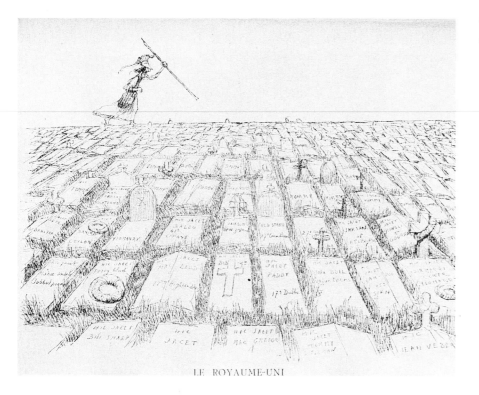

LE ROYAUME-UNI

'The United Empire.' From *L'Assiette au Beurre*, November 1901.

The fruits of victory tasted sweet and sour to the British army. The old class-conscious British army was not destroyed, as Wolseley had hoped. On the other hand, the antiquated War Office machine was given new premises, a new general staff, and a thorough overhaul. The Cabinet decided the partnership with the Commander-in-Chief was impossible and created a Chief of the Imperial General Staff instead, without warning the incumbent C-in-C, Roberts. He arrived one morning in 1904 to find that he had officially ceased to exist.

Among the younger generation of Roberts's and Kitchener's officers there were many future field-marshals, including the leaders of the BEF in the First World War, French and Haig. They had learnt something from their days in the veld, but the central tactical lesson of the Boer War eluded them. The reason for those humiliating reverses was not the marksmanship of the Boers, nor their better guns, nor the crass stupidity of the British generals – all myths which British people found it convenient to believe. It was that the smokeless-propellant, long-range, high-velocity, small-calibre bullet from magazine rifle or machine-gun, plus the trench, had decisively tilted the balance in favour of defence. The world learnt this lesson the hard way, in the bloody stalemates of the First World War.

In politics, too, the war brought results no one could have predicted. Milner's crèche started their race to rebuild the Transvaal and Free State on British lines, before the British Parliament handed them back to the volk. The careful work of reconstruction partially redeemed for many Boers the wanton destruction that had made it necessary.

But Milner's plans to anglicize the old republics rested on one crucial foundation: the need for British immigrants. The first census, taken in 1904, showed that potential Boer and potential British voters in the Transvaal roughly balanced each other. Hence Milner's desperate need for British immigration, which depended, in turn, on the expansion of the Rand. The alliance with Wernher-Beit, indispensable to the making of the war, now proved Milner's undoing. The deep-level mines, controlled by Wernher-Beit and other British magnates, were still short of African miners prepared to work underground at low wages. Milner agreed that the best expedient was to import indentured labourers from China. The British Cabinet also agreed – provided the Chinese were not liable to be flogged, as Africans were. But the white miners' hostility towards Chinese immigration was such that Milner lost the support of the mass of British Uitlanders; their political representatives formed an alliance with the emergent pan-Afrikaner party (Het Volk) of Botha and Smuts. When it became known in Britain that Chinese labourers were being flogged after all, a vote of censure was passed on Milner in the House of Commons. He resigned as Governor in 1905. His fall – and the hullabaloo over 'Chinese slavery' – helped sweep CB and the Liberals to power in 1906.

In fact, Milner's experiment in building a Greater Britain on the veld was already doomed. The blunt demographical facts undermined all his hopes. There was so little immigration that the Boers remained in the majority. In 1906, CB and the Liberals gave the two Crown Colonies self-governing status. When the votes were counted after the first general elections, Het Volk had swept the board. This set the seal on the failure of Milnerism. From now on, there would be a series of shifting alliances in South Africa. The loyalist party, led by Sir Percy Fitzpatrick (knighted, along with other Randlords or ex-Randlords, including Julius Wernher), would have no chance.

On the other hand, CB's grant of self-government transformed Smuts's and Botha's own attitude to the Empire. While Milner exchanged public service for international banking (re-emerging only in December 1916 as the man of destiny in Lloyd George's War Cabinet), Botha and Smuts travelled the world as imperial statesmen. In fact, the paradox of the war was that, despite the bitterness it created among the volk, it gave Britain during the same period an apparently contented addition to its Empire. In two world wars, South Africa stuck by its mother (and stepmother). The naval base at Simonstown, hinge of Britain's global strategy, remained under British control until 1955.

Then, in 1961, the Great Trek happened all over again. Dr Verwoerd led the volk out of the Commonwealth, taking all other South Africans, black, brown and white, with them. He declared the Union a republic fifty-nine years to the day after the Peace of Vereeniging. But the new governments were heirs to the old uncompromising republican tradition of Steyn and De Wet – tempered in the fire of war. After that the Nationalists ruled white

South Africa on their own terms, and the memory of the *Tweede Vryheidsoorlog* (the 'Second War of Independence') was kept green. It was a reminder to English-speaking South Africans that they did not belong to the volk, and must earn their place in the white laager. The war helped to weaken white opposition to the Nationalists.

Perhaps the worst legacy of the war was the political price it exacted from Africans to pay for white unity. Bringing two new states into the Empire made urgent the need to reconcile the white communities. The war made that process a great deal more difficult. It has taken ninety-odd years and is still not fully accomplished. And the price of attempting that reconciliation was paid by the blacks and browns. In fact, the result of Milner's destruction of the old republics was not only to lose the two old colonies, but to cast away that priceless Liberal legacy, the no-colour-bar tradition of the Cape.

The first payment of the price was at Vereeniging. Milner had inserted that subtle preposition 'after' into Clause 9 of the peace terms: no franchise for the natives until *after* the introduction of self-government – that is, never. And down the years, the spirit of this contempt for the black majority grew and throve. It was to this that Milner's short-cut had led South Africa.

By 1979 the wheel had turned full circle. With the Second War of Independence finally won, the volk were facing a third. The new adversary, black nationalism, could match Afrikaner nationalism in stamina, and perhaps even in bitterness. Otherwise, there were many parallels between the situation in 1979 and in 1899. 'There is only one way out of the troubles in South Africa: reform or war. And of the two war is more likely.' Milner's phrase was grimly prophetic. But, this time, no one expected the war to be over by Christmas.

Milner did not live to see the complete overthrow of all he had tried to accomplish. The Higher Powers had reserved a more ironic fate for him. With Violet (they married in 1921), he made a trip to South Africa in 1924 to revisit the scene of his labours. He was bitten by a tsetse fly, caught sleeping sickness, and died. Africa had had its revenge on him.

'The Scout on the Veldt', as forecast by
Carruthers Gould.

Important Dates
Before and During the Boer War

1652	Dutch East India Company found shipping station at Cape
1795	Dutch lose Cape to British
1803	Dutch (Batavian Republic) resume control
1806	Second British occupation begins
1815	Slachter's Nek Rebellion by Afrikaans-speaking settlers. British rule at Cape confirmed
1820	4,000 British settlers arrive at Cape
1834	Slavery abolished at Cape, following decision of British Parliament
1835–7	The Great Trek. Frontier farmers (Boers) pour across Orange River. But majority of the Afrikaans-speaking settlers (Afrikaners) remain in the Cape
1838	(16 Dec) Pretorius beats Dingaan, Zulu king, at Battle of Blood River
1838–43	Boers concentrate in Natal
1843	British annex Natal as colony
1848	Transorangia annexed as Orange River Sovereignty. Smith defeats Pretorius at Battle of Boomplaatz
1852	Sand River Convention confirms independence of Transvaal Republic
1854	Bloemfontein Convention restores independence of Transorangia as Orange Free State
1868–9	British annex Basutoland as Crown Colony at request of King Mosweshwe
1870–1	Diamond rush to Kimberley
1871	Annexation of Kimberley to Cape Colony, now self-governing. Cecil Rhodes, aged 18, joins diamond rush, followed by Alfred Beit (in 1875)
1877	Proclamation of Transvaal as British Crown Colony. Arrival of Frere
1879	British forces invade and (1887) annex Zululand, soon incorporated in Natal, now self-governing
1880–1	Kruger leads Transvaal rebellion against British rule: First Boer War (alias 'First War of Independence')
1881	Peace talks after Battle of Majuba (27 Feb). Pretoria Convention: Transvaal Republic obtains limited independence
1884	London Convention: Transvaal (South African Republic) obtains greater independence
1886	Gold rush to Witwatersrand begins
1888	Cecil Rhodes obtains British Royal Charter for his British South Africa Co. to exploit Lobengula's territory (Mashonaland and Matabeleland)
1889	Formation of Wernher, Beit & Co, soon to become the principal Rand mining house
1890	Rhodes's BSA Co. (Chartered Company) sends pioneers to occupy Lobengula's country, renamed Rhodesia

1895	(29 Dec) Dr Jameson launches Raid into Transvaal with 500 Chartered Company police from Pitsani and Mafeking
1896	Battle of Doornkop. Jameson surrenders. Arrest and trial of Johannesburg Reform Committee. Rhodes resigns as Prime Minister at the Cape. Cape Enquiry into Raid
1897	London Enquiry into Raid. Sir Alfred Milner takes over as British High Commissioner at the Cape
1898	Kruger elected for fourth term as President of Transvaal
1898–9	Milner back in London for 'holiday'

1899:

31 May –

5 Jun	Bloemfontein Conference
8 Sep	British Cabinet decides to send 10,000 men to defend Natal
26 Sep	Penn Symons pushes up troops to Dundee
27 Sep	Kruger calls up Transvaal burghers, and persuades Steyn to follow suit in Free State
7 Oct	British mobilize 1st Army Corps etc. White lands at Durban
9 Oct	Kruger sends ultimatum
11 Oct	Expiry of ultimatum and outbreak of war
14–16 Oct	Boers begin siege of Kekewich at Kimberley and of Baden-Powell at Mafeking
20 Oct	Penn Symons gives battle at Talana. Möller surrenders
21 Oct	Battle of Elandslaagte
24 Oct	Battle of Rietfontein
30 Oct	'Mournful Monday': Joubert outmanoeuvres White at Battle of Ladysmith (Modderspruit) and Carleton is forced to surrender at Nicholson's Nek
31 Oct	Buller lands at Cape Town
2 Nov	White's 'field force' accepts siege at Ladysmith
15 Nov	Botha wrecks armoured train between Frere and Chieveley
22–3 Nov	Battle of Willow Grange
23 Nov	End of Botha's and Joubert's raid southwards into Natal. Methuen's first battle: Belmont
25 Nov	Methuen's second battle: Graspan
26 Nov	Holdsworth, with Linchwe's Africans, attack Boer laager at Deerdepoort
28 Nov	Methuen's third battle: Modder River
7 Dec	Hunter's night raid on Long Tom besieging Ladysmith
10 Dec	Gatacre's mishap at Stormberg
11 Dec	Methuen's repulse at Magersfontein
15 Dec	Buller's first reverse: Colenso
18 Dec	Roberts appointed to succeed Buller as C-in-C in South Africa, with Kitchener as Chief of Staff
26 Dec	Baden-Powell's abortive attack on Game Tree Fort
29 Dec	German mail-steamer *Bundesrath* seized by Royal Navy

1900:

6 Jan	Boers attack Caesar's Camp and Wagon Hill (Platrand) at Ladysmith
10 Jan	Roberts and Kitchener land at Cape Town
24 Jan	Battle of Spion Kop
5–7 Feb	Vaal Krantz captured, then evacuated
11 Feb	Roberts begins great flank march
14–27 Feb	Buller's fourth attempt to relieve Ladysmith
15 Feb	French relieves Kimberley
18 Feb	Battle of Paardeberg
27 Feb	Surrender of Cronje at Paardeberg
28 Feb	Buller relieves Ladysmith
7 Mar	Battle of Poplar Grove. Kruger escapes
10 Mar	Battle of Driefontein
13 Mar	Capture of Bloemfontein
15 Mar	Roberts's first proclamation: amnesty except for leaders
17 Mar	Boer council of war at Kroonstad
27 Mar	Death of Joubert
31 Mar	De Wet ambushes Broadwood at Sannah's Post
4 Apr	Surrender of Royal Irish at Reddersburg
3 May	Roberts resumes march to Pretoria
4 May	Mahon's relief column sets out for Mafeking
11 May	Buller resumes advance
12 May	Roberts occupies Kroonstad, B-P beats off Eloff's attack on Mafeking
14 May	Buller outmanoeuvres Boers from Biggarsberg
17 May	Mahon and Plumer relieve Mafeking
28 May	Annexation of Orange Free State proclaimed: renamed Orange River Colony
31 May	Roberts captures Johannesburg
	Piet De Wet captures Spragge and Irish Yeomanry at Lindley
5 Jun	Roberts captures Pretoria. Release of prisoners
7 Jun	Christiaan De Wet's success at Roodewal
11–12 Jun	Battle of Diamond Hill
12 Jun	Buller turns Drakenberg position and occupies Volksrust
11 Jul	Surrender of Scots Greys at Zilikat's Nek
15 Jul	Steyn and De Wet escape from Brandwater Basin
21 Jul	Roberts begins advance towards Komati Poort
31 Jul	Surrender of Prinsloo to Hunter in Brandwater Basin
14 Aug	Ian Hamilton fails to prevent De Wet's escape
27 Aug	Buller defeats Botha at Bergendal (Dalmanutha)
30 Aug	Release of last 2,000 British prisoners at Nooitgedacht
6 Sep	Buller captures Lydenburg
25 Sep	Pole-Carew reaches Komati Poort
19 Oct	Kruger sails for France on Dutch cruiser
24 Oct	Buller sails for England
25 Oct	Formal proclamation at Pretoria of annexation of Transvaal
6 Nov	De Wet defeated at Bothaville

29 Nov	Kitchener succeeds Roberts as C-in-C in South Africa.
	Roberts to succeed Wolseley as C-in-C at home
13 Dec	De la Rey and Smuts surprise Clements at Nooitgedacht
16 Dec	Kritzinger enters Cape Colony

1901

27 Jan –	
26 Mar	French's drive in E. Transvaal
31 Jan	Smuts captures Modderfontein. Massacre of Africans
10–28 Feb	De Wet's 'invasion' of Cape Colony
28 Feb	Abortive Middelburg peace talks between Kitchener and Botha
10 Apr	First drive in N. Free State begins
8 May	Milner sails for leave in England
18 Jul	First drive in Cape Colony northwards
7 Aug	Kitchener's proclamation of banishment for Boer leaders captured armed after 15 Sep
12 Aug	Kritzinger driven out of Cape Colony
3 Sep	Smuts's invasion of Cape Colony via Kiba Drift
5 Sep	Scobell captures Lotter's commando
17 Sep	Smuts cuts up 17th Lancers at Elands River Poort; Botha cuts up Gough's force at Blood River Poort
26 Sep	Botha attacks Forts Itala and Prospect
6 Oct	Botha escapes northward
11 Oct	Execution of Commandant Lotter. Capture of Scheepers
30 Oct	Benson killed at Bakenlaagte
7 Nov	Ian Hamilton appointed Kitchener's Chief of Staff
7 Dec	National Scouts inaugurated
16 Dec	Kritzinger captured
23 Dec	Kroonstad-Lindley blockhouse line completed
25 Dec	De Wet captures Yeomanry at Tweefontein

1902:

17 Jan	Scheepers executed
6–8 Feb	New drive in E. Orange River Colony. De Wet breaks out
13–26 Feb	Second drive in E. Orange River Colony. Rawlinson's success
7 Mar	De la Rey captures Methuen at Tweebosch
24 Mar	First drive in W. Transvaal
26 Mar	Death of Cecil Rhodes
11 Apr	Battle of Rooiwal
12–18 Apr	Boer peace delegates' first meeting at Pretoria
1–10 May	Last drives in N.E. Orange River Colony
6 May	Zulu attack on Holkrantz
11 May	End of Ian Hamilton's last drive in W. Transvaal
15–18 May	First meeting of Boer delegates at Vereeniging
31 May	Final meeting at Vereeniging. Surrender terms signed at Pretoria

ACKNOWLEDGEMENTS

I am deeply grateful to the following:

For family papers, etc: the Marquess of Lansdowne, the Marquess of Salisbury, the Earl Haig, Lord Allenby, Lady Lucas, the late Lord Methuen, the late Captain Michael Buller, the late Miss Daisy Bigge, Brigadier Shamus Hickie, Myles Hildyard, Owen Keane, Major Trotter, Harry Oppenheimer, Mrs Rosemary Parker, Mrs Frances Pym (*née* Gough), Mrs Mackeson-Sandbach and the late Mrs Mackie Niven (*née* Fitzpatrick).

For official records: the Army Museums Ogilby Trust (Spenser Wilkinson), Bodleian Library, Birmingham University (Chamberlain), British Museum (Balfour, Campbell-Bannerman and others), Christ Church (Lord Salisbury), Devon and Dorset Regimental Museum, Household Brigade Museum, Hove Central Library (Wolseley), India Office Library (White), King's College, London (Hamilton etc.), Liverpool Museum (Steavenson), Manchester Public Library, New College (Milner), National Army Museum (Baden-Powell and others), National Library of Scotland (Haldane and others), North Lancs. Regimental Museum, Sherwood Foresters Regimental Museum (Smith-Dorrien), Public Record Office (Ardagh and others), Rhodes House (Rhodes), John Rylands Library (Bromley Davenport), Scottish Record Office (Dundonald), Society for the Propagation of the Gospel in Foreign Parts, University of St Andrews (Alford), Ministry of Defence Library, Westfield College (Lyttelton); the Africana Museum, Cape Archives, Natal Archives, Orange Free State Archives, Rhodesian National Archives, Transvaal Archives, De Beers Archives, Killie Campbell Museum, University of Witwatersrand; the National Library of Australia.

For general help and encouragement: my wife Valerie, my parents, Fiona Barbour, Professor Johann Barnard, Zac De Beer, Brian Bond, the Camerer family, Janet Carleton, Ron Clark, Anna Collins, Donald and Anita Fabian, Ryno Greenwall, Coralie Hepburn, Elaine Katz, Laurence and Linda Kelly, Dennis Kiley, Joy Law, Kevin MacDonnell, Dr Shula Marks, Jane Martineau, Godfrey Le May, Richard Mendelsohn, the late Tertius Myburgh, Kevin Nowlan, Anthony Sampson, Julian Symons, Enid de Waal, Emma Way and Jenny Wilson.

PICTURE SOURCES

Numbers in **bold** refer to page numbers

Front endpaper H. F. Mackern for Underwood and Underwood (Author's collection). **Frontispiece** *Le Petit Journal*, Brussels, November 1899. **3** *Manchester Evening Mail*, 30 August 1899. **8** (National Army Museum/Author's collection). **18–19** Horace Nicholls (Kevin MacDonnell). **21** (**left**) (Author's collection). **21** (**right**) Mortimer Menpes. *War Impressions*, 1901. **22** E. H. Mills (P. Fitzpatrick, *South African Memories* 1932). **24** (Africana Museum, Johannesburg). **26** 'Drawl'. *Vanity Fair*, 8 March 1900 (Ryno Greenwall). **27** Mortimer Menpes. *War Impressions*, 1901. **30** (from J. H. Breytenbach, *Tweede Vryheidsoorlog*, 1967–7). **31** (from W. K. Hancock, *Smuts*, 1962). **34** F. Carruthers Gould for *The Political Struwwelpeter*, 1899. **36** (Transvaal Archives Depot, Pretoria. TAD 30471). **37** Mrs Chapin (from C. Headlam, *The Milner Papers*, 1931). **38** F. Carruthers Gould. Harold Begbie *The Struwwelpeter Alphabet*, 1900 (Ryno Greenwall). **41** (**left**) (Hulton-Deutsch Collection). **41** (**right**) F. Hollyer (Hulton-Deutsch Collection.

P3543). **44** (Hulton-Deutsch Collection. P32570). **47** (R. Chester Master collection). **50** (**left**) (from J. H. Breytenbach, *Tweede Vryheidsoorlog*, 1967–7). **50** (**right**) Hulton-Deutsch Collection. P28731). **53** D. Barnett (Hulton-Deutsch Collection. H11512). **54** H. F. Mackern for Underwood and Underwood (Author's Collection). **55** (Cape Archives, Cape Town. J498). **56** (**top**) (National Cultural History Museum, Pretoria. HKF435). **56** (**below**) M. Bennett (Cape Archives, Cape Town. J452). **57** Horace Nicholls (Kevin MacDonnell). **59** (**top**) Horace Nicholls (Kevin MacDonnell. #760). **59** (**below**) Horace Nicholls (Kevin MacDonnell. 1386/8A). **60** (Author's collection). **61** Horace Nicholls (Kevin MacDonnell). **62** (Cape Archives, Cape Town. J489). **63** 'Spy'. *Vanity Fair*, 1899. **66–67** Horace Nicholls (Kevin MacDonnell). **69** (National Cultural History Museum, Pretoria. **71** (**top**) (Cape Archives, Cape Town. J696). **71** (**below**) Horace Nicholls (Kevin MacDonnell). **72** Horace Nicholls (Kevin MacDonnell). **75** (National Cultural History Museum, Pretoria. 13316).

76 Horace Nicholls (Kevin MacDonnell). **77** (Africana Museum, Johannesburg. **80** Horace Nicholls (Kevin MacDonnell). **81** Horace Nicholls (Kevin MacDonnell) **83** Horace Nicholls (Kevin MacDonnell). **84** Horace Nicholls (Kevin MacDonnell). **87** (**top**) Reinhold Thiele (Hulton-Deutsch Collection. H63176). **87** (**below left**) Horace Nicholls (Kevin MacDonnell). **87** (**below right**) (Kevin MacDonnell). **88** Horace Nicholls (Kevin MacDonnell). **90** D. Barnett (Africana Museum, Johannesburg). **92** (Africana Museum, Johannesburg). **95** (Natural Cultural History Museum, Pretoria. 128). **96** (Author's collection). **97** (**top**) (Transvaal Archives Depot, Pretoria. TAD 13097). **97** (**below**) *Amsterdamsche Courant*, 17 November 1899 (Ryno Greenwall). **98** *Le Rire*, 14 February 1900 (Ryno Greenwall). **100** (Reinhold Thiele (Hulton-Deutsch Collection. H63356). **102** (Africana Museum, Johannesburg). **103** *L'Assiette au Beurre*, 28 September 1901. **104** (**top**) (Africana Museum, Johannesburg). **104** (**below left**) F. H. Hancox (National Army Museum).

104 (below right) (McGregor Museum, Kimberley. MMKP 1317). 108 (top) Reinhold Thiele (Hulton-Deutsch Collection. H63353). 108 (below) Reinhold Thiele (Hulton-Deutsch Collection. H63359). 110 J. McNeill (Ryno Greenwall). 112 Reinhold Thiele (Hulton–Deutsch Collection. H62946). 113 Reinhold Thiele (Hulton–Deutsch Collection. H63192). 114 Reinhold Thiele (Hulton–Deutsch Collection). 116 Reinhold Thiele (Hulton–Deutsch Collection. H62763. 119 D. Barnett (National Army Museum. O/PH 1502K). 124 (National Cultural History Museum, Pretoria. 13480). 127 R. Steger (from J. H. Breytenbach, *Tweede Vryheidsoorlog*). 128–9 J. E. Middlebrook (Author's collection). 132 Reinhold Thiele (Hulton-Deutsch Collection. H63360). 133 (top) (National Cultural History Museum, Pretoria. 13480). 133 (below) Reinhold Thiele (Hulton–Deutsch Collection. H24506). 134 (top left) F. Carruthers Gould. *The Political Sruwwelpeter*, 1899. 134 (top right) Eugene Damblans. *Le Petit Journal*, 24 December 1899. 134 (below left) August Rubille (Ryno Greenwall). 134 (below right) (Ryno Greenwall). 138 C. M. Dixon. *The Leaguer of Ladysmith*, 1900. 141 (Africana Museum, Johannesburg). 142 (Africana Museum, Johannesburg). 147 Horace Nicholls (Kevin MacDonnell). 148 Horace Nicholls (Kevin MacDonnell). 151 (Hulton-Deutsch Collection). 156 (Cape Archives, Cape Town. J340). 157 (Africana Museum, Johannesburg). 158 W. Dixon (British Film Institute). 159 Mortimer Menpes. *War Impressions*, 1901. 160–1 Reinhold Thiele (Hulton-Deutsch Collection. H40746). 163 (top) 'Spy'. *Vanity Fair*, 23 February 1899 (Ryno Greenwall). 163 (below left) *Vanity Fair*, 29 November 1900 (Ryno Greenwall). 163 (below right) 'Spy'. *Vanity Fair*, 21 June 1900 (Ryno Greenwall). 164 (Author's collection). 165 H. F. Mackern for Underwood and Underwood (Author's collection). 167 (above) (McGregor Museum, Kimberley. MMKP 6393). 167 (below) M. Bennett (Cape Archives, Cape Town. J446). 168 (Cape Archives, Cape Town. JS301). 169 M. Bennett (Cape Archives, Cape Town. J967). 170 Mortimer Menpes. *War Impressions*, 1901 (Ryno Greenwall). 171 (above) Stratford St Leger. *War Sketches in Colour*, 1903. 171 (below) Stratford St Leger. *War Sketches in Colour*, 1903. 172 (top) (McGregor Museum, Kimberley. MMKP 1203).

172(below) (McGregor Museum, Kimberley. MMKP 1512). 173 (top) (McGregor Museum, Kimberley. MMKP 5054). 173 (below) (McGregor Museum, Kimberley. MMKP 5179). 176 Reinhold Thiele (Hulton-Deutsch Collection. H24510). 177 Reinhold Thiele (Hulton-Deutsch Collection. H24523). 178 Perceval Landon (National Army Museum. 76703). 179 (top) Reinhold Thiele (Hulton-Deutsch Collection. P42164). 179 (below) H. F. Mackern for Underwood and Underwood (Author's collection). 182 C. M. Dixon. *The Leaguer of Ladysmith*, 1900. 187 (top) (Cape Archives, Cape Town. J5301). 187 (below) J. E. Middlebrook (Cape Archives, Cape Town. J5301). 190 Melton Prior. *The Siege of Ladysmith*. 193 (top) H. F. MacKern for Underwood and Underwood (Author's collection). 193 (below) Reinhold Thiele (Hulton-Deutsch Collection. H62629). 195 (top) Reinhold Thiele (Hulton-Deutsch Collection. H63185). 195 (below)H. F. MacKern for Underwood and Underwood (Author's collection). 196 Horace Nicholls (Royal Photographic Society. #982). 198 Horace Nicholls (Royal Photographic Society. #1018). 202 Stratford St Leger. *War Sketches in Colour*, 1903 (Ryno Greenwall). 204 (above) (Cape Archives, Cape Town. J7735). 204 (below) (Cape Archives, Cape Town. AG2614). 206 (National Army Museum. 23611). 207 Van Hoepen (Author's collection). 208 E. Ross from H. W. Wilson *With the Flag to Pretoria*. 209 (Africana Museum, Johannesburg). 214 Max Beerbohm (Africana Museum, Johannesburg). 215 Raphael Tuck (Ryno Greenwall). 217 (Cape Archives, Cape Town. AG2615). 218 (above) H. F. Mackern for Underwood and Underwood (Author's collection). 218 (below) H. F. Mackern for Underwood and Underwood (Author's collection). 219 (above) H. F. Mackern for Underwood and Underwood (Author's collection). 219 (below) H. F. Mackern for Underwood and Underwood (Author's collection). 221 (Africana Museum, Johannesburg). 222 Horace Nicholls (Kevin MacDonnell. 1386/13A). 223 J. H. Cuthbert, 1st Scots Guards (Author's collection). 224 (Africana Museum, Johannesburg). 227 detail of cartoon from *L'Assiette au Beurre*, 28 September 1901. 228 (National Army Museum. 25769). 229 Horace Nicholls (Royal Photographic Society. #1025). 230 (National Army Museum. 17436).

231 *Le Rire*, c.1900 (Author's collection). 233 (Hulton-Deutsch Collection. H61674). 234 H. F. MacKern for Underwood and Underwood (Author's collection). 236–7 (Africana Museum, Johannesburg). 239 (above) (The Wellcome Institute Library, London. L22431). 239 (below) Horace Nicholls (Kevin MacDonnell). 240 (Africana Museum, Johannesburg). 241 (Africana Museum, Johannesburg). 245 (National Cultural History Museum, Pretoria. 14299). 247 (Author's collection). 248 (Africana Museum, Johannesburg). 249 (above) (Africana Museum, Johannesburg). 249 (centre) The War Museum, Bloemfontein). 249 (below) (Foreign and Commonwealth Office). 250 (above) *L'Assiette au Beurre*, 28 November 1901. 250 (below) *L'Assiette au Beurre*, 28 November 1901. 251 (above and below) *L'Assiette au Beurre*, 28 September 1901. 254–5 Basil Blackwood (Private collection). 258 (above) Eardley Norton. *Vanity Fair*, 31 July 1902 (Ryno Greenwall). 258 (below) (Private collection/Ryno Greenwall). 259 'L' (Ryno Greenwall). 262 (above) Turnbull (Africana Museum, Johannesburg). 262 (below) (Africana Museum, Johannesburg). 264 Africana Museum, Johannesburg). 265 (Mrs F. Maxwell, *Frank Maxwell*, 1921). 268 (R. Adelson, *Mark Sykes*). 269 (National Cultural History Museum, Pretoria. 13314). 270 (Africana Museum, Johannesburg). 271 (above) (Cape Archives, Cape Town. E8227). 271 (below) (National Cultural History Museum, Pretoria. 13297). 277 (The Wellcome Institute Library, London. L22428). 278 (Africana Museum, Johannesburg). 282 (Emmanuel Lee collection). 283 'S.A.H.' (Africana Museum, Johannesburg). 284 (above) Horace Nicholls (Kevin MacDonnell). 284 (below) Horace Nicholls (Kevin MacDonnell). 285 (above) (Hulton-Deutsch Collection. H22922). 285 (below) Horace Nicholls (Royal Photographic Society. #1111). 286 Caron d'Ache (Ryno Greenwall). 288 *L'Assiette au Beurre*, 28 September 1901. 290 F. Carruthers Gould. *Westminster Gazette*, 4 October 1899. Back endpaper (Foreign and Commonwealth Office).

Every attempt has been made to trace copyright owners. We will be glad to correct any errors in a reprint, if notified.

INDEX

Numbers in *italics* refer to illustration captions

à Court, Lt-Col Charles, 149, 152, 153, 181, 190
Abdy, Major A. J., 144
Abon Dam cavalry charge, 163, 170, *171*
Africans (blacks), 10, 32, 60, 64, 65; cost of war to, 9, 10, 287, 290; labour, 32–3, 64–5, 98, *102*, 113, 121, 141, 169, 269, 274, 275, 289; native levies in Cape, 89; Hart's guide, 124, 125, 128; in Mafeking, 208–12, 213, 215; civil rights of, 247; flogging of, *266*, 289; repairing railway lines, *267*; arming of, *268*, 270; role in armies, 269–70; new pass laws for, 274; Modderfontein massacre of, 281, 294; threat to Boers of, 281
Alford, Lieut Henry, 180
Aloe Knoll, Spion Kop, 149, 150, 151, 153, 155
Altham, Major, 50
Amery, Leo, 9, 123, 191, 235
Ardagh, Major-Gen Sir John, 42
Argyll and Sutherland Highlanders, 117
artillery, Boer, 39, 76, 143, 149; Creusot, 29, 30, 68, *127*; Long Toms, 79, 83, 88, 142, 143, 168, *168*, 169, 170, 207, *207*, 210, 292; Krupp 5-inch howitzer, 121, 125
Artillery, Royal Field, 68, 74, *100*, 109, 116; 53rd Battery, 144; 67th Battery, 73; 69th Battery, 68; 82nd Battery, 177; at Colenso, 120–1, 125, 126, 127, 129–30, *133*; 'Joe Chamberlain', *114*; 'Lady Anne', 143, 145; 'Long Cecil', 168, *168*, *169*, 207; 'Lord Nelson', 207–8; naval guns, *114*, 116, 121, 125, 126, 129, 143, *148*, 188; 'Wolf', 207
Artillery, Royal Horse, 146, 163; Q and U Batteries, 200, 202–3
Asquith, Henry, Lord, 28, 64
Asquith, Margot (*née* Tennant), Lady, 28
Atkins, John, 185, 188
Australian contingent, 136, 215

Badenhorst, Commandant, 242–3
Baden-Powell, Col R. S. S., 46, 63, *63*, 64, *206*; at Mafeking, *205*, 205–15, 292; attack on Game Tree Fort, 210, 292
Bakenlaagte, Benson killed at, 264–5, 294

Balfour, Arthur, 28, 48–9, 135, 252
balloon, observation, 72
Baralongs in Mafeking, 208, 211–12, 213, 215
Baring, Sir Evelyn (later Lord Cromer), 21
Barnard, Professor Johann, 10
Barton, Major-Gen Geoffrey, 120, 187
Bechuanaland Protectorate Regiment, at Mafeking, 205–6, 209, 210, 212, 213
Beerbohm's cartoon of Mafeking Night in London, 214
Beit, Alfred, 12, 13, 22, 23–4, 25, 28, 32, 33, 35, 199, 291
Belfast (Bergendal), 231; Buller defeats Botha at (Aug. 1900), 232–3, 235, 293
Bell, Moberly, 123
Belmont, 101; battle of (1899), 105, 106, 109, 112, 292
Benson, Lieut-Col G. E., 264, 294
Bethlehem (OFS), 226, 266
Beyers, Gen Christiaan, 242, 243
Biggarsberg, 50, 80, 217, 232, 293
Bigge, Sir Arthur, 185
Blaauw Kranz River, 95
Black Watch, 115, 117
'Black Watch' (African force at Mafeking), 209
Black Week, 136, 137, 142, 163
Blackwood, Lord Basil, 254
blockhouse and barbed wire system, Kitchener's, 251, 257, 263, 265, 266, 268–9, 270, 272, 282, 294
Bloemfontein, 37, 63, 86, 87, 88, 193, 196–7, 200, 281; Kruger-Milner Conference (1899), 37, 39, 40, 43, 44, 46, 52, 55, 292; Roberts' advance on, 162, 163–4, *163*, 170; fall of (13 March 1900), 192, 194, 198, 293; typhoid epidemic, 197–8; Milner's visit to, 198–9; De Wet's victory at Sannah's Post, 200–3; British soldiers' graves at, *196*; annexation of Free State proclaimed in, *217*; concentration camp, 253
Bloemfontein Convention 1854, 291
Blomfield, Col, 151
Blood River, battle of (1838), 139, 291
Blood River Poort, 294

Boer commandos: Carolina, 149, 150, 155; Christiana, 57; Ermelo, 122; Heidelberg, 122; Johannesburg, 75, 79, 122, 212; Krugersdorp, 122; Lichtenburg, 109, 220; Lydenburg, 155; Middelburg, 122; Pretoria, 150; Standerton, 122; Vryheid, 122; Wakkerstroom, 122; Zoutpansberg, 122; leaving for the front (1899), 21; in Johannesburg (1896), 24; backveld Boer, 56; commandant posing for photographer, 57; eastern, 68, 69, 74; scouts on Talana Hill, 71; the spade as secret weapon of, 121, 141
Boer War, First (1880–1), 11, 291
Boomplatz, battle of (1848), 56, 291
Boschbult, battle of (1902), 275
Bosman's Drift (Modder River), 107
Botha, Gen Louis, 10, 93, *93*, 95, 118, 140, 141, 146, 180, 181, 186, 216, 223–4, 231, 235, 257, 277, 289, 294; takes over Joubert's command at Natal, 93, 96; as Joubert's right-hand man, 94; attack on armoured train, 95–6, 292; fortifies Tugela line, 92, 98; at Colenso, 120, 121–2, 125, 127, 129, 130, 139; and battle of Spion Kop, 119, 145–50, 152, 153, 155; outmanoeuvred by Buller, 186–7, 188; withdraws from Jo'burg and Rand, 221, 222, 223; battle of Diamond Hill, 224; at Machadodorp, 230; British armies march against, 232–2; defeated at Belfast by Buller, 232–3, 235, 293; flight of, 234, 235; Cypherfontein meeting with Steyn, 240–1; abortive peace talks at Middelburg, 246–51, 247, 294; consults Kruger about peace terms, 254; Standerton war council, 257, 260; plan to invade Natal, 259–61; attacks on Fort Itala and Fort Prospect, 60–1, 294; battle of Bakenlaagte, 264–5; Pretoria peace talks, 279, 282
Botha, Philip, 200
Bothaville, Boer disaster at, 241, 293
Bowers, Trooper, 266, 268
Brabant's Horse, 203
Brandwater Basin, Boers surrender at, 226, 227–9, 230, 293

Breytenbach, Dr J. H., 10
Bridle Drift (Tugela River), 120, 122, 123, 124, 125, 127
Brigades, British Infantry: Guards, 4, 99, 109, 115, 117; Rifle, 127, 142, 144; 1st, 83; 2nd, 83; 4th, 188; 5th Irish, 120, 121, 123, 125, 127–8, 127, 129, 185–6, 188; 6th Fusilier, 187; 9th Highland, 99, 109, 115. 116, 117, 163, 175, 176, 219, 220, 225, 226, 228; 11th Lancashire, 181, 185; 12th, 226; 13th, 175; 18th, 175; 19th, 163, 175, 176, 177, 219; 20th, 226; 21st, 219, 226
British South Africa Company (BSA: Charter Co.), 13, 16, 23, 291
Broad Bottom Camp, Boer PoWs at, 248
Broadwood, Brig-Gen Robert, 200–2, 203, 219, 226, 242, 243, 254, 293
Brodrick, St John, 28, 235, 236, 240, 247, 248, 250, 251, 252, 255, 263
Buchan, John, 20, 274
Buckle, George, 28
Buffalo River, 74, 260
Buffelshoek, Smuts and De la Rey ambush convoy at (1900), 242
Buller, Gen Sir Redvers, 9, 10, 40, 41, 42, 43, 50, 51, 58, 63, 66, 86, 94, 106, 119, 136, 141, 145, 150, 163, 164, 227, 293; advises against advancing beyond Tugela River, 51, 57, 61, 82–3; sails for South Africa on Dunottar Castle, 60, 60–1, 86–7; plan of campaign, 82, 87–8, 89, 90, 91; siege of Ladysmith, 88–9, 92, 131–2; and siege of Kimberley, 101, 102, 105, 293; battle of Colenso, 117, 119–31, 123, 127–8, 133, 133, 142; and after Colenso, 131–3; cables to Lansdowne, 131–2, 135, 137; replaced as GOC by Roberts, 133, 135, 146; remains in charge of Natal army, 135, 197, 217; and Spion Kop, 146, 150, 159, 183; suffers reverse at Vaal Krantz, 159, 164; Roberts refuses to send reinforcements to, 164–5, 180; new tactics and strategy of, 180, 186–7, 188, 194; Ladysmith relieved by, 188–91, 293; White's bitterness towards, 189–90; and campaign against, 190–1; march against Botha, 231–4, 235; feud between Roberts and, 232–3, 235; defeats Botha at Belfast, 232–3, 235, 293; returns to England (Oct. 1900), 234, 293; Press campaign against, 263
Bullock, Lieut-Col G. M., 129, 130
Bulwana Hill, 189; Long Tom on, 142, 189
Burger, Schalk, 149, 155, 156, 246, 272, 281, 283
Burn-Murdoch, Lieut-Col John, 120
Bushman's Kop (near Sannah's Post, 201
Butler, Lt-Gen Sir William, 35, 39, 42, 50

Byng, Lieut-Col Julian (later Field-Marshal Lord), 268

Caesar's Camp, Boer attack on (1900), 141, 143–5, 293
Campbell-Bannerman, Sir Henry, 28, 44, 58, 238, 252, 253, 289
Canadian contingent, 136, 215
Cape Colony, 11, 13, 20, 23, 24, 32, 37, 44, 45, 51, 52, 63, 65, 86, 87, 90, 93, 99, 102, 140, 164, 205, 241, 247, 294; map (1899), 14–15; defence of, 45–6, 51, 63, 89, 91, 93, 206; and Boer ultimatum, 61; British refugees from Rand in, 61–2; martial law, 89; officers' hospital, 132; Steenkamp raiding party starts Afrikaner rising, 196; guerrilla warfare, 241, 243, 245, 259, 265; Kritzinger's 'invasion' of, 245, 254, 256, 294; martial law, 245; loyalist militia raised in, 245; Smuts' raid into, 256, 257–9, 261, 294; amnesty for rebels in, 279
Cape Coloureds, 13, 31, 32, 33, 60, 65
Cape Town, 35, 50, 51, 61, 86, 87, 89, 91, 146
Cardwell, Edward, 1st Viscount, 136
Carleton, Lt-Col R. F. C., 84–5, 292
Carter's Ridge, Kimberley, 105
Cecil, Lady Edward (Violet; later Viscountess Milner), 86, 183; Milner's friendship with, 46–7, 47, 64; and marriage to Milner (1921), 290
Cecil, Major Lord Edward, 46, 208, 209
Chamberlain, Sir Austen, 28
Chamberlain, Joseph, (Colonial Secretary), 16, 20, 21, 21, 23, 25–7, 30, 34, 35, 36, 37, 39, 50, 63, 64, 65, 222, 252, 255, 257; 'no-war' policy of, 25, 27, 28; Milner's visit to (1898), 25–7; and Kruger, 27, 29, 35, 37, 43–4, 45, 46, 47, 48, 52–3; Helot Despatch approved by, 36, 37, 43; policy differences between Milner and, 43, 45, 46, 52–3; sends troops to Natal, 47–51, 53–4, 54–5; and Kruger's ultimatum, 54–5, 58, 60, 63; and colonial contingents sent to South Africa, 136; Khaki election, 238, 239; Middelburg peace talks, 247; and Pretoria peace talks, 273, 279, 280
Chieveley, 95, 121, 180, 181; Africans repairing railway lines at, 267
Chinese labourers in Rand, 289
Chisholme, Col John Scott, 77–8
Christian Victor, Major Prince, 130, 235
Churchill, Winston, 60, 157, 159, 181, 188; as Morning Post correspondent, 86, 87, 156; captured and imprisoned at Pretoria, 96; escapes from gaol, 156; at Spion Kop, 156–7, 159
Cingolo, 181, 186

City Imperial Volunteers (CIV), 22
Clements, Major-Gen R. A. P., 226, 228, 242–3, 294
Clery, Lt-Gen Sir Francis, 90, 91, 190
Coke, Major-Gen J. Talbot, 153, 154, 156, 157, 158
Coldstream Guards, 109
Colenso, 82, 95, 118, 145, 181; battle of (15 Dec. 1899), 119–31, 119, 127, 128, 133, 134, 136, 137, 139, 140, 142, 143, 185, 191, 292; Buller's occupation of (19 Feb. 1900), 181
Colesberg, 91, 164, 195, 196
Colley, Gen Sir G. P., 16, 39
Coloureds, 11, 64, 222, 279
Colvile, Major-Gen Sir Henry, 106, 109, 163, 175, 176, 177, 201, 203, 219, 220, 225
Commando Nek, 227
Conan Doyle, Arthur, 87, 107
concentration camps, 10, 244, 248, 250, 257, 274, 281, 282, 286, 287; Boer families in, 248; Norvals Pont, 249; Kitchener's policy on, 248, 250, 251, 270; Emily Hobhouse's campaign against, 251, 252–3; and Fawcett Commission Report, 254, 255; deconcentration of, 270, 274
Congreve, Capt Walter, 130
Conical Hill, Spion Kop, 149, 150, 151
Consolidated Goldfields, 35
Craigavon, Lord, 225
Cranborne, Lady, 86
Crofton, Col Malby, 151, 152, 153
Cronje, Gen Andries, 266
Cronje, Gen Piet, 105, 107, 113, 117, 140, 170, 199, 205; battle of Modder River, 107, 109, 111; at Magersfontein, 162, 163, 164, 170; at Paardeberg, 170, 173, 178–9, 293; surrenders to Roberts, 178–9, 179, 185, 224, 293; and Mafeking, 206, 207
Curzon, George Nathaniel, Lord, 28
Cypherfontein meeting of Boer leaders (October 1900), 240–1, 243, 256

De Aar railway junction, 63
De Beers Mining Corporation, 99, 102, 104, 105, 166, 168, 169, 169
De Jager's Drift, Gough's disaster at, 260
De la Rey, Adriaan, 111
De la Rey, Gen Koos, 112, 196, 199, 220, 222, 235, 240, 257, 272; battle of Modder River, 107, 109, 111, 117; battle of Magersfontein, 113, 117, 121; at Zilikat's Nek, 230; Cypherfontein meeting, 240; ambushes convoy at Buffelshoek, 242; at Nooitgedacht, 242–3, 294; captures Methuen at Tweebosch, 272, 294; battle of Rooiwal, 275, 277; Pretoria peace talks, 279, 282, 282
De Wet, Gen Christiaan, 164, 192, 196, 197,

199, 216–17, 224, 227, 230, 231, 232, 235, 236, 240, 256, 257, 258, 269, 289, 293, 294; ambushes Roberts at Waterval Drift, 165, 194; at Paardeberg, 173–5, 178–9; and Poplar Grove, 193; at Kroonstad council, 199, 200; victory at Sannah's Post, 200–3, 293; and at Reddersberg, 203; guerrilla warfare of, 224–5, 226, 231, 240, 242, 243, 245, 265; escape Hunter's trap, 229; flight to Magaliesberg, 230; British failure to hunt down, 231; Bothaville defeat of, 241–2, 293; success at Tweefontein, 266, 268, 294; eludes capture by Kitchener, 268, 272; Pretoria peace talks, 279, 280, 281, 282, 283, 283

De Wet, Piet, 219, 224, 225, 266, 282, 282, 293

Deerdeport, raid on, 208, 292

Delagoa Bay, 89

Devonshire Regiment, 76, 77, 78, 83, 129, 130, 145, 147

Diamond Hill, battle of (11–12 June 1900), 224, 226, 293

diamond mines, Kimberley, 11, 64, 102, 104, 169–70-, 291

Digby-Jones, Lieut, 143, 144

Dingaan's Day (16 December), 139

Divisions, British Infantry: Colonial, 226; 1st, 91, 99; 2nd, 89, 90, 91; 3rd, 91; 4th, 231; 5th, 131, 135; 6th, 163, 175, 176, 194; 7th, 137, 163, 220; 8th, 137, 226; 9th, 163, 175, 176; 11th, 220

Dixon, Lieut Charles, 139, 182

Dixon, Brigadier-Gen H. G., 254

Donoughmore, Lord, 225

Doornkop, Jameson's surrender at (1896), 17, 20, 23, 75, 220, 292; Hamilton's storming of (1900), 220

Dorset Regiment, 152, 156

Dragoon Guards, 78–9

Driefontein, battle of (1900), 194, 293

Drielingkoppe, Spion Kop, 155, 156

Dublin Fusiliers, 68, 83, 187

Duke of Cornwall's Light Infantry, 166, 176, 177

Duncan, Patrick, 274

Dundee, 59, 76, 79, 86, 94; Symons' forces at, 51, 54, 57–8, 61, 65, 68, 292; Boer attack on, 68–9; Talana Hill action, 69–75; Yule's withdrawal from, 79–82, 80–1

Dundonald, Col Lord, 120, 127, 163, 181, 231

Dunottar Castle, 60, 60, 61, 86–7, 89

Durban, 50, 51, 53, 55, 57, 82, 87, 89, 91, 93, 94, 96, 156, 235

Dutch East India Company, 11, 291

dysentery, 184, 249

East London, 58, 87

Edgar, Tom, shooting of, 33, 79, 233

Edward VII, King, 28, 251, 251, 279

Elands River Poort, battle of (September 1900), 257–8, 294

Elandsfontein, 220

Elandslaagte, battle of (October 1899), 75–9, 75, 82, 83, 93–4, 145, 292

Elliot, Major-Gen E. L., 268

Ellis, John, 252, 253

Eloff, Commandant Sarel, 212–13, 293

Ennismore, Lord, 225

Erasmus, Gen Daniel, 69

Essex Regiment, 175, 203

Estcourt (Natal), 87, 90, 91, 94–5, 146

Exham, Lt-Col Richard, 184, 198, 219

farm-burning by British, 230, 231, 232, 235, 239, 240–1, 242

Fawcett Commission report on concentration camps, 253, 255

Ferreirs, F. S., 175

Fiddes, George, 35

Fingoes in Mafeking, 208

1st Army Corps, British, 40, 42, 44, 50, 51, 54, 58, 61, 63, 86, 87, 88, 89, 91, 98, 137, 206, 292

Fischer, Maria, diary of, 244

FitzClarence, Capt C., 209, 213

Fitzpatrick, Sir Percy, 32–4, 35–6, 289

Fleet St (London) peace celebrations, 285

Fort Itala and Fort Prospect, Botha's attacks on, 260–1, 294

Fort Wylie, 122

Fouriesburg, 227, 228

Fraser, Edmund, 31, 33

Free Staters (Boer Commandos), 107, 109, 113, 122, 143, 144, 155, 196, 200, 216–17, 232, 241, 257; alleged cowardice of, 111–12; Roberts offers amnesty to, 194, 196, 197, 199, 224

French, Major Gen John (later Field-Marshal Lord), 85, 163, 192–3, 201, 259, 268, 288, 294; battle of Elandslaagte, 75–9; and siege of Ladysmith, 88; dash to, and relief of Kimberley by, 162–3, 165, 170, 293; at Poplar Grove, 193–4; and guerrilla war in Cape, 259

Frere (Natal), 118, 132–3, 146, 180

Game Tree Fort (Mafeking), 210, 292

Gatacre, Lt-Gen Sir William, 91, 119, 131, 292

Gell, Sir Philip, 22

Germany, anglophobia in, 136

Gladstone, W. E., 1, 11, 22, 23, 31, 58

Gloucestershire Regiment, 141

Godley, Major Alick, 209, 213

gold mines at Witwatersrand, 10, 12, 23, 24, 29, 31–3, 35, 46, 62, 77, 102, 141, 199, 207, 216, 246, 251, 274–5, 289, 291; black labour force, 32–3, 65, 169, 274, 275; British refugees flee from, 61–2, 61, 62; Shangans expelled from, 207; surrender of Boers to British, 221, 222, 223; mine dynamited by commandos, 254; white miners return to (1902), 274–5; Chinese labourers, 289

Golden Gate pass, 227, 228, 229

Gordon Highlanders, 75, 76, 77, 83, 143, 144, 220

Goschen, G. J., 21

Gough, Lt-Col Hubert, 189, 260, 294

Gough, Capt John, 142, 144, 145, 183

Graspan, battle of (1899), 105, 106, 109, 112, 292

Great Hart's River, 276

Great Trek (1835–7), 11, 291

Green Hill, Spion Kop, 150

Greene, Conyngham, 46, 54, 55, 64

Grenadier Guards, 105, 109

Grey, Sir Edward (later Lord Grey of Falloden), 64

Grey, Raleigh, 16

Grimwood, Col Geoffrey, 83, 85

Groenloof, battle of (Sept. 1901), 259

Guards Brigade see Brigades

guerrilla warfare, Boer, 10, 141, 164, 170, 194, 199, 230, 235, 240, 241, 242, 243, 245, 246, 248, 254, 256, 257, 258–9, 259, 263, 265, 266–7, 270, 275, 281; De Wet's, 224–5, 226, 230, 236, 240, 245

Gun Hill (Ladysmith), raid on, 142–3, 143

Gun Hill (Modder River), 177

Haig, Col Douglas, later Field-Marshal Lord), 88–9, 162, 158–9, 288

Haldane, Richard (later Lord), 64, 238, 244

Hamilton, Major-Gen Bruce, 219, 226, 227, 228

Hamilton, Col Ian, 50, 83, 85, 230, 231, 235, 294; at Elandslaagte, 76–7, 78; at Ladysmith, 144, 145; campaign against Buller, 190, 191; advance on Johannesburg and Pretoria, 216, 217, 219–20; appointed acting Lt-Gen, CO of new division, 219; crosses Vaal River, 219–20; storming of Doornkop by, 220; breaks collar bone, 226; fails to hunt down De Wet, 231, 293; appointed Chief of Staff to Kitchener, 264, 294; battle of Rooiwal, 275–7; Pretoria peace talks, 278–9, 285

'handsuppers', 280, 282, 286

Hannay, Lt-Col O. C., 176–7

Harcourt, Sir William, 21, 58

Hart, Major-Gen Fitzroy, 152; at Colenso, 120, 121, 123–5, 126, 127–8, 131; at

Hart's Hill, 185–6
Hart's Hill action (Feb. 1900), 185–6, *187*, *188*
Hay, Trooper, with Eloff, 212, *213*
Hayes, Dr (PMO at Mafeking), 209
Heilbron, 225
Hely-Hutchinson, Sir Walter, 57, 62
Henry, Col St G., 220
Hertzog, Judge Barry, 245, 256, 279
Het Volk, Afrikaner party, 289
Hicks Beach, Sir Michael, 45, 48
Highland Light Infantry, 117
Hildyard, Major-Gen Henry, 120, 122, 126, 127, 129
Hill, Lt-Col A. W., 157
Hlangwane Hill (Bosch Kop), 120, 121, 122, 127; Buller's capture of, 180–1
Hobhouse, Emily, 251, 252–3, *253*, 255
Hofmeyr, Jan, 37
Holdsworth, Col G., 208, 292
Holkrantz, Zulu attack on, 281, 294
Hore, Lt-Col C. O., 209, 212, 213
'Horse Hill' kopje, 173
Horse Shoe Hill, 185
hospitals, 73, 74, 81, 84, 111, *132*, 184, 198, *198*, 219, 238; 18th Field Hospital, 73, 184; 20th Field Hospital, 74
Houtnek action, 219
Hunter, Major-Gen Sir Archibald, 144, 145, 183, 217, 228, 231, 232, 272, 292; Brandwater Basin action, 226–9, 293
Hussar Hill, near Chieveley, 181
Hussars, 18th, 74

Imperial Light Horse (Beit's Horse: ILH), 65, 77–8, 79, 142, 143, 144, 152, 214
Imperial Light Infantry, 152
Imperial Yeomanry, 137, 225, 228, 239
Indians, 32, 60, 73, 131, 279
intelligence, British (FID), 99, 101, 106, 118, 124, 196, 226, 250, 254, 259, 260, 266, 268, 286
Intombi Camp, 144
Intombi hospital, 184
Irish Hunt Contingent, 225, 293

Jacobsdal, Boers' base hospital, 111
James, David, 9
Jameson Raid (Dr Jameson: 1895–6), 13–18, 20, 21, 23–4, 24, 25, 27, 29, 32, 33, 45, 53, 64, 65, 75, 206, 220, 292
Johannesburg, 24, 31, 32, 220, 246; Jameson Raid on, 13–18; burghers off to war front from, 53; British refugees fleeing from, *61*, 62; Roberts's advance on, 216–17; surrender of (May 1900), 220–2, 221, 223, 293; parade of Rand Rifles in, 239; British Uitlander refugees return to, 283
Johannesburg Reformers/Reform

Committee, 13, 24, 32, 33, 34, 214, 292
'John Bull as Gulliver', Dutch cartoon, 96
Joubert, Commandant-General Piet, 10, 29, 30, *30*, 56, 85, 93, 121, 149; offensive against Natal, 57, 58, 59, 64, 68–9, 73, 76, 82, 93–4; breakfasting with staff, 69; occupation of Impati by, 79; and siege of Ladysmith, 94, 292; raid on south Natal, 94, 96; thrown from horse, 92, 96; and Botha takes over his command, 92; death of (1900), 293
Jowett, Dr Benjamin, Master of Balliol, 21

Kekewich, Lt-Col Robert, 102, *104*, 105, 109, 135, 166–8, *167*, 173, 292; battle of Rooiwal, 275, 276, 277
Kelly-Kenny, Lt-Gen Thomas, 163, 192–3, 194; at Paardeberg, 174–6, 178, 179
Kemp, Boer Gen, 254, 276–7
Kentish, Lieut Reggie, 68, 139
Kerin, Major, 74
Khaki election, British (1900), 238–40
Kiba Drift, 256, 259, 294
Kimberley, 39, 45, 57, 63, 64, 87, 88, 91, 93, 98, 103, 135, 207; diamond mines, 12, 64, 102, *104*, 169–70, 291; Rhodes besieged at, 86, 88, 91, 98, *98*, *104*; Methuen's march to relieve, 98, 99–106; siege of, 101, 102–5, *103*, 112, 142, 164, 172, 173, 292; conning tower at De Beers mine, 102, 105; attacks on Carter's Ridge, 105; struggle between Rhodes and Kekewich in, 105, 166–8; French's dash to, 162–3, 165, 170; Boer shelling of, 168, 169; starvation and disease in, 160; relief of (15 Feb. 1900), 170, 181, 293; 'Shrapnel Hotel' dug-out, 166
King's Royal Rifles, 69
Kipling, Rudyard, 9, 160, 192, *193*, 216, 273
Kitchener of Khartoum, Field-Marshal Lord, 162, *163*, 164, 165, 200, 229, 230, 235, 236, 239, 246, 250, 259, 260, 261, 263, 264–5, *265*, 272, 275, 285, 293, 294; COS to Roberts, 135, *163*, 292; overrules Kelly-Kenny at Paardeberg, 174–9; fails to hunt down De Wet, 231; rift between Milner and, 240, 244, 251–2, 278; succeeds Roberts as C-in-C South Africa, 244, 294; Middelburg peace talks, 246–51, *247*, 263, 294; promised post of C-in-C India, once war is over, 247–8; and concentration camps, 248, 250, 251, 270; blockhouse and barbed wire policy of, 251, 257, 263, 265, 266, 268–9, 270, 272, 294; appointed acting High Commissioner (1901), 251; Cabinet's ultimatum, and his counter-attack, 253, 254–5, 263–4; and Milner's 'protection' policy, 253, 265; sweep-and-scour policy

of, 254, 257, 269; forecasts end of war by April 1902, 263; Ian Hamilton appointed COS to, 264, 294; Steyn and De Wet elude capture by, 268, 272; arming of Africans by, 269–70; and Pretoria peace talks, 272, 273, 274, 278, 279, 281, 282, 283, 285; battle of Rooiwal, 275–7
Kitchener, Col Walter, 188, 275
'Kitchener's Kopje', Paardeberg, 176–8, 179, 185
Klip Drift, wounded Tommies in waggon house at, *112*
Knox, Major-Gen Charles, 175, 176, 241–2
Knox, Col William, 85
Kock, Gen J. H. M., 76, 78, 79, 94
Kock, Judge, 79
Kock, Philip, 79
Koffyfontein, 173
Komati Poort, 235, 293
Korn Spruit (Sannah's Post), 201, 202, 203
Krause, Commandant, conditional surrender of Johannesburg by, 220–1, 223
Kritzinger, Gen P. H., 245, 257, 259; 'invasion' of Cape Colony by, 245, 254, 256, 294; capture of, 294
Kroonstad, *218*, 225, 266, 268, 294; Boer Council (17 March 1900), 199–200, 293; fall of, 217, 219, 293
Kruger, Paul, Pres of Transvaal, 4, 12, 20, 23, 25, 26, 27, 28, 33, 34, 35, 37, 39, 96, 118, 139–41, 193, 194, 203, 216, 225, 292; First Boer War, 11, 291; and Jameson Raid, 17, 23–4, 25, 29–30; re-elected President, 24, 27, 292; and Chamberlain, 27, 29, 37, 43–4, 45, 46, 47, 48–9, 52–3; arming of Transvaal, 30, *30*; and modernizing of Transvaal, 30–1; Uitlanders' franchise, 33, 35–6, 37, 43, 46, 47, 52; 'Great Deal' offer, 35–6; Bloemfontein conference with Milner (1899), 37, 39, 40, 43, 46, 52, 281; political concessions offered by, 43, 44, 45, 46, 47, 52; ultimatum to Britain by, 54–5, 57, 58, 60, 62; strategic war plans of, 56–7, 141, 143; and main political objectives, 93, 140; concerned over cowardice of Free Staters, 111–12; and battle of Colenso, 121–2, 139, 140; Dingaan's Day speech of, 139; war of attrition policy of, 140, 141; at Kroonstad council, 199–200; withdraws from Pretoria to Machadodorp, 222; Steyn rejects his suggestion of surrender, 223; goes into exile, 235, 243, 293; Botha consults him about peace terms, 254

Labram, George, 105, 168, *169*
Ladysmith, 43, 49, 51, 57, 65, 66, *71*, 75, 76,

82, 83, 87, 118, 120, 121, 146, *148*, 150, 159, 164, 207, 226; siege of, 69, *81*, 82, 85, 87, 88–9, 91, *92*, 93, 94, 131–2, 133, 134, 135, *139*, 142–3, 183, 292; British soldiers brought out for burial at, *76*; Yule withdraws from Dundee to, 79–81, *80–1*; White's reasons for not withdrawing from, 82–3; battle of ('Mournful Monday'), 83–5, *84*, 87, 88, 94, 183, 292; and surrender of Carleton's column, 85, 87; Boer attack on Wagon Hill and Caesar's Camp (Platrand), 141, *141*, 143–5, 293; British raids on Gun Hill and Surprise Hill, 142–3; White's HQ hit by shell, *142*; Buller's advance on, 180–1, 183, 185–8, *187*; food supplies, 183–4; typhoid and dysentery in, 184, 197; relief of, 188–91, *190*, 232, 293
Laing's Nek, battle of (1900), 232
Lancashire Fusiliers, 151, 154
Lancers, 5th, 78–9; 9th, 101; 17th, 257, 294
Landon, Perceval, *178*
Lang Riet, Rawlinson surrounds laager, 272
Lansdowne, 5th Marquess of, 9, 40–4, *41*, 48, 60–1, 120, 131, 191, 217, 219, 230, 252; and Milner's military proposals, 40, 41–2; and Wolseley, 40, 41–2, 43, 44, 89, 135, 137; war preparations and despatch of troops, 41–4, 48–51; and Buller, 131–2, 133, 135; appoints Roberts as GOC South Africa, 133, 135–6; appointed Foreign Secretary, 240
Le May, Godfrey, 10
Leicester Regiment, 68, *70*, 73, *80–1*, 83
Leitrim, Earl of, 225
Lennox Hill, *70*, 73, 74
Leyds, Dr, 140
Liberal Party, British, 28, 44, 238–9, 251, 253, 257, 270, 289
Linchwe, Chief, 208, 292
Lincoln Regiment, 230
Lindley, 219, 220, 225, 294; Irish Hunt Contingent captured at, 225, 293
Little Hart's River, 276
Liverpool Regiment, 83, 145
Lloyd George, David, 239, 252, 253, 289
Lombard's Kop, 143
London Convention (1884), 12, 23, 27, 54, 55, 291
Long, Col Charles, 95, 122, 126, 127, 129, 130, 131, *133*
Longford, Capt Earl of, 225
Lotter, Commandant, 259, 278, 294
Lyttelton, Major-Gen Neville, 120, 121, 127–8, 153, 155, 156, 159, 181, 190, 231, 233

MacDonald, Major-Gen Hector ('Fighting Mac'), 163, *163*, 170, 175, 176

McGrigor, Major, 223
Machadodorp, 222, 230, 231, 233
McKenzie, Col C. J., 216
Mafeking, 13, 16, 29, 46, 57, 63, 64, 99, 105, 113, 170, 272; siege of, 93, 135, *204*, 205–13, 292; relief of, 203, 212, 214–15, *214–15*, 293; map of, *206*; treatment of Africans in, 208–12, 213, 215; food rationing, 210–12; Eloff's attack on, 212–13, 293
Magaliesberg, 230, 272
Magersfontein, 101, 111, 112, 117, 164; battle of (11 Dec. 1899), 110, 113, *114*, 115–17, 119, 121, 124, 136, 139, 162, 163, 164, 170, 176, 292
Mahon, Col Bryan, relief of Mafeking by, 203, 212, 214–15, 293
Majuba, battle of (1881), 11, 12, 16, 20, 21, 22, 23, 31, 39, 51, 58, 75, 139, 140, 179, 220, 291
Malan, A. H., 259
Malmani, 17
Manchester Regiment, 75, 77, 83, 144
Maritzburg, 57, 82, 91, 94
Massey, Major, 148, 151
Maurice, Major-Gen Sir F., 9
Maxwell, Capt Frank, *265*
Menpes, Mortimer, sketches by, *21*, *27*, *159*, *170*
Methuen, Lt-Gen Lord, 91, 98, 131, *163*, 164, 230, 272, 275; march to relieve Kimberley, 98, 99–106; minor victories at Belmont and Graspan, 105, 106, 292; battle of Modder River, 106, 107, *108*, 109–12, 292; tactics at Modder River and Magersfontein, *110*; wounded, *111*; battle of Magersfontein, 115–17, 119, 162, 292; replaced by Sir Charles Warren, 131; captured at Tweebosch by De la Rey, 272, 294
Methuen's Force, 99
Meyer, Lucas, 68, 69, 73, 74–5, 94
MI (mounted infantry), 73, 74, 101, 136, 137, 148, 163, *171*, 175, 197, 200, 202, 205, 219, 220, 226, 260, 276, 277
Middelburg, abortive peace talks at (February 1901), 246–51, *247*, 254, 263, 273–4, 279, 280, 294
Middlesex Regiment, 152, 154
Miller-Walnut, Major, 144, 145
Milner, Sir Alfred (later Baron Milner), High Commissioner for South Africa and Governor of Cape Colony, 20–8, 29, 33, 34, 35–7, 44, *44*, 51, 93, 119, 131, 142, 215, 222, 238, 244, 255, 263, 275, 289, 292; background and early career, 20–1; Menpes sketch of, *21*; South African policy of, 22–3, 24, 28, 35–7, 43, 46, 64–5; secret alliance with Beit and Wernher, 22,

199; working holiday in England (1898), 20, 25–8; and his meeting with Chamberlain, 25–7; Kruger's 'Great Deal' offer to, 35–6; Helot Despatch, 36, 37, 43; Bloemfontein Conference (1899), 37, 39, 40, 43, 46; military proposals to War Office of, 40, 41–2, 51, 57; and defence of Cape Colony, 45–6; Violet Cecil's friendship with, 46–7, 47, 64, 86; appeals to Chamberlain for troops to be sent, 47–9; and Boer ultimatum, 62; his worries about military situation, 62–4, 65, 87, 89, 90, 91, 164; and siege of Kimberley, 102, 135; at Bloemfontein, 198–9; seeks to revise official Proclamation, 231; at parade of Rand Rifles, 239; warns Brodrick about ongoing guerrilla war, 240; rift between Kitchener and, 240, 244, 251–2, 278; as civil administrator of Transvaal and ORC, 244; military plan (protection policy) of, 244–6, 253, 265; and Middelburg peace talks, 246, 247, *247*, 251; home leave, 251–2, 294; receives peerage, 252; Pretoria peace talks, 273, 274, 278–80, 281, 283; 'Kindergarten' of, 274, 288; black labour policy of, 274; plans to rebuild Transvaal and ORC on British lines, 288–9; resigns as Governor, 289; death of (1924), 290
Modder River, *100*, 101, 105, 106, *112*, 115, 131, *160*, 163, 164, 193, 200; Boers entrenched on, 106, 107; battle of (Nov. 1899), 106, 107, *109*, 109–12, *110*, 117, 292; Methuen's troops fording, *109*; mess of 3rd Grenadier Guards at, *109*; Methuen's tactics at, *110*; graffiti dialogue on walls of house at, *113*; railway bridge, 115; battle of Paardeberg, 170–9; Roberts's gunners and infantry crossing, *177*; Sannah's Post action, 200–3; sorting mail for troops at, *195*
Modderfontein, Boer massacre of Africans at, 281, 294
Modderspruit, battle of *see* Ladysmith, battle of; Boer council of war, 93, 94
Moller, Lt-Col B. D., 73, 74; surrender of, 74, 75, 82, 292
Molopo River (Mafeking), 207
Monte Cristo (near Ladysmith), 190; Buller's capture of, 180–1, 186
Mooi River (Natal), 91
Mount Alice, 153
Mount Impati, 68, 69, 74, 79
Mouton, Dr J. A., 10

Naauwpoort, 63, 91, 227
Naauwpoort Nek, 228
Natal, 11, 32, 39, 40, 42, 43, 49, 63, 65, 86,

87, 88, 140, 164, 205, 217, 241, 247, 265, 279; British annex as colony (1843), 11, 291; map of, *14–15*; defence of, 42, 44, 51, 63, 87, 88, 90, *90*, 94, 142, 197; British troops sent to, 47–51, 53–5, 58, 137; Joubert's offensive against, 57, *59*, 64, 66, 68–9, 73, 76, 82, 93–4, *196*; British refugees from Rand in, 62; Boer invasion force in, *196*; concentration camps, 252; Botha's plan to invade, 259–61
Natal Carbineers, 142
Natal Volunteers, 189
National Scouts ('handsuppers': Boers fighting for British), 266, 280, 282, 294
Nationalist Party, South African, 289–90
Naval Brigade in Johannesburg, *221*
Naval Gun Hill (Colenso), 121, 125
Nevinson, Henry, 79
New Zealand contingent, 136
Nicholls, Horace, war photographer, *83, 87*
Nicholson's Nek, fiasco at, 84, 85, 87, 292
'Night of the Great Rain', 257
Nooitgedacht, release of last British PoWs at, 233, 293; Boers attack Clements at, 242–3, 260, 294
Norcott, Major-Gen, *188*
North Lancashire Regiment, 102
Norvals Pont concentration camp, 249
Nugent, Capt, 74

Ogilvy, Lieut, RN, 126, 129
Old Wagon Drift, 120, 122
Olifant's Nek, 230, 231
Olivier, Gen J. H., 196, 197, 200, 201, 229
Omdurman, battle of (1898), 135
Opperman, Commandant, 150, 155, 159, 265
Orange Free State (Orange River Colony), 11, 29, 30, 37, 39, 42–3, 45, 46, 52, 64, 93, 99, 107, 217, 220, 226, 254, 256, 272, 291, 294; British annexation of (1877), 11, 291; map of, *14–15*; mobilization, and ultimatum to Britain, 54–5, *55*, 56, 57, 58, 61, 62; war plans, 56–7; Roberts's invasion of, 162, 163–4, 181, 197; fall of Bloemfontein, 192, 194, 198; Roberts's offer of amnesty, 194, 196, 197, 199, 224; Boer forces remaining in, 196; Kroonstad council, 199–200; British annexation of, and renamed Orange River Colony (May 1900), 216, 217, 293; guerrilla warfare in, 224–5, 226, 231, 240, 265, 266; Milner's military plan in, 244–6; concentration camps, 252, 255; Pretoria peace talks, 278–83; native rights in, 279–80; British financial help for, 280; Milner's plan to rebuild on British lines, 288–9; self-government granted to (1906), 289
Orange River, 11, 34, 64, 89, 91, 99, 105,

111, 164, 236, 245, 256; railway bridge, 63, 99, 164
Oxfordshire Light Infantry, 175

Paardeberg, battle of (1900), 170, 173–9, *174*, 193, 293; Cronje's surrender at, 179, *179*, 185, 293
Packer, Private Joe, 146
Paget, Major-Gen Arthur, 226, 228
Paris, Private Prosper, 75
Parsons, Lt-Col L. W., 120, 125, 128, 187
peace negotiations: Middleburg (Feb. 1901), 246–51, *251*, 254, 263, 273–4, 279, 280; Pretoria (April–May 1902), 272, 273–4, 278–83, 294; signing of Peace Treaty (31 May), 283, 294
Pepworth Hill, 83, 85
Phillips, Capt, *158*
Phipps-Hornby, Major Edward, 202–3
Pieters Hill (near Ladysmith), 181, 186, 187, 188
Pitsani Camp (Bechuanaland), 13, 16, 206
Platrand (Wagon Hill and Caesar's Camp), Boer attack on, 141, 143–5, 149–50, 242
Plomer, William, 287
Plumer, Lt-Col Herbert, 205, 211, 215, 293
Pole-Carew, Major-Gen Reggie, 109, 111, 163, 220, 235, 293
Poplar Grove, battle of (7 March 1900), 193–4, 201, 293
Potgieter, Commandant, 276–7, *277*
Potgieter's Drift, 118, 119, 146, 153
Power, Sir John, *225*
PoWs, British, 81, 96, 97, 139, 233, 259, 293; Boer, 88, 94, 248, 253
Pretoria, 18, 46, 81, 86, 87, 97, 139, 194, 222; Transvaal burghers off to war front from, *55*; Palace of Justice used as hospital, *198*; Roberts's advance on, 203, 216–19, *219*, typhoid epidemic in, *208*; Roberts's occupation of (5 June 1900), 222, *222*–3, 224, 232, 293; peace negotiations in (April–May 1902), 272, 273–4, 278–83, *283*, 294; victory parade 8 June (1902), *285*
Pretoria Convention (1881), 12, 291
Pretorius, Andries, 291
Prieska, Afrikaner rising at, 196
Prinsloo, Commandant Henrik, 149, 150
Prinsloo, Commandant-Gen Marthinus, 96, 98, 272; battle of Modder River, 107, 109, 111; surrenders at Brandwater Basin, 229, 230, 232, 293
Prior, Melton, war artist, *190*
Progressives, Transvaal, 29, 30
Punt Drift (Tugela River), 122

Queen's Regiment, 129
Queenstown, 90

Railway Hill (near Ladysmith), 186, 187–8
Ralph, Julian, 101
Ramdam (Orange Free State), 162–3
Rand Rifles, 239
Rawlinson, Col Sir Henry, 50, 57, 85, 143, 144, 145, 183, 190, 191, 201, 216, 217, 263, 265, 268, 272, 275, 278
Reddersberg, British garrison surrenders to De Wet, 203, 240, 293
Reitz, Deneys, 57, 150, 155, 159, 257–8
Reitz, Francis, 54
Retief's Nek, 227, 228
Rhodes, Cecil, 12, 21, 22, 23, 24, 25, 33, 35, 36, 45, 64, 65, 99, 164, *168*, 291, 292; and Jameson Raid, 13–18, 23, 27; Menpes sketch of, *27*; besieged in Kimberley, 86, 88, 91, 98, *98*, 102, *103, 105*, 162; struggle between Kekewich and, 105, 166–8; offers diamond mines as shelter against shelling, 169–70; relief of Kimberley, 170; death of (1902), 294
Rhodesia, 12, 13, 16, 99, 291
Rhodesian Regiment, 205, 206, 211, 215
Ridley, Col C. P., 219, 226
Riet River, 106, 107, 109, 111, 117, 163, 165
Rietfontein, battle of (1899), 292
Rifle Brigade *see* Brigades
Rifles, 60th, 68, 74, 83, 144
Rimington, Major Mike, 101, 234, 268
Roberts, Field-Marshal Frederick Lord, 11, 41, 50, 159, *162*, 163, 165, 175, 191, 192–8, 201, 210, 211, 229, 230–1, 231, 239, 252, 263, 264, 277, 281, 288, 293; learns of Buller's reverse at Colenso and sends 'radical change' cable to Lansdowne, 133, 135; death of his son at Colenso, 133, 136; appointed GOC South Africa, 133, 135–6, 146, 292; advances on Bloemfontein, 162, 163–4, *163*, 170, 181; and French's dash to Kimberley, 162, 168; transport system of, 162, 165, 194, 197; decides not to send reinforcements to Buller, 164–5, 180; and battle of Paardeberg, 175, 178, 179; surrender of Cronje to, 179, *179*, 185; fall of Bloemfontein to, 192, 194; and battle of Poplar Grove, 193–4; letter to Queen Victoria, 194; amnesty offered to Freestaters by, 194, 196, 197, 199, 224, 293; miscalculates Boer weakness and British strength, 194, 197; defects in military system of, 197; and typhoid in Bloemfontein, 197–8; advance northward to Pretoria, 203, 216–19, *218–19*, 293; Johannesburg surrenders to, 220–1, 223, 293; Pretoria occupied by, 222–3, 224, 232, 293; battle of Diamond Hill, 224;

fails to hunt down De Wet, 230–1; march against Botha, 230, 231–3; farm-burning policy of, 231, 232, 235, 240–1; feud between Buller and, 231–2, 235; returns home to England, 234, 235, 244; and succeeds Wolseley as C-in-C at home, 234, 294; believes mistakenly war to be 'practically over', 235, 240, 244; proclaims annexation of Transvaal, 235
Roberts, Lieut Frederick, killed at Colenso, 130, 133, 136, 235
Roberts, Lady Nora, 136, 224
Roberts ('Indian') vs Wolseley ('African') Rings in British Army, 41–2, 41, 50, 50, 133, 137, 234–5
Robinson, Geoffrey, 274
Robinson's Drift (Tugela River), 122
Rochfort, Col A. N., 275
Roodeval railway station, De Wet's attack on, 225, 293
Rooiwal, battle of (1902), 275–7, 275, 294
Roslin Castle (troopship), 89
Rosmead Drift (Modder River), 107, 109, 111
Rowntree, Joshua, 252
Royal Canadians, 176, 177
Royal Commission Report on South African War (1903), 40
Royal Dragoons, 124
Royal Inniskilling Fusiliers, 125
Royal Irish Fusiliers, 68, 84, 228, 293
Royal Lancaster Regiment, 151
Royal Munster Fusiliers, 193
Royal Navy, British, 89–90, 292
Rundle, Lt-Gen Sir Leslie, 226, 227, 266, 268

St Leger, Capt Stratford, sketches by, 171
Salisbury, Lord (British Prime Minister and Foreign Secretary), 9, 44, 44, 48–9, 89, 134, 135, 238, 151, 280; Kruger and Steyn's joint appeal to, 199–200; Khaki election, 238, 240
Sand River Convention (1852), 291
Sandbach, Lt-Col Arthur, 153, 154, 181, 183, 186
Sandeman, Capt, 257
Sandspruit, 56, 57, 58
Sannah's Post, De Wet's victory at, 200–3, 240, 293
Scheepers, Capt Gideon, 259, 278, 294
Schoeman's Drift (Vaal), 230
Schofield, Capt H. N., 130
Schreiner, William, 37, 45–6, 63, 89, 102
Scobell, Col Harry, 259, 294
Scott-Turner, Lt-Col, 105
Scots Fusiliers, 187
Scots Greys, 170, 230, 293
Scots Guards, 107, 109, 223

'The Scout on the Veldt', 290
Seaforth Highlanders, 117
Selborne, William Palmer, Lord, 28
Shangans, living in Mafeking, 208
Shropshire Regiment, 177
Sim, Lt-Col G. H., 156
Simonstown naval base, 289
Sims, naval gunner, 143, 145
Slabbert's Nek, 226, 227–8
Slachter's Nek Rebellion (1815), 291
Slap Kranz, Boers handing in rifles, 228
slavery, abolition of (1834), 11, 291
Smith, Private, of Black Watch, 115
Smith-Dorrien, Major-Gen Horace, 163, 166, 175, 176–8, 219, 230
Smuts, Jan, 18, 33, 37, 46, 52, 53, 222, 223, 240–1, 242, 289, 294; appointed State Attorney (1898), 30, 31; 'Great Deal' offer of, 33–4, 35; secret memo for Transvaal Executive (1899), 52; his plan for offensive against Natal, 53, 56; and surrender of Johannesburg, 223; at Cypherfontein meeting, 240, 243; appointed Assistant Commandant-General, 242; ambushes convoy at Buffelshoek, 242; at Nooitgedacht, 242–3, 294; raid into Cape Colony, 256, 257–9, 261, 294; and 'Night of the Great Rain', 257; battle of Elands River Poort, 257–8; birthday party for, 278; Pretoria peace talks, 279, 282
Snyman, Gen J. P., 206, 211, 212, 213
South African League, 33, 35
South African Light Horse, 65, 156, 214
South African Republic see Transvaal
South African Women and Children Distress Fund, 252, 253
South Lancashire Regiment, 188
Spion Kop, 146; battle of (Jan. 1900), 146, 147, 148–59, 151, 157, 158, 164, 183, 293
Spragge, Lt-Col Basil, 225, 293
Springfield, 118, 146
Springfontein, 164, 197
Spytfontein, 101, 106, 111, 112
Standerton, 232; war council at, 257, 260
State Artillery Corps, Transvaal, 30
Steavenson, Capt C. J., 145
Steenkamp, Gen, 196
Stephenson, Brigadier-Gen T. E., 175, 176
Steyn, Marthinus, President of Orange Free State, 36, 39, 107, 140, 203, 217, 219, 225, 229, 241, 265, 268, 289, 293; ultimatum to Britain from Kruger and, 53–4, 55, 58; and war plans, 56–7; visits Free Staters at front, 111–12; fall of Bloemfontein, and flees northwards, 192; at Kroonstad council, 199–200; rejects Kruger's suggestion of surrender, 223; provisional government at Fouriesburg, 227;

Cypherfontein meeting, 240–1; against peace agreement, 254; eludes capture by Kitchener, 268, 272; Pretoria peace talks, 279, 280, 281
Stinkfontein, Farm, 176
Stopford, Col S., 126
Stormberg, railway junction, 63; battle of (1899), 119, 136, 139, 292
Surprise Hill, raid on, 143
Symons, Major-Gen Sir Penn, 44, 57–8, 79, 80, 82; appointed GOC Natal, 42, 50; moves brigade to Dundee, 51, 57, 61, 292; Boer attack on Dundee, 68–9; and Talana Hill action, 69–74, 75, 292; wounded, 71, 74, 75; left behind by Yule, 79, 80, 81; and death, 81, 87

Tabanyama (Rangeworthy), 150, 152, 153, 155
Talana Hill, 68, 79, 80; battle of, 69–75, 93–4, 106, 292; Boer scouts on, 71
Thabanchu, 197, 200, 201
Thackeray, Lt-Col Thomas, 125, 128
Thiele, Reinhold, war photographer, 83
Thorneycroft, Lt-Col Alec, at Spion Kop, 148, 152, 153–4, 155, 156–8, 159
'Tigers' (colonial scouts), 101, 170, 200, 216; house at Yassfontein looted by, 234
trains, armoured, 87, 95–6, 96–7, 204
transport, 163, 164, 219, 269; regimental or decentralized system of, 162, 165; Roberts's system of, 162, 165, 194, 197
Transvaal (South African Republic), 11, 12, 22, 25, 28, 194, 256, 272; British annexation of (1877), 11, 291; Jameson Raid, 13–18, 20, 21, 23–4, 24, 25, 27, 29, 32, 33, 45, 53, 64; map of, 14–15; Volksraad, 29, 35; arming and defence of, 30, 30, 31, 39, 42–3; modernization of, 30–1; Zarps, 31, 33; Uitlanders' franchise, 33, 35–6, 37, 43, 44, 46, 47, 52; 'Great Deal' offer, 33–4, 35–6; burghers off to war front, 53, 55; mobilization, 54, 55, 56, 56; ultimatum to Britain, 54–5, 57, 58, 60, 61, 62, 93; British refugees leave, 61–2, 61; birth rate, 141; vrouw as cornerstone of, 141; surrender of Jo'burg to Roberts, 220–2, 223; and of Pretoria, 222–3, 224; Roberts proclaims annexation of (Oct. 1900), 235, 293; guerrilla warfare in, 240, 246, 265; Milner's military plan, 244–6; concentration camps, 252; Pretoria peace talks, 272, 273–4, 278–83; native rights in, 279–80; British financial help for, 280; Milner's plan to rebuild on British lines, 288–9; census (1904), 289; Chinese immigration to, 289; self-government granted to (1906), 289

Trikhardt's Drift, 146
Trotter, Capt Algy, 60, 118, 125, 126
Tucker, Major-Gen Charles, 163, 220
Tugela River, 51, 57, 83, 85, 87, 88, 94, 95,
    96, 98, 141, 146, 180, 181, 186; Buller
    advised against advancing beyond, 51,
    57, 61, 82–3; Botha's fortification of, 92,
    98, 121; Joubert crosses, 94; Buller
    crosses at Colenso, 118–20; and battle of
    Colenso, 119, 120–31, 133, 134
Tweebosch, De la Rey captures Methuen at
    (1902), 272, 274, 275, 294
Tweefontein, De Wet's success at (1901),
    266, 268, 272, 294
Twyfelaar (near Belfast), 231
typhoid, 82, 184, 196, 197–8, 198, 219, 235,
    249, 255

Uitlanders in Transvaal, 12, 16, 24, 27, 28,
    30, 31, 32, 33–4, 35–6, 39, 47–8, 51, 60,
    64, 136, 141, 222, 246, 274, 283; franchise
    for, 33, 35–6, 37, 43, 44, 46, 47, 52, 55, 60;
    shooting of Tom Edgar, 33; 'Great Deal'
    offer, 33–4, 35–6; Helot Despatch, 36, 37,
    43; refugees flee to Cape and Natal from,
    61–2, 61, 62; volunteer corps raised from
    refugees, 65, 214; pro-Boer, 141; refugees
    return home to Jo'burg, 285; hostility to
    Chinese immigration, 289

Vaal River, 11, 217, 219, 225, 230, 231, 232,
    240, 275, 276
Vaal Krantz, battle of (1900), 159, 164, 184,
    293
Vereeniging, 278; Boer delegates agree
    peace terms at (1902), 279, 280–3, 289,
    290, 294
Verwoerd, Dr Hendrik, 289
Victoria, Queen, 27, 28, 130, 135, 191, 194,
    195, 221, 238, 247
Viljoen, Commandant Ben, 79, 220

Vivian, Capt Lord, 257
Vlakfontein Camp, Boer attack on, 254
vrouw (Boer housewife), 248, 268; as
    cornerstone in Transvaal, 141

Wagon Hill, 183; Gloucesters on picket
    duty at, 141; Boer attack on (6 Jan. 1900),
    141, 141, 143–5, 293
Walrond, Ozzy, 62
War Office, 40, 49; files on Boer War, 9;
    Secret Journal of the war, 9; 'Indian' vs
    'African Rings' in Army, 41–2, 50, 50,
    133, 137, 234–5; Military Notes on the
    Dutch Republics, handbook, 42–3, 50,
    81, 200; despatch of army reinforcement,
    49–50; mistakes and deficiencies in
    supplies, 137; regimental system of
    transport, 162, 165; CIGS created (1904),
    288
Warren, Lt-Gen Sir Charles, 131, 135, 146,
    190; at Spion Kop, 148, 150, 152–3,
    154–6, 157, 158, 159
Watermeier, Capt, 179
Waterval Drift, 163, 165, 194, 199
Waterval Onder (PoW camp for British
    soldiers), 'Ladysmith Street' at, 233
Wauchope, Major-Gen Andrew, 115–16,
    117, 117, 124
Welsh Regiment, 175
Wepener, siege of, 203
Wernher, Julius, 22, 28, 32, 35, 199, 289
Wernher-Beit (Wernher, Beit & Co.), 32–3,
    34, 46, 47, 49, 65, 221, 289, 291
West Yorkshire Regiment, 188
White, Bobby, 16
White, Lt-Gen Sir George, 50, 51, 57, 61, 62,
    75, 76, 79, 82, 88, 99, 133, 163, 181;
    appointed GOC Natal, 50, 51; and Yule's
    withdrawal from Dundee, 79–80, 82; his
    reasons for not withdrawing from
    Ladysmith, 82–3; and Pepworth Hill

disaster, 83–5, 84, 292; siege of
    Ladysmith, 85, 88–9, 91, 93, 94, 121,
    131–2, 135, 142, 143, 144, 145, 164,
    183–4; relief of Ladysmith, 188–91, 190;
    his resentment towards Buller, 189–90;
    invalided home, 191
Wilkinson, Spenser, 28, 191
Willoughby, Col Sir John, 16
Willow Grange, battle (1899), 98, 292
Wilson, Surgeon-Gen W. D., 198, 219
Witwatersrand (Rand) see gold mines
Wolseley, Field-Marshal Lord, 40, 41, 44,
    48, 133, 135, 136, 288; and Lansdowne,
    40, 41–2, 43, 89, 134, 137; and British
    troops sent to Natal, 48, 49, 58; and
    Kruger's ultimatum, 58; Roberts
    succeeds him as C-in-C at home, 234, 294
Woodgate, Major-Gen E. R. P., 148, 151,
    152
Woolls-Sampson, Col A., 78, 79, 265, 275
Wyndham, George, 137
Wynne, Major-Gen Arthur, 181, 185, 188
Wynne's Hill, 185, 186

Yassfontein, house looted by Tigers, 234
Yeomanry Hill, Noortgedacht, 243
Yorkshire Light Infantry, 54
Yorkshire Regiment, 175
Yule, Brig-Gen James, 73, 74, 83; retreat
    from Dundee, 79–82, 80–1
Yzer Spruit, De la Rey captures convoy at,
    272, 275

Zand River action, 219
Zarps (Transvaal police), 31, 33, 232–3
Zilikat's Nek, De la Rey's success at, 230,
    240, 293
Zulus, Zululand, 139, 189, 260, 261, 282,
    292, 294